ALCOHOL, TOBACCO, AND ILLICIT DRUGS

ISSN 1938-8896

ALCOHOL, TOBACCO, AND ILLICIT DRUGS

Stephen Meyer

INFORMATION PLUS® REFERENCE SERIES
Formerly Published by Information Plus, Wylie, Texas

GALE
CENGAGE Learning·

Farmington Hills, Mich • San Francisco • New York • Waterville, Maine
Meriden, Conn • Mason, Ohio • Chicago

Alcohol, Tobacco, and Illicit Drugs

Stephen Meyer

Kepos Media, Inc.: Steven Long and Janice
Jorgensen, Series Editors

Project Editor: Laura Avery

Rights Acquisition and Management:
 Ashley Maynard, Carissa Poweleit

Composition: Evi Abou-El-Seoud,
 Mary Beth Trimper

Manufacturing: Rita Wimberley

Product Design: Kristine Julien

For product information and technology assistance, contact us at
Gale Customer Support, 1-800-877-4253.
For permission to use material from this text or product,
submit all requests online at **www.cengage.com/permissions.**
Further permissions questions can be e-mailed to
permissionrequest@cengage.com

Cover photograph: © Lee O'Dell/Shutterstock.com.

While every effort has been made to ensure the reliability of the information presented in this publication, Gale, a Cengage Company, does not guarantee the accuracy of the data contained herein. Gale accepts no payment for listing; and inclusion in the publication of any organization, agency, institution, publication, service, or individual does not imply endorsement of the editors or publisher. Errors brought to the attention of the publisher and verified to the satisfaction of the publisher will be corrected in future editions.

Gale
27500 Drake Rd.
Farmington Hills, MI 48331-3535

ISBN-13: 978-0-7876-5103-9 (set)
ISBN-13: 978-1-4103-2538-9

ISSN 1938-8896

This title is also available as an e-book.
ISBN-13: 978-1-4103-3268-4 (set)
Contact your Gale sales representative for ordering information.

Printed in the United States of America
1 2 3 4 5   21 20 19 18 17

TABLE OF CONTENTS

PREFACE

Alcohol, Tobacco, and Illicit Drugs is part of the *Information Plus Reference Series*. The purpose of each volume of the series is to present the latest facts on a topic of pressing concern in modern American life. These topics include the most controversial and studied social issues of the 21st century: abortion, capital punishment, care of senior citizens, crime, the environment, health care, immigration, national security, social welfare, water, women, youth, and many more. Although this series is written especially for high school and undergraduate students, it is an excellent resource for anyone in need of factual information on current affairs.

By presenting the facts, it is the intention of Gale, a Cengage Company, to provide its readers with everything they need to reach an informed opinion on current issues. To that end, there is a particular emphasis in this series on the presentation of scientific studies, surveys, and statistics. These data are generally presented in the form of tables, charts, and other graphics placed within the text of each book. Every graphic is directly referred to and carefully explained in the text. The source of each graphic is presented within the graphic itself. The data used in these graphics are drawn from the most reputable and reliable sources, such as from various branches of the U.S. government and from private organizations and associations. Every effort has been made to secure the most recent information available. Readers should bear in mind that many major studies take years to conduct and that additional years often pass before the data from these studies are made available to the public. Therefore, in many cases the most recent information available in 2017 is dated from 2014 or 2015. Older statistics are sometimes presented as well if they are landmark studies or of particular interest and no more-recent information exists.

Although statistics are a major focus of the *Information Plus Reference Series*, they are by no means its only content. Each book also presents the widely held positions and important ideas that shape how the book's subject is discussed in the United States. These positions are explained in detail and, where possible, in the words of their proponents. Some of the other material to be found in these books includes historical background, descriptions of major events related to the subject, relevant laws and court cases, and examples of how these issues play out in American life. Some books also feature primary documents or have pro and con debate sections that provide the words and opinions of prominent Americans on both sides of a controversial topic. All material is presented in an evenhanded and unbiased manner; readers will never be encouraged to accept one view of an issue over another.

HOW TO USE THIS BOOK

Both legal and illicit drugs—substances that can affect a person's mood or physiology—are used by people from all segments of American society. Legal drugs include prescription medications as well as popular and widely available substances such as alcohol, tobacco, and caffeine. Illegal drugs include those with no currently accepted medical use in the United States, such as heroin, LSD, ecstasy, and inhalants. This book provides an overview of legal and illicit drugs, including their health impact, addictive nature, and potential for abuse. Also discussed are the political and economic ramifications of such substances, their use among youth, possible treatments, drug trafficking, and antidrug efforts and campaigns.

Alcohol, Tobacco, and Illicit Drugs consists of nine chapters and three appendixes. Each chapter is devoted to a particular aspect of alcohol, tobacco, and illicit drugs in the United States. For a summary of the information that is covered in each chapter, please see the synopses that are provided in the Table of Contents. Chapters generally begin with an overview of the basic facts and background information on the chapter's topic, then proceed to examine subtopics of particular interest. For example, Chapter 5: Alcohol

Tobacco, Illicit Drugs, and Youth opens with an assessment of various risk factors underlying illicit drug use among young people. An overview of trends in current alcohol use among high school and college students follows, with a focus on incidences of heavy alcohol use and binge drinking in these age groups. The chapter proceeds to discuss demographic factors involved with alcohol use trends in young people, accounting for geography, the educational attainment of parents, and racial and ethnic backgrounds. Similar considerations are used to analyze data relating to the current use of various tobacco products by young people, before the chapter concludes with an in-depth survey of current, annual, and lifetime illicit drug use among high school students, college undergraduates, and young adults. Readers can find their way through a chapter by looking for the section and subsection headings, which are clearly set off from the text. They can also refer to the book's extensive Index if they already know what they are looking for.

Statistical Information

The tables and figures featured throughout *Alcohol, Tobacco, and Illicit Drugs* will be of particular use to readers in learning about this issue. These tables and figures represent an extensive collection of the most recent and valuable statistics on alcohol, tobacco, illicit drugs, and related issues—for example, graphics cover trends in cigarette use, alcohol's involvement in fatal motor accidents, health consequences associated with tobacco use, the number of youth who use illicit drugs, and the prevalence of hallucinogen use among students. Gale, a Cengage Company, believes that making this information available to readers is the most important way to fulfill the goal of this book: to help readers understand the issues and controversies surrounding alcohol, tobacco, and illicit drugs in the United States and to reach their own conclusions.

Each table or figure has a unique identifier appearing above it for ease of identification and reference. Titles for the tables and figures explain their purpose. At the end of each table or figure, the original source of the data is provided.

To help readers understand these often complicated statistics, all tables and figures are explained in the text. References in the text direct readers to the relevant statistics. Furthermore, the contents of all tables and figures are fully indexed. Please see the opening section of the Index at the back of this volume for a description of how to find tables and figures within it.

Appendixes

Besides the main body text and images, *Alcohol, Tobacco, and Illicit Drugs* has three appendixes. The first is the Important Names and Addresses directory. Here, readers will find contact information for a number of government and private organizations that can provide further information on alcohol, tobacco, and/or illicit drugs. The second appendix is the Resources section, which can also assist readers in conducting their own research. In this section the author and editors of *Alcohol, Tobacco, and Illicit Drugs* describe some of the sources that were most useful during the compilation of this book. The final appendix is the Index. It has been greatly expanded from previous editions and should make it even easier to find specific topics in this book.

COMMENTS AND SUGGESTIONS

The editors of the *Information Plus Reference Series* welcome your feedback on *Alcohol, Tobacco, and Illicit Drugs*. Please direct all correspondence to:

Editors
Information Plus Reference Series
Gale, a Cengage Company
27500 Drake Rd.
Farmington Hills, MI 48331-3535

CHAPTER 1
DRUGS: A DEFINITION

Drugs are nonfood chemicals that alter the way a person thinks, feels, functions, or behaves. This includes everything from prescription medications, to illegal chemicals such as heroin, to popular and widely available substances such as alcohol, tobacco, and caffeine. A wide variety of laws, regulations, and government agencies exist to control the possession, sale, and use of drugs. Different drugs are held to different standards based on their perceived dangers and usefulness, a fact that sometimes leads to disagreement and controversy.

Illegal drugs are those with no currently accepted medical use in the United States, such as heroin, lysergic acid diethylamide (LSD), and marijuana. It is illegal to buy, sell, possess, and use these drugs except for research purposes. They are supplied only to registered, qualified researchers. (Some states and local jurisdictions have decriminalized certain uses of specific amounts of marijuana, but federal laws supersede these state and local marijuana decriminalization laws. For a more detailed discussion on the legalization of marijuana, see Chapter 9.)

By contrast, legal drugs are drugs whose sale, possession, and use as intended are not forbidden by law. Their use may be restricted, however. For example, the U.S. Drug Enforcement Administration (DEA) controls the use of legal psychoactive (mood- or mind-altering) drugs that have the potential for abuse. These drugs, which include narcotics, depressants, and stimulants, are available only with a prescription and are called controlled substances. The term *illicit drugs* is used by the Substance Abuse and Mental Health Services Administration to describe both controlled substances that are used in violation of the law and drugs that are completely illegal.

The goal of the DEA is to ensure that controlled substances are readily available for medical use or research purposes while preventing their illegal sale and abuse. The agency works toward accomplishing this goal by requiring people and businesses that manufacture, distribute, prescribe, and dispense controlled substances to register with the DEA. Registrants must abide by a series of requirements that relate to drug security, records accountability, and adherence to standards. The DEA also enforces the controlled substances laws and regulations of the United States by investigating and prosecuting those who violate these laws.

The U.S. Food and Drug Administration (FDA) also plays a role in drug control. This agency regulates the manufacture and marketing of prescription and nonprescription drugs. It also requires that the active ingredients in a product be safe and effective before allowing the drug to be sold.

Alcohol and tobacco are monitored and specially taxed by the Alcohol and Tobacco Tax and Trade Bureau (TTB). The TTB was formed in January 2003 as a provision of the Homeland Security Act of 2002, which split the Bureau of Alcohol, Tobacco, and Firearms (ATF) into two new agencies. One of these agencies, the TTB, took over the taxation duties for alcohol, tobacco, and firearms and remained a part of the U.S. Department of the Treasury. The TTB also ensures that alcohol and tobacco products are legally labeled, advertised, and marketed; regulates the qualification and operations of distilleries, wineries, and breweries; tests alcoholic beverages to ensure that their regulated ingredients are within legal limits; and screens applicants who wish to manufacture, import, or export tobacco products.

The other agency split from the former ATF is the reformed ATF: the Bureau of Alcohol, Tobacco, Firearms, and Explosives. The ATF has become a principal law enforcement agency within the U.S. Department of Justice, enforcing federal criminal laws and regulating the firearms and explosives industries. It also investigates illegal trafficking of alcohol and tobacco products.

In June 2009 Congress and President Barack Obama (1961–) enacted legislation that gave the FDA authority to oversee the sale and advertising of tobacco. The legislation granted the FDA various liberties, including regulating the levels of nicotine and other ingredients in cigarettes, banning tobacco manufacturers from selling candy-flavored or menthol cigarettes, requiring larger warning signs on tobacco packaging, and preventing the sale of so-called mild or light cigarettes.

FIVE CATEGORIES OF DRUGS

Drugs may be classified into five categories:

- Depressants, including alcohol and tranquilizers—these substances slow down the activity of the nervous system. They produce sedative (calming) and hypnotic (trancelike) effects as well as drowsiness. If taken in large doses, depressants can cause intoxication (drunkenness).

- Hallucinogens, including marijuana, phencyclidine, and LSD—hallucinogens produce abnormal and unreal sensations such as seeing distorted and vividly colored images. Hallucinogens can also produce frightening psychological responses such as anxiety, depression, and the feeling of losing control of one's mind.

- Narcotics, including heroin and opium, from which morphine and codeine are derived—narcotics are drugs that alter the perception of pain and induce sleep and euphoria (an intense feeling of well-being; a "high").

- Stimulants, including caffeine, nicotine, cocaine, amphetamine, and methamphetamine—these substances speed up the processing rate of the central nervous system. They can reduce fatigue, elevate mood, increase energy, and help people stay awake. In large doses stimulants can cause irritability, anxiety, sleeplessness, and even psychotic behavior. Caffeine is the most commonly used stimulant in the world.

- Other compounds, including anabolic steroids and inhalants—anabolic steroids are a group of synthetic substances that are chemically related to testosterone and are promoted for their muscle-building properties. Inhalants are solvents and aerosol products that produce vapors that have psychoactive effects. These substances dull pain and can produce euphoria.

Table 1.1 provides an overview of alcohol, nicotine, and other selected psychoactive substances. It includes the DEA schedule for each drug listed. Developed as part of the Controlled Substances Act (CSA) of 1970, the DEA drug schedules are categories into which controlled substances are placed depending on their characteristics such as medical use, potential for abuse, safety, and danger of dependence. Table 1.2 provides a list of commonly abused prescription drugs, along with their DEA

schedules. The types of drugs categorized in each of the five schedules, with examples, are shown in Table 1.3.

DRUGS DISCUSSED IN THIS BOOK

This book focuses on substances that are widely used throughout the world: alcohol, tobacco, and illicit drugs. Not only are alcohol and tobacco legal, relatively affordable, and more or less socially acceptable (depending on time, place, and circumstance) but also they are important economic commodities. Industries exist to produce, distribute, and sell these products, creating jobs and income and contributing to economic well-being. Thus, whenever discussions of possible government regulation of alcohol and tobacco arise, the topic brings with it significant economic and political issues.

Illicit drugs are those that are unlawful to possess or distribute under the CSA. Some controlled substances can be taken under the supervision of health care professionals who are licensed by the DEA. The CSA provides penalties for the unlawful manufacture, distribution, and dispensing of controlled substances, based on the schedule of the drug or substance. Nonetheless, illicit drugs have fostered huge illicit drug marketing and drug trafficking (buying and selling) networks. (See Chapter 8.) Tobacco, beer, wine, and spirits (hard liquor) are exempt from the CSA and the DEA drug schedules.

Figure 1.1, Table 1.4, and Figure 1.2 show trends in cigarette, illicit drug, and alcohol use from various periods in the 20th century to the second decade of the 21st century. They also provide an overview of the ebb and flow of the use and abuse of these substances in the United States. This chapter takes a historical look at the use and abuse of each substance, and the chapters that follow present more up-to-date information.

WHAT ARE ABUSE AND ADDICTION?

Many drugs, both legal and illicit, have the potential for abuse and addiction. Research and treatment experts identify three general levels of interaction with drugs: use, abuse, and dependence (or addiction). In general, abuse involves a compulsive use of a substance and impaired social or occupational functioning. Dependence (addiction) includes these traits, plus evidence of physical tolerance (a need to take increasingly higher doses to achieve the same effect) or withdrawal symptoms when use of the drug is stopped.

The progression from use to dependence is complex, as are the abused substances themselves. Researchers find no standard boundaries between using a substance, abusing a substance, and being addicted to a substance. They believe these lines vary widely from substance to substance and from individual to individual.

TABLE 1.1

Commonly abused drugs

Substances: category and name	Examples of commercial and street names	DEA schedule[a]/how administered[b]	Acute effects/health risks
Tobacco			
Nicotine	Found in cigarettes, cigars, bidis, and smokeless tobacco (snuff, spit tobacco, chew)	Not scheduled/smoked, snorted, chewed	Increased blood pressure and heart rate/chronic lung disease; cardiovascular disease; stroke; cancers of the mouth, pharynx, larynx, esophagus, stomach, pancreas, cervix, kidney, bladder, and acute myeloid leukemia; adverse pregnancy outcomes; addiction
Alcohol			
Alcohol (ethyl alcohol)	Found in liquor, beer, and wine	Not scheduled/swallowed	In low doses, euphoria, mild stimulation, relaxation, lowered inhibitions; in higher doses, drowsiness, slurred speech, nausea, emotional volatility, loss of coordination, visual distortions, impaired memory, sexual dysfunction, loss of consciousness/increased risk of injuries, violence, fetal damage (in pregnant women); depression; neurologic deficits; hypertension; liver and heart disease; addiction; fatal overdose
Cannabinoids			
Marijuana	Blunt, dope, ganja, grass, herb, joint, bud, Mary Jane, pot, reefer, green, trees, smoke, sinsemilla, skunk, weed	I/smoked, swallowed	Euphoria; relaxation; slowed reaction time; distorted sensory perception; impaired balance and coordination; increased heart rate and appetite; impaired learning, memory; anxiety; panic attacks; psychosis/cough; frequent respiratory infections; possible mental health decline; addiction
Hashish	Boom, gangster, hash, hash oil, hemp	I/smoked, swallowed	
Opioids			
Heroin	Diacetylmorphine: smack, horse, brown sugar, dope, H, junk, skag, skunk, white horse, China white; cheese (with OTC cold medicine and antihistamine)	I/injected, smoked, snorted	Euphoria; drowsiness; impaired coordination; dizziness; confusion; nausea; sedation; feeling of heaviness in the body; slowed or arrested breathing/constipation; endocarditis; hepatitis; HIV; addiction; fatal overdose
Opium	Laudanum, paregoric: big O, black stuff, block, gum, hop	II, III, V/swallowed, smoked	
Stimulants			
Cocaine	Cocaine hydrochloride: blow, bump, C, candy, Charlie, coke, crack, flake, rock, snow, toot	II/snorted, smoked, injected	Increased heart rate, blood pressure, body temperature, metabolism; feelings of exhilaration; increased energy, mental alertness; tremors; reduced appetite; irritability; anxiety; panic; paranoia; violent behavior; psychosis/weight loss; insomnia; cardiac or cardiovascular complications; stroke; seizures; addiction
Amphetamine	Biphetamine, Dexedrine: bennies, black beauties, crosses, hearts, LA turnaround, speed, truck drivers, uppers	II/swallowed, snorted, smoked, injected	Also, for cocaine—nasal damage from snorting
Methamphetamine	Desoxyn: meth, ice, crank, chalk, crystal, fire, glass, go fast, speed	II/swallowed, snorted, smoked, injected	Also, for methamphetamine—severe dental problems
Club drugs			
MDMA (methylenedioxymethamphetamine)	Ecstasy, Adam, clarity, Eve, lover's speed, peace, uppers	I/swallowed, snorted, injected	MDMA—mild hallucinogenic effects; increased tactile sensitivity, empathic feelings; lowered inhibition; anxiety; chills; sweating; teeth clenching; muscle cramping/sleep disturbances; depression; impaired memory; hyperthermia; addiction
Flunitrazepam[c]	Rohypnol: forget-me pill, Mexican Valium, R2, roach, Roche, roofies, roofinol, rope, rophies	IV/swallowed, snorted	Flunitrazepam—sedation; muscle relaxation; confusion; memory loss; dizziness; impaired coordination/addiction
GHB[c]	Gamma-hydroxybutyrate: G, Georgia home boy, grievous bodily harm, liquid ecstasy, soap, scoop, goop, liquid X	I/swallowed	GHB—drowsiness; nausea; headache; disorientation; loss of coordination; memory loss/unconsciousness; seizures; coma
Dissociative drugs			
Ketamine	Ketalar SV: cat Valium, K, Special K, vitamin K	III/injected, snorted, smoked	Feelings of being separate from one's body and environment; impaired motor function/anxiety; tremors; numbness; memory loss; nausea
PCP and analogs	Phencyclidine: angel dust, boat, hog, love boat, peace pill	I, II/swallowed, smoked, injected	Also, for ketamine—analgesia; impaired memory; delirium; respiratory depression and arrest; death
Salvia divinorum	Salvia, Shepherdess's Herb, Maria Pastora, magic mint, Sally-D	Not scheduled/chewed, swallowed, smoked	Also, for PCP and analogs—analgesia; psychosis; aggression; violence; slurred speech; loss of coordination; hallucinations
Dextromethorphan (DXM)	Found in some cough and cold medications: Robotripping, Robo, Triple C	Not scheduled/swallowed	Also, for DXM—euphoria; slurred speech; confusion; dizziness; distorted visual perceptions

TABLE 1.1

Commonly abused drugs [CONTINUED]

Substances: category and name	Examples of commercial and street names	DEA schedule[a]/how administered[b]	Acute effects/health risks
Hallucinogens			
LSD	Lysergic acid diethylamide: acid, blotter, cubes, microdot, yellow sunshine, blue heaven	I/swallowed, absorbed through mouth tissues	Altered states of perception and feeling; hallucinations; nausea
Mescaline	Buttons, cactus, mesc, peyote	I/swallowed, smoked	Also, for LSD and mescaline—increased body temperature, heart rate, blood pressure; loss of appetite; sweating; sleeplessness; numbness; dizziness; weakness; tremors; impulsive behavior; rapid shifts in emotion
Psilocybin	Magic mushrooms, purple passion, shrooms, little smoke	I/swallowed	Also, for LSD—flashbacks, Hallucinogen Persisting Perception Disorder
			Also, for psilocybin—nervousness; paranoia; panic
Other compounds			
Anabolic steroids	Anadrol, Oxandrin, Durabolin, Depo-Testosterone, Equipoise: roids, juice, gym candy, pumpers	III/injected, swallowed, applied to skin	Steroids—no intoxication effects/hypertension; blood clotting and cholesterol changes; liver cysts; hostility and aggression; acne; in adolescents—premature stoppage of growth; in males—prostate cancer, reduced sperm production, shrunken testicles, breast enlargement; in females—menstrual irregularities, development of beard and other masculine characteristics
Inhalants	Solvents (paint thinners, gasoline, glues); gases (butane, propane, aerosol propellants, nitrous oxide); nitrites (isoamyl, isobutyl, cyclohexyl): laughing gas, poppers, snappers, whippets	Not scheduled/inhaled through nose or mouth	Inhalants (varies by chemical)—stimulation; loss of inhibition; headache; nausea or vomiting; slurred speech; loss of motor coordination; wheezing/cramps; muscle weakness; depression; memory impairment; damage to cardiovascular and nervous systems; unconsciousness; sudden death

[a]Schedule I and II drugs have a high potential for abuse. They require greater storage security and have a quota on manufacturing, among other restrictions. Schedule I drugs are available for research only and have no approved medical use; Schedule II drugs are available only by prescription (unrefillable) and require a form for ordering. Schedule III and IV drugs are available by prescription, may have five refills in 6 months, and may be ordered orally. Some Schedule V drugs are available over the counter.

[b]Some of the health risks are directly related to the route of drug administration. For example, injection drug use can increase the risk of infection through needle contamination with staphylococci, HIV, hepatitis, and other organisms.

[c]Associated with sexual assaults.

SOURCE: Adapted from "Commonly Abused Drugs," National Institutes of Health, National Institute on Drug Abuse, March 2011, https://www.drugabuse.gov/sites/default/files/cadchart_2.pdf (accessed January 9, 2017)

TABLE 1.2

Commonly abused prescription drugs

Substances: category and name	Examples of commercial and street names	DEA schedule[a]/how administered	Intoxication effects/health risks
Depressants			
Barbiturates	Amytal, Nembutal, Seconal, Phenobarbital: barbs, reds, red birds, phennies, tooies, yellows, yellow jackets	II, III, IV/injected, swallowed	Sedation/drowsiness, reduced anxiety, feelings of well-being, lowered inhibitions, slurred speech, poor concentration, confusion, dizziness, impaired coordination and memory/slowed pulse, lowered blood pressure, slowed breathing, tolerance, withdrawal, addiction; increased risk of respiratory distress and death when combined with alcohol
Benzodiazepines	Ativan, Halcion, Librium, V alium, Xanax, Klonopin: candy, downers, sleeping pills, tranks	IV/swallowed	
Sleep medications	Ambien (zolpidem), Sonata (zaleplon), Lunesta (eszopiclone)	IV/swallowed	For barbiturates—euphoria, unusual excitement, fever, irritability/life-threatening withdrawal in chronic users
Opioids and morphine derivatives[b]			
Codeine	Empirin with Codeine, Fiorinal with Codeine, Robitussin A-C, Tylenol with Codeine: Captain Cody, Cody, schoolboy; (with glutethimide: doors & fours, loads, pancakes and syrup)	II, III, IV/injected, swallowed	Pain relief, euphoria, drowsiness, sedation, weakness, dizziness, nausea, impaired coordination, confusion, dry mouth, itching, sweating, clammy skin, constipation/slowed or arrested breathing, lowered pulse and blood pressure, tolerance, addiction, unconsciousness, coma, death; risk of death increased when combined with alcohol or other CNS depressants
Morphine	Roxanol, Duramorph: M, Miss Emma, monkey, white stuff	II, III/injected, swallowed, smoked	
Methadone	Methadose, Dolophine: fizzies, amidone (with MDMA: chocolate chip cookies)	II/swallowed, injected	For fentanyl—80-100 times more potent analgesic than morphine
Fentanyl and analogs	Actiq, Duragesic, Sublimaze: Apache, China girl, dance fever, friend, goodfella, jackpot, murder 8, TNT, Tango and Cash	II/injected, smoked, snorted	For oxycodone—muscle relaxation/twice as potent analgesic as morphine; high abuse potential
Other opioid pain relievers: Oxycodone HCL Hydrocodone Bitartrate Hydromorphone Oxymorphone Meperidine Propoxyphene	Tylox, Oxycontin, Percodan, Percocet: Oxy, O.C., oxycotton, oxycet, hillbilly heroin, percs Vicodin, Lortab, Lorcet: vike, Watson-387 Dilaudid: juice, smack, D, footballs, dillies Opana, Numorphan, Numorphone: biscuits, blue heaven, blues, Mrs. O, octagons, stop signs, O Bomb Demerol, meperidine hydrochloride: demmies, pain killer Darvon, Darvocet	II, III, IV/chewed, swallowed, snorted, injected, suppositories	For codeine—less analgesia, sedation, and respiratory depression than morphine For methadone—used to treat opioid addiction and pain; significant overdose risk when used improperly
Stimulants			
Amphetamines	Biphetamine, Dexedrine, Adderall: bennies, black beauties, crosses, hearts, LA turn around, speed, truck drivers, uppers	II/injected, swallowed, smoked, snorted	Feelings of exhilaration, increased energy, mental alertness/increased heart rate, blood pressure, and metabolism, reduced appetite, weight loss, nervousness, insomnia, seizures, heart attack, stroke
Methylphenidate	Concerta, Ritalin: JIF, MPH, R-ball, Skippy, the smart drug, vitamin R	II/injected, swallowed, snorted	For amphetamines—rapid breathing, tremor, loss of coordination, irritability, anxiousness, restlessness/delirium, panic, paranoia, hallucinations, impulsive behavior, aggressiveness, tolerance, addiction For methylphenidate—increase or decrease in blood pressure, digestive problems, loss of appetite, weight loss
Other compounds			
Dextromethorphan (DXM)	Found in some cough and cold medications: Robotripping, Robo, Triple C	Not scheduled/swallowed	Euphoria, slurred speech/increased heart rate and blood pressure, dizziness, nausea, vomiting, confusion, paranoia, distorted visual perceptions, impaired motor function

[a]Schedule I and II drugs have a high potential for abuse. They require greater storage security and have a quota on manufacturing, among other restrictions. Schedule I drugs are available for research only and have no approved medical use. Schedule II drugs are available only by prescription and require a new prescription for each refill. Schedule III and IV drugs are available by prescription, may have five refills in 6 months, and may be ordered orally. Most Schedule V drugs are available over the counter.

[b]Taking drugs by injection can increase the risk of infection through needle contamination with staphylococci, HIV, hepatitis, and other organisms. Injection is a more common practice for opioids, but risks apply to any medication taken by injection.

SOURCE: Adapted from "Commonly Abused Prescription Drugs," National Institutes of Health, National Institute on Drug Abuse, October 2011, https://www.drugabuse.gov/sites/default/files/rx_drugs_placemat_508c_10052011.pdf (accessed January 9, 2017)

TABLE 1.3

Drug schedules established by the Controlled Substance Act, 1970

Schedule I

- The drug or other substance has a high potential for abuse.
- The drug or other substance has no currently accepted medical use in treatment in the United States.
- There is a lack of accepted safety for use of the drug or other substance under medical supervision.
- Examples of Schedule I substances include heroin, gamma hydroxybutyric acid (GHB), lysergic acid diethylamide (LSD), marijuana, and methaqualone.

Schedule II

- The drug or other substance has a high potential for abuse.
- The drug or other substance has a currently accepted medical use in treatment in the United States or a currently accepted medical use with severe restrictions.
- Abuse of the drug or other substance may lead to severe psychological or physical dependence.
- Examples of Schedule II substances include morphine, phencyclidine (PCP), cocaine, methadone, hydrocodone, fentanyl, and methamphetamine.

Schedule III

- The drug or other substance has less potential for abuse than the drugs or other substances in Schedules I and II.
- The drug or other substance has a currently accepted medical use in treatment in the United States.
- Abuse of the drug or other substance may lead to moderate or low physical dependence or high psychological dependence.
- Anabolic steroids, codeine and hydrocodone products with aspirin or Tylenol®, and some barbiturates are examples of Schedule III substances.

Schedule IV

- The drug or other substance has a low potential for abuse relative to the drugs or other substances in Schedule III.
- The drug or other substance has a currently accepted medical use in treatment in the United States.
- Abuse of the drug or other substance may lead to limited physical dependence or psychological dependence relative to the drugs or other substances in Schedule III.
- Examples of drugs included in Schedule IV are alprazolam, clonazepam, and diazepam.

Schedule V

- The drug or other substance has a low potential for abuse relative to the drugs or other substances in Schedule IV.
- The drug or other substance has a currently accepted medical use in treatment in the United States.
- Abuse of the drug or other substances may lead to limited physical dependence or psychological dependence relative to the drugs or other substances in Schedule IV.
- Cough medicines with codeine are examples of Schedule V drugs.

SOURCE: Adapted from *Drugs of Abuse, 2015 Edition*, U.S. Department of Justice, Drug Enforcement Administration, 2015, https://www.dea.gov/pr/multimedia-library/publications/drug_of_abuse.pdf (accessed January 9, 2017)

In addition, scientists have been working to understand why some people who use addictive substances become addicted and why others do not or can more easily break the addiction. The results of many studies of identical and fraternal (nonidentical) twins and families with histories of substance abuse and addiction indicate that there is a genetic component to addiction. For example, the American Society of Addiction Medicine indicates in "Definition of Addiction" (April 19, 2011, http://www.asam.org/quality-practice/definition-of-addiction) that inheritance accounts for approximately 50% of an individual's probability of developing a substance abuse problem. Other factors, such as gender, age, social influences, and cultural characteristics, interact with one's genetics, resulting in an individual's susceptibility to addictive behavior.

Physiological, Psychological, and Sociocultural Factors

Some researchers maintain that the principal causes of substance use are external social influences, such as peer pressure, whereas the principal causes of substance abuse and/or dependence are psychological and physiological needs and pressures, including inherited tendencies. Additionally, psychoactive drug use at an early age may be a risk factor (a characteristic that increases likelihood) for subsequent dependence. This phenomenon is called the gateway theory and suggests that experimentation with substances such as alcohol and marijuana during adolescence can lead to the abuse of more addictive drugs such as cocaine, heroin, and methamphetamine in adulthood. However, Stephen Nkansah-Amankra and Mark Minelli assert in "'Gateway Hypothesis' and Early Drug Use: Additional Findings from Tracking a Population-Based Sample of Adolescents to Adulthood" (*Preventive Medicine Reports*, vol. 4, December 2016) that the correlation between early drug experimentation and later abuse remains unproven. As a result of their findings, they suggest that "proven multi-sectoral prevention strategies," rather than treatments that focus "only on individual behaviors," should form the basis of prevention programs aimed at adolescent drug abuse.

Physically, mood-altering substances affect brain processes. Most drugs that are abused stimulate the reward or pleasure center of the brain by causing the release of dopamine, which is a neurotransmitter (a chemical in the brain that relays messages from one nerve cell to another).

Psychologically, a person may become dependent on a substance because it relieves pain, offers escape from real or perceived problems, or makes the user feel more relaxed or confident in certain social settings. A successful first use of a substance may reduce the user's fear of the drug and thus lead to continued use and even dependence.

Socially, substance use may be widespread in some groups or environments. The desire to belong to a special group is a strong human characteristic, and those who use one or more substances may become part of a subculture that encourages and promotes use. An individual may be influenced by one of these groups to start using a substance, or he or she may be drawn to such a group after starting use somewhere else. In addition, a person—especially a young person—may not have access to alternative rewarding or pleasurable groups or activities that do not include substance use.

Researchers have identified complex relationships between physiological, psychological, and cultural factors that influence drinking and drinking patterns. Constraints (inhibitory factors) and motivations influence drinking patterns. In turn, drinking patterns influence the relationship between routine activities that are related to drinking and acute (immediate) consequences of drinking.

FIGURE 1.1

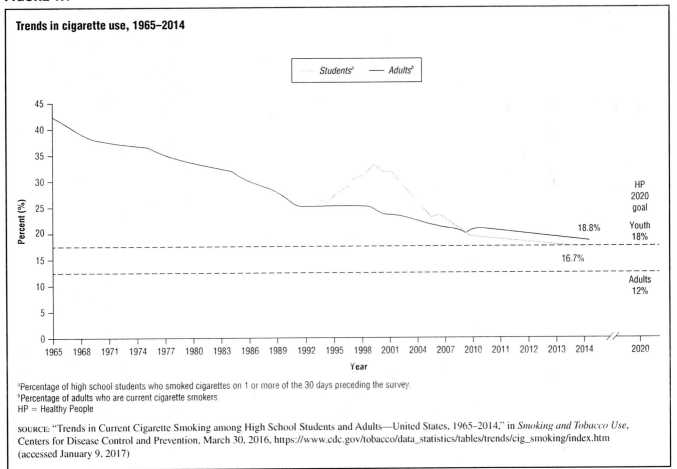

Trends in cigarette use, 1965–2014

[a]Percentage of high school students who smoked cigarettes on 1 or more of the 30 days preceding the survey.
[b]Percentage of adults who are current cigarette smokers.
HP = Healthy People

SOURCE: "Trends in Current Cigarette Smoking among High School Students and Adults—United States, 1965–2014," in *Smoking and Tobacco Use*, Centers for Disease Control and Prevention, March 30, 2016, https://www.cdc.gov/tobacco/data_statistics/tables/trends/cig_smoking/index.htm (accessed January 9, 2017)

Definitions of Abuse and Dependence

Two texts provide the most commonly used medical definitions of substance abuse and dependence. The *Diagnostic and Statistical Manual of Mental Disorders (DSM)* is published by the American Psychiatric Association (APA). The *International Classification of Diseases (ICD)* is published by the World Health Organization (WHO). Although the definitions of dependence in these two manuals are almost identical, the definitions of abuse are not.

THE *DSM* DEFINITION OF ABUSE. Published in 2013, the fifth edition of the *DSM (DSM-5)* combines substance dependence and substance abuse into a single category, substance use disorder, which is measured on a scale ranging between mild and severe. Some symptoms of substance use disorder include:

- Failure to fulfill major obligations at home, school, or work (e.g., repeated absences, poor performance, or neglect)

- Use in hazardous or potentially hazardous situations, such as driving a car or operating a machine while impaired

- Continued use in spite of social or interpersonal problems caused by the use of the substance, such as fights or family arguments

The *DSM-5* lists 11 symptoms of substance use disorder. In *Highlights of Changes from DSM-IV-TR to DSM-5* (August 6, 2015, https://www.psychiatry.org/File%20 Library/Psychiatrists/Practice/DSM/APA_DSM_Changes _from_DSM-IV-TR_-to_DSM-5.pdf), the APA reports that the presence of two to three of these criteria indicates a mild case of substance use disorder, four to five are evidence of a moderate disorder, and six or more signify a severe substance use disorder.

THE *ICD* DEFINITION OF HARMFUL USE. The 10th and most recent revision (as of March 2017) of the *ICD (ICD-10)*, which was endorsed by the 43rd World Health Assembly in May 1990 and has been used by WHO member states since 1994, uses the term *harmful use* rather than *abuse*. (The publication of the *ICD-11* in its final form is expected in 2018.) It defines harmful use as "a pattern of psychoactive substance use that is causing damage to health," either physical or mental.

Because the *ICD-10* manual is targeted toward international use, its definition must be broader than the *DSM-5* definition, which is intended for use in the United States. Cultural customs of substance use vary widely, sometimes even within the same country.

TABLE 1.4

Trends in illicit drug use, 1979–2014

[Thousands]

Year	Ages 12 or older					Adolescent (Ages 12–17)		
	Current use of any illicit drug[b]	Current marijuana use[b]	Current cocaine use[b]	Life time methamphetamine use	Life time heroin use	Current use of any illicit drug[b]	Current marijuana use[b]	Life time inhalant use[c]
1979	25,400	23,800	4,700	NA	2,300	3,900	3,374	NA
1982	NA	21,500	4,500	NA	1,800	2,800	2,199	NA
1985	23,300	18,600	5,700	NA	1,800	2,800	2,189	NA
1988	15,000	12,400	3,100	NA	1,700	1,900	1,102	NA
1990	13,500	10,900	1,700	NA	1,500	1,600	875	NA
1991	13,400	10,400	2,000	NA	2,400	1,200	722	NA
1992	12,000	9,700	1,400	NA	1,700	1,100	696	NA
1993	12,300	9,600	1,400	NA	2,100	1,200	845	NA
1994	12,600	10,100	1,400	NA	2,100	1,800	1,315	1,500
1995	12,800	9,800	1,500	NA	2,500	2,400	1,828	1,600
1996	13,000	10,100	1,700	NA	2,400	2,000	1,600	1,300
1997	13,900	11,100	1,500	NA	2,000	2,600	2,116	1,600
1998	13,600	11,000	1,800	NA	2,400	2,300	1,878	1,400
1999[a]	13,829	10,458	1,552	NA	3,054	2,265	1,676	2,118
2000	14,027	10,714	1,213	NA	2,779	2,264	1,678	2,079
2001	15,910	12,122	1,676	NA	3,091	2,556	1,889	2,038
2002[a]	19,522	14,584	2,020	15,365	3,668	2,878	2,023	2,605
2003	19,470	14,638	2,281	15,139	3,744	2,811	1,971	2,670
2004	19,071	14,576	2,021	14,512	3,145	2,674	1,909	2,762
2005	19,720	14,626	2,397	12,663	3,534	2,511	1,730	2,658
2006	20,387	14,849	2,426	14,226	3,788	2,488	1,695	2,559
2007	19,892	14,470	2,077	13,081	3,806	2,415	1,693	2,428
2008	20,123	15,269	1,865	12,634	3,795	2,312	1,668	2,326
2009	21,930	16,826	1,642	12,908	3,680	2,484	1,813	2,283
2010	22,648	17,409	1,472	13,060	4,144	2,468	1,802	2,015
2011	22,454	18,071	1,369	11,928	4,162	2,522	1,967	1,877
2012	23,863	18,855	1,650	12,259	4,565	2,377	1,800	1,613
2013	24,573	19,810	1,549	12,257	4,812	2,197	1,762	1,327
2014	26,983	22,188	1,530	12,943	4,813	2,338	1,830	1,307

NA = Data not available

[a]In 1999, the survey methodology changed from a paper-and-pencil interview (PAPI) to a computer–assisted interview (CAI). Estimates based on the new CAI methodology are not directly comparable to previous years. In 2002, the survey was renamed the National Survey on Drug Use and Health, and methodological changes were implemented that significantly affected reported prevalence rates. Therefore, estimates since 2002 are not directly comparable to previous years.

[b]Data for past-month (current) use.

[c]Prior to a 1994 questionnaire change, data did not allow separate reporting for this age group.

Note: "Any illicit drug use" includes use of marijuana, cocaine, hallucinogens, inhalants (except in 1982), heroin, or nonmedical use of sedatives, tranquilizers, stimulants, or analgesics. The exclusion of inhalants in 1982 is believed to have resulted in underestimates of any illicit use for that year, especially for adolescents.

SOURCE: "Table 1. Estimated Number of Users of Selected Illegal Drugs, 1979–2014 (Thousands)," in *National Drug Control Strategy: Data Supplement 2016*, Executive Office of the President, Office of National Drug Control Policy, 2016, https://obamawhitehouse.archives.gov/sites/default/files/ondcp/policy-and-research/2016_ndcs_data_supplement_20170110.pdf (accessed March 13, 2017)

THE HISTORY OF ALCOHOL USE

Ethyl alcohol (ethanol), the active ingredient in beer, wine, and other liquors, is the oldest known psychoactive drug. It is also the only type of alcohol that is used as a beverage. Other alcohols, such as methanol and isopropyl alcohol, when ingested even in small amounts can produce severe negative health effects and often death.

The basic characteristics of alcoholic beverages have remained unchanged from early times. Beer and wine are created through the natural chemical process called fermentation. Fermentation can produce beverages with an alcohol content of up to 14%. More potent drinks, such as rum or vodka (known as spirits or hard liquor), can be produced through distillation. This is a process that involves using heat to separate and concentrate the alcohol found in fermented beverages and can result in drinks that have an alcoholic content of 40% or more.

Early Uses and Abuses of Alcohol

Beer and wine have been used since ancient times in religious rituals, celebrations of councils, coronations, war, peacemaking, festivals, and the rites of birth, initiation, marriage, and death. In ancient times, just as in the 21st century, the use of beer and wine sometimes led to drunkenness. One of the earliest works on temperance (controlling one's drinking or not drinking at all) was written in Egypt nearly 3,000 years ago. These writings can be thought of as similar to present-day pamphlets that espouse moderation in alcohol consumption. Similar recommendations have been found in early Greek, Roman, Indian, Japanese, and Chinese writings, as well as in the Bible.

Drinking in Colonial America

In colonial America people drank much more alcohol than they do in the 21st century, with estimates ranging

FIGURE 1.2

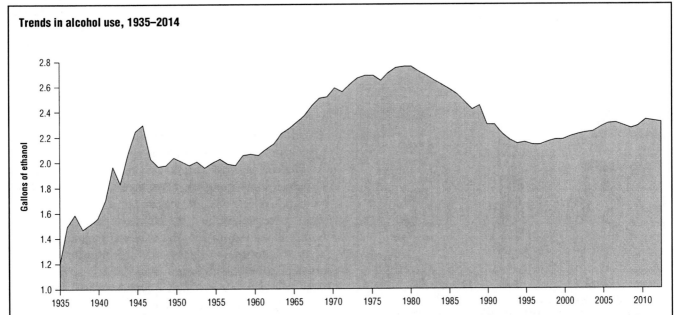

Trends in alcohol use, 1935–2014

SOURCE: Sarah P. Haughwout, Robin A. LaVallee, and I-Jen P. Castle, "Figure 1. Total per Capita Ethanol Consumption, United States, 1935–2014," in *Surveillance Report #104: Apparent per Capita Alcohol Consumption: National, State, and Regional Trends, 1977–2014*, U.S. Department of Health and Human Services, Public Health Service, National Institutes of Health, National Institute on Alcohol Abuse and Alcoholism, March 2016, https://pubs.niaaa.nih.gov/publications/surveillance104/CONS14.pdf (accessed January 9, 2017)

from three to seven times more alcohol per person per year. Liquor was used to ease the pain and discomfort of many illnesses and injuries such as the common cold, fever, broken bones, toothaches, and frostbite. In addition, a lack of clean water led many American colonists to view alcoholic beverages as healthier to consume. Furthermore, because beer was considered to be a food, its consumption was as a sign of social status in colonial society, while water was reserved for the lower classes. Parents often gave liquor to children to relieve their minor aches and pains or to help them sleep. Until 1842, when modern surgical anesthesia began with the use of ether, only heavy doses of alcohol were consistently effective to ease pain during operations.

As early as 1619 drunkenness was illegal in the Virginia Colony. It was punished in various ways: whipping, placement in the stocks, fines, and even wearing a red D (for "Drunkard"). By the 18th century all classes of people were getting drunk with greater frequency, even though it was well known that alcohol affected the senses and motor skills and that drunkenness led to increased crime, violence, accidents, and death.

Temperance

In 1784 Benjamin Rush (1746–1813), a physician and signer of the Declaration of Independence, published the booklet *An Inquiry into the Effects of Ardent Spirits on the Mind and Body*. The pamphlet became popular among the growing number of people who were concerned about the excessive drinking of many Americans. Such concern gave rise to the temperance movement.

The temperance movement in the United States spanned the 19th and early 20th centuries. Initially, the goal of the movement was to promote moderation in the consumption of alcohol. By the 1850s large numbers of people were completely giving up alcohol, and by the 1870s the goal of the temperance movement was to promote abstinence from alcohol. Reformers were concerned about the effects of alcohol on the family, the labor force, and the nation, all of which needed sober participants if they were to remain healthy and productive. Temperance supporters also saw alcoholism as a problem of personal immorality.

Prohibition

Temperance organizations lobbied for the prohibition of alcohol in the United States during the early years of the 20th century. One of the leading temperance organizations was the Anti-Saloon League, which created print materials to convince the public that alcohol should be banned. Figure 1.3 is one of the league's flyers, which showed that families that drank alcohol had a higher rate of child death than families that abstained from alcohol. However, the Anti-Saloon League's research did not take into account other factors that might affect the rate of child death among families, such as poverty. In addition, the league used sensationalist images in its print materials, such as children with gravestones above their heads, to sway public opinion.

In 1919 reform efforts led to the passage of the 18th Amendment of the U.S. Constitution, which prohibited the "manufacture, sale, or transportation of intoxicating

FIGURE 1.3

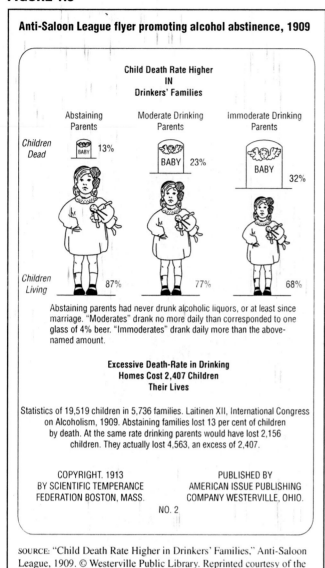

Anti-Saloon League flyer promoting alcohol abstinence, 1909

Child Death Rate Higher
IN
Drinkers' Families

| Abstaining Parents | Moderate Drinking Parents | Immoderate Drinking Parents |

Children Dead   13%   BABY 23%   BABY 32%

Children Living   87%   77%   68%

Abstaining parents had never drunk alcoholic liquors, or at least since marriage. "Moderates" drank no more daily than corresponded to one glass of 4% beer. "Immoderates" drank daily more than the above-named amount.

Excessive Death-Rate in Drinking Homes Cost 2,407 Children Their Lives

Statistics of 19,519 children in 5,736 families. Laitinen XII, International Congress on Alcoholism, 1909. Abstaining families lost 13 per cent of children by death. At the same rate drinking parents would have lost 2,156 children. They actually lost 4,563, an excess of 2,407.

COPYRIGHT. 1913
BY SCIENTIFIC TEMPERANCE
FEDERATION BOSTON, MASS.

PUBLISHED BY
AMERICAN ISSUE PUBLISHING
COMPANY WESTERVILLE, OHIO.

NO. 2

SOURCE: "Child Death Rate Higher in Drinkers' Families," Anti-Saloon League, 1909. © Westerville Public Library. Reprinted courtesy of the Westerville Public Library, Westerville, OH.

liquors" and their importation and exportation. The Volstead Act of 1919, which passed over President Woodrow Wilson's (1856–1924) veto, was the Prohibition law that enforced the 18th Amendment.

Outlawing alcohol did not stop most people from drinking; instead, alcohol was manufactured and sold illegally by gangsters, who organized themselves efficiently and gained considerable political influence from the money they earned. In addition, many individuals illegally brewed alcoholic beverages at home or smuggled alcohol from Canada and Mexico. Ultimately, the 18th Amendment was repealed in 1933 with the passage of the 21st Amendment.

Understanding the Dangers of Alcohol

As the decades passed, recognition of the dangers of alcohol increased. In 1956 the American Medical Association endorsed classifying and treating alcoholism as a disease. In 1970 Congress created the National Institute on Alcohol Abuse and Alcoholism, which established a public commitment to alcohol-related research. During the 1970s, however, many states lowered their drinking age to 18 when the legal voting age was lowered to this age.

Traffic fatalities rose after these laws took effect, and many such accidents involved people between the ages of 18 and 21 years who had been drinking and driving. Organizations such as Mothers against Drunk Driving and Students against Drunk Driving sought to educate the public about the great harm drunk drivers had done to others. As a result, and because of pressure from the federal government, by 1988 all states raised their minimum drinking age to 21. The National Highway Traffic Safety Administration of the U.S. Department of Transportation estimates in *Traffic Safety Facts, 2014 Data: Young Drivers* (May 2016, https://crashstats.nhtsa.dot .gov/Api/Public/ViewPublication/812278) that laws making 21 the minimum drinking age saved an estimated 30,323 lives between 1975 and 2014. By 1989 warning labels noting the deleterious effects of alcohol on health were required on all retail containers of alcoholic beverages. Nonetheless, the misuse and abuse of alcohol remain major health and social problems in the 21st century.

THE HISTORY OF TOBACCO USE

Tobacco is a commercially grown plant that contains nicotine, an addictive drug. Tobacco is native to North America, where since ancient times it has played an important part in Native American social and religious customs. Additionally, Native Americans believed that tobacco had medicinal properties, so it was used to treat pain, epilepsy, colds, and headaches.

From Pipes to Cigarettes

As European explorers and settlers came to North America during the 15th and 16th centuries, Native Americans introduced them to tobacco. Its use soon spread among the settlers, and then throughout Europe and Asia, although some rulers and nations opposed it and sought to outlaw it. At that point tobacco was smoked in pipes, chewed, or taken as snuff. Snuff is finely powdered tobacco that can be chewed, rubbed on the gums, or inhaled through the nose.

Cigar smoking was introduced to the United States in about 1762. Cigars are tobacco leaves that are rolled and prepared for smoking. The U.S. consumption of cigars exceeded 4 billion in 1898, according to various tobacco-related websites. However, cigarettes (cut tobacco rolled in a paper tube) would soon become the choice of most smokers, thanks to the 1881 invention of a cigarette-making machine that allowed them to be mass-produced and sold inexpensively.

Early Antismoking Efforts in the United States

The first antismoking movement in the United States was organized during the 1830s (just as the temperance movement was growing in the country). Reformers characterized tobacco as an unhealthy and even fatal habit. Tobacco use was linked to increased alcohol use and lack of cleanliness. Antismoking reformers also suggested that tobacco exhausted the soil, wasted money, and promoted laziness, promiscuity, and profanity. Their efforts to limit or outlaw smoking were met with only small, temporary successes until well into the 20th century.

A Boom in Smoking in the United States

The Centers for Disease Control and Prevention reports in "Surveillance for Selected Tobacco-Use Behaviors—United States, 1900–1994" (*Morbidity and Mortality Weekly Report*, vol. 43, no. SS03, November 18, 1994) that cigarette usage increased dramatically during the early 1900s, with the total consumption increasing from 2.5 billion cigarettes in 1901 to 13.2 billion cigarettes in 1912. In 1913 the R. J. Reynolds Company introduced Camel cigarettes, an event that is often called the birth of the modern cigarette. During World War I (1914–1918) cigarettes were shipped to U.S. troops fighting overseas (this also occurred during World War II [1939–1945]). They were included in soldiers' rations and were dispensed by groups such as the American Red Cross and the Young Men's Christian Association. Women began openly smoking in larger numbers as well, which was something that tobacco companies noticed; in 1919 the first advertisement featuring a woman smoking cigarettes appeared.

Cigarette smoking was very common and an accepted part of society, but doubts about its safety were growing. On July 12, 1957, following a joint report by the National Cancer Institute, the National Heart Institute, the American Cancer Society, and the American Heart Association, the U.S. surgeon general Leroy E. Burney (1906–1998), a smoker himself, delivered the official statement "Lung Cancer and Excessive Cigarette Smoking" (http://www.traumaf.org/Lung%20Cancer%20and%20Excessive%20Cigarette%20Smoking.pdf), in which he declared that "the weight of the evidence is increasingly pointing in one direction: that excessive smoking is one of the causative factors in lung cancer." Nevertheless, cigarette ads of the 1950s touted cigarette smoking as pleasurable, sexy, relaxing, flavorful, and fun.

Health Risks Lead to Diminished Smoking

In 1964 the U.S. surgeon general Luther L. Terry (1911–1985) released *Smoking and Health: Report of the Advisory Committee to the Surgeon General of the Public Health Service* (https://profiles.nlm.nih.gov/NN/B/B/M/Q/_/nnbbmq.pdf). This landmark document was the first widely publicized official recognition that cigarette smoking is a cause of lung cancer and laryngeal cancer in men, a probable cause of lung cancer in women, and the most important cause of chronic bronchitis.

Increased attention was paid to the potential health risks of smoking throughout the rest of the 1960s and 1970s. The first health warnings appeared on cigarette packages in 1966. In 1970 the WHO took a public stand against smoking. On January 2, 1971, the Public Health Cigarette Smoking Act of 1969 went into effect, removing cigarette advertising from radio and television in the United States. A growing number of individuals, cities, and states filed lawsuits against U.S. tobacco companies. Some individuals claimed they had been deceived about the potential harm of smoking. A few states filed lawsuits to recoup money spent on smokers' Medicaid bills. In 1998, 46 states, five territories, and the District of Columbia signed the Master Settlement Agreement (https://oag.ca.gov/tobacco/msa) with the major tobacco companies to settle all state lawsuits for $206 billion. Excluded from the settlement were Florida, Minnesota, Mississippi, and Texas, which had already concluded previous settlements with the tobacco industry. Chapter 7 includes more information on the Master Settlement Agreement and its long-term effects.

As awareness of the hazards of smoking increased, researchers began reporting the dangers of secondhand smoke (also known as environmental tobacco smoke or passive smoke). State and federal regulators responded to these studies by imposing strict new laws that regulated smoking, particularly in public places. In 1995 California became the first state to pass a law that prohibited smoking in restaurants and bars; the statute went into effect in 1998. Delaware passed a similar restriction in 2002, and by 2017 half of all U.S. states had implemented public smoking bans. According to Ryan Jaslow, in "Anti-smoking Laws Prevent Heart Attacks, Research Suggests" (CBS News.com, October 30, 2012), Mayo Clinic researchers reported in 2012 that the number of heart attacks caused by exposure to secondhand smoke dropped 33% due to public smoking bans. Chapter 3 provides a more detailed overview of antismoking legislation in the United States, as well as a more thorough analysis of shifting public attitudes toward smoking since the late 20th century.

THE EARLY HISTORY OF NARCOTIC, STIMULANT, AND HALLUCINOGEN USE

Humans have experimented with narcotic and hallucinogenic plants since before recorded history, discovering their properties as they tested plants for edibility or were attracted by the odors of some leaves when the leaves were burned. Ancient cultures used narcotic plants to relieve pain or to heighten pleasure and hallucinogenic plants to induce trancelike states during religious ceremonies. Natural substances, used directly or in refined extracts, have also served simply to increase or dull alertness, to invigorate the body, or to change the mood.

Narcotic Use through the 19th Century

As mentioned earlier, narcotics, including heroin and opium, are drugs that alter the perception of pain and induce sleep and euphoria. Opium is a dried powdered extract that is derived from the opium poppy plant *Papaver somniferum*. Morphine and heroin are made from opium, and all three of these addicting narcotics are called opiates.

Opium itself has been used as a pain reliever in Europe and Asia for thousands of years. In 1805 Friedrich Sertürner (1793–1841), a German pharmacist, discovered how to isolate the highly potent morphine from opium. In 1832 the French chemist Pierre-Jean Robiquet (1780–1840) isolated codeine from opium, which is milder than morphine. It came to be used in cough remedies. The development of the hypodermic needle during the early 1850s made it easier to use morphine. It became a common medicine for treating severe pain, such as battlefield injuries. During the U.S. Civil War (1861–1865) so many soldiers became addicted to morphine that the addiction was later called soldier's disease.

The most potent narcotic that is derived from opium is heroin, which was first synthesized in 1874 by Charles Romley Alder Wright (1844–1894) at St. Mary's Hospital in London, England. In 1898 the Bayer Company of Elberfeld, Germany, began marketing the drug as a cough remedy and painkiller under the brand-name Heroin; the word was derived from the German word for "heroic," which was intended to convey the drug's power and potency. The drug was an instant success and was soon exported.

Stimulant Use through the 19th Century

The use of stimulants dates back to about 3000 BC with South American societies. Even then, the people of this region knew that cocaine, which is extracted from the leaves of the coca tree *Erythroxylon coca*, was capable of producing euphoria, hyperactivity, and hallucinations. This small coca tree is native to tropical mountain regions in Peru and Bolivia.

After the Spanish conquest of the Incas during the early 1500s and the ensuing Spanish immigration into South America, coca was grown on plantations and used as wages to pay workers. The drug seemed to negate the effects of exhaustion and malnutrition, especially at high altitudes. Many South Americans still chew coca leaves to alleviate the effects of high altitudes.

The spread of the use of coca is attributed to Paolo Mantegazza (1831–1910), an Italian physician who came to value the restorative powers of coca while living in Lima, Peru, during the 1850s. He praised the drug, which led to interest in coca in the United States and Europe. In 1863 the French chemist Angelo Mariani (1838–1914) extracted cocaine from coca leaves and used it as the main ingredient in his coca wine, called Vin Mariani. Shortly thereafter, cough syrups and tonics holding drops of cocaine in solution became popular. Eventually, extracts from coca leaves not only appeared in wine but also in chewing gum, tea, and throat lozenges.

The temperance movement in the United States from 1800 to 1890 helped fuel the public's fondness for nonalcoholic products containing coca. During the mid-1880s Atlanta, Georgia, became one of the first major U.S. cities to forbid the sale of alcohol. It was there that the American inventor John Pemberton (1831–1888) first marketed Coca-Cola, a syrup that then contained extracts of both coca and the kola nut, as a "temperance drink."

Hallucinogen Use through the 19th Century

Naturally occurring hallucinogens, which are derived from plants, have been used by various cultures for magical, religious, recreational, and health-related purposes for thousands of years. For more than 2,000 years Native American societies often used hallucinogens, such as the psilocybin mushroom (*Psilocybe mexicana*) of Mexico and the peyote cactus (*Lophophora williamsii*) of the U.S. Southwest, in religious ceremonies. Although scientists were slow to discover the medicinal possibilities of hallucinogens, by 1919 they had isolated mescaline from the peyote cactus and recognized its resemblance to the adrenal hormone epinephrine (adrenaline).

Cannabis, also a hallucinogen, is the term generally applied to the hemp plants *Cannabis sativa* and *Cannabis indica*, from which marijuana, bhang, and hashish are derived. Bhang is equivalent to the U.S.-style marijuana, consisting of the leaves, fruits, and stems of the plant. Hashish is prepared by crushing the flowering tips of cannabis into a resinous paste.

Cannabis dates back more than 5,000 years to Central Asia and China; from there it spread to India and the Near East. Cannabis was highly regarded as a medicinal plant used in folk medicines. It was long valued as an analgesic (painkiller), topical anesthetic, antispasmodic, antidepressant, appetite stimulant, antiasthmatic, and antibiotic.

NARCOTIC, STIMULANT, AND HALLUCINOGEN USE AT THE END OF THE 19TH CENTURY AND BEYOND

In late 19th-century America it was possible to buy, in a store or by mail order, many medicines (or alleged medicines) that contained morphine, cocaine, and even heroin. Until 1903 the soft drink Coca-Cola contained cocaine. The cocaine was removed and more caffeine (which was already present in the drink from the kola nut) was added. Pharmacies sold cocaine in pure form, as well as many drugs made from opium, such as morphine and heroin.

Beginning in 1898 heroin became widely available when the Bayer Company marketed it as a powerful cough suppressant. According to the Office of Technology Assessment, in *Technologies for Understanding and Preventing Substance Abuse and Addiction* (September 1994, http://www.princeton.edu/~ota/disk1/1994/9435/9435.PDF), physician prescriptions of these drugs increased from 1% of all prescriptions in 1874 to between 20% and 25% in 1902. These drugs were readily available and widely used, with little concern for negative health consequences.

Soon, however, cocaine, heroin, and other drugs were taken off the market for a number of reasons. A growing awareness of the dangers of drug use and food contamination led to the passage of laws such as the Pure Food and Drug Act of 1906. Among other things, the act required the removal of false claims from patent medicines. Medical labels also had to state the amount of any narcotic ingredient the medicine contained and whether that medicine was habit-forming. A growing temperance movement, the development of safe painkillers (such as aspirin), and more alternative medical treatments contributed to the passage of laws that limited drug use, although these laws did not completely outlaw the drugs.

Besides health-related worries, drug use had come to be associated with "undesirables" by the mid- to late 1800s. When drug users were thought to live only in the slums, drug use was considered solely a criminal problem; but when it was finally recognized in middle-class neighborhoods, it came to be seen as a mental health problem. By the start of the 20th century the use of narcotics was considered to be an international problem. In 1909 the International Opium Commission met to discuss worldwide drug use. This meeting led to the signing of a treaty two years later in the Netherlands requiring all signatories to pass laws that limited the use of narcotics for medicinal purposes. After nearly three years of debate, Congress passed the Harrison Narcotic Act of 1914, which called for the strict control of opium and coca (although coca is a stimulant and not a narcotic).

Regulating Narcotics, Stimulants, and Hallucinogens

During the 1920s the federal government regulated drugs through the Department of the Treasury. In 1930 President Herbert Hoover (1874–1964) created the Federal Bureau of Narcotics and selected Harry J. Anslinger (1892–1975) to head it. Believing that all drug users were deviant criminals, Anslinger vigorously enforced the law for the next 32 years. Marijuana, for example, was presented as a "killer weed" that threatened the very fabric of American society.

Marijuana is thought to have been introduced to the United States by Mexican immigrants. Thus, according to the Office of Technology Assessment, in *Technologies*

for Understanding and Preventing Substance Abuse and Addiction, it was widely believed that anti-Mexican attitudes, as well as Anslinger's considerable influence, prompted the passage of the Marijuana Tax Act of 1937. The act made the use or sale of marijuana without a tax stamp a federal offense. Because by this time the sale of marijuana was illegal in most states, buying a federal tax stamp would alert the authorities in a particular state to who was selling drugs. Naturally, no marijuana dealer wanted to buy a stamp and expose his or her identity to the authorities.

From the 1940s to the 1960s the FDA, based on the authority granted by the Food, Drug, and Cosmetic Act of 1938, began policing the sale of certain drugs. The act required the FDA to stipulate if specific drugs, such as amphetamines (stimulants) and barbiturates (depressants), were safe for self-medication.

After studying most amphetamines and barbiturates, the agency concluded that it simply could not declare them safe for self-medication. (See Table 1.1 for listings of stimulants and depressants.) Therefore, it ruled that these drugs could only be used under medical supervision—that is, with a physician's prescription. For all pharmaceutical products other than narcotics, this marked the beginning of the distinction between prescription and over-the-counter (without a prescription) drugs.

For 25 years undercover FDA inspectors identified pharmacists who sold amphetamines and barbiturates without a prescription and doctors who wrote illegal prescriptions. During the 1950s, with the growing sale of amphetamines, barbiturates, and, eventually, LSD and other hallucinogens at cafés, truck stops, flophouses, and weight-reduction salons and by street-corner pushers, FDA authorities went after these other illegal dealers. In 1968 the drug-enforcement responsibilities of the FDA were transferred to the Department of Justice.

War on Drugs

From the mid-1960s to the late 1970s the demographic profile of drug users changed. Previously, drug use had generally been associated with minorities, lower classes, or young "hippies" and "beatniks." During this period drug use among middle- and upper-class whites became widespread and more generally accepted. Many of them began using cocaine, an expensive drug, which they considered to be nonaddictive and a status symbol. In addition, drugs had become much more prevalent in the military because they were cheap and plentiful in Vietnam.

Whereas some circles viewed drug use with wider acceptance, other public sectors came to see drugs as a threat to their communities—much as, 40 years earlier, alcohol had acquired a negative image, leading to Prohibition. Drugs not only symbolized poverty but also were associated with protest movements against the Vietnam War (1954–1975) and the so-called Establishment. Many parents began perceiving the widespread availability of drugs as a threat to their children. By the end of the 1960s such views were beginning to acquire a political expression.

When Richard M. Nixon (1913–1994) ran for president in 1968, he included a strong antidrug plank in his law-and-order platform, calling for a War on Drugs. After he was elected president, Nixon created the President's National Commission on Marihuana and Drug Abuse, which published its findings in *Marihuana: A Signal of Misunderstanding* (March 1972, http://www.druglibrary .org/Schaffer/Library/studies/nc/ncmenu.htm). Nixon ignored the commission's findings, which called for the legalization of marijuana. Since that time the U.S. government has been waging the War on Drugs. In 1973 Congress authorized the formation of the DEA to reduce the supply of drugs. The following year the National Institute on Drug Abuse (NIDA) was created to lead the effort to reduce the demand for drugs and to direct research, federal prevention, and treatment services.

Under the Nixon, Ford, and Carter administrations federal spending tended to emphasize the treatment of drug abusers. Meanwhile, a growing number of parents, fearing that their children were being exposed to drugs, began pressuring elected officials and government agencies to do more about the growing use of drugs. In response, the NIDA began widely publicizing the dangers of marijuana and other drugs once thought not to be particularly harmful.

President Ronald Reagan (1911–2004) favored a strict approach to drug use, popularized the phrase "War on Drugs," and increased enforcement efforts. In *Technologies for Understanding and Preventing Substance Abuse and Addiction*, the Office of Technology Assessment states that the budget to fight drugs rose from $1.5 billion in fiscal year (FY) 1981 to $4.2 billion in FY 1989. By the end of the Reagan administration two-thirds of all drug control funding went for law enforcement and one-third went for treatment and prevention. First Lady Nancy Reagan (1921–2016) vigorously campaigned against drug use, urging children to "just say no!" The Crime Control Act of 1984 dramatically increased the penalties for drug use and drug trafficking.

INTRODUCTION OF CRACK COCAINE. Cocaine use increased dramatically during the 1960s and 1970s, but the drug's high cost restricted its use to the more affluent. During the early 1980s cocaine dealers discovered a way to prepare cocaine so that it could be smoked in small and inexpensive but powerful and highly addictive amounts. The creation of this so-called crack cocaine meant that poor people could now afford to use the drug and led to the creation of a new market. In addition, the acquired immunodeficiency syndrome (AIDS) epidemic caused some injection drug users to switch to smoking crack to avoid exposure to the human immunodeficiency virus (HIV), which can be contracted by sharing needles with an infected user.

Battles for control of the distribution and sale of the drug led to a violent black market. The easy availability of firearms and the huge amounts of money to be made selling crack and other drugs transformed many areas of the nation—but particularly the inner cities—into dangerous places.

The widespread fear of crack cocaine led to increasingly harsh laws and penalties. Authorities warned that crack was highly addictive and spreading rapidly, and they predicted a subsequent generation of "crack babies"—that is, babies born addicted to crack because their mothers were using it during pregnancy.

HEROIN GETS CHEAPER AND PURER. The dangers associated with crack cocaine caused changes in the use of heroin during the 1980s. Many reported deaths from heroin overdosing had lessened the drug's attraction. In addition, heroin had to be injected by syringe, and concerns regarding HIV infection contributed to the dangers of using the drug. During the 1990s an oversupply of heroin, innovations that produced a smokable variety of the drug, and the appearance of purer forms of the drug restored its attractiveness to the relatively small number of people who were addicted to so-called hard drugs. It was no longer necessary to take the drug intravenously—it could be sniffed like cocaine—although many users continued to use needles.

The War Continues: The Office of National Drug Control Policy

The Anti-drug Abuse Act of 1988 created the Office of National Drug Control Policy (ONDCP), to be headed by a director—popularly referred to as the drug czar—who would coordinate the nation's drug policy. The Office of Technology Assessment reports in *Technologies for Understanding and Preventing Substance Abuse and Addiction* that spending for drug control rose from $4.2 billion in FY 1989 under President Reagan to $12.7 billion in FY 1993 under President George H. W. Bush (1924–). As was the case during the Reagan administration, the monetary split was roughly two-thirds for law enforcement and one-third for treatment and prevention. By 1990 every state that had once decriminalized the use of marijuana had repealed those laws.

The Office of Technology Assessment indicates that when President Bill Clinton (1946–) took office in 1993, he cut the ONDCP staff from 146 to 25, while at the same time raising the director of the ONDCP to cabinet status. Clinton called for 100,000 more police officers on the streets and advocated drug treatment on demand. According to the ONDCP, in *The National Drug Control Strategy, FY 2004 Budget Summary* (February 2003, https://www.ncjrs.gov/pdffiles1/ondcp/198157.pdf), drug control funding totaled $8.2 billion in FY 1998, with the split 52% for law enforcement and 48% for treatment and prevention. (It is important to note that during the mid-1990s changes were made in the list of expenditures included in this tally and that in 2003 the national drug control budget was restructured, thus making it difficult to analyze historical drug control spending trends before and after 1995. The FY 2004 budget summary provides a recalculation of historical tables from FYs 1995 to 2004.)

When he took office in 2001, President George W. Bush (1946–) promised to continue national efforts to eradicate illicit drugs in the United States and abroad. In May 2001 he appointed John P. Walters (1952?–) as the new drug czar. Together, they pledged to continue to reduce illicit drug use in the United States. Their proposed goals included increased spending on treatment, intensified work with foreign nations, and an adamant opposition to the legalization of any currently illicit drugs. The Bush administration also wove its antidrug message into its arguments for invading Afghanistan. Although Bush's case was built primarily on the notion that Afghanistan's Taliban leaders were harboring the terrorist Osama bin Laden (1957?–2011), Bush regularly referred to Afghanistan's role as the world's biggest producer of opium poppies.

By 2008, however, some foreign policy experts viewed the Bush administration's opium poppy eradication program as both an economic and political disaster. In "Still Wrong in Afghanistan" (WashingtonPost.com, January 23, 2008), the veteran diplomat Richard Holbrooke (1941–2010) described the policy as arguably "the single most ineffective program in the history of American foreign policy." Citing the program's annual cost at roughly $1 billion, Holbrooke suggested that the policy actually helped strengthen "the Taliban and al-Qaeda, as well as criminal elements within Afghanistan," largely by driving "farmers with no other source of livelihood into the arms of the Taliban."

In June 2009 President Obama announced a major change in the United States' drug strategy for Afghanistan, in which resources were shifted from the eradication of poppy fields to the prohibition of supplies needed to grow opium and to more vigorous efforts to curtail drug smuggling operations. At the same time, the new policy aimed to help Afghan farmers with the cultivation of alternative crops. Nevertheless, these new efforts to curb the production of opium in Afghanistan also proved ineffective. According to the article "Afghanistan Sees Rise in Poppy Cultivation" (Aljazeera.com, November 12, 2014), opium production in Afghanistan reached 7,000 tons (6,400 t) in 2014, an increase of roughly 17% over the previous year. Dawood Azami reports in "Why Afghanistan May Never Eradicate Opium" (BBC.com,

February 25, 2013) that the rise in poppy production was driven by a combination of factors. Notable among these were the Afghan government's repeated failures to distribute the seeds and other materials necessary to promote the cultivation of alternative crops, as well as the high prices commanded by opium in the world market, a factor that made poppy growing too lucrative to resist for many Afghan farmers. In "U.S. Kicks Drug-War Habit, Makes Peace with Afghan Poppies" (Wired.com, May 9, 2013), David Axe notes that by 2013 the U.S. military had adopted a policy of nonintervention in regard to poppy farming in Afghanistan, as opium production came to be seen as having a relatively stabilizing influence on the war-torn nation.

Questioning the War on Drugs

By 2007 there was considerable controversy surrounding the necessity and effectiveness of the War on Drugs. Decades of effort had led to large numbers of people serving prison sentences for manufacturing, selling, or using drugs. However, the illicit drug trade continued to thrive. Many critics argued that a different approach was necessary and questioned whether illicit drugs were an enemy worth waging war against, especially such a costly war during a time of rapidly rising federal budget deficits.

The American public also appeared to view the War on Drugs as a low priority. Jeffrey M. Jones of Gallup, Inc., indicates in *Economy Runaway Winner as Most Important Problem* (November 21, 2008, http://www.gallup.com/poll/112093/Economy-Runaway-Winner-Most-Important-Problem.aspx) that in 2008, 58% of adult Americans rated the economy as the top problem in the United States; drugs were not listed among the top-13 most important problems. Other problems seen as having a higher priority than drugs were the war in Iraq, unemployment, dissatisfaction with government leaders, national security, education, and terrorism.

In November 2008 the Partnership for the Americas Commission of the Brookings Institution released *Rethinking U.S.-Latin American Relations: A Hemispheric Partnership for a Turbulent World* (https://www.brookings.edu/wp-content/uploads/2016/06/1124_latin_america_partnership.pdf). The report noted that "current U.S. counternarcotics policies are failing by most objective measures" and that "the only long-run solution to the problem of illegal narcotics is to reduce the demand for drugs in the major consuming countries, including the United States." The report also suggested that the United States should work to reduce the flow of guns to Mexico, which would help curb the flow of drugs to the United States; expand drug prevention programs in schools, especially those that emphasize drugs' disfiguring attributes to young people; and promote drug courts, which merge treatment with incarceration.

In the months that followed President Obama's inauguration, the new administration began showing signs of rethinking existing drug policy in the United States. Gil Kerlikowske (1949–), who was named the director of the ONDCP, called for an end to the War on Drugs and favored treatment over prison time for drug offenders. In its inaugural *National Drug Control Strategy* (2010, https:// obamawhitehouse.archives.gov/sites/default/files/ondcp/ policy-and-research/ndcs2010.pdf), the Obama administration outlined a "new, balanced approach" to drug policy, one that prioritized prevention and treatment efforts, while also maintaining strong law enforcement policies aimed at curbing the distribution of illegal substances, particularly on the U.S. border with Mexico. In a notable shift from previous administrations, Obama's drug strategy also set out to address inequalities in drug sentencing laws, in particular the discrepancy between penalties for crack cocaine and cocaine powder possession. The administration notes that, beginning in the 1980s, first-time possession of 5 grams of crack cocaine had carried the same mandatory five-year prison term as possessing 500 grams of cocaine powder; because 85% of crack cocaine offenders were African American, this policy was perceived to have a "disproportionate racial impact" on U.S. drug laws. Obama addressed this imbalance in August 2010, when he signed the Fair Sentencing Act, a new law that repealed mandatory sentences for crack cocaine possession, while significantly reducing the disparity between penalties for crack and powder cocaine.

Despite indications that it was prepared to scale back the War on Drugs, the Obama administration remained staunchly opposed to drug decriminalization and legalization efforts, notably those relating to marijuana. Citing data from the FDA and the Institute of Medicine, the Obama administration's 2012 *National Drug Control Strategy* (https://obamawhitehouse.archives.gov/sites/default/ files/ondcp/2012_ndcs.pdf) rebuffs claims that marijuana is either effective as medicine or safe to use. Furthermore, the report asserts that "legalizing marijuana would not provide the answer to any of the health, social, youth education, criminal justice, and community quality of life challenges associated with drug use."

In 2013, after Washington and Colorado voted to legalize the sale and consumption of marijuana for recreational purposes, the administration's policy toward the drug began to shift. Ryan J. Reilly and Ryan Grim report in "Eric Holder Says DOJ Will Let Washington, Colorado Marijuana Laws Go into Effect" (Huffington Post.com, August 29, 2013) that in August 2013 the U.S. attorney general Eric Holder Jr. (1951–) announced that the Department of Justice would not intervene in the regulation of marijuana use in these states, provided that certain federal standards were met. Key stipulations included prevention of the sale of marijuana to minors, as well as a prohibition on trafficking the drug across state lines. In "State Department Official Calls for 'Flexibility' on Drug Control Treaties" (HuffingtonPost.com, October 14, 2014), Matt Sledge reveals that by 2014 the Obama administration had adopted a more "flexible" attitude toward international drug treaties, relaxing its traditionally uncompromising prohibitionist stance to grant signatory nations greater freedom to determine their own legalization policies. Meanwhile, a number of other states began passing laws that legalized marijuana for medical and recreational purposes. Alaska, Oregon, and the District of Columbia legalized recreational marijuana in 2014. California, Maine, Massachusetts, and Nevada voted to legalize recreational marijuana in 2016. That same year the use of marijuana for medicinal purposes became legal in Florida, North Dakota, Ohio, and Pennsylvania.

Although this shift in federal strategy was praised by legalization advocates, it also sparked opposition from both Democrats and Republicans in Congress. Matt Ferner notes in "Senators Rip Obama's 'Flexible' Interpretation of U.N. Drug Controls" (HuffingtonPost.com, January 13, 2015) that in January 2015 the U.S. senators Dianne Feinstein (1933–; D-CA) and Chuck Grassley (1933–; R-IA) wrote letters to Holder and the U.S. secretary of state John Kerry (1943–) that criticized the administration's new policy, asserting that it undermined the country's leadership in relation to international drug laws, while also conveying that the federal government had adopted a more tolerant attitude toward drug use. Despite these complaints, the Obama administration remained firmly opposed to marijuana legalization. However, with the inauguration of Donald J. Trump (1946–), a Republican, as the nation's 45th president in January 2017, the future of federal policy toward marijuana legalization remained unclear.

CHAPTER 2
ALCOHOL

Contrary to popular belief, ethanol (the alcohol in alcoholic beverages) is not a stimulant, but a depressant. Although many of those who drink alcoholic beverages feel relaxation, pleasure, and stimulation, these feelings are caused by the depressant effects of alcohol on the brain.

WHAT CONSTITUTES A DRINK?

In the United States a standard drink contains about 0.5 ounces (14.8 mL) of pure alcohol. The following beverages contain nearly equal amounts of alcohol and are approximately standard drink equivalents:

- One shot (1.5 ounces, or 44.4 mL) of spirits (80-proof whiskey, vodka, gin, and so on)

- One 2.5-ounce (73.9-mL) glass of a cordial, liqueur, or aperitif

- One 5-ounce (147.9-mL) glass of table wine

- One 3- to 4-ounce (88.7- to 118.3-mL) glass of fortified wine, such as sherry or port

- One 12-ounce (354.9-mL) bottle or can of beer

- One 8- to 9-ounce (236.6- to 266.2-mL) bottle or can of malt liquor

ALCOHOL CONSUMPTION IN THE UNITED STATES

After caffeine, alcohol is the most commonly used drug in the United States. Although researchers frequently count how many people are drinking and how often, the statistics do not necessarily reflect the true picture of alcohol consumption in the United States. People tend to underreport their drinking. Furthermore, survey interviewees are typically people living in households; therefore, the results of survey research may not include the homeless, a portion of the U.S. population that is traditionally at risk for alcoholism (alcohol dependence).

Alcohol: A Lucrative Business

As Table 2.1 shows, yearly expenditures on alcoholic beverages have increased steadily since 1935. In 1980 annual total expenditures on alcoholic beverages topped $45.4 billion; by 2014 this figure nearly quadrupled, to $176.1 billion. Overall, in 2014 consumers spent $92.8 billion on packaged alcoholic beverages, or beverages to be consumed at home, compared with $83.3 billion spent on alcoholic beverages consumed away from home. Restaurants and bars represented the largest share of alcoholic beverage sales in 2014, accounting for $66.9 billion (38%). By comparison, liquor stores accounted for $47.5 billion (27%) of alcoholic beverage sales.

Individual Consumption of Alcohol

The data for alcohol consumption mentioned in the previous section are per capita figures, which are determined by taking the total consumption of alcohol per year and dividing by the total resident population, including children. This figure is useful for showing how consumption changes from year to year because it takes into account changes in the size of the resident population. Nonetheless, babies and small children generally do not consume alcohol, so it is also useful to look at consumption figures that are based on U.S. residents aged 12 years and older.

Table 2.2 shows the percentage of respondents aged 12 years and older who reported consuming alcohol in the past month in 2014 and 2015 when questioned for the annual National Survey on Drug Use and Health, which is conducted by the Substance Abuse and Mental Health Services Administration. In 2015, 51.7% of this total population had consumed alcohol in the month before the survey, a figure that was slightly lower than the percentage of the total population that had consumed alcohol within the previous month in 2014 (52.7%). A higher percentage of males had consumed alcoholic beverages in the past month than did females in both

TABLE 2.1

Total alcoholic beverage expenditures, 1935–2014

[Million dollars]

Year	Packaged alcoholic beverages at home				Eating and drinking places[b]	Alcoholic drinks away from home			All alcoholic beverages
	Liquor stores	Food stores	All other	Total[a]		Hotels and motels[b]	All other	Total[a]	Total[a]
1935	305	65	199	569	964	81	20	1,065	1,634
1936	435	95	220	750	1,195	97	24	1,316	2,066
1937	504	113	235	852	1,299	109	28	1,436	2,288
1938	479	111	227	817	1,246	98	26	1,370	2,187
1939	517	122	237	876	1,365	103	28	1,496	2,372
1940	602	131	244	977	1,459	113	30	1,602	2,579
1941	758	151	271	1,180	1,753	124	37	1,914	3,094
1942	1,081	194	311	1,586	2,176	145	47	2,368	3,954
1943	1,395	225	361	1,981	2,744	194	60	2,998	4,979
1944	1,734	252	393	2,379	3,144	219	69	3,432	5,811
1945	2,070	272	422	2,764	3,609	236	79	3,924	6,688
1946	2,443	368	472	3,283	3,984	272	91	4,347	7,630
1947	2,540	341	481	3,362	4,178	274	96	4,548	7,910
1948	2,487	475	484	3,446	4,172	272	100	4,544	7,990
1949	2,359	550	479	3,388	4,029	258	110	4,397	7,785
1950	2,399	569	487	3,455	4,028	259	126	4,413	7,868
1951	2,646	617	526	3,789	4,341	272	152	4,765	8,554
1952	2,786	668	545	3,999	4,442	281	176	4,899	8,898
1953	2,830	698	552	4,080	4,482	282	196	4,960	9,040
1954	2,942	685	562	4,189	4,454	274	218	4,946	9,135
1955	3,060	717	584	4,361	4,552	290	226	5,068	9,429
1956	3,408	756	616	4,780	4,753	309	238	5,300	10,080
1957	3,642	806	645	5,093	4,861	325	252	5,438	10,531
1958	3,841	868	656	5,365	4,910	330	261	5,501	10,866
1959	4,056	919	678	5,653	5,014	356	289	5,659	11,312
1960	4,137	966	690	5,793	5,039	378	317	5,734	11,527
1961	4,120	979	695	5,794	4,975	395	337	5,707	11,501
1962	4,494	1,071	714	6,279	5,172	427	365	5,964	12,243
1963	4,665	1,169	725	6,559	5,306	458	385	6,149	12,708
1964	4,958	1,272	761	6,991	5,465	493	408	6,366	13,357
1965	5,247	1,382	809	7,438	5,681	541	440	6,662	14,100
1966	5,676	1,535	864	8,075	5,981	593	487	7,061	15,136
1967	6,005	1,539	904	8,448	6,222	623	551	7,396	15,844
1968	6,576	1,708	955	9,234	6,642	667	587	7,896	17,130
1969	7,034	1,834	987	9,855	6,878	691	624	8,193	18,048
1970	7,671	2,110	1,064	10,845	7,652	760	657	9,069	19,914
1971	8,506	2,297	1,102	11,905	8,026	849	678	9,553	21,458
1972	8,810	2,702	1,113	12,625	7,911	961	704	9,576	22,201
1973	9,236	3,105	1,254	13,595	8,747	1,069	757	10,573	24,168
1974	9,948	3,600	1,355	14,903	9,371	1,167	778	11,316	26,219
1975	10,681	4,080	1,519	16,280	10,324	1,315	887	12,526	28,806
1976	11,170	4,209	1,717	17,096	11,088	1,555	947	13,590	30,686
1977	11,686	4,603	1,946	18,235	11,981	1,713	1,266	14,960	33,195
1978	12,179	5,211	2,222	19,612	13,342	2,023	1,303	16,668	36,280
1979	13,528	5,903	2,480	21,911	15,152	2,306	1,435	18,893	40,804
1980	14,977	6,995	2,816	24,788	16,722	2,450	1,484	20,656	45,444
1981	15,648	7,629	3,141	26,418	17,976	2,751	1,528	22,255	48,673
1982	15,984	8,147	3,378	27,509	18,371	2,849	1,488	22,708	50,217
1983	16,818	8,999	3,878	29,695	19,038	3,051	1,620	23,709	53,404
1984	15,997	10,132	4,158	30,287	19,863	3,220	1,691	24,774	55,061
1985	17,058	10,361	4,152	31,571	20,659	3,371	1,816	25,846	57,417
1986	17,350	10,755	5,031	33,136	22,291	3,406	1,935	27,632	60,768
1987	17,283	9,164	4,156	30,603	23,232	3,108	2,527	28,867	59,470
1988	17,007	9,436	4,404	30,846	24,227	3,237	2,802	30,267	61,113
1989	17,292	10,073	4,913	32,278	24,748	3,214	3,077	31,039	63,317
1990	18,597	10,844	5,428	34,869	26,528	3,186	3,429	33,144	68,013
1991	19,123	10,770	5,800	35,693	27,200	3,059	3,606	33,866	69,559
1992	18,418	10,700	6,647	35,764	27,727	3,124	3,823	34,674	70,438
1993	18,370	11,146	6,801	36,318	28,393	3,111	3,917	35,421	71,739
1994	18,846	11,735	6,940	37,520	29,227	3,175	4,010	36,413	73,933
1995	18,850	12,280	7,135	38,264	30,194	3,187	4,152	37,534	75,798
1996	19,922	12,953	7,467	40,343	31,379	3,197	4,270	38,846	79,189
1997	20,864	12,798	6,759	40,421	33,427	3,491	4,436	41,354	81,775
1998	21,859	14,139	6,934	42,931	35,688	5,173	4,741	45,603	88,534
1999	22,725	15,159	7,439	45,322	38,090	7,043	5,447	50,580	95,902

years. Table 2.2 also shows that alcohol consumption varies by race. A higher percentage of whites had used alcohol within the month before the survey than had other races and ethnic groups.

Prevalence of Problem Drinking

Table 2.2 also shows the percentages of Americans aged 12 years and older who engaged in binge drinking or heavy alcohol use in the month before the survey. Binge drinking means a male had five or more drinks and a female had four or more drinks on the same occasion, that is, within a couple hours of each other. Heavy alcohol use means a person had participated in binge drinking on the same occasion on each of five or more days in the past 30 days. All heavy alcohol users are binge drinkers, but not all binge drinkers are heavy alcohol users.

TABLE 2.1

Total alcoholic beverage expenditures, 1935–2014 [CONTINUED]

[Million dollars]

Year	Packaged alcoholic beverages at home				Eating and drinking places[b]	Alcoholic drinks away from home			All alcoholic beverages
	Liquor stores	Food stores	All other	Total[a]		Hotels and motels[b]	All other	Total[a]	Total[a]
2000	24,350	15,847	8,022	48,218	41,533	6,404	5,468	53,405	101,623
2001	25,168	16,888	8,214	50,270	44,174	4,942	5,297	54,412	104,682
2002	27,951	17,356	10,161	55,468	47,180	4,320	5,862	57,362	112,830
2003	28,623	17,520	11,074	57,217	49,068	4,333	6,585	59,986	117,203
2004	30,613	18,056	11,905	60,575	49,943	4,575	7,365	61,883	122,458
2005	32,103	18,603	12,809	63,515	51,248	4,707	7,602	63,556	127,071
2006	34,600	18,968	13,486	67,054	53,570	4,770	9,083	67,423	134,477
2007	36,791	19,545	13,406	69,743	53,201	4,730	10,061	67,992	137,735
2008	38,018	20,336	20,677	79,031	54,827	4,822	10,236	69,884	148,915
2009	39,025	20,297	18,980	78,303	53,989	4,669	9,997	68,655	146,958
2010	40,245	20,728	20,326	81,299	55,153	4,721	10,183	70,057	151,356
2011	40,829	21,803	22,398	85,030	57,936	4,774	10,449	73,159	158,189
2012	43,337	22,463	23,646	89,446	61,508	4,882	10,947	77,337	166,783
2013	44,994	22,922	22,447	90,363	62,861	4,899	11,415	79,175	169,538
2014	47,524	23,523	21,786	92,833	66,860	4,926	11,483	83,269	176,102

[a]Computed from unrounded data.
[b]Includes tips.

SOURCE: "Table 4. Alcoholic Beverages: Total Expenditures," in *Food Expenditures*, U.S. Department of Agriculture, Economic Research Service, January 26, 2016, https://www.ers.usda.gov/webdocs/DataFiles/Food_Expenditures__17981/FoodExpenditures_table4.xls?v=42395 (accessed January 9, 2017)

TABLE 2.2

Percentage of past-month alcohol use, binge alcohol use, and heavy alcohol use among drinkers aged 12 and older, by age, sex, and race and Hispanic origin, 2014 and 2015

Demographic characteristic	Alcohol use (2014)	Alcohol use (2015)	Binge alcohol use (2014)	Binge alcohol use (2015)	Heavy alcohol use (2014)	Heavy alcohol use (2015)
Total	52.7[a]	51.7	nc	24.9	nc	6.5
Age						
12–17	11.5[b]	9.6	nc	5.8	nc	0.9
18 or older	56.9[a]	56.0	nc	26.9	nc	7.0
18–25	59.6	58.3	nc	39.0	nc	10.9
26 or older	56.5	55.6	nc	24.8	nc	6.4
Gender						
Male	57.3	56.2	30.0	29.6	9.3	8.9
Female	48.4	47.4	nc	20.5	nc	4.2
Hispanic origin and race						
Not Hispanic or Latino	54.3	53.5	nc	24.8	nc	6.8
White	57.7	57.0	nc	26.0	nc	7.6
Black or African American	44.2	43.8	nc	23.4	nc	4.8
American Indian or Alaska Native	42.3	37.9	nc	24.1	nc	4.7
Native Hawaiian or other Pacific Islander	37.9	33.8	nc	17.8	nc	3.0
Asian	38.7	39.7	nc	14.0	nc	2.2
Two or more races	49.5[a]	42.8	nc	22.9	nc	6.8
Hispanic or Latino	44.4	42.4	nc	25.7	nc	4.8

nc = not comparable due to methodological changes
[a]The difference between this estimate and the 2015 estimate is statistically significant at the 0.05 level. Rounding may make the estimates appear identical.
[b]The difference between this estimate and the 2015 estimate is statistically significant at the 0.01 level. Rounding may make the estimates appear identical.
Note: "Binge alcohol use" is defined as drinking five or more drinks (for males) or four or more drinks (for females) on the same occasion (i.e., at the same time or within a couple of hours of each other) on at least 1 day in the past 30 days. In 2015, the definition for females changed from five to four drinks. "Heavy alcohol use" is defined as binge drinking on the same occasion on each of 5 or more days in the past 30 days; all heavy alcohol users are also binge alcohol users.

SOURCE: "Table 2.46B. Alcohol Use, Binge Alcohol Use, and Heavy Alcohol Use in Past Month among Persons Aged 12 or Older, by Demographic Characteristics: Percentages, 2014 and 2015," in *2015 National Survey on Drug Use and Health: Detailed Tables*, U.S. Department of Health and Human Services, Substance Abuse and Mental Health Services Administration, September 8, 2016, https://www.samhsa.gov/data/sites/default/files/NSDUH-DetTabs-2015/NSDUH-DetTabs-2015/NSDUH-DetTabs-2015.pdf (accessed January 9, 2017)

In 2015 people aged 18 to 25 years were more likely than people in other age groups to be binge drinkers and heavy alcohol users. Much higher percentages of males binge drank and used alcohol heavily than females in the month before each of these surveys. Whites (26%) were the most likely to have engaged in binge drinking in

2015, followed by Hispanics (25.7%) and Native Americans or Alaskan Natives (24.1%). Whites (7.6%) were also more likely than all other groups to have engaged in heavy alcohol use in 2015. By comparison, only 2.2% of Asian Americans were heavy drinkers in 2015.

DEFINING ALCOHOLISM

Most people consider an alcoholic to be someone who drinks too much alcohol and cannot control his or her drinking. Alcoholism, however, does not merely refer to heavy drinking or getting drunk a certain number of times. The diagnosis of alcoholism applies only to those who show specific symptoms of addiction, which the Institute of Medicine defines in *Dispelling the Myths about Addiction: Strategies to Increase Understanding and Strengthen Research* (1997) as a brain disease "manifested by a complex set of behaviors that are the result of genetic, biological, psychological, and environmental interactions."

In "The Definition of Alcoholism" (*Journal of the American Medical Association*, vol. 268, no. 8, August 26, 1992), Robert M. Morse and Daniel K. Flavin define alcoholism as "a primary, chronic disease with genetic, psychosocial, and environmental factors influencing its development and manifestations. The disease is often progressive and fatal. It is characterized by impaired control over drinking, preoccupation with the drug alcohol, use of alcohol despite adverse consequences, and distortions in thinking, most notably denial. Each of these symptoms may be continuous or periodic."

"Primary" refers to alcoholism as a disease independent from any other psychological disease (e.g., schizophrenia), rather than as a symptom of some other underlying disease. "Adverse consequences" for an alcoholic can include physical illness (such as liver disease or withdrawal symptoms), psychological problems, interpersonal difficulties (such as marital problems or domestic violence), and problems at work. "Denial" includes a number of psychological maneuvers by the drinker to avoid the fact that alcohol is the cause of his or her problems. Family and friends may reinforce an alcoholic's denial by covering up his or her drinking (e.g., calling an employer to say the alcoholic has the flu rather than a hangover). Such behavior is also known as enabling. In other words, family and friends make excuses for the drinker and enable him or her to continue drinking as opposed to having to face the repercussions of his or her alcohol abuse. Denial is a major obstacle in recovery from alcoholism.

The Mayo Clinic provides in "Alcohol Use Disorder" (July 25, 2015, http://www.mayoclinic.org/diseases -conditions/alcohol-use-disorder/basics/definition/con-20020 866) a very simple and straightforward definition of alcoholism: "Alcohol use disorder (which includes a level that's sometimes called alcoholism) is a pattern of alcohol use that involves problems controlling your drinking, being preoccupied with alcohol, continuing to use alcohol even when it causes problems, having to drink more to get the same effect, or having withdrawal symptoms when you rapidly decrease or stop drinking."

ALCOHOLISM AND ALCOHOL ABUSE

The American Psychiatric Association (APA), which publishes the *Diagnostic and Statistical Manual of Mental Disorders* (*DSM*), first defined alcoholism in 1952. The *DSM-III* (1980), the third edition of the APA's publication, renamed alcoholism as alcohol dependence and introduced the term *alcohol abuse*. According to the *DSM-III*'s definition of alcohol abuse, the condition involves a compulsive use of alcohol and impaired social or occupational functioning, whereas alcohol dependence includes physical tolerance and withdrawal symptoms when the drug is stopped. Although the *DSM-IV* (1994) retained these definitions, the *DSM-5* (2013) combined alcohol dependence and alcohol abuse into a single category, alcohol use disorder (AUD), which was subsequently divided into degrees of mild, moderate, and severe. The *DSM-5* lists 11 symptoms of AUD, including repeated failures to curb alcohol consumption; the curtailment of social, professional, and recreational activities due to alcohol use; and symptoms of alcohol withdrawal syndrome. (See Table 2.3.)

Prevalence of Alcohol Use Disorder, Binge Drinking, and Heavy Drinking

The National Institute on Alcohol Abuse and Alcoholism (NIAAA) reports in "Alcohol Use Disorder" (2017, http://www.niaaa.nih.gov/alcohol-health/overview -alcohol-consumption/alcohol-use-disorders) that 17 million Americans (7.2% of the population aged 18 years and older) had AUD in 2012. In addition, the NIAAA notes that roughly 855,000 adolescents between the ages of 12 and 17 years suffered from AUD that year.

Figure 2.1 shows the percentages of people who engaged in alcohol use, binge drinking, and heavy alcohol use in 2015. Of the 138.3 million current alcohol users that year, nearly half (66.7 million, or 48.2%) were binge drinkers. In addition, slightly more than a quarter (17.3 million, or 26%) of binge drinkers in 2015 were also heavy alcohol users.

RISK FACTORS OF ALCOHOL USE DISORDERS

The development of AUD is the result of a complex mix of biological, psychological, and social factors, including genetics, alcohol reactivity (sensitivity), and psychosocial factors. Genetics and alcohol reactivity are biological factors. The rest are psychosocial factors.

TABLE 2.3

Symptoms of alcohol use disorder (AUD)

DSM–IV	DSM–5	
Any 1 = Alcohol abuse	In the past year, have you:	The presence of at least 2 of these symptoms indicates an **Alcohol Use Disorder (AUD).**
1 Found that drinking—or being sick from drinking—often interfered with taking care of your home or family? Or caused job troubles? Or school problems?	Had times when you ended up drinking more, or longer, than you intended?	The severity of the AUD is defined as:
2 More than once gotten into situations while or after drinking that increased your chances of getting hurt (such as driving, swimming, using machinery, walking in a dangerous area, or having unsafe sex)?	More than once wanted to cut down or stop drinking, or tried to, but couldn't?	**Mild:** The presence of 2 to 3 symptoms
3 More than once gotten arrested, been held at a police station, or had other legal problems because of your drinking?	Spent a lot of time drinking? Or being sick or getting over other aftereffects?	**Moderate:** The presence of 4 to 5 symptoms
This is not included in DSM–5	Wanted a drink so badly you couldn't think of anything else?	**Severe:** The presence of 6 or more symptoms
4 Continued to drink even though it was causing trouble with your family or friends?	****This is new to DSM–5****	
Any 3 = Alcohol dependence		
5 Had to drink much more than you once did to get the effect you want? Or found that your usual number of drinks had much less effect than before?	Found that drinking—or being sick from drinking—often interfered with taking care of your home or family? Or caused job troubles? Or school problems?	
6 Found that when the effects of alcohol were wearing off, you had withdrawal symptoms, such as trouble sleeping, shakiness, restlessness, nausea, sweating, a racing heart, or a seizure? Or sensed things that were not there?	Continued to drink even though it was causing trouble with your family or friends?	
7 Had times when you ended up drinking more, or longer, than you intended?	Given up or cut back on activities that were important or interesting to you, or gave you pleasure, in order to drink?	
8 More than once wanted to cut down or stop drinking, or tried to, but couldn't?	More than once gotten into situations while or after drinking that increased your chances of getting hurt (such as driving, swimming, using machinery, walking in a dangerous area, or having unsafe sex)?	
9 Spent a lot of time drinking? Or being sick or getting over other aftereffects?	Continued to drink even though it was making you feel depressed or anxious or adding to another health problem? Or after having had a memory blackout?	
10 Given up or cut back on activities that were important or interesting to you, or gave you pleasure, in order to drink?	Had to drink much more than you once did to get the effect you want? Or found that your usual number of drinks had much less effect than before?	
11 Continued to drink even though it was making you feel depressed or anxious or adding to another health problem? Or after having had a memory blackout?	Found that when the effects of alcohol were wearing off, you had withdrawal symptoms, such as trouble sleeping, shakiness, restlessness, nausea, sweating, a racing heart, or a seizure? Or sensed things that were not there?	

DSM = Diagnostic and Statistical Manual of Mental Disorders

SOURCE: "A Comparison between DSM–IV and DSM–5," in *Alcohol Use Disorder: A Comparison between DSM–IV and DSM–5*, U.S. Department of Health and Human Services, National Institutes of Health, National Institute on Alcohol Abuse and Alcoholism, July 2016, https://pubs.niaaa.nih.gov/publications/dsmfactsheet/dsmfact.pdf (accessed January 9, 2017)

Biological Factors

GENETICS. A variety of studies investigating family history, adopted versus biological children living in the same families, and twins separated and living in different families all indicate that genetics play a substantial role in some forms of AUD. For example, R. Dayne Mayfield, R. Adron Harris, and Marc A. Schuckit indicate in "Genetic Factors Influencing Alcohol Dependence" (*British Journal of Pharmacology*, vol. 154, no. 2, May 2008) that relatives of alcoholics have four times the risk of developing alcohol dependence than do nonrelatives of alcoholics and that the identical twins of those dependent on alcohol have a higher risk of developing alcohol dependence than do fraternal twins or nontwin siblings. Most likely, many genes influence a range of characteristics that affect risk. Marc A. Schuckit of the University of California, San Diego, states in "An Overview of Genetic Influences in Alcoholism" (*Journal of Substance Abuse Treatment*, vol. 36, no. 1, January 2009) that "genes explain about 50% of the vulnerabilities leading to heavy drinking and associated problems." In "Assessing the Genetic Risk for Alcohol Use Disorders" (*Alcohol Research: Current Reviews*, vol. 34, no. 3, 2012), Tatiana Foroud and Tamara J. Phillips discuss the link between alcoholism and the human genome, asserting that alcoholism is determined by complex interactions between genes, rather than by individual genes themselves. Emily C. Williams et al. suggest in "Primary Care Providers' Interest in Using a Genetic Test to Guide Alcohol Use Disorder Treatment" (*Journal of Substance Abuse Treatment*, vol. 70, November 2016) that genetic testing could prove effective in

FIGURE 2.1

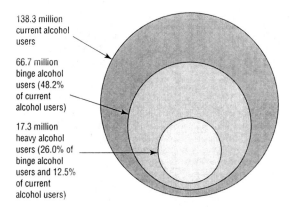

Alcohol use by individuals aged 12 and older, by degree of use, 2015

138.3 million current alcohol users

66.7 million binge alcohol users (48.2% of current alcohol users)

17.3 million heavy alcohol users (26.0% of binge alcohol users and 12.5% of current alcohol users)

Note: In 2015, the threshold for determining binge alcohol use for females changed from five or more drinks on an occasion to four or more drinks on an occasion.

SOURCE: "Figure 21. Current, Binge, and Heavy Alcohol Use among People Aged 12 or Older: 2015," in *Key Substance Use and Mental Health Indicators in the United States: Results from the 2015 National Survey on Drug Use and Health*, U.S. Department of Health and Human Services, Substance Abuse and Mental Health Services Administration, September 2016, https://www.samhsa.gov/data/sites/default/files/NSDUH-FFR1-2015/NSDUH-FFR1-2015/NSDUH-FFR1-2015.pdf (accessed January 9, 2017)

enabling health care providers to develop specific, personalized AUD treatment approaches for individual patients.

ALCOHOL REACTIVITY. Alcohol reactivity refers to the sense of intoxication one has when drinking alcohol. Without early signals of intoxication, an individual may tend to drink more before feeling drunk and thus may develop a high physiological tolerance for alcohol. An individual with low alcohol reactivity to moderate doses of alcohol may be more likely to become an alcoholic over time than an individual with greater reactivity. Typically, the children of alcoholics report a lower sense of intoxication and show fewer signs of intoxication when given moderate amounts of alcohol, compared with the children of nonalcoholics, showing a likely genetic link to alcoholism.

Psychosocial Factors

SOCIAL SANCTIONS, GENDER ROLES, BIOLOGICAL DIFFERENCES, AND CULTURAL FACTORS. Social sanctions are a mechanism of social control for enforcing a society's standards. Social sanctions may be one factor explaining why men drink more alcohol than women. Besides social sanctions against women drinking as heavily as men, American culture appears to identify alcohol consumption as more of a part of the male gender role than of the female gender role. However, gender differences in alcohol consumption are seen not only in the United States but also around the world.

Richard W. Wilsnack et al. explain in "Gender and Alcohol Consumption: Patterns from the Multinational GENACIS Project" (*Addiction*, vol. 104, no. 9, September 2009):

> Gender differences in alcohol consumption remain universal [among countries], although the sizes of gender differences vary. More drinking and heavy drinking occur among men, more long-term abstention occurs among women, and no cultural differences or historical changes have entirely erased these differences. As there are relatively few universals in human social behavior, these findings suggest that biological differences play some role in how men and women drink. However, because the gender differences vary in magnitude across cultures and across different drinking patterns, it is also very likely that gender differences in drinking behavior are modified by cultural and not just biological factors.

DRINKING MOTIVES, EXPECTATIONS, AND DEPRESSION/ DISTRESS. People consume alcohol for various reasons: as part of a meal, to celebrate certain occasions, and to reduce anxiety in social situations. People also consume alcohol to cope with distress or depression or to escape from negative feelings. Those who have positive expectations for their drinking, such as the belief that alcohol will reduce distress, tend to drink more than those who have negative expectations, such as the belief that alcohol will interfere with the ability to cope with distress. In general, Shelly F. Greenfield et al. indicate in "Substance Abuse in Women" (*Psychiatric Clinics of North America*, vol. 33, no. 2, June 2010) that men have more positive expectations concerning alcohol consumption than women. In addition, women are more likely than men to drink alcohol in response to distress and negative emotions. The researchers note, however, that although these generalizations can be made, the relationships among depression, general distress, and alcohol consumption are quite complex.

IMPULSIVITY, SENSATION-SEEKING, BEHAVIORAL UNDERCONTROL, AND ANTISOCIALITY. In "Sex Difference in Alcoholism: Who Is at a Greater Risk for Development of Alcoholic Complication?" (*Life Sciences*, vol. 87, nos. 5–6, July 31, 2010), Asli F. Ceylan-Isik, Shawna M. McBride, and Jun Ren of the University of Wyoming, Laramie, indicate that impulsivity, sensation-seeking, and behavioral undercontrol (not controlling one's behavior well) are consistently associated with alcohol use and problems in men rather than in women. The researchers suggest this may occur because "women perceive greater social and health sanctions for drinking while alcohol and alcoholism may counter desirable feminine traits."

Antisociality is a personality disorder that includes a chronic disregard for the rights of others and an absence of remorse for the harmful effects of these behaviors on others. People with this disorder are usually involved in aggressive and illegal activities. They are often impulsive and reckless and are more likely to become alcohol dependent. Males are more likely than females to demonstrate antisociality.

ALCOHOL USE AND INTERPERSONAL RELATIONSHIPS, CHILD ABUSE, SEXUAL ASSAULT, AND RAISING CHILDREN. Married couples often have strongly similar levels of drinking. Philip H. Smith et al. observe in "Women Ending Marriage to a Problem Drinking Partner Decrease Their Own Risk for Problem Drinking" (*Addiction*, vol. 107, no. 8, August 2012) that the drinking habits of one partner in a marriage can play a direct role in determining the drinking habits of the other partner. The researchers note that women who are in a relationship with a problem drinker are five times more likely to develop an AUD than women who are in a relationship with a nonproblem drinker. It is unclear whether men and women with problem drinking patterns seek out partners with similar drinking patterns or whether either is influenced by the other to drink during the marriage. However, marital discord is often present when spouses' drinking patterns differ significantly.

Being a victim of sexual assault and/or child abuse is a risk factor for AUD. Both men and women who were sexually assaulted during childhood are at an increased risk for problem drinking and alcohol abuse. Daniel F. Becker and Carlos M. Grilo, in investigating the psychosocial factors of drug and alcohol abuse in adolescents, note that women are not the only victims of this abuse/misuse cycle. The researchers suggest in "Prediction of Drug and Alcohol Abuse in Hospitalized Adolescents: Comparisons by Gender and Substance Type" (*Behaviour Research and Therapy*, vol. 44, no. 10, October 2006) that a history of child abuse is a risk factor for drug and alcohol abuse in both males and females. In "Vulnerability to Alcohol Use Disorders Following Early Sexual Abuse: The Role of Effortful Control" (*Addiction Research and Theory*, vol. 21, no. 2, April 2013), Alicia K. Klanecky and Dennis E. McChargue report that 43.5% of women who were sexually abused as children or adolescents go on to demonstrate symptoms of AUD by the age of 21, compared with 7.9% of women who were not victims of sexual abuse at an early age. Among male victims of childhood or adolescent sexual abuse, well over one-third (38.7%) develop a lifelong dependency on alcohol, which is more than double the 19.2% of men who become dependent on alcohol after having never suffered early sexual abuse.

Researchers have also studied the ways that alcohol abuse adversely affects the ability of parents to raise their children effectively. For example, in "Explicating the Social Mechanisms Linking Alcohol Use Behaviors and Ecology to Child Maltreatment" (*Journal of Sociology and Social Welfare*, vol. 39, no. 4, December 2012), Bridget Freisthler and Megan R. Holmes of the University of California, Los

Angeles, analyze the link between alcoholism and child abuse. The researchers focus on the ways in which certain social situations (such as weddings or other special occasions) are tied to alcohol consumption and in turn how these situations can lead to inadequate supervision, disruptive and unsafe household environments, and other circumstances that put children at risk of abuse or neglect. Freisthler and Holmes conclude that increasing understanding of the "specific social mechanisms" by which alcohol consumption leads to child maltreatment can help lead to improved intervention techniques and practices.

EFFECTS OF PARENTAL ALCOHOLISM ON CHILDREN

Living with someone who has an alcohol problem affects every member of the family. Children often suffer many problems as a result. In the fact sheet "Children of Addicted Parents: Important Facts" (October 30, 2015, http://nacoa.org/wp-content/uploads/2016/08/Children-of-Addicted-Parents-Important-Facts-NACoA.pdf), the National Association for Children of Alcoholics (NACoA) estimates that there are more than 28 million children of alcoholics in the United States, including 11 million under the age of 18 years.

As mentioned earlier, relatives of alcoholics have four times the risk of alcoholism than do nonrelatives. Jodi M. Gilman, James M. Bjork, and Daniel W. Hommer of the NIAAA note in "Parental Alcohol Use and Brain Volumes in Early and Late-Onset Alcoholics" (*Biological Psychiatry*, vol. 62, no. 6, September 15, 2007) that many factors contribute to this increased risk. Some of these contributing factors are a genetic predisposition to alcoholism as well as a poor diet, unstable parental relationships, and alcohol exposure in the womb. Their research adds another factor, however: the effect of a family history of heavy drinking on brain volume. Gilman, Bjork, and Hommer find that alcoholic patients who had a family history of heavy drinking had significantly smaller brain volumes than did alcoholic patients with no family history of heavy drinking. The researchers conclude that "parental alcohol use may increase risk for alcoholism in offspring in part by a genetic and/or environmental effect that may be related to reduced brain growth."

The NACoA also notes that children of alcoholics are more likely to suffer from attention-deficit/hyperactivity disorder, behavioral problems, and anxiety disorders. They tend to score lower on tests that measure cognitive and verbal skills. Furthermore, children of alcoholics are more likely to be truant, repeat grades, drop out of school, or be referred to a school counselor or psychologist.

UNDERAGE DRINKING, THE LAW, AND ADVERTISING

One issue of particular concern to health experts, regulators, and parents is the prevalence of underage drinking. In the United States, the consumption of alcohol by anyone under the age of 21 years is illegal. Furthermore, possession of alcohol by anyone under 21 is illegal in all 50 states; these statutes are typically referred to as minor-in-possession laws. Related laws also prohibit adults from providing alcohol to minors.

The Johns Hopkins Bloomberg School of Public Health reports in "Alcohol Advertising and Youth" (April 2007, http://www.camy.org/resources/fact-sheets/alcohol-advertising-and-youth/) that many factors help shape the underage drinking culture in the United States, including parental behavior, peer pressure, and the pervasiveness of alcohol in popular culture. It also indicates that alcohol advertising plays a key role in encouraging teenagers to drink. Indeed, according to the Bloomberg School, advertisements for alcoholic beverages often appeal to the adolescent desire for "immediate gratification, thrills and/or social status." A number of studies show that this type of advertising can be very effective. For example, in "Does Alcohol Advertising Promote Adolescent Drinking? Results from a Longitudinal Assessment" (Addiction, vol. 100, no. 2, February 2005), Phyllis L. Ellickson et al. identify a link between high school drinking and exposure to in-store beer marketing and alcohol advertisements in magazines. David Jernigan et al. reinforce this idea in "Alcohol Marketing and Youth Alcohol Consumption: A Systematic Review of Longitudinal Studies Published since 2008" (Addiction, vol. 112, Suppl. 1, January 2017), drawing further evidence of the correlation between alcohol marketing and youth drinking from a dozen long-range studies that were conducted between 2008 and 2016.

In the position paper "Alcohol Advertising and Youth" (2010, http://www.aafp.org/about/policies/all/alcohol-advertising.html), the American Academy of Family Physicians examines the ways that alcohol advertising targets youth. According to the academy, such marketing often tries to establish a link between consuming alcoholic beverages and aspects of everyday life that are valued by young people, such as friendships, sexual relationships, and social status. Meanwhile, the alcohol industry sometimes incorporates animals and cartoon characters into advertising campaigns, with the aim of appealing directly to young audiences.

SHORT-TERM EFFECTS OF ALCOHOL ON THE BODY

When most people think about how alcohol affects them, they think of a temporary light-headedness or a hangover the next morning. Many are also aware of the serious damage that continuous, excessive alcohol use can do to the liver. Alcohol, however, affects many organs of the body and has been linked to cancer, mental and/or physical retardation in newborns, heart disease, and other health problems.

Low to moderate doses of alcohol produce a slight, brief increase in heartbeat and blood pressure. Large doses can reduce the pumping power of the heart and produce irregular heartbeats. In addition, blood vessels within muscles constrict, but those at the surface expand, causing rapid heat loss from the skin and a flushing or reddening. Thus, large doses of alcohol decrease body temperature and, additionally, may cause numbness of the skin, legs, and arms, creating a false feeling of warmth.

Alcohol affects the endocrine system (a group of glands that produce hormones) in several ways. One effect is increased urination. Urination increases not only because of fluid intake but also because alcohol stops the release of vasopressin (an antidiuretic hormone) from the pituitary gland. This hormone controls how much water the kidneys reabsorb from the urine as it is being produced and how much water the kidneys excrete. Therefore, heavy alcohol intake can result in both dehydration and an imbalance in electrolytes, which are chemicals dissolved in body fluids that conduct electrical currents. Both of these conditions are serious health hazards.

Alcohol is sometimes believed to be an aphrodisiac (sexual stimulant). Nicole Prause, Cameron Staley, and Peter Finn identify in "The Effects of Acute Ethanol Consumption on Sexual Response and Sexual Risk-Taking Intent" (Archives of Sexual Behavior, vol. 40, no. 2, April 2011) a link between alcohol consumption and both an increase in sexual arousal and a decrease in sexual inhibition. It is also known that excessive alcohol consumption tends to impair sexual performance, with alcoholics sometimes reporting difficulties in their sex life.

Intoxication

The speed of alcohol absorption affects the rate at which one becomes intoxicated. Intoxication occurs when alcohol is absorbed into the blood faster than the liver can oxidize it (or break it down into water, carbon dioxide, and energy). In a 160-pound (72.6- kg) man, alcohol is metabolized at a rate of about one drink every two hours. The absorption of alcohol is influenced by several factors:

- Body weight—heavier people are less affected than lighter people by the same amount of alcohol because there is more blood and water in their system to dilute the alcohol intake. In addition, the greater the body muscle weight, the lower the blood alcohol concentration (BAC) for a given amount of alcohol. For example, on average a man weighing 120 pounds (54 kg) will achieve a BAC of 0.08 grams (g) of alcohol per 1 deciliter (dL) of blood—the legal limit for operating a motor vehicle—after consuming three alcoholic beverages, whereas a 200-pound (91 kg) man will typically need to consume five alcoholic drinks to achieve the same BAC.

- Speed of drinking—the faster alcohol is drunk, the faster the BAC level rises.

- Presence of food in the stomach—eating while drinking slows down the absorption of alcohol by increasing the amount of time it takes the alcohol to get from the stomach to the small intestine.

- Drinking history and body chemistry—the longer a person has been drinking, the greater his or her tolerance (in other words, the more alcohol it takes him or her to get drunk). An individual's physiological functioning or "body chemistry" may also affect his or her reactions to alcohol. Women are more easily affected by alcohol regardless of weight because women metabolize alcohol differently than men. Women are known to have less body water than men of the same body weight, so equivalent amounts of alcohol result in higher concentrations of alcohol in the blood of women than men.

As a person's BAC rises, there are somewhat predictable responses in behavior:

- At 0.05 g/dL, thought processes, judgment, and restraint are more lax. The person may feel more at ease socially. Also, reaction time to visual or auditory stimuli slows down as the BAC rises. (It should be noted that a measurement of g/dL—a mass/volume measure—is approximately equal to a volume/volume—or a percentage—measurement when calculating BAC and that the two are often used interchangeably; so a BAC of 0.05 g/dL can also mean a BAC of 0.05%.)

- At 0.10 g/dL, voluntary motor actions become noticeably clumsy. (It is illegal to drive with a BAC of 0.08 g/dL or higher.)

- At 0.20 g/dL, the entire motor area of the brain becomes significantly depressed. The person staggers, may want to lie down, may be easily angered, or may shout or weep.

- At 0.30 g/dL, the person generally acts confused or may be in a stupor.

- At 0.40 g/dL, the person usually falls into a coma.

- At 0.50 g/dL or more, the medulla is severely depressed, and death generally occurs within several hours, usually from respiratory failure. The medulla is the portion of the brainstem that regulates many involuntary processes, such as breathing.

Without immediate medical attention, a person whose BAC reaches 0.50 g/dL will almost certainly die. Death may even occur at a BAC of 0.40 g/dL if the alcohol is consumed quickly and in a large amount, causing the BAC to rise rapidly.

Sobering Up

Time is the only way to rid the body of alcohol. The more slowly a person drinks, the more time the body has to process the alcohol, so less alcohol accumulates in the bloodstream. In addition, having food in the stomach slows the absorption of alcohol. Drinking slowly while eating and alternating nonalcoholic beverages with alcoholic beverages helps keep the BAC at lower levels than drinking more quickly on an empty stomach.

Hangovers

Hangovers cause a great deal of misery as well as absenteeism and loss of productivity at school or work. A person with a hangover can experience several physical symptoms after drinking and fully metabolizing alcohol. The major symptoms of a hangover include headaches, fatigue, and difficulty concentrating. However, the causes of these symptoms are not well known. Gemma Prat, Ana Adan, and Miguel Sánchez-Turet of the University of Barcelona review explanations of hangovers in "Alcohol Hangover: A Critical Review of Explanatory Factors" (*Human Psychopharmacology: Clinical and Experimental*, vol. 24, no. 4, June 2009). The primary hypotheses as to the causes of hangovers are that they are a physiological response to withdrawal from alcohol, impurities produced during fermentation that are present in alcoholic beverages, or by-products that are produced by the body during the metabolism of alcohol. Fluctuations in body hormones and dehydration intensify hangover symptoms. Genetic disposition can also be a factor. In "Genetic Influences on Alcohol-Related Hangover" (*Addiction*, vol. 109, no. 12, December 2014), Wendy S. Slutske et al. note that hereditary factors play a key role in determining an individual's susceptibility to hangovers.

There is no scientific evidence to support popular hangover cures, such as black coffee, raw egg, chili pepper, steak sauce, "alkalizers," and vitamins. To treat a hangover, health care practitioners usually prescribe bed rest as well as eating food and drinking nonalcoholic fluids.

LONG-TERM EFFECTS OF ALCOHOL ON THE BODY

The results of scientific research help health care practitioners and the general public understand both the positive and negative health consequences of drinking alcohol. Thomas F. Babor and Katherine Robaina identify in "Public Health, Academic Medicine, and the Alcohol Industry's Corporate Social Responsibility Activities" (*American Journal of Public Health*, vol. 103. no. 2, February 2013) a link between alcohol consumption and a range of health problems and diseases, including breast cancer, cirrhosis of the liver, heart disease, and tuberculosis. Citing statistics from the World Health Organization, the researchers state that alcohol consumption causes 3.8% of all deaths worldwide. In "Alcohol-Attributable Cancer Deaths and Years of Potential Life Lost in the United States" (*American Journal of Public Health*, vol. 103, no. 4, April 2013),

David E. Nelson et al. report that alcohol consumption resulted in 19,500 cancer deaths in 2009, greater than the number of deaths due to ovarian cancer or melanoma and roughly two-thirds the number of deaths due to prostate cancer that year.

Not all the effects of alcohol consumption are harmful to health, however. Ronald C. Hamdy and Melissa McManama Aukerman list in "Alcohol on Trial: The Evidence" (*Southern Medical Journal*, vol. 98, no. 1, January 2005) levels of alcohol consumption and the relative risk for total mortality (death) for a variety of diseases and conditions. Their data show that men aged 40 to 85 years who drank up to, and possibly slightly more than, two drinks per day had a lower total mortality risk than those who did not drink. That is, this level of drinking was good for the men's overall health and life expectancy. According to David M. Goldberg and George E. Soleas of the University of Toronto, in "Wine and Health: A Paradigm for Alcohol and Antioxidants" (*Journal of Medical Biochemistry*, vol. 30, no. 2, June 2011), the ethanol found in alcoholic beverages has been found to reduce clotting of the arteries, while also diminishing the risk of type 2 diabetes, which is a major cause of arteriosclerotic vascular disease.

Benjamin Taylor et al. compare in "Alcohol and Hypertension: Gender Differences in Dose-Response Relationships Determined through Systematic Review and Meta-Analysis" (*Addiction*, vol. 104, no. 12, December 2009) alcohol consumption versus relative risk of hypertension (chronic high blood pressure) in women versus men. Alcohol consumption of between two and four drinks per week, with only one drink per day on any occasion, lowered the risk of hypertension in women. Once that level of alcohol consumption was reached, however, the risk of hypertension in women rose as their alcohol consumption rose. With men, low levels of alcohol consumption were not protective against hypertension as in women. Furthermore, the more men drank, the higher their risk of hypertension. Conversely, reducing alcohol consumption can help alleviate symptoms of hypertension. According to Chrysi Koliaki and Nicholas Katsilambros, in "Dietary Sodium, Potassium, and Alcohol: Key Players in Pathophysiology, Prevention, and Treatment of Human Hypertension" (*Nutrition Reviews*, vol. 71, no. 6, June 2013), decreasing alcohol consumption by 76% is shown to reduce blood pressure readings in both hypertensive and nonhypertensive subjects.

In "Effects of Beer, Wine, and Liquor Intakes on Bone Mineral Density in Older Men and Women" (*American Journal of Clinical Nutrition*, February 25, 2009), Katherine L. Tucker et al. of Tufts University indicate that bone density can also benefit from alcohol consumption. In reporting on Tucker et al.'s study, Anne Harding explains in "Moderate Drinking May Help Bone

Density" (Reuters.com, March 20, 2009) that "people who enjoy a glass or two of wine or beer every day could be helping to keep their bones strong." Alcohol consumption can also play a role in promoting bone density among older individuals, particularly women. Isolde Sommer et al. observe in "Alcohol Consumption and Bone Mineral Density in Elderly Women" (*Public Health Nutrition*, vol. 16, no. 4, April 2013) that elderly women who drink three or more alcoholic beverages a week are shown to have 12% higher bone density in the femoral neck region and 9.2% higher bone density in the lumbar spine region than elderly women who refrain from drinking alcohol altogether.

The studies mentioned in this section provide only a small sample of the wide variety and large number of studies that have been conducted on the long-term effects of alcohol consumption on health. With so many studies and so many health-related factors to take into account, how does a person know how much alcohol is beneficial and how much is too much? The World Cancer Research Fund and the American Institute for Cancer Research state in *Food, Nutrition, Physical Activity, and the Prevention of Cancer: A Global Perspective* (2007, http://discovery.ucl.ac.uk/4841/1/4841.pdf): "If alcoholic drinks are consumed, limit consumption to no more than two drinks a day for men and one drink a day for women." Their justification for this statement is as follows: "The evidence on cancer justifies a recommendation not to drink alcoholic drinks. Other evidence shows that modest amounts of alcoholic drinks are likely to reduce the risk of coronary heart disease."

In "Alcohol and Heart Health" (January 12, 2015, http://www.heart.org/HEARTORG/HealthyLiving/Healthy Eating/Nutrition/Alcohol-and-Heart-Health_UCM_305173 _Article.jsp), the American Heart Association notes that drinking alcohol in moderation can help lead to increases in high-density lipoproteins, or "good cholesterol," which has been shown to promote "anti-clotting properties" in the blood. However, it also stresses that even moderate alcohol consumption is not a substitute for more "conventional measures" of preventing heart disease, such as "lowering your cholesterol and lowering high blood pressure, controlling your weight, getting enough physical activity and following a healthy diet."

EFFECTS OF ALCOHOL ON SEX AND REPRODUCTION

Alcohol consumption can affect sexual response and reproduction in profound ways. Many alcoholics suffer from erectile dysfunction (impotence) and/or reduced sexual drive. Valentina Boddi et al. suggest in "Priapus Is Happier with Venus Than with Bacchus" (*Journal of Sexual Medicine*, vol. 7, no. 8, August 2010) that male alcohol consumption of four or more drinks per day was associated with a greater risk of erectile dysfunction as shown by a reduction in penile blood flow. The researchers also note that this level of alcohol consumption "was associated with low perceived partner's sexual desire, worse couple relationship, and smoking abuse." Many alcoholics suffer from depression, which may further impair their sexual function. In addition, Jerrold S. Greenberg, Clint E. Bruess, and Sarah C. Conklin report in *Exploring the Dimensions of Human Sexuality* (2017) that alcohol use is associated with poor sperm quality in men.

In premenopausal women chronic heavy drinking can contribute to a variety of reproductive disorders. According to Greenberg, Bruess, and Conklin, these disorders include the cessation of menstruation, irregular menstrual cycles, failure to ovulate, early menopause, increased risk of spontaneous miscarriages, and lower rates of conception. Some of these disorders can be caused directly by the interference of alcohol with the hormonal regulation of the reproductive system. They may also be caused indirectly through other disorders that are associated with alcohol abuse, such as liver disease, pancreatic disease, malnutrition, or fetal abnormalities.

Fetal Alcohol Spectrum Disorders

Alcohol consumption during pregnancy can result in severe harm to the fetus (unborn child). The development of such defects can begin early in pregnancy when the mother-to-be may not even know that she is pregnant, and such defects are likely to be exacerbated by binge drinking. For example, Lisa A. DeRoo et al. reveal in "First-Trimester Maternal Alcohol Consumption and the Risk of Infant Oral Clefts in Norway: A Population-Based Case-Control Study" (*American Journal of Epidemiology*, vol. 168, no. 6, September 15, 2008) that women who binge drank during their first trimester of pregnancy were twice as likely as nondrinkers to give birth to an infant having a cleft lip, cleft palate, or both. Other alcohol-related birth defects include malformations and abnormal development of the heart, bones, and kidneys.

It should be noted that drinking during pregnancy can cause more than physical alcohol-related birth defects. Exposure to alcohol in the womb can cause a variety of conditions that are collectively called fetal alcohol spectrum disorders (FASDs). Alcohol-related birth defects make up only one aspect of FASDs. Children with FASDs can exhibit not only physical birth defects but also a complex pattern of behavioral and cognitive dysfunctions, including delayed motor development and hyperactivity. Together, FASDs include effects that are physical, cognitive, and behavioral; cannot be cured; and last throughout the life of the affected individual.

Fetal alcohol syndrome (FAS) is the most severe FASD. An individual with FAS has characteristic facial anomalies, growth deficiency, and central nervous system abnormalities. Children with these facial anomalies and the central nervous system abnormalities of FAS but who have normal growth patterns are said to have partial FAS. Children exposed to alcohol before birth who do not have the facial characteristics typical of FAS, but who have severe central nervous system dysfunction have the FASD called alcohol-related neurodevelopmental disorder.

In "Fetal Alcohol Spectrum Disorders (FASDs): Data and Statistics" (March 23, 2016, https://www.cdc.gov/ncbddd/fasd/data.html), the Centers for Disease Control and Prevention (CDC) notes that FAS rates range from 0.2 to 1.5 infants per 1,000 live births in results of CDC studies. In the 21st century all prenatal alcohol-related conditions are collectively known as FASD.

In February 2005 the U.S. surgeon general Richard Carmona (1949–) issued an advisory on alcohol use during pregnancy. Key points of the advisory are listed in Table 2.4. As noted in the advisory, there is no known safe level of alcohol consumption during pregnancy. The CDC emphasizes, along with the surgeon general, that FAS and other prenatal alcohol-related disorders are 100% preventable if a woman does not drink alcohol while she is pregnant or if she is of reproductive age and is using birth control. Even so, data show that some women who might become pregnant, or who are pregnant, consume alcohol and put themselves at risk for having a child with FASD.

Table 2.5 shows that 9.3% of pregnant women consumed alcohol in the past month in 2015 when questioned

TABLE 2.4

Key points in the U.S. surgeon general's advisory on alcohol use during pregnancy, 2005

Based on the current, best science available we now know the following:

- Alcohol consumed during pregnancy increases the risk of alcohol related birth defects, including growth deficiencies, facial abnormalities, central nervous system impairment, behavioral disorders, and impaired intellectual development.
- No amount of alcohol consumption can be considered safe during pregnancy.
- Alcohol can damage a fetus at any stage of pregnancy. Damage can occur in the earliest weeks of pregnancy, even before a woman knows that she is pregnant.
- The cognitive deficits and behavioral problems resulting from prenatal alcohol exposure are lifelong.
- Alcohol-related birth defects are completely preventable.

For these reasons:

1. A pregnant woman should not drink alcohol during pregnancy.
2. A pregnant woman who has already consumed alcohol during her pregnancy should stop in order to minimize further risk.
3. A woman who is considering becoming pregnant should abstain from alcohol.
4. Recognizing that nearly half of all births in the United States are unplanned, women of childbearing age should consult their physician and take steps to reduce the possibility of prenatal alcohol exposure.
5. Health professionals should inquire routinely about alcohol consumption by women of childbearing age, inform them of the risks of alcohol consumption during pregnancy, and advise them not to drink alcoholic beverages during pregnancy.

SOURCE: Adapted from "Surgeon General's Advisory on Alcohol Use in Pregnancy," in *U.S. Surgeon General Releases Advisory on Alcohol Use in Pregnancy*, U.S. Department of Health and Human Services, Office of the Surgeon General, February 21, 2005, http://come-over.to/FAS/SurGenAdvisory.htm (accessed January 9, 2017)

TABLE 2.5

Percentage of past-month alcohol use among females aged 15–44, by pregnancy status, 2014 and 2015

Demographic/pregnancy characteristic	Total[c]		Pregnancy status			
			Pregnant		Not pregnant	
	2014	2015	2014	2015	2014	2015
Total	54.5[a]	53.1	8.8	9.3	56.3[a]	54.8
Age						
15–17	20.0[b]	16.8	*	*	20.1[b]	16.8
18–25	57.6	57.2	6.4[a]	11.8	60.1	59.4
26–44	58.7	57.1	9.9	7.8	60.7[a]	59.0
Hispanic origin and race						
Not Hispanic or Latino	56.8	56.0	9.6	9.3	58.6	57.7
White	60.7	59.7	10.6	9.3	62.6	61.6
Black or African American	50.7	50.3	8.7	12.8	52.4	51.9
American Indian or Alaska Native	43.6	47.3	*	*	44.7	48.5
Native Hawaiian or other Pacific Islander	*	*	*	*	*	
Asian	38.3	38.0	*	*	39.9	*
Two or more races	58.8	60.3	*	*	60.3	
Hispanic or Latino	45.5[a]	41.9	5.2	9.4	47.1[b]	39.1
						61.9
						43.2
Trimester[d]						
First	da	da	21.5	16.4	da	da
Second	da	da	4.5	6.1	da	da
Third	da	da	2.2	4.3	da	da

*low precision. da = does not apply.

[a]The difference between this estimate and the 2015 estimate is statistically significant at the 0.05 level. Rounding may make the estimates appear identical.
[b]The difference between this estimate and the 2015 estimate is statistically significant at the 0.01 level. Rounding may make the estimates appear identical.
[c]Estimates in the total column represent all females in the specified subgroup, including those with unknown pregnancy status.
[d]Pregnant females aged 15 to 44 not reporting trimester were excluded.

SOURCE: "Table 6.76B. Alcohol Use in Past Month among Females Aged 15 to 44, by Pregnancy Status, Demographic Characteristics, and Pregnancy Characteristics: Percentages, 2014 and 2015," in *2015 National Survey on Drug Use and Health: Detailed Tables*, U.S. Department of Health and Human Services, Substance Abuse and Mental Health Services Administration, September 8, 2016, https://www.samhsa.gov/data/sites/default/files/NSDUH-DetTabs-2015/NSDUH-DetTabs-2015/NSDUH-DetTabs-2015.pdf (accessed January 9, 2017)

for the annual National Survey on Drug Use and Health. This figure was slightly higher than the 8.8% recorded among pregnant women in 2014. In 2014, 21.5% of pregnant women drank during their first trimester of pregnancy, a time when all the organ systems of the fetus are developing; in 2015 this figure decreased to 16.4%. In contrast, the percentage of pregnant women who drank during their second trimester rose, from 4.5% in 2014 to 6.1% in 2015.

ALCOHOL'S INTERACTION WITH OTHER DRUGS

Because alcohol is easily available and such an accepted part of American social life, people often forget that it is a drug. When someone takes a medication while drinking alcohol, he or she is taking two drugs. Alcohol consumed with other drugs—for example, an illegal drug such as cocaine, an over-the-counter (without a prescription) drug such as cough medicine, or a prescription drug such as an antibiotic—may make the combination harmful or even deadly or may counteract the effectiveness of a prescribed medication.

To promote the desired chemical or physical effects, a medication must be absorbed into the body and must reach its site of action. Alcohol may prevent an appropriate amount of the medication from reaching its site of action. In other cases alcohol can alter the drug's effects once it reaches the site. Alcohol interacts negatively with more than 150 medications. Table 2.6 shows some possible interactions when combining alcohol and other types of drugs.

The U.S. Food and Drug Administration recommends that anyone who regularly has three alcoholic drinks per day should check with a physician before taking aspirin, acetaminophen, or any other over-the-counter painkiller. Combining alcohol with aspirin, ibuprofen, or related pain relievers may promote stomach bleeding. Combining alcohol with acetaminophen may promote liver damage.

ALCOHOL-RELATED DEATHS

According to Kenneth D. Kochanek et al. of the CDC, in "Deaths: Final Data for 2014" (*National Vital Statistics Reports*, vol. 65, no. 4, June 30, 2016), 30,722 people in the United States died from alcohol-induced causes in 2014. This category includes deaths from dependent use of alcohol, nondependent use of alcohol, and accidental alcohol poisoning. It excludes accidents, homicides, and other causes indirectly related to alcohol use, as well as deaths because of FAS. In 2014, 19,388 people died from alcoholic liver disease.

TABLE 2.6

Interactions between alcohol and various medications

Symptoms/disorders	Medication (brand name)	Medication (generic name)	Some possible reactions with alcohol
Allergies/colds/flu	• Alavert®	Loratadine	Drowsiness, dizziness; increased risk for overdose
	• Atarax®	Hydroxyzine	
	• Benadryl®	Diphenhydramine	
	• Clarinex®	Desloratadine	
	• Claritin®, Claritin-D®	Loratadine	
	• Dimetapp® Cold & Allergy	Brompheniramine	
	• Sudafed® Sinus & Allergy	Chlorpheniramine	
	• Triaminic® Cold & Allergy	Chlorpheniramine	
	• Tylenol® Allergy Sinus	Chlorpheniramine	
	• Tylenol® Cold & Flu	Chlorpheniramine	
	• Zyrtec®	Cetirizine	
Angina (chest pain), coronary heart disease	• Isordil®	Isosorbide Nitroglycerin	Rapid heartbeat, sudden changes in blood pressure, dizziness, fainting
Anxiety and epilepsy	• Ativan®	Lorazepam	Drowsiness, dizziness; increased risk for overdose; slowed or dificulty breathing; impaired motor control; unusual behavior; memory problems
	• BuSpar®	Buspirone	
	• Klonopin®	Clonazepam	
	• Librium®	Chlordiazepoxide	
	• Paxil®	Paroxetine	
	• Valium®	Diazepam	
	• Xanax®	Alprazolam	
	• Herbal preparations (Kava Kava)		Liver damage, drowsiness
Arthritis	• Celebrex®	Celecoxib	Ulcers, stomach bleeding, liver damage
	• Naprosyn®	Naproxen	
	• Voltaren®	Diclofenac	
Attention and concentration (attention deficit/hyperactivity disorder)	• Adderall®	Amphetamine/dextro-amphetamine	Dizziness, drowsiness, impaired concentration (methylphenidate, dexmethylphenidate); possible increased risk for heart problems (amphetamine, dextroamphetamine, lisdexamfetamine); liver damage (atomoxetine)
	• Concerta®, Ritalin®	Methylphenidate	
	• Dexedrine®	Dextroamphetamine	
	• Focalin®	Dexmethylphenidate	
	• Strattera®	Atomo xetine	
	• Vyvanse®	Lisdexamfetamine	
Blood clots	• Coumadin®	Warfarin	Occasional drinking may lead to internal bleeding; heavier drinking also may cause bleeding or may have the opposite effect, resulting in possible blood clots, strokes, or heart attacks
Cough	• Delsym®, Robitussin Cough®	Dextromethorpan	Drowsiness, dizziness; increased risk for overdose
	• Robitussin A–C®	Guaifenesin + codeine	
Depression	• Abilify®	Aripriprazone	Drowsiness, dizziness; increased risk for overdose; increased feelings of depression or hopelessness (all medications); impaired motor control (quetiapine, mirtazapine); increased alcohol effect (bupropion); liver damage (duloxetine)
	• Anafranil®	Clomipramine	
	• Celexa®	Citalopram	
	• Clozaril®	Clozapine	
	• Cymbalta®	Duloxetine	
	• Desyrel®	Trazodone	
	• Effexor®	Venlafaxine	
	• Elavil®	Amitriptyline	
	• Geodon®	Ziprasidone	
	• Invega®	Paliperidone	
	• Lexapro®	Escitalopram	Monoamine oxidase inhibitors (MAOIs), such as tranylcypromine and phenelzine, when combined with alcohol, may result in serious heart-related side effects. Risk for dangerously high blood pressure is increased when MAOIs are mixed with tyramine, a byproduct found in beer and red wine
	• Luvox®	Fluvoxamine	
	• Nardil®	Phenelzine	
	• Norpramin®	Desipramine	
	• Parnate®	Tranylcypromine	
	• Paxil®	Paroxetine	
	• Pristiq®	Desevenlaf axine	
	• Prozac®	Fluoxetine	
	• Remeron®	Mirtazapine	
	• Risperdal®	Risperidone	
	• Seroquel®	Quetiapine	
	• Serzone®	Nefazodone	
	• Symbyax®	Fluoxetine/Olanzapine	
	• Wellbutrin®	Bupropion	
	• Zoloft®	Sertraline	
	• Zyprexa	Olanzapine	
	• Herbal preparations (St. John's Wort)		

MOTOR VEHICLE AND PEDESTRIAN ACCIDENTS

In *Traffic Safety Facts 2014* (2016, https://crashstats.nhtsa.dot.gov/Api/Public/Publication/812261), the National Highway Traffic Safety Administration (NHTSA) of the U.S. Department of Transportation defines a fatal traffic crash as alcohol related if either

Symptoms/disorders	Medication (brand name)	Medication (generic name)	Some possible reactions with alcohol
Diabetes	• Diabinese®	Chlorpropamide	Abnormally low blood sugar levels, flushing reaction (nausea, vomiting, headache, rapid heartbeat, sudden changes in blood pressure); symptoms of nausea and weakness may occur (metformin)
	• Glucotrol®	Glipizide	
	• Glucophage®	Metformin	
	• Glynase®, DiaBeta®, Micronase®	Glyburide	
	• Orinase®		
	• Tolinase®	Tolbutamide	
		Tolazamide	
Enlarged prostate	• Cardura®	Doxazosin	Dizziness, light headedness, fainting
	• Flomax®	Tamsulosin	
	• Hytrin®	Terazosin	
	• Minipress®	Prazosin	
Heartburn, indigestion, sour stomach	• Axid®	Nizatidine	Rapid heartbeat; increased alcohol effect; sudden changes in blood pressure (metoclopramide)
	• Reglan®	Metoclopramide	
	• Tagamet®	Cimetidine	
	• Zantac®	Ranitidine	
High blood pressure	• Accupril®	Quinapril	Dizziness, fainting, drowsiness; heart problems such as changes in the heart's regular heartbeat (arrhythmia)
	• Calan®	Verapamil	
	• Capozide®	Hydrochlorothiazide	
	• Cardura®	Doxazosin	
	• Catapres®	Clonidine	
	• Cozaar®	Losartan	
	• Hytrin®	Terazosin	
	• Lopressor® HCT	Hydrochlorothiazide	
	• Lotensin®	Benzapril	
	• Minipress®	Prazosin	
	• Norvasc®	Amlodipine mesylate	
	• Prinivil®, Zestril®	Lisinopril	
	• Vaseretic®	Enalapril	
High cholesterol	• Advicor®	Lovastatin + Niacin	Liver damage (all medications); increased flushing and itching ((niacin), increased stomach bleeding (pravastatin + aspirin)
	• Altocor®	Lovastatin	
	• Crestor®	Rosuvastatin	
	• Lipitor®	Atorvastatin	
	• Mevacor®	Lovastatin	
	• Niaspan®	Niacin	
	• Pravachol®	Pravastatin	
	• Pravigard™	Pravastatin + Aspirin	
	• Vytorin™	Ezetimibe + Simvastatin	
	• Zocor®	Simvastatin	
Infections	• Acrodantin®	Nitrofurantoin	Fast heartbeat, sudden changes in blood pressure; stomach pain, upset stomach, vomiting, headache, or flushing or redness of the face; liver damage (isoniazid, ketoconazole)
	• Flagyl®	Metronidazole	
	• Grisactin®	Griseofulvin	
	• Nizoral®	Ketoconazole	
	• Nydrazid®	Isoniazid	
	• Seromycin®	Cycloserine	
	• Tindamax®	Tinidazole	
	• Zithromax®	Azithromycin	
Mood stabilizers	• Depakene®, Depakote®	Valproic acid	Drowsiness, dizziness; tremors; increased risk for side effects, such as restlessness, impaired motor control; loss of appetite; stomach upset; irregular bowel movement; joint or muscle pain; depression; liver damage (valproic acid)
	• Eskalith®, Eskalith®CR, Lithobid	Lithium	
Muscle pain	• Flexeril®	Cyclobenzaprine	Drowsiness, dizziness; increased risk of seizures; increased risk for overdose; slowed or difficulty breathing; impaired motor control; unusual behavior; memory problems
	• Soma®	Carisoprodol	
Nausea, motion sickness	• Antivert®	Meclizine	Drowsiness, dizziness; increased risk for overdose
	• Dramamine®	Dimenhydrinate	
	• Phenergan®	Promethazine	
Pain (such as muscle ache, minor arthritis pain), fever, inflammation	• Advil®	Ibuprofen	Stomach upset, bleeding and ulcers; liver damage (acetaminophen); rapid heartbeat
	• Aleve®	Naproxen Aspirin	
	• Excedrin®	Acetaminophen	
	• Motrin®	Ibuprofen	
	• Tylenol®	Acetaminophen	

the driver or an involved pedestrian has a BAC of 0.01 g/dL or greater. If either the driver or an involved pedestrian has a BAC of 0.08 g/dL or greater, the individual is considered to be intoxicated and the crash is classified as alcohol impaired. However, neither definition means that alcohol is necessarily the cause of the accident.

The NHTSA reports that 32,675 people were killed in traffic accidents in 2014, with 9,967 of them in alcohol-impaired crashes. (See Table 2.7.) These alcohol-impaired traffic deaths represented 31% of all car crash fatalities in 2014. The percentage of alcohol-impaired traffic fatalities has declined somewhat steadily from a high

TABLE 2.6

Interactions between alcohol and various medications [CONTINUED]

Symptoms/disorders	Medication (brand name)	Medication (generic name)	Some possible reactions with alcohol
Seizures	• Dilantin® • Horizant®, Neurontin® • Keppra® • Klonopin® • Lamictal® • Lyrica® • Tegretol® • Topamax® • Trileptal®	Phenytoin Gabapentin Levetiracetam Clonazepam Phenobarbital Lamotrigine Pregabalin Carbamazepine Topiramate Oxcarbazepine Barbiturates	Drowsiness, dizziness; increased risk of seizures (levetiracetam, phenytoin); unusual behavior and changes in mental health (such as thoughts of suicide) (topiramate)
Severe pain from injury, postsurgical care, oral surgery, migraines	• Darvocet–N® • Demerol® • Fiorinal® with codeine • Percocet® • Vicodin®	Propoxyphene Merepidine Butalbital + codeine Oxycodone Hydrocodone	Drowsiness, dizziness; increased risk for overdose; slowed or difficulty breathing; impaired motor control; unusual behavior; memory problems
Sleep problems	• Ambien® • Lunesta™ • Prosom™ • Restoril® • Sominex® • Unisom® • Herbal preparations (chamomile, valerian, lavender)	Zolpidem Eszopiclone Estazolam Temazepam Diphenhydramine Doxylamine	Drowsiness, sleepiness, dizziness; slowed or difficulty breathing; impaired motor control; unusual behavior; memory problems Increased drowsiness

SOURCE: "Commonly Used Medicines (Both Prescription and Over-the-Counter) That Interact with Alcohol," in *Harmful Interactions*, U.S. Department of Health and Human Services, National Institute on Alcohol Abuse and Alcoholism, 2014, https://pubs.niaaa.nih.gov/publications/Medicine/Harmful_Interactions .pdf (accessed January 9, 2017)

of 48% in 1982, and leveled out from about the mid-1990s to 2014. The peak number of fatalities occurred in 1988, when 47,087 traffic accident deaths occurred, of which 18,611 (40%) involved instances of alcohol-impaired driving.

The Department of Transportation reports in *2015 Motor Vehicle Crashes: Overview* (August 2016, https://crashstats.nhtsa.dot.gov/Api/Public/ViewPublication/812318) that alcohol-impaired car crash fatalities rose to 10,265 in 2015. (See Table 2.8.) As Table 2.9 shows, Rhode Island (43%) had the highest rate of alcohol-impaired car crash fatalities among all U.S. states in 2015.

A number of important factors have contributed to the decline of drunk driving fatalities. Mothers against Drunk Driving was founded in 1980. This organization's most significant achievement was lobbying to get the legal drinking age raised to 21 in all states, which occurred in 1988. There were also successful campaigns such as "Friends Don't Let Friends Drive Drunk." The use of seat belts has also helped reduce deaths in motor vehicle accidents.

By August 2005 all 50 states, the District of Columbia, and Puerto Rico had lowered the BAC limit for drunk driving from 0.1 g/dL to 0.08 g/dL. According to the Insurance Institute for Highway Safety, in "DUI/DWI" (http://www.iihs.org/iihs/topics/laws/dui), as of March 2017, 41 states and the District of Columbia also had administrative license revocation laws, which require

prompt, mandatory suspension of driver's licenses when drivers fail or refuse to take the BAC test. This suspension, before conviction and independent of criminal procedures, is invoked immediately after arrest.

In 2014 drivers aged 25 to 34 years were the most likely to be involved in fatal crashes in which the driver had a BAC of 0.08 g/dL or higher. (See Table 2.10.) Among the 8,972 fatal crashes involving drivers aged 25 to 34 that year, 2,586 (29%) involved drivers with a BAC of 0.08 g/dL or higher. By contrast, only 6% of fatal crashes involving drivers over the age of 74 years involved drivers who were legally intoxicated at the time of the accident.

Cases involving drivers with a BAC of 0.08 g/dL or higher accounted for a higher percentage of fatal crashes by motorcycles (29%) in 2014 than of crashes involving automobiles and light trucks (22% each). (See Table 2.11.) Fatal crashes involving large trucks were very unlikely to involve drivers with a BAC of 0.08 g/dL or higher (2%). In 2014, 42% each of all fatal car-crash victims aged 21 to 24 years and 25 to 34 years were involved in traffic accidents in which the driver had a BAC of 0.08 g/dL or higher, the highest percentage of any age group that year. (See Table 2.12.)

ALCOHOL-RELATED OFFENSES

Doris J. James of the Bureau of Justice Statistics (BJS) mentions in *Profile of Jail Inmates, 2002* (July 2004,

TABLE 2.7

Fatalities in motor accidents, by blood-alcohol concentration at time of crash, 1982–2014

Year	BAC = 0.00		BAC = 0.01–0.07		Alcohol-impaired driving fatalities (BAC = 0.08+)		BAC = 0.01+		Total fatalities*	
	Number	Percent	Number	Percent	Number	Percent	Number	Percent	Number	Percent
1982	19,771	45	2,912	7	21,113	48	24,025	55	43,945	100
1983	19,787	46	2,588	6	20,051	47	22,639	53	42,589	100
1984	21,429	48	3,007	7	19,638	44	22,645	51	44,257	100
1985	22,589	52	2,974	7	18,125	41	21,098	48	43,825	100
1986	22,896	50	3,487	8	19,554	42	23,041	50	46,087	100
1987	24,186	52	3,238	7	18,813	41	22,051	48	46,390	100
1988	25,164	53	3,156	7	18,611	40	21,767	46	47,087	100
1989	25,152	55	2,793	6	17,521	38	20,314	45	45,582	100
1990	23,823	53	2,901	7	17,705	40	20,607	46	44,599	100
1991	23,025	55	2,480	6	15,827	38	18,307	44	41,508	100
1992	22,726	58	2,352	6	14,049	36	16,401	42	39,250	100
1993	23,979	60	2,300	6	13,739	34	16,039	40	40,150	100
1994	24,948	61	2,236	5	13,390	33	15,626	38	40,716	100
1995	25,768	62	2,416	6	13,478	32	15,893	38	41,817	100
1996	26,052	62	2,415	6	13,451	32	15,866	38	42,065	100
1997	26,902	64	2,216	5	12,757	30	14,973	36	42,013	100
1998	26,477	64	2,353	6	12,546	30	14,899	36	41,501	100
1999	26,798	64	2,235	5	12,555	30	14,790	35	41,717	100
2000	26,082	62	2,422	6	13,324	32	15,746	38	41,945	100
2001	26,334	62	2,441	6	13,290	31	15,731	37	42,196	100
2002	27,080	63	2,321	5	13,472	31	15,793	37	43,005	100
2003	27,328	64	2,327	5	13,096	31	15,423	36	42,884	100
2004	27,413	64	2,212	5	13,099	31	15,311	36	42,836	100
2005	27,423	63	2,404	6	13,582	31	15,985	37	43,510	100
2006	26,633	62	2,479	6	13,491	32	15,970	37	42,708	100
2007	25,611	62	2,494	6	13,041	32	15,534	38	41,259	100
2008	23,499	63	2,115	6	11,711	31	13,826	37	37,423	100
2009	21,051	62	1,972	6	10,759	32	12,731	38	33,883	100
2010	21,005	64	1,771	5	10,136	31	11,906	36	32,999	100
2011	20,848	64	1,662	5	9,865	30	11,527	35	32,479	100
2012	21,563	64	1,782	5	10,336	31	12,118	36	33,782	100
2013	20,843	63	1,831	6	10,110	31	11,941	36	32,894	100
2014	20,856	64	1,764	5	9,967	31	11,731	36	32,675	100

BAC = Blood alcohol concentration
*Totals include fatalities in crashes in which there was no driver present.
Note: The National Highway Traffic Safety Administration estimates alcohol involvement when alcohol test results are unknown.

SOURCE: "Table 13. Persons Killed, by Highest Driver Blood Alcohol Concentration (BAC) in the Crash, 1982–2014," in *Traffic Safety Facts: 2014*, U.S. Department of Transportation, National Highway Traffic Safety Administration, National Center for Statistics and Analysis, 2016, https://crashstats.nhtsa.dot.gov/Api/Public/Publication/812261 (accessed January 9, 2017)

TABLE 2.8

Alcohol-related motor vehicle fatalities, by vehicle type, 2014 and 2015

	2014	2015	Change	% change
Total fatalities	**32,744**	**35,092**	**+2,348**	**+7.2%**
AI-driving fatalities	9,943	10,265	+322	+3.2%
Alcohol-impaired drivers in fatal crashes by vehicle type				
Passenger cars	3,892	4,085	+193	+5.0%
Light truck—vans	246	214	−32	−13.0%
Light truck—utility	1,494	1,529	+35	+2.3%
Light truck—pickups	1,936	1,900	−36	−1.9%
Motorcycles	1,370	1,365	−5	−0.4%
Large trucks	68	60	−8	−11.8%

SOURCE: "Table 4. Total and Alcohol-Impaired Driving Fatalities, 2014 and 2015," in *2015 Motor Vehicle Crashes: Overview*, U.S. Department of Transportation, National Highway Traffic Safety Administration, August 2016, https://crashstats.nhtsa.dot.gov/Api/Public/ViewPublication/812318 (accessed January 9, 2017)

https://www.bjs.gov/content/pub/pdf/pji02.pdf) that in 2002, 33.4% of convicted jail inmates reported that they had been under the influence of alcohol alone (not in combination with any other drug) when they committed their offenses. This figure had decreased since 1996. A higher percentage of jail inmates used alcohol when committing a violent offense than did those committing other types of crimes, such as property or drug offenses. As of March 2017, these data were the most recent from the BJS.

TABLE 2.9

Alcohol-related motor vehicle fatalities, by state, 2014 and 2015

State	2014 Total fatalities	Alcohol-impaired-driving fatalities #	Alcohol-impaired-driving fatalities %	2015 Total fatalities	Alcohol-impaired-driving fatalities #	Alcohol-impaired-driving fatalities %	2014 to 2015 change Total fatalities Change	Total fatalities % change	Alcohol-impaired-driving fatalities Change	Alcohol-impaired-driving fatalities % change
Alabama	820	265	32%	849	247	29%	+29	+3.5%	−18	−6.8%
Alaska	73	22	30%	65	23	36%	−8	−11.0%	+1	+4.5%
Arizona	773	200	26%	893	272	31%	+120	+15.5%	+72	+36.0%
Arkansas	470	136	29%	531	149	28%	+61	+13.0%	+13	+9.6%
California	3,102	876	28%	3,176	914	29%	+74	+2.4%	+38	+4.3%
Colorado	488	160	33%	546	151	28%	+58	+11.9%	−9	−5.6%
Connecticut	248	97	39%	266	103	39%	+18	+7.3%	+6	+6.2%
Delaware	124	52	42%	126	41	33%	+2	+1.6%	−11	−21.2%
Dist of Columbia	23	5	23%	23	6	26%	0	0.0%	+1	+20.0%
Florida	2,494	694	28%	2,939	797	27%	+445	+17.8%	+103	+14.8%
Georgia	1,164	279	24%	1,430	366	26%	+266	+22.9%	+87	+31.2%
Hawaii	95	30	31%	94	33	35%	−1	−1.1%	+3	+10.0%
Idaho	186	53	28%	216	70	32%	+30	+16.1%	+17	+32.1%
Illinois	924	302	33%	998	307	31%	+74	+8.0%	+5	+1.7%
Indiana	745	160	21%	821	178	22%	+76	+10.2%	+18	+11.3%
Iowa	322	91	28%	320	78	24%	−2	−0.6%	−13	−14.3%
Kansas	385	108	28%	355	84	24%	−30	−7.8%	−24	−22.2%
Kentucky	672	171	25%	761	192	25%	+89	+13.2%	+21	+12.3%
Louisiana	740	247	33%	726	245	34%	−14	−1.9%	−2	−0.8%
Maine	131	37	28%	156	52	33%	+25	+19.1%	+15	+40.5%
Maryland	442	130	29%	513	159	31%	+71	+16.1%	+29	+22.3%
Massachusetts	354	143	40%	306	96	31%	−48	−13.6%	−47	−32.9%
Michigan	901	212	23%	963	267	28%	+62	−6.9%	+55	+25.9%
Minnesota	361	108	30%	411	115	28%	+50	+13.9%	+7	+6.5%
Mississippi	607	172	28%	677	175	26%	+70	+11.5%	+3	+1.7%
Missouri	766	205	27%	869	224	26%	+103	+13.4%	+19	+9.3%
Montana	192	73	38%	224	75	34%	+32	+16.7%	+2	+2.7%
Nebraska	225	60	27%	246	65	26%	+21	+9.3%	+5	+8.3%
Nevada	291	93	32%	325	97	30%	+34	+11.7%	+4	+4.3%
New Hampshire	95	29	30%	114	33	29%	+19	+20.0%	+4	+13.8%
New Jersey	556	161	29%	562	111	20%	+6	+1.1%	−50	−31.1%
New Mexico	386	117	30%	298	98	33%	−88	−22.8%	−19	−16.2%
New York	1,041	312	30%	1,121	311	28%	+80	+7.7%	−1	−0.3%
North Carolina	1,284	363	28%	1,379	411	30%	+95	+7.4%	+48	+13.2%
North Dakota	135	55	41%	131	50	38%	−4	−3.0%	−5	−9.1%
Ohio	1,006	302	30%	1,110	313	28%	+104	+10.3%	+11	+3.6%
Oklahoma	669	156	23%	643	170	27%	−26	−3.9%	+14	+9.0%
Oregon	357	99	28%	447	155	35%	+90	+25.2%	+56	+56.6%
Pennsylvania	1,195	349	29%	1,200	364	30%	+5	+0.4%	+15	+4.3%
Rhode Island	51	17	32%	45	19	43%	−6	−11.8%	+2	+11.8%
South Carolina	823	331	40%	977	301	31%	+154	+18.7%	−30	−9.1%
South Dakota	136	44	32%	133	43	33%	−3	−2.2%	−1	−2.3%
Tennessee	963	273	28%	958	252	26%	−5	−0.5%	−21	−7.7%
Texas	3,536	1,446	41%	3,516	1,323	38%	−20	−0.6%	−123	−8.5%
Utah	256	57	22%	276	43	16%	+20	+7.8%	−14	−24.6%
Vermont	44	8	19%	57	15	27%	+13	+29.5%	+7	+87.5%
Virginia	703	216	31%	753	208	28%	+50	+7.1%	−8	−3.7%
Washington	462	132	29%	568	148	26%	+106	+22.9%	+16	+12.1%
West Virginia	272	84	31%	268	71	27%	−4	−1.5%	−13	−15.5%
Wisconsin	506	165	33%	566	189	33%	+60	+11.9%	+24	+14.5%
Wyoming	150	48	32%	145	56	38%	−5	−3.3%	+8	+16.7%
National	32,744	9,943	30%	35,092	10,265	29%	+2,348	+7.2%	+322	+3.2%
Puerto Rico	304	94	31%	309	104	34%	+5	+1.6%	+10	+10.6%

SOURCE: "Table 6. Total and Alcohol-Impaired-Driving Fatalities, by State, 2014 and 2015," in *2015 Motor Vehicle Crashes: Overview*, U.S. Department of Transportation, National Highway Traffic Safety Administration, August 2016, https://crashstats.nhtsa.dot.gov/Api/Public/ViewPublication/812318 (accessed January 9, 2017).

TABLE 2.10

Drivers and motorcycle riders involved in fatal motor vehicle crashes, by age and blood alcohol concentration, 2014

| | Driver's BAC | | | | | | | | | | | |
| | 0.00 | | 0.01–0.07 | | 0.08 or higher* | | 0.01 and higher | | Total | |
Age (years)	Number	Percent	Number	Percent	Number	Percent	Number	Percent	Number	Percent
<16	126	92	1	1	10	7	11	8	137	100
16–20	2,967	78	175	5	662	17	836	22	3,803	100
21–24	2,967	64	283	6	1,404	30	1,687	36	4,654	100
25–34	5,957	66	429	5	2,586	29	3,015	34	8,972	100
35–44	4,978	72	264	4	1,652	24	1,916	28	6,894	100
45–54	5,571	76	286	4	1,493	20	1,779	24	7,350	100
55–64	4,855	81	197	3	945	16	1,142	19	5,997	100
65–74	2,906	88	81	2	327	10	408	12	3,314	100
>74	2,442	92	47	2	152	6	199	8	2,641	100
Unknown	582	71	52	6	187	23	239	29	821	100
Total	**33,352**	**75**	**1,814**	**4**	**9,417**	**21**	**11,231**	**25**	**44,583**	**100**

BAC = Blood alcohol concentration

SOURCE: "Table 78. Drivers and Motorcycle Riders Involved in Fatal Crashes, by Age and Driver's Blood Alcohol Concentration (BAC)," in *Traffic Safety Facts: 2014*, U.S. Department of Transportation, National Highway Traffic Safety Administration, National Center for Statistics and Analysis, 2016, https://crashstats.nhtsa.dot.gov/Api/Public/Publication/812261 (accessed January 9, 2017)

TABLE 2.11

Drivers and motorcycle riders involved in fatal motor vehicle crashes, by vehicle type and blood alcohol concentration, 2014

| | Driver's BAC | | | | | | | | | | | |
| | 0.00 | | 0.01–0.07 | | 0.08 or higher* | | 0.01 and higher | | Total | |
Vehicle type	Number	Percent	Number	Percent	Number	Percent	Number	Percent	Number	Percent
Passenger car	13,095	74	741	4	3,922	22	4,662	26	17,757	100
Light truck	12,697	75	626	4	3,694	22	4,320	25	17,017	100
Large truck	3,585	97	45	1	68	2	112	3	3,697	100
Bus	209	90	6	3	18	8	24	10	232	100
Other/unknown	776	65	68	6	344	29	412	35	1,188	100
Subtotal	**30.361**	**76**	**1,485**	**4**	**8,045**	**20**	**9,530**	**24**	**39,891**	**100**
Motorcycle	2,991	64	329	7	1,372	29	1,701	36	4,692	100
Total	**33,352**	**75**	**1,814**	**4**	**9,417**	**21**	**11,231**	**25**	**44,583**	**100**

BAC = Blood alcohol concentration
*BAC of 0.08 g/dl or higher indicates alcohol-impaired driving.
Note: The National Highway Traffic Safety Administration (NHTSA) estimates alcohol involvement when alcohol test results are unknown.

SOURCE: "Table 81. Drivers and Motorcycle Riders Involved in Fatal Crashes, by Vehicle Type and Driver's Blood Alcohol Concentration (BAC)," in *Traffic Safety Facts: 2014*, U.S. Department of Transportation, National Highway Traffic Safety Administration, National Center for Statistics and Analysis, 2016, https://crashstats.nhtsa.dot.gov/Api/Public/Publication/812261 (accessed January 9, 2017)

TABLE 2.12

Persons killed in fatal motor vehicle accidents, by age of victim and driver blood alcohol concentration, 2014

	Highest driver BAC in crash								Total[b]	
	0.00		0.01–0.07		0.08 or higher[a]		0.01 and higher			
Age (years)	Number	Percent	Number	Percent	Number	Percent	Number	Percent	Number	Percent
<5	246	72	16	5	79	23	95	28	340	100
5–9	273	78	15	4	59	17	74	21	350	100
10–15	434	77	26	5	102	18	128	23	562	100
16–20	1,970	66	204	7	812	27	1,016	34	2,998	100
21–24	1,657	50	232	7	1,390	42	1,622	49	3,292	100
25–34	2,983	51	354	6	2,463	42	2,816	48	5,817	100
35–44	2,327	55	244	6	1,640	39	1,884	45	4,222	100
45–54	3,064	62	258	5	1,578	32	1,836	37	4,908	100
55–64	3,074	70	218	5	1,089	25	1,306	30	4,390	100
65–74	2,181	79	114	4	445	16	559	20	2,745	100
>74	2,592	87	80	3	288	10	367	12	2,964	100
Unknown	57	65	5	6	23	27	28	32	87	100
Total	**20,856**	**64**	**1,764**	**5**	**9,967**	**31**	**11,731**	**36**	**32,675**	**100**

BAC = Blood alcohol concentration
[a]BAC of 0.08 g/dl or higher indicates alcohol-impaired driving.
[b]Total includes fatalities in crashes in which there was no driver present.
Note: The National Highway Traffic Safety Administration (NHTSA) estimates alcohol involvement when alcohol test results are unknown.

SOURCE: "Table 82. Persons Killed, by Age and Highest Driver Blood Alcohol Concentration (BAC) in the Crash," in *Traffic Safety Facts: 2014*, U.S. Department of Transportation, National Highway Traffic Safety Administration, National Center for Statistics and Analysis, 2016, https://crashstats.nhtsa.dot .gov/Api/Public/Publication/812261 (accessed January 9, 2017)

CHAPTER 3
TOBACCO

During the mid-20th century smoking in the United States was often associated with adventure, relaxation, and romance; movie stars oozed glamour on-screen while smoking, and movie tough guys were never more masculine than when lighting up. Songs such as "Smoke Gets in Your Eyes" topped the list of most popular songs. Smoking became a rite of passage for young males and a sign of increasing independence for young females.

Since the 1990s, however, there has been an increase in opposition to tobacco use. Health authorities warn of the dangers of smoking and chewing tobacco, and nonsmokers object to secondhand smoke—because of both the smell and the health dangers of breathing smoke from other people's cigarettes. In the 21st century a smoker is more likely to ask for permission before lighting up, and the answer is often "no." Because of health concerns, smoking has been banned on airplanes, in hospitals, and in many workplaces, restaurants, and bars. Justin McCarthy of Gallup, Inc., notes in *Ban on Smoking in Public Retains Majority Support in U.S.* (July 30, 2015, http://www.gallup.com/poll/184397/ban-smoking-public-retains-majority-support.aspx) that in 2015, 58% of Americans supported a ban on smoking in public places, while 24% believed smoking should be made "totally illegal" in the United States.

This increased awareness of the dangers of cigarettes has coincided with a steady decline in the percentage of Americans who smoke. In *In U.S., Smoking Dips, but Fewer Eating Healthy since '09* (August 31, 2016, http://www.gallup.com/poll/195161/smoking-dips-fewer-eating-healthily.aspx), Nader Nekvasil of Gallup reports that smoking rates in the United States fell steadily between 2008 and 2016, from 21.1% to 18%.

PHYSICAL PROPERTIES OF NICOTINE

Cultivated tobacco (*Nicotiana tabacum*) is a plant native to the Western Hemisphere. It belongs to the nightshade family *Solanaceae*. Tobacco contains nicotine, a drug that is classified as a stimulant, although it has some depressive effects as well. Nicotine is a poisonous alkaloid that is the major psychoactive (mood-altering) ingredient in tobacco. Alkaloids are carbon- and nitrogen-containing compounds that are found in some families of plants. They have both poisonous and medicinal properties.

Nicotine's effects on the body are complex. The drug affects the brain and central nervous system as well as the hypothalamus and pituitary glands of the endocrine (hormone) system. Nicotine easily crosses the blood–brain barrier (a series of capillaries and cells that control the flow of substances from the blood to the brain). It accumulates in the brain faster than caffeine or heroin but slower than Valium (a sedative that is used to treat anxiety). In the brain nicotine imitates the actions of the hormone epinephrine (adrenaline) and the neurotransmitter acetylcholine, both of which heighten awareness. Nicotine also triggers the release of dopamine, which enhances feelings of pleasure, and endorphins, which have a calming effect.

As noted earlier, nicotine acts as both a stimulant and a depressant. By stimulating certain nerve cells in the spinal cord, nicotine relaxes the nerves and slows some reactions, such as the knee-jerk reflex. Small amounts of nicotine stimulate some nerve cells, but these cells are depressed by large amounts of nicotine. In addition, nicotine stimulates the brain cortex (the outer layer of the brain) and affects the functions of the heart and lungs.

TRENDS IN TOBACCO USE
Cigarettes

CONSUMPTION DATA. Each year the Substance Abuse and Mental Health Services Administration (SAMHSA) surveys U.S. households on drug use for the National Survey on Drug Use and Health. According to the

SAMHSA, in *Results from the 2015 National Survey on Drug Use and Health: Detailed Tables* (September 8, 2016, https://www.samhsa.gov/data/sites/default/files/NSDUH-Det Tabs-2015/NSDUH-DetTabs-2015/NSDUH-DetTabs-2015 .pdf), in 2015, 58.5% of Americans aged 12 years and older had smoked cigarettes at some point during their lifetime, and 19.4% were current smokers (meaning they had smoked within the month preceding the survey). (See Table 3.1.)

In 2015 men (21.8%) were more likely than women (17.1%) to be current smokers. (See Table 3.1.) Additionally, Native Americans or Alaskan Natives (29.5%) were considerably more likely to be current smokers than African Americans (21.3%), whites (20.7%), Hispanics (15.3%), or Asian Americans (10%). Those aged 18 to 25 years had the highest rate of current smoking, at 26.7%, compared with 4.2% for those aged 12 to 17 years and 20% for those aged 26 years and older.

Meanwhile, smoking rates declined steadily during the first decade and a half of the 21st century. According a poll conducted by Gallup, between 2001 and 2005 a quarter (25%) of all U.S. adults had smoked at some point during the week before being surveyed; between 2011 and 2015 this figure fell to one out of five (20%). (See Table 3.2.) As Figure 3.1 shows, current smoking rates fell steadily among all age groups between 2002 and 2015. The percentage of current cigarette smokers who smoked every day also declined during that span, dropping from 63.4% in 2002 to 58.1% in 2015. (See Table 3.3.)

At the same time, the quantity of cigarettes consumed by smokers in the United States has declined dramatically. As Figure 3.2 shows, during the late 1970s nearly two-thirds (65%) of U.S. smokers consumed a pack or more of cigarettes per day. By 2015 this figure fell to just over a quarter (26%). During the early 21st century the percentage of young smokers who smoked a pack or more of cigarettes per day fell considerably. As Figure 3.3 shows, the percentage of smokers aged 18 to 25 years who

TABLE 3.2

Percentage of adults who smoke cigarettes, by age group, 2001–15

HAVE YOU, YOURSELF, EVER SMOKED CIGARETTES IN THE PAST WEEK?

(% yes)

	2001–2005	2006–2010	2011–2015	Change over past decade
	%	%	%	(pct. pts.)
18 to 29	34	28	22	-12
30 to 49	28	25	23	-5
50 to 64	24	22	21	-3
65+	11	11	11	0
National average	25	22	20	-5

SOURCE: Nader Nekvasil and Diana Liu, "Percentage of U.S. Adults Who Smoke Cigarettes, by Age Group," in *In U.S., Young Adults' Cigarette Use Is Down Sharply*, Gallup, Inc., December 10, 2015, http://www.gallup.com/poll/187592/young-adults-cigarette-down-sharply.aspx?g_source=cigarettes&g_medium=search&g_campaign=tiles (accessed January 9, 2017). Copyright © 2017. Republished with permission of Gallup, Inc.; permission conveyed through Copyright Clearance Center, Inc.

TABLE 3.1

Percentage of lifetime, past year, and past-month cigarette users, by age group, gender, and race and Hispanic origin, 2014 and 2015

Demographic characteristic	Lifetime (2014)	Lifetime (2015)	Past year (2014)	Past year (2015)	Past month (2014)	Past month (2015)
Total	61.0[b]	58.5	24.8[b]	23.1	20.8[b]	19.4
Age						
12–17	14.2[a]	13.2	8.9[a]	8.1	4.9[a]	4.2
18 or older	65.9[b]	63.1	26.5[b]	24.6	22.5[b]	21.0
18–25	56.1[b]	53.3	37.7[b]	35.0	28.4[a]	26.7
26 or older	67.5[b]	64.7	24.6[b]	22.9	21.5[b]	20.0
Gender						
Male	65.8[b]	63.8	27.8[b]	26.0	23.2[b]	21.8
Female	56.5[b]	53.4	22.1[b]	20.4	18.6[b]	17.1
Hispanic origin and race						
Not Hispanic or Latino	63.4[b]	60.6	25.5[b]	23.7	21.6[b]	20.2
White	68.3[b]	65.6	26.3[b]	24.2	22.3[b]	20.7
Black or African American	50.2[a]	47.2	25.6	24.7	22.5	21.3
American Indian or Alaska Native	65.7	65.3	37.7	34.9	32.5	29.5
Native Hawaiian or other Pacific Islander	61.0[b]	39.5	29.1	20.9	25.4	16.3
Asian	32.8	31.8	12.5	12.6	9.2	10.0
Two or more races	64.4	63.1	29.1	31.4	24.4	26.8
Hispanic or Latino	48.6	47.3	21.6	20.1	16.7	15.3

[a]The difference between this estimate and the 2015 estimate is statistically significant at the 0.05 level. Rounding may make the estimates appear identical.
[b]The difference between this estimate and the 2015 estimate is statistically significant at the 0.01 level. Rounding may make the estimates appear identical.

SOURCE: "Table 2.26B, Cigarette Use in Lifetime, Past Year, and Past Month among Persons Aged 12 or Older, by Demographic Characteristics: Percentages, 2014 and 2015," in *2015 National Survey on Drug Use and Health: Detailed Tables*, U.S. Department of Health and Human Services, Substance Abuse and Mental Health Services Administration, September 8, 2016, https://www.samhsa.gov/data/sites/default/files/NSDUH-DetTabs-2015/NSDUH-DetTabs-2015/NSDUH-DetTabs-2015.pdf (accessed January 9, 2017)

FIGURE 3.1

Past-month cigarette use among persons aged 12 and older, by age group, 2002–15

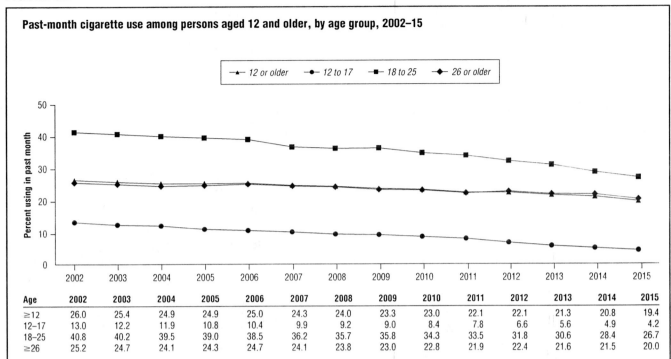

Age	2002	2003	2004	2005	2006	2007	2008	2009	2010	2011	2012	2013	2014	2015
≥12	26.0	25.4	24.9	24.9	25.0	24.3	24.0	23.3	23.0	22.1	22.1	21.3	20.8	19.4
12–17	13.0	12.2	11.9	10.8	10.4	9.9	9.2	9.0	8.4	7.8	6.6	5.6	4.9	4.2
18–25	40.8	40.2	39.5	39.0	38.5	36.2	35.7	35.8	34.3	33.5	31.8	30.6	28.4	26.7
≥26	25.2	24.7	24.1	24.3	24.7	24.1	23.8	23.0	22.8	21.9	22.4	21.6	21.5	20.0

SOURCE: "Figure 15. Past Month Cigarette Use among People Aged 12 or Older, by Age Group: Percentages, 2002–2015," in *Key Substance Use and Mental Health Indicators in the United States: Results from the 2015 National Survey on Drug Use and Health*, U.S. Department of Health and Human Services, Substance Abuse and Mental Health Services Administration, September 2016, https://www.samhsa.gov/data/sites/default/files/NSDUH-FFR1-2015/NSDUH-FFR1-2015/NSDUH-FFR1-2015.pdf (accessed January 9, 2017)

TABLE 3.3

Daily cigarette use among past-month cigarette smokers aged 12 and older, by age group, 2002–15

Age group	2002	2003	2004	2005	2006	2007	2008	2009	2010	2011	2012	2013	2014	2015
12 or older	63.4	62.9	62.3	63.0	62.3	61.3	61.5	61.0	59.5	60.7	60.7	59.6	58.8	58.1
12 to 17	31.8	29.7	27.6	25.8	26.5	26.4	22.3	23.0	22.5	22.7	22.0	19.4	24.1	20.0
18 to 25	51.8	52.7	51.6	50.1	48.8	49.2	47.8	45.3	45.8	45.3	45.1	43.1	43.0	42.0
26 or older	68.8	68.0	67.8	68.9	67.9	66.3	67.0	67.2	64.8	66.5	66.0	64.9	63.3	62.7

SOURCE: "Table 1. Daily Cigarette Use among Past Month Cigarette Smokers Aged 12 or Older, by Age Group: Percentages, 2002–2015," in *Key Substance Use and Mental Health Indicators in the United States: Results from the 2015 National Survey on Drug Use and Health*, U.S. Department of Health and Human Services, Substance Abuse and Mental Health Services Administration, September 2016, https://www.samhsa.gov/data/sites/default/files/NSDUH-FFR1-2015/NSDUH-FFR1-2015/NSDUH-FFR1-2015.pdf (accessed January 9, 2017)

---

smoked a pack or more of cigarettes per day fell from 39.1% in 2002 to 22.5% in 2015. The rate of decline was also high among daily smokers between the ages of 12 and 17 years. In 2002, 21.8% of smokers in that age group smoked a pack or more of cigarettes per day; by 2015 this figure fell to 7.8%.

Table 3.4 provides a breakdown of lifetime, annual, and current smoking rates in the United States, by geographic location and county characteristics. The Midwest had the highest proportion of current smokers in 2015, with 21.5% of people aged 12 years and older living in the region claiming to have smoked at some point during the previous month. The South (20.8%) had a comparable proportion of current smokers in 2015, while the Northeast

(18.2%) and the West (16.2%) had notably lower smoking rates that year. At the same time, there appears to be a correlation between population density and smoking rates. In 2015, 17.5% of people living in large metropolitan areas (areas with populations of 1 million or more) were current smokers; by contrast, more than a quarter (25.9%) of people living in rural areas were current smokers that year.

Cigars, Pipes, and Other Forms of Tobacco

SAMHSA reports in *Key Substance Use and Mental Health Indicators in the United States: Results from the 2015 National Survey on Drug Use and Health* (September 2016, https://www.samhsa.gov/data/sites/default/files/NSDUH-FFR1-2015/NSDUH-FFR1-2015/NSDUH-FFR1

FIGURE 3.2

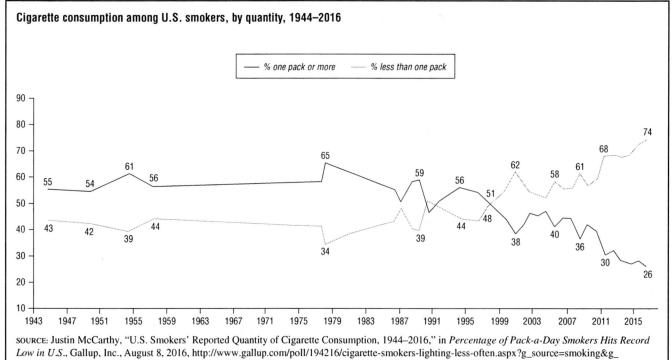

Cigarette consumption among U.S. smokers, by quantity, 1944–2016

— % one pack or more   ⋯⋯ % less than one pack

SOURCE: Justin McCarthy, "U.S. Smokers' Reported Quantity of Cigarette Consumption, 1944–2016," in *Percentage of Pack-a-Day Smokers Hits Record Low in U.S.*, Gallup, Inc., August 8, 2016, http://www.gallup.com/poll/194216/cigarette-smokers-lighting-less-often.aspx?g_source=smoking&g_medium=search&g_campaign=tiles (accessed January 9, 2017). Copyright © 2017. Republished with permission of Gallup, Inc.; permission conveyed through Copyright Clearance Center, Inc.

FIGURE 3.3

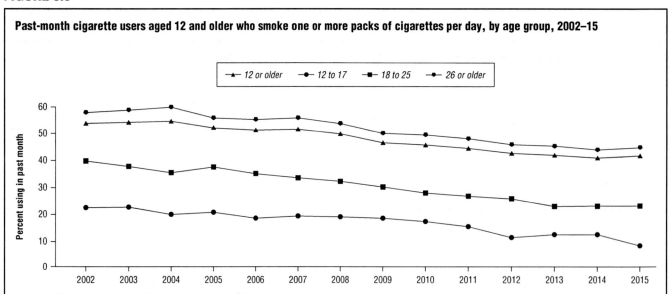

Past-month cigarette users aged 12 and older who smoke one or more packs of cigarettes per day, by age group, 2002–15

▲ 12 or older   ● 12 to 17   ■ 18 to 25   ● 26 or older

SOURCE: "Figure 17. Smokers of One or More Packs of Cigarettes per Day among Past Month Daily Cigarette Smokers Aged 12 or Older, by Age Group: Percentages, 2002–2015," in *Key Substance Use and Mental Health Indicators in the United States: Results from the 2015 National Survey on Drug Use and Health*, U.S. Department of Health and Human Services, Substance Abuse and Mental Health Services Administration, September 2016, https://www.samhsa.gov/data/sites/default/files/NSDUH-FFR1-2015/NSDUH-FFR1-2015/NSDUH-FFR1-2015.pdf (accessed January 9, 2017)

-2015.pdf) that of the 64 million people aged 12 years and older who were current tobacco users in 2015, more than four out of five (52 million, or 81.3%) smoked cigarettes. (See Figure 3.4.) Another 12.5 million smoked cigars that year, while 9 million used smokeless tobacco and 2.3 million smoked tobacco out of a pipe. Overall, people who smoked only cigarettes accounted for two-thirds (66.3%) of all past-month tobacco users in 2015. (See Figure 3.5.) Nearly one out of five (18.8%) of current tobacco users did not smoke cigarettes, while 15% of current tobacco users both smoked cigarettes and used some other tobacco product during the past month.

TABLE 3.4

Percentage of lifetime, past year, and past-month cigarette users aged 12 and older, by geographic location, 2014 and 2015

Geographic characteristic	Lifetime (2014)	Lifetime (2015)	Past year (2014)	Past year (2015)	Past month (2014)	Past month (2015)
Total	61.0[b]	58.5	24.8[b]	23.1	20.8[b]	19.4
Geographic division						
Northeast	60.9[b]	57.6	23.4	21.9	19.8	18.2
New England	62.5	61.6	21.2	20.9	17.8	17.3
Middle Atlantic	60.3[b]	56.1	24.2	22.2	20.5	18.6
Midwest	65.6[b]	62.6	27.6[b]	24.9	23.5[b]	21.5
East North Central	65.4[a]	62.9	27.9[b]	25.1	24.0[a]	21.9
West North Central	66.0[b]	61.9	26.7	24.5	22.3	20.7
South	60.6[b]	58.2	26.3[b]	24.6	22.4[b]	20.8
South Atlantic	61.5[b]	58.3	25.7[b]	22.9	21.9[b]	19.4
East South Central	62.8	60.0	28.6	28.9	25.0	25.3
West South Central	58.0	57.2	26.1	25.3	22.1	20.9
West	57.6	55.8	21.2	20.0	16.7	16.2
Mountain	60.6	58.7	23.5	21.9	19.3	18.2
Pacific	56.3	54.5	20.2	19.2	15.5	15.3
Country type[c]						
Large metro	58.5[b]	55.9	22.9[b]	21.3	18.9[b]	17.5
Small metro	63.1[b]	60.9	26.4[b]	24.6	22.3[a]	21.0
250K–1 mil. pop.	62.4[a]	60.3	25.2	24.4	21.2	20.8
<250K pop.	64.8[a]	62.1	29.1[b]	25.0	25.0[b]	21.4
Nonmetro	66.6[b]	63.5	29.3[a]	26.9	25.4	23.7
Urbanized	65.9	63.4	28.1	26.4	23.7	23.1
Less urbanized	67.3[b]	63.2	30.7[b]	26.9	27.3[a]	23.7
Completely rural	66.9	65.2	27.5	28.5	23.3	25.9

[a]The difference between this estimate and the 2015 estimate is statistically significant at the 0.05 level. Rounding may make the estimates appear identical.
[b]The difference between this estimate and the 2015 estimate is statistically significant at the 0.01 level. Rounding may make the estimates appear identical.
[c]Due to the use of the 2013 Rural-Urban Continuum Codes in the creation of the county type variables, the 2014 estimates may differ from previously published estimates.

SOURCE: "Table 2.56B. Cigarette Use in Lifetime, Past Year, and Past Month among Persons Aged 12 or Older, by Geographic Characteristics: Percentages, 2014 and 2015," in *2015 National Survey on Drug Use and Health: Detailed Tables*, U.S. Department of Health and Human Services, Substance Abuse and Mental Health Services Administration, September 8, 2016, https://www.samhsa.gov/data/sites/default/files/NSDUH-DetTabs-2015/NSDUH-DetTabs-2015/NSDUH-DetTabs-2015.pdf (accessed January 9, 2017)

FIGURE 3.4

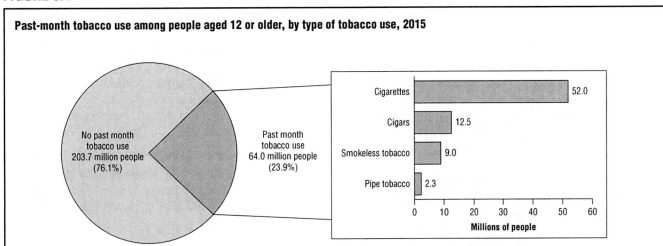

Past-month tobacco use among people aged 12 or older, by type of tobacco use, 2015

Note: The estimated numbers of current users of different tobacco products are not mutually exclusive because people could have used more than one type of tobacco product in the past month.

SOURCE: "Figure 13. Past Month Tobacco Use among People Aged 12 or Older: 2015," in *Key Substance Use and Mental Health Indicators in the United States: Results from the 2015 National Survey on Drug Use and Health*, U.S. Department of Health and Human Services, Substance Abuse and Mental Health Services Administration, September 2016, https://www.samhsa.gov/data/sites/default/files/NSDUH-FFR1-2015/NSDUH-FFR1-2015/NSDUH-FFR1-2015.pdf (accessed January 9, 2017)

ADDICTIVE NATURE OF NICOTINE

Is tobacco addictive? In *The Health Consequences of Smoking—Nicotine Addiction: A Report of the Surgeon General* (1988, https://profiles.nlm.nih.gov/NN/B/B/Z/D/_/nnbbzd.pdf), researchers first examined this question. They determined that the pharmacological (chemical and

FIGURE 3.5

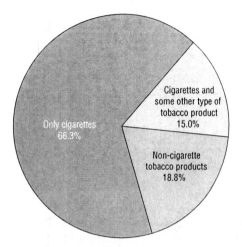

Types of tobacco use among past-month tobacco users aged 12 and older, 2015

- Only cigarettes 66.3%
- Cigarettes and some other type of tobacco product 15.0%
- Non-cigarette tobacco products 18.8%

Note: The percentages do not add to 100 percent due to rounding.

SOURCE: "Figure 14. Type of Past Month Tobacco Use among Current Tobacco Users Aged 12 or Older: Percentages, 2015," in *Key Substance Use and Mental Health Indicators in the United States: Results from the 2015 National Survey on Drug Use and Health*, U.S. Department of Health and Human Services, Substance Abuse and Mental Health Services Administration, September 2016, https://www.samhsa.gov/data/sites/default/files/NSDUH-FFR1-2015/NSDUH-FFR1-2015/NSDUH-FFR1-2015.pdf (accessed January 9, 2017)

physical) effects and behavioral processes that contribute to tobacco addiction are similar to those that contribute in the addiction to drugs such as heroin and cocaine. Many researchers consider nicotine to be as potentially addictive as cocaine and heroin and note that it can create dependence quickly in some users. According to Frank Newport of Gallup, in *Most U.S. Smokers Want to Quit, Have Tried Multiple Times* (July 31, 2013, http://www.gallup.com/poll/163763/smokers-quit-tried-multiple-times.aspx), in 2013 nearly three-quarters (72%) of all smokers considered themselves addicted to cigarettes.

Cigarette smoking results in the rapid distribution of nicotine throughout the body, reaching the brain within 10 seconds of inhalation. However, the intense effects of nicotine disappear in a few minutes, causing smokers to continue smoking frequently throughout the day to maintain its pleasurable effects and to prevent withdrawal. Tolerance develops after repeated exposure to nicotine, and higher doses are required to produce the same initial stimulation. Because nicotine is metabolized (chemically processed) fairly quickly, disappearing from the body in a few hours, some tolerance is lost overnight. Smokers often report that the first cigarette of the day is the most satisfying. The more cigarettes smoked during the day, the more tolerance develops, and the less effect subsequent cigarettes have.

Is There a Genetic Basis for Nicotine Addiction?

Smoking is influenced by both environment and genetics, as are all addictions. (See Chapter 1.) The results of many scientific studies, such as M. K. Ho and Rachel F. Tyndale's "Overview of the Pharmacogenomics of Cigarette Smoking" (*Pharmacogenomics Journal*, vol. 7, no. 2, April 2007), show that between 11% and 78% of the initiation of smoking and between 28% and 84% of the maintenance of dependent smoking behavior are genetically influenced. In addition, 28% to 84% of the number of cigarettes an individual smokes is genetically influenced as is 31% to 75% of nicotine dependence. The ranges in these data are due to the variations in the results of numerous studies. Ho and Tyndale conclude that "taken together, these studies suggest a substantial genetic contribution to most aspects of smoking."

Nicotine May Not Be the Only Substance in Cigarettes Linked to Addiction

Research results suggest that nicotine may not be the only ingredient in tobacco involved with addiction. Various compounds called monoamine oxidase (MAO) inhibitors are found in high concentrations in cigarette smoke. MAO is an enzyme that is responsible for breaking down the brain chemical dopamine. The decrease in MAO results in higher dopamine levels and may be another reason that smokers continue to smoke—to sustain the high dopamine levels that result in pleasurable effects and the desire for repeated cigarette use.

One issue that complicates any efforts by a longtime smoker to quit is nicotine withdrawal, which is often referred to as craving. This urge for nicotine is not well understood by researchers. Withdrawal may begin within a few hours after the last cigarette. According to the National Institute on Drug Abuse, high levels of craving may persist six months or longer. Besides craving, withdrawal can include irritability, attention deficits, interruption of thought processes, sleep disturbances, and increased appetite.

Some researchers also point out the behavioral aspects that are involved in smoking. The purchasing, handling, and lighting of cigarettes may be just as pleasing psychologically to the user as the chemical properties of the tobacco itself.

HEALTH CONSEQUENCES OF TOBACCO USE
Respiratory System Effects

Cigarette smoke contains almost 4,000 different chemical compounds, many of which are toxic, mutagenic (capable of increasing the frequency of mutation, or change, in the genetic material), and carcinogenic (cancer causing). At least 43 carcinogens have been identified in tobacco smoke. Besides nicotine, the most damaging substances are tar and carbon monoxide. Cigarette smoke also contains hydrogen cyanide and other chemicals that can damage the respiratory system. These substances and nicotine are absorbed into the body through the linings of the mouth, nose, throat, and lungs. About 10 seconds later they are delivered by the bloodstream to the brain.

Tar, which adds to the flavor of cigarettes, is released by the burning of tobacco. As it is inhaled, it enters the alveoli (air cells) of the lungs. There, the tar hampers the action of cilia (small, hairlike extensions of cells that clean foreign substances from the lungs), allowing the substances in cigarette smoke to accumulate.

Carbon monoxide affects the blood's ability to distribute oxygen throughout the body. Carbon monoxide is chemically similar to carbon dioxide, which bonds with the hemoglobin in blood so that the carbon dioxide can be carried to the lungs for elimination. Hemoglobin has two primary functions: to carry oxygen to all parts of the body and to remove excess carbon dioxide from the body's tissues. Carbon monoxide bonds to hemoglobin more tightly than carbon dioxide and leaves the body more slowly, which allows carbon monoxide to build up in the hemoglobin, in turn reducing the amount of oxygen the blood can carry. The lack of adequate oxygen is damaging to most of the body's organs, including the heart and brain.

Diseases and Conditions Linked to Tobacco Use

The results of medical research show an association between smoking and cancer, as well as heart and circulatory disease, fetal growth retardation, and low birth weight babies. The 1983 *Health Consequences of Smoking—Cardiovascular Disease: Report of the Surgeon General* (https://profiles.nlm.nih.gov/NN/B/B/T/D/_/nnbbtd.pdf) linked cigarette smoking to cerebrovascular disease (strokes) and associated it with cancer of the uterine cervix. Two 1992 studies showed that people who smoke double their risk of forming cataracts, the leading cause of blindness. Several other studies linked smoking to unsuccessful pregnancies, increased infant mortality, and peptic ulcer disease. In 2004 the U.S. surgeon general Richard Carmona (1949–) released *The Health Consequences of Smoking: A Report of the Surgeon General* (https://www.cdc.gov/tobacco/data_statistics/sgr/2004/complete_report/index.htm), which revealed for the first time that cigarette smoking causes diseases in nearly every organ of the body. In 2014 the acting U.S. surgeon general Boris D. Lushniak released *The Health Consequences of Smoking—50 Years of Progress: A Report of the Surgeon General* (https://www.surgeongeneral.gov/library/reports/50-years-of-progress/full-report.pdf). This report pictorially shows the long list of health consequences and diseases that are caused by smoking, as well as the health consequences of exposure to secondhand smoke. (See Figure 3.6 and Figure 3.7.)

The National Cancer Institute notes in "Cigar Smoking and Cancer" (October 27, 2010, https://www.cancer.gov/about-cancer/causes-prevention/risk/tobacco/cigars-fact-sheet) that cigar smoking is associated with cancers of the lip, tongue, mouth, throat, larynx (voice box), lungs, esophagus (food tube), and possibly the pancreas. Those who smoke cigars daily and inhale the smoke have an increased risk for developing heart and lung disease.

Smokeless tobacco, which includes chewing tobacco and snuff, also creates health hazards for its users. The National Cancer Institute explains that smokeless tobacco is associated with cancers of the lip, gum, mouth, esophagus, and pancreas. It can also cause heart disease, gum disease, and precancerous white patches in the mouth. It is not a safer alternative to smoking. In addition, smokeless tobacco use can lead to nicotine addiction and may, therefore, lead to smoking.

Premature Aging

Smoking cigarettes contributes to premature aging in a variety of ways. The results of research conducted over nearly four decades, such as Akimichi Morita et al.'s "Molecular Basis of Tobacco Smoke-Induced Premature Skin Aging" (*Journal of Investigative Dermatology Symposium Proceedings*, vol. 14, no. 1, August 2009), show that smoking enhances facial aging and skin wrinkling. The researchers also note that cigarette smoking results in "smoker's face," which consists of a gray pallor and deep wrinkles. Cigarette smoking is also associated with the development of gray hair, cataracts, diabetes, weak bones, and atherosclerosis (a hardening of the walls of the arteries caused by the buildup of fatty deposits on the inner walls of the arteries that interferes with blood flow).

Why do these changes occur? Lowell Dale of the Mayo Clinic explains in "Is It True That Smoking Causes Wrinkles?" (October 10, 2014, http://www.mayoclinic.org/healthy-lifestyle/quit-smoking/expert-answers/smoking/faq-20058153) that nicotine tightens blood vessels, which decreases blood flow to the body's organs, depriving them of the proper amount of oxygen and nutrients that they need for good health. The skin, which is the body's largest organ, also receives less oxygen and nutrients than it needs, especially vitamin A. This vitamin is critical to regenerating new skin cells, which are essential to healthy, youthful-looking skin. In addition, the lack of proper skin nutrition damages structural proteins within the skin, resulting in skin sagging and wrinkling. Dale states a startling fact: "Smoking can speed up the normal aging process of your skin, contributing to wrinkles. These skin changes may occur after only 10 years of smoking."

In "Cigarette Smoke Induces Cellular Senescence via Werner's Syndrome Protein Down-Regulation" (*American Journal of Respiratory and Critical Care Medicine*, vol. 179, no. 4, February 15, 2009), Toru Nyunoya et al. report that cigarette smokers have the same cell defect as individuals with the genetic premature

FIGURE 3.6

Health consequences linked to smoking

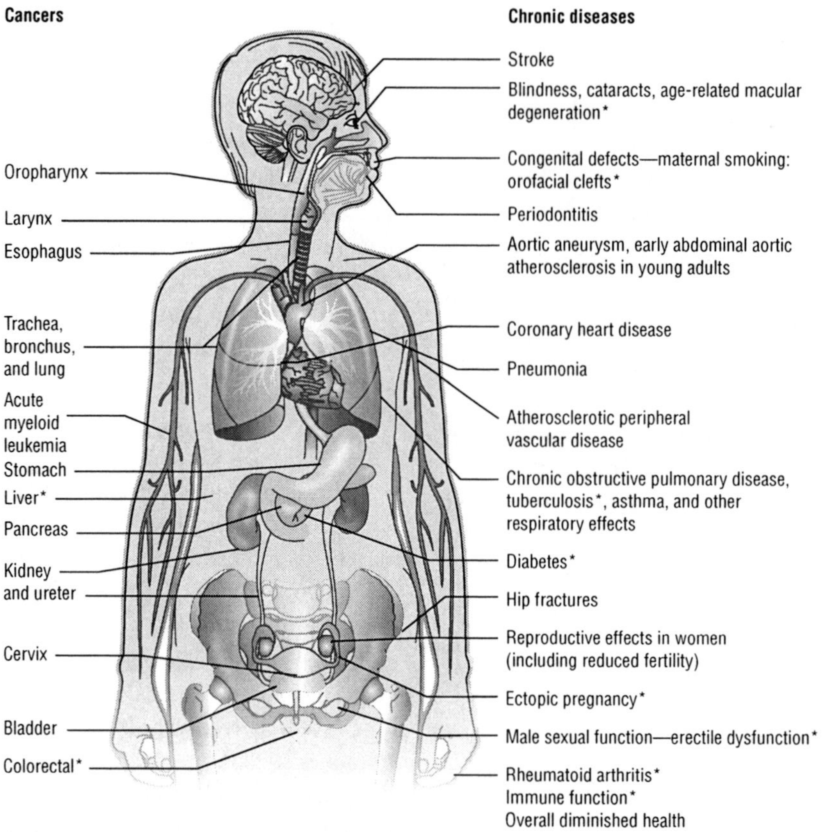

Cancers

Oropharynx
Larynx
Esophagus
Trachea, bronchus, and lung
Acute myeloid leukemia
Stomach
Liver*
Pancreas
Kidney and ureter
Cervix
Bladder
Colorectal*

Chronic diseases

Stroke
Blindness, cataracts, age-related macular degeneration*
Congenital defects—maternal smoking: orofacial clefts*
Periodontitis
Aortic aneurysm, early abdominal aortic atherosclerosis in young adults
Coronary heart disease
Pneumonia
Atherosclerotic peripheral vascular disease
Chronic obstructive pulmonary disease, tuberculosis*, asthma, and other respiratory effects
Diabetes*
Hip fractures
Reproductive effects in women (including reduced fertility)
Ectopic pregnancy*
Male sexual function—erectile dysfunction*
Rheumatoid arthritis*
Immune function*
Overall diminished health

*The condition is a new disease that has been causally linked to smoking in *The Health Consequences of Smoking—50 Years of Progress: A Report of the Surgeon General.*

SOURCE: "Figure 1.1A. The Health Consequences Causally Linked to Smoking," in *The Health Consequences of Smoking—50 Years of Progress: A Report of the Surgeon General*, U.S. Department of Health and Human Services, Centers for Disease Control and Prevention, National Center for Chronic Disease Prevention and Health Promotion, Office on Smoking and Health, 2014, http://www.surgeongeneral.gov/library/reports/50-years-of-progress/full-report.pdf (accessed January 9, 2017)

aging disease Werner's syndrome. Research results show that both cigarette smokers and individuals with Werner's syndrome do not produce enough of a protein called WRN, which protects and repairs genetic material in the body. In addition, an extract of cigarette smoke is found to reduce WRN production in cultured lung cells in the laboratory. Not enough of WRN leads to premature aging. This information may help researchers develop a treatment for premature aging in smokers.

Although smoking is damaging to the body, research shows that the body begins to rebound shortly after a smoker quits smoking. For example, in "Quit Smoking Improves Gastroesophageal Reflux Symptoms and Quality of Life" (*Health*, vol. 3, no. 11, November 2011), Kou Nakajima et al. report that even though cigarettes have been linked to gastroesophageal reflux disease, quitting smoking can lead to dramatic improvements in a patient's condition, in many cases even eliminating the need for a medical procedure to remedy the disorder. According to Toshiji Ishiwata et al., in "Improvement in Skin Color

Achieved by Smoking Cessation" (*International Journal of Cosmetic Science*, vol. 35, no. 2, April 2013), studies show that skin discoloration associated with smoking can begin to show signs of reversal as early as four to 12 weeks after a smoker quits.

Interactions with Other Drugs

Smoking can have adverse effects when combined with over-the-counter (without a prescription) and prescription medications that a smoker may be taking. In many cases smoking reduces the effectiveness of medications, such as pain relievers (acetaminophen), antidepressants, tranquilizers, sedatives, ulcer medications, and insulin. With estrogen and oral contraceptives, smoking may increase the risk of heart and blood vessel disease and can cause strokes and blood clots.

Robert G. Smith notes in "An Appraisal of Potential Drug Interactions in Cigarette Smokers and Alcohol Drinkers" (*Journal of the American Podiatric Medical Association*, vol. 99, no. 1, January–February 2009) that

FIGURE 3.7

Health consequences linked to secondhand smoke

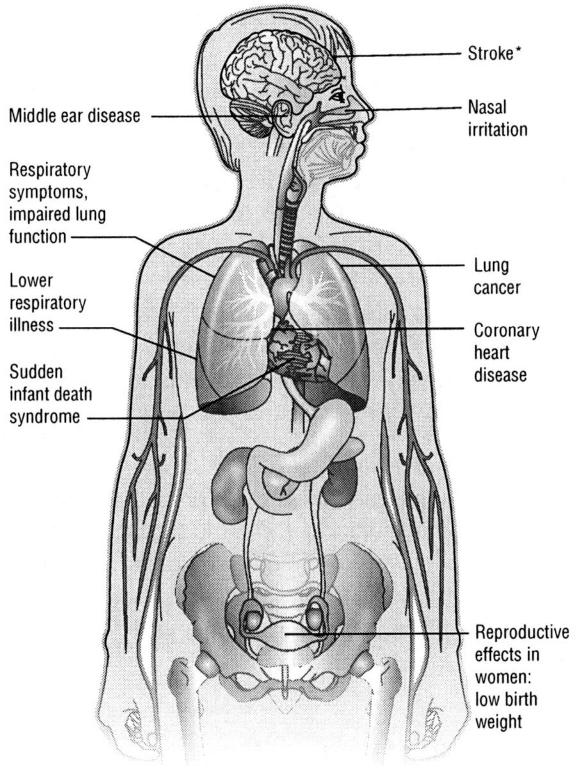

Children

Adults

- Stroke*
- Middle ear disease
- Nasal irritation
- Respiratory symptoms, impaired lung function
- Lower respiratory illness
- Lung cancer
- Coronary heart disease
- Sudden infant death syndrome
- Reproductive effects in women: low birth weight

*The condition is a new disease that has been causally linked to smoking in *The Health Consequences of Smoking—50 Years of Progress: A Report of the Surgeon General.*

SOURCE: "Figure 1.1B. The Health Consequences Causally Linked to Exposure to Secondhand Smoke," in *The Health Consequences of Smoking—50 Years of Progress: A Report of the Surgeon General*, U.S. Department of Health and Human Services, Centers for Disease Control and Prevention, National Center for Chronic Disease Prevention and Health Promotion, Office on Smoking and Health, 2014, http://www .surgeongeneral.gov/library/reports/50-years-of-progress/full-report.pdf (accessed January 9, 2017)

TABLE 3.5

Surgeon General's reports on smoking and health, 1964–2016

1964: Smoking and Health: Report of the Advisory Committee to the Surgeon General of the Public Health Service
1967: The Health Consequences of Smoking: A Public Health Service Review
1968: The Health Consequences of Smoking: 1968 Supplement to the 1967 Public Health Service Review
1969: The Health Consequences of Smoking: 1969 Supplement to the 1967 Public Health Service Review
1971: The Health Consequences of Smoking
1972: The Health Consequences of Smoking
1973: The Health Consequences of Smoking
1974: The Health Consequences of Smoking
1975: The Health Consequences of Smoking
1976: The Health Consequences of Smoking: A Reference Edition
1979: The Health Consequences of Smoking, 1977–1978
1979: Smoking and Health
1980: The Health Consequences of Smoking for Women
1981: The Health Consequences of Smoking: The Changing Cigarette
1982: The Health Consequences of Smoking: Cancer
1983: The Health Consequences of Smoking: Cardiovascular Disease
1984: The Health Consequences of Smoking: Chronic Obstructive Lung Disease
1985: The Health Consequences of Smoking: Cancer and Chronic Lung Disease in the Workplace
1986: The Health Consequences of Involuntary Smoking
1988: The Health Consequences of Smoking: Nicotine Addiction
1989: Reducing the Health Consequences of Smoking: 25 Years of Progress
1990: Smoking and Health: A National Status Report
1990: The Health Benefits of Smoking Cessation
1992: Smoking and Health in the Americas
1994: SGR 4 Kids: The Surgeon General's Report for Kids about Smoking
1995: Preventing Tobacco Use among Young People
1998: Tobacco Use among U.S. Racial/Ethnic Minority Groups
2000: Reduce Tobacco Use
2001: Women and Smoking
2004: The Health Consequences of Smoking
2006: The Health Consequences of Involuntary Exposure to Tobacco Smoke
2007: Children and Secondhand Smoke Exposure: Excerpts from the Health Consequences of Involuntary Exposure to Tobacco Smoke
2008: Treating Tobacco Use and Dependence: 2008 Update
2010: How Tobacco Smoke Causes Disease: The Biology and Behavioral Basis for Smoking-Attributable Disease
2012: Preventing Tobacco Use among Youth and Young Adults
2014: The Health Consequences of Smoking—50 Years of Progress
2016: E-Cigarette Use Among Youth and Young Adults

SOURCE: Created by Stephen Meyer for Gale, © 2017

many drug interactions with smoking have been identified, and therefore smokers should be screened by their physicians for potential harmful drug interactions. In addition, individuals may need to take higher doses of some medications while they are current smokers and may need to reduce dosages when they quit.

SMOKING AND PUBLIC HEALTH

A study during the 1920s found that men who smoked two or more packs of cigarettes per day were 22 times more likely than nonsmokers to die of lung cancer. At the time, these results surprised researchers and medical authorities alike. Roughly 40 years later the U.S. government first officially recognized the negative health consequences of smoking. In 1964 the Advisory Committee to the Surgeon General released *Smoking and Health: Report of the Advisory Committee to the Surgeon General of the Public Health Service*, which was a groundbreaking survey of studies on tobacco use. In the report the U.S. surgeon general Luther L. Terry (1911–1985) stated that cigarette smoking increased overall mortality in men and caused lung and laryngeal cancer, as well as chronic bronchitis. Terry concluded, "Cigarette smoking is a health hazard of sufficient importance in the United States to warrant appropriate remedial action," but what action should be taken was left unspecified at that time.

Later surgeons general issued additional reports on the health effects of smoking and the dangers to nonsmokers of secondhand smoke. Besides general health concerns, the reports addressed specific health consequences and populations. Table 3.5 shows a listing of reports of the surgeons general and the years in which they were published. The later reports concluded that smoking increases the morbidity (proportion of diseased people in a particular population) and mortality (proportion of deaths in a particular population) of both men and women. In addition, the surgeon general released *E-Cigarette Use among Youth and Young Adults: A Report of the Surgeon General* (https://e-cigarettes.surgeongeneral .gov/documents/2016_SGR_Full_Report_non-508.pdf) in 2016, the first federal report that addressed the potential health risks involved with electronic cigarette use.

In 1965 Congress passed the Federal Cigarette Labeling and Advertising Act, which required the following health warning on all cigarette packages: "Caution: Cigarette smoking may be hazardous to your health." The Public Health Cigarette Smoking Act of 1969 strengthened the warning to read: "Warning: The Surgeon General has determined that cigarette smoking is dangerous to your health." Still later acts resulted in four different health warnings to be used in rotation.

In June 2009 President Barack Obama (1961–) signed the Family Smoking Prevention and Tobacco Control Act. The act gave the U.S. Food and Drug Administration (FDA) regulatory authority over tobacco products and required that cigarette packages and advertisements have larger and more visible graphic health warnings. The FDA reveals in "FDA Unveils New Cigarette Health Warnings" (June 2011, https://www.fda .gov/downloads/ForConsumers/ConsumerUpdates/UCM 259865.pdf) that two of the proposed warnings were "Smoking can kill you," with an accompanying photo of a dead person, and "Cigarettes cause cancer," with an accompanying photo of a smoker suffering from mouth cancer. Responding to the new regulations, the major tobacco companies filed a legal challenge, arguing that the rules violated basic protections of their right to free speech. In "FDA Changes Course on Graphic Warning Labels for Cigarettes" (CNN.com, March 20, 2013), Steve Almasy reports that in March 2012 a federal judge ruled in favor of the tobacco companies; in August of that year the U.S. Court of Appeals for the District of Columbia Circuit upheld the ruling by a 2–1 vote. Almasy notes that in March 2013 the FDA announced that it would not appeal the verdict to the U.S. Supreme Court, opting instead to "create new warning labels to comply with the 2009 law." As of March 2017, however, the FDA had still not followed up on its intention to release new labels relating to the dangers of tobacco use.

DEATHS ATTRIBUTED TO TOBACCO USE

According to the 2014 surgeon general's report *Health Consequences of Smoking—50 Years of Progress,* cigarette smoking is the leading cause of preventable death and disability in the United States and produces substantial health-related economic costs to society. The report reveals that smoking and exposure to secondhand smoke cause more than 480,000 deaths each year. It also notes that between 1964 and 2014 smoking was the cause of 20 million premature deaths in the United States.

In 2015 diseases linked to smoking accounted for four of the top-five causes of death in the United States. (See Figure 3.8.) The CDC explains in "Health Effects of Cigarette Smoking" (December 1, 2016, https://www .cdc.gov/tobacco/data_statistics/fact_sheets/health_effects/ effects_cig_smoking/) that smoking can double, and in some cases quadruple, a person's risk of developing coronary heart disease, which is the leading cause of death in the United States. According to the CDC, each year smoking kills more people than the human immunodeficiency virus, illegal drug abuse, alcohol abuse, motor vehicle accidents, and firearm-related incidents combined. It also reports that smoking is responsible for roughly 90% of all lung cancer deaths and 80% of all deaths caused by chronic obstructive pulmonary disease.

In *Cancer Facts and Figures, 2016* (2016, https://www .cancer.org/content/dam/cancer-org/research/cancer-facts -and-statistics/annual-cancer-facts-and-figures/2016/cancer -facts-and-figures-2016.pdf), the American Cancer Society estimates that 188,800 of 595,690 cancer deaths were smoking related in 2016. That same year 224,390 new cases of lung cancer were diagnosed.

SECONDHAND SMOKE

Secondhand smoke, also known as environmental tobacco smoke or passive smoke, is a health hazard for nonsmokers who live or work with smokers. In the fact sheet "Secondhand Smoke and Cancer" (January 12, 2011, https://www.cancer.gov/about-cancer/causes-prevention/risk/ tobacco/second-hand-smoke-fact-sheet), the National Cancer Institute defines secondhand smoke as "the smoke given off by a burning tobacco product" and "the smoke exhaled by a smoker."

The article "Non-smoking Wives of Heavy Smokers Have a Higher Risk of Lung Cancer: A Study from Japan" (*British Medical Journal*, vol. 282, no. 6259, January 17, 1981) by Takeshi Hirayama of the National Cancer Centre Research Institute was the first scientific paper on the harmful effects of secondhand smoke. Hirayama studied 91,540 nonsmoking wives of smoking husbands and a similarly sized group of nonsmoking women who were married to nonsmokers. He discovered that nonsmoking wives of husbands who smoked faced a 40% to 90% elevated risk of lung cancer (depending on how frequently their husband smoked) compared with the wives of nonsmoking husbands.

Other studies followed. The U.S. Environmental Protection Agency (EPA) concluded in *Respiratory Health Effects of Passive Smoking: Lung Cancer and Other Disorders* (December 1992, https://oaspub.epa.gov/eims/ eimscomm.getfile?p_download_id=36793) that the "widespread exposure to environmental tobacco smoke (ETS) in

FIGURE 3.8

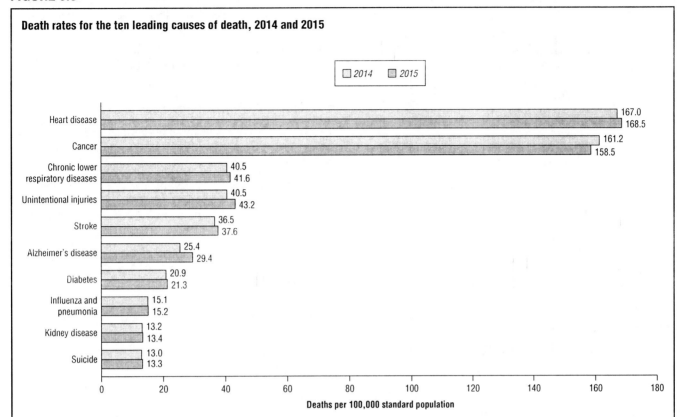

Death rates for the ten leading causes of death, 2014 and 2015

□ *2014* ▨ *2015*

Cause	2014	2015
Heart disease	167.0	168.5
Cancer	161.2	158.5
Chronic lower respiratory diseases	40.5	41.6
Unintentional injuries	40.5	43.2
Stroke	36.5	37.6
Alzheimer's disease	25.4	29.4
Diabetes	20.9	21.3
Influenza and pneumonia	15.1	15.2
Kidney disease	13.2	13.4
Suicide	13.0	13.3

Deaths per 100,000 standard population

Notes: A total of 2,712,630 resident deaths were registered in the United States in 2015. The 10 leading causes accounted for 74.2% of all deaths in the United States in 2015. Causes of death are ranked according to number of deaths.

SOURCE: Jiaquan Xu et al., "Figure 3. Age-Adjusted Death Rates for the 10 Leading Causes of Death in 2015: United States, 2014 and 2015," in *Data Brief 267: Mortality in the United States, 2015*, Centers for Disease Control and Prevention, National Center for Health Statistics, December 2016, https://www.cdc.gov/nchs/data/databriefs/db267.pdf (accessed January 9, 2017)

the United States presents a serious and substantial public health impact." In 2000 the Environmental Health Information Service's *Ninth Report on Carcinogens* classified secondhand smoke as a Group A (human) carcinogen. According to the EPA, there is no safe level of exposure to such Group A toxins.

In 2005 more evidence accumulated on the risks of secondhand smoking. Paolo Vineis et al. revealed in "Environmental Tobacco Smoke and Risk of Respiratory Cancer and Chronic Obstructive Pulmonary Disease in Former Smokers and Never Smokers in the EPIC Prospective Study" (*British Medical Journal*, vol. 330, no. 7486, February 5, 2005) that those who had been exposed to secondhand smoke during childhood for many hours each day had more than triple the risk of developing lung cancer compared with people who were not exposed. In addition, Sarah M. McGhee et al. showed in "Mortality Associated with Passive Smoking in Hong Kong" (*British Medical Journal*, vol. 330, no. 7486, February 5, 2005) that there is a correlation between an increased risk of dying from various causes (including lung cancer and other lung diseases, heart disease, and stroke) and the number of smokers in the home. The risk increased by

24% when one smoker lived in the home and by 74% with two smokers in the household.

In 2006 the 31st report of the surgeon general on smoking—*The Health Consequences of Involuntary Exposure to Tobacco Smoke: A Report of the Surgeon General* (https://www.ncbi.nlm.nih.gov/books/NBK44324/pdf/Bookshelf_NBK44324.pdf)—was published. The report noted that:

With regard to the involuntary exposure of nonsmokers to tobacco smoke, the scientific evidence now supports the following major conclusions:

1. Secondhand smoke causes premature death and disease in children and in adults who do not smoke.

2. Children exposed to secondhand smoke are at an increased risk for sudden infant death syndrome (SIDS), acute respiratory infections, ear problems, and more severe asthma. Smoking by parents causes respiratory symptoms and slows lung growth in their children.

3. Exposure of adults to secondhand smoke has immediate adverse effects on the cardiovascular system and causes coronary heart disease and lung cancer.

4. The scientific evidence indicates that there is no risk-free level of exposure to secondhand smoke.

5. Many millions of Americans, both children and adults, are still exposed to secondhand smoke in their homes and workplaces despite substantial progress in tobacco control.

6. Eliminating smoking in indoor spaces fully protects nonsmokers from exposure to secondhand smoke. Separating smokers from nonsmokers, cleaning the air, and ventilating buildings cannot eliminate exposures of nonsmokers to secondhand smoke.

The 2014 surgeon general's report *Health Consequences of Smoking—50 Years of Progress* notes that secondhand smoke has also been shown to increase the risk of stroke, the second-leading cause of death in the world. In addition, secondhand smoke has been linked to thrombosis (clotting in the blood vessels), atherosclerosis, and inflammation.

THIRDHAND SMOKE

According to Jonathan P. Winickoff et al., in "Beliefs about the Health Effects of 'Thirdhand' Smoke and Home Smoking Bans" (*Pediatrics*, vol. 123, no. 1, January 2009), "Thirdhand smoke is residual tobacco smoke contamination that remains after the cigarette is extinguished." The researchers find an association between parents believing that thirdhand smoke harms children and their banning smoking in the home.

Discussions and research results regarding thirdhand smoke have appeared in the medical literature only since 2009. Just a few studies on the existence and harmfulness of thirdhand smoke were available as of March 2017. For example, Marie-Hélène Becquemin et al. were the first to show that particles from cigarette smoke that fall onto furniture and other surfaces can become airborne long after a cigarette is extinguished. Once airborne, these potentially harmful particles can be inhaled and enter the lungs. The researchers published their findings in "Third-Hand Smoking: Indoor Measurements of Concentration and Sizes of Cigarette Smoke Particles after Resuspension" (*Tobacco Control*, vol. 19, no. 4, August 2010). In "Thirdhand Tobacco Smoke: A Tobacco-Specific Lung Carcinogen on Surfaces in Smokers' Homes" (*Nicotine and Tobacco Research*, vol. 16, no. 1, January 2014), Janet L. Thomas et al. present the results of a study in which they found high levels of nicotine-derived nitrosamine ketone (NNK), a carcinogen commonly found in tobacco, in 33 out of 37 smokers' residences. The researchers note the presence of NNK in a dwelling poses a considerable health risk to prospective renters or home buyers.

Meanwhile, researchers have identified potential damaging effects of thirdhand smoke at the cellular level. Vasundhra Bahl et al. analyze in "Thirdhand Cigarette Smoke Causes Stress-Induced Mitochondrial Hyperfu-

sion and Alters the Transcriptional Profile of Stem Cells" (*Toxicological Sciences*, vol. 153, no. 1, September 2016) evidence suggesting that thirdhand smoke might alter the behavior of mitochondria (organelles primarily responsible for producing energy in animal cells).

TOBACCO AND SMOKING LAWS

The legal age for using and purchasing tobacco products varies by state and municipality. The minimum age for purchasing tobacco products ranges between 18 and 21 years throughout the United States. For example, the legal age for purchasing tobacco in Illinois is 18 years old, but stricter laws have been implemented in Chicago and Evanston, where the legal age is 21. As of March 2017, 20 states—Alabama, Arkansas, California, Colorado, Hawaii, Idaho, Iowa, Maine, Michigan, Minnesota, Mississippi, Nebraska, New Hampshire, North Dakota, Rhode Island, Texas, Utah, Virginia, West Virginia, and Wyoming—also had statewide age requirements for smoking. In June 2016 California raised the legal age for smoking or purchasing tobacco to 21, the most restrictive tobacco law in the country; however, the new law exempted active military personnel, who were still permitted to use or purchase tobacco at the age of 18.

A MOVEMENT TO BAN SMOKING

Many efforts have been initiated over the years to control public smoking or to separate smokers and non-smokers. In 1975 Minnesota became the first state in the nation to require the separation of smokers and non-smokers following passage of the Clean Indoor Air Act. The purpose of the law was to protect public health, public comfort, and the environment by banning smoking in public places and at public meetings, except in designated smoking areas. Other states soon followed.

In 1977 Berkeley became the first community in California to limit smoking in restaurants and other public places. In 1990 San Luis Obispo, California, became the first city to ban smoking in all public buildings, bars, and restaurants. In 1994 smoking was restricted in many government buildings in California. That same year the fast-food giant McDonald's banned smoking in all of its establishments. In 1995 New York City banned smoking in the dining areas of all restaurants with more than 35 seats. As of July 2003, all public and private workplaces in New York City became smoke-free, including bars and restaurants. Laws vary from state to state and from city to city, but by 2005 smoking was banned in most workplaces, hospitals, government buildings, museums, schools, theaters, and restaurants throughout the United States. Meanwhile, organizations such as the Campaign for Tobacco-Free Kids have spearheaded efforts to raise the smoking age to 21 years old nationwide.

STOPPING SMOKING

In "Current Cigarette Smoking among Adults—United States, 2005–2015" (*Morbidity and Mortality Weekly Report*, vol. 65, no. 44, November 11, 2016), the CDC estimates that there were 36.5 million current smokers in 2015. Although this figure represented a decline from 45.1 million Americans who smoked in 2005, it was still high, given that smoking-related illnesses continued to place enormous financial strain on the nation's health care system. Regardless, the CDC notes that antismoking initiatives have proven effective over time, stating, "Sustained comprehensive state tobacco control programs funded at CDC-recommended levels could accelerate progress in reducing adult smoking prevalence and smoking-related disease, death, and economic costs." In an effort to further promote its antismoking efforts, the CDC launched in 2012 the campaign Tips from Former Smokers (https://www.cdc.gov/tobacco/campaign/tips/). The testimonials featured in this campaign are from former smokers, who share their personal struggles with heart failure, cancer, and other health issues related to long-term smoking.

Global Efforts to Reduce Tobacco Use

According to the World Health Organization (WHO), in *WHO Report on the Global Tobacco Epidemic, 2015: Raising Taxes on Tobacco* (2015, http://apps.who.int/iris/bitstream/10665/178574/1/9789240694606_eng.pdf?ua=1&ua=1), tobacco use kills approximately 6 million people worldwide annually, while tobacco-related health problems result in an economic cost of hundreds of billions of dollars each year. According to the WHO, most tobacco-related deaths occur in low- and middle-income countries.

The WHO is working diligently to curb smoking around the world. In May 2003 member states of the WHO adopted the world's first international public health treaty for global cooperation in reducing the negative health consequences of tobacco use. The WHO Framework Convention on Tobacco Control (FCTC; 2003, http://www.who.int/tobacco/framework/WHO_FCTC_english.pdf) was designed to reduce tobacco-related deaths and disease worldwide. In February 2005 the treaty came into force after 40 member countries had ratified it (become bound by it). The treaty has many measures, including requiring countries to impose restrictions on tobacco advertising, sponsorship, and promotion; creating new packaging and labeling of tobacco products; establishing clean indoor air controls; and promoting taxation as a way to cut consumption and fight smuggling.

The WHO notes in "Parties to the WHO Framework Convention on Tobacco Control" (http://www.who.int/fctc/signatories_parties/en/) that as of March 2017 there were 168 signatories to the treaty. The United States signed the treaty in May 2004, indicating its general acceptance, but as of March 2017 it had not yet ratified the treaty. Although it was not entirely clear why the United States had not ratified the FCTC more than a decade after signing the treaty, some commentators have suggested that pressure from the tobacco industry has been largely to blame. For example, in "Has the U.S. Commitment against Smoking Gone Down in Flames?" (Fredericksburg.com, November 29, 2005), Kathryn Mulvey asserts that the tobacco industry continued to maintain a "stranglehold on top-level U.S. officials" at the time of the treaty's passage, noting that tobacco company executives had spent more than $45 million in political campaign contributions between 1995 and 2005. The Campaign for Tobacco-Free Kids reports in "Toll of Tobacco in the United States" (January 27, 2017, http://www.tobaccofreekids.org/facts_issues/toll_us) that the tobacco industry spent $20 million lobbying Congress in 2015, while donating an additional $1.2 million to political campaigns at the federal level in 2016. According to Tim K. Mackey et al., in "Call to Action: Promoting Domestic and Global Tobacco Control by Ratifying the Framework Convention on Tobacco Control in the United States" (*PLoS Medicine*, vol. 11, no. 5, May 2014), delays in ratifying the FCTC are linked to the tobacco industry's lobbying efforts against tobacco regulation in the United States, in particular its successful legal challenge to the FDA's requirement that cigarette companies include graphic warnings on their products under the Family Smoking Prevention and Tobacco Control Act. Noting that the act actually includes a number of key provisions outlined in the FCTC, Mackey et al. contend that ratification of the treaty would represent a crucial first step in granting the federal government greater power to impose stricter tobacco regulations at home.

In *WHO Report on the Global Tobacco Epidemic, 2008: The MPOWER Package* (2008, http://www.who.int/tobacco/mpower/mpower_report_full_2008.pdf), the WHO configures the primary measures of the treaty into the acronym MPOWER, which stands for:

- Monitor tobacco use and prevention policies
- Protect people from tobacco smoke
- Offer help to quit tobacco use
- Warn about the dangers of tobacco
- Enforce bans on tobacco advertising, promotion, and sponsorship
- Raise taxes on tobacco

The WHO indicates in *WHO Report on the Global Tobacco Epidemic, 2015* that by 2015, 2.8 billion people in 103 countries were covered by at least one MPOWER measure.

Benefits of Stopping

The 1990 *Health Benefits of Smoking Cessation: A Report of the Surgeon General* (https://profiles.nlm.nih .gov/NN/B/B/C/T/_/nnbbct.pdf) noted that quitting offers major and immediate health benefits for both sexes and for all ages. This first comprehensive report on the benefits of quitting showed that many of the ill effects of smoking can be reversed. According to the 2014 surgeon general's report *Health Consequences of Smoking—50 Years of Progress*, smokers who quit after being diagnosed with cancer demonstrate a lower mortality rate than those who continue to smoke following their diagnosis.

Nevertheless, health experts concede that giving up smoking poses a significant challenge to most smokers. The surgeon general's report *How Tobacco Smoke Causes Disease: The Biology and Behavioral Basis for Smoking-Attributable Disease* (2010, https://www.ncbi .nlm.nih.gov/books/NBK53017/pdf/Bookshelf_NBK53017 .pdf) states that of smokers who try to quit at any one time, fewer than 5% are successful. According to the report, smokers who quit early in life (aged 25 to 34 years) reduce their risk of dying from all causes to the same level as lifetime nonsmokers. Those who quit slightly later in life (aged 35 to 44 years) reduce their

risk of dying from all causes to nearly the same level as nonsmokers. Even those who quit after the age of 45 years reduce their risk of dying to a level in between that of nonsmokers and smokers. Nonetheless, for lung cancer alone, "there is a persistent elevated risk in former smokers compared with lifetime nonsmokers of the same age even after a long abstinence." The report adds, "Evidence indicates that lung cancer risk increases far more strongly with each additional year of smoking than it increases for a higher average number of cigarettes smoked per day."

Quitting and Pregnancy

In *Results from the 2015 National Survey on Drug Use and Health: Detailed Tables*, SAMHSA finds that in 2015, 13.6% of pregnant women smoked cigarettes in the month before the survey. (See Table 3.6.) This percentage of smokers represented an increase from the 11.4% of pregnant women who reported smoking during the past month in 2014.

Smoking during pregnancy can compromise the health of the developing fetus (unborn child). According to the 2010 surgeon general's report *How Tobacco Smoke Causes Disease*, evidence suggests the possibility of a causal relationship between maternal smoking and

TABLE 3.6

Percentage of past-month cigarette use among women aged 15–44, by pregnancy status, pregnancy characteristics, age, and race and Hispanic origin, 2014 and 2015

| Demographic/pregnancy characteristic | Total[c] | | Pregnancy status | | | |
| | | | Pregnant | | Not Pregnant | |
	2014	2015	2014	2015	2014	2015
Total	22.2	21.1	11.4	13.6	22.5[a]	21.4
Age						
15–17	7.6	6.6	*	*	7.6	6.5
18–25	23.1	22.7	17.7	22.9	23.3	22.7
26–44	24.1	22.7	7.9	8.1	24.7	23.3
Hispanic origin and race						
Not Hispanic or Latino	23.8	23.1	13.1	15.9	24.1	23.3
White	26.6	25.6	15.1	16.5	26.9	25.9
Black or African American	20.0	19.2	10.6	14.0	20.5	19.3
American Indian or Alaska Native	37.1	33.5	*	*	36.7	33.8
Native Hawaiian or other Pacific Islander	*	*	*	*	*	*
Asian	6.7	6.7	*	*	7.0	6.8
Two or more races	25.3[a]	33.4	*	*	25.3[a]	33.1
Hispanic or Latino	15.7	13.7	4.1	4.8	16.2	14.0
Trimester[d]						
First	da	da	15.5	16.6	da	da
Second	da	da	8.5	13.4	da	da
Third	da	da	11.2	10.1	da	da

* = low precision. da = does not apply.
[a]The difference between this estimate and the 2015 estimate is statistically significant at the 0.05 level. Rounding may make the estimates appear identical.
[b]The difference between this estimate and the 2015 estimate is statistically significant at the 0.01 level. Rounding may make the estimates appear identical.
[c]Estimates in the total column represent all females in the specified subgroup, including those with unknown pregnancy status.
[d]Pregnant females aged 15 to 44 not reporting trimester were excluded.

SOURCE: "Table 6.75B. Cigarette Use in Past Month among Females Aged 15 to 44, by Pregnancy Status, Demographic Characteristics, and Pregnancy Characteristics: Percentages, 2014 and 2015," in *2015 National Survey on Drug Use and Health: Detailed Tables*, U.S. Department of Health and Human Services, Substance Abuse and Mental Health Services Administration, September 8, 2016, https://www.samhsa.gov/data/sites/default/files/NSDUH-DetTabs-2015/NSDUH-DetTabs-2015/NSDUH-DetTabs-2015.pdf (accessed January 9, 2017)

ectopic pregnancy, a situation in which the fertilized egg implants in the fallopian tube rather than in the uterus. This situation is quite serious and is life-threatening to the mother. Smoking by pregnant women is also linked to an increased risk of miscarriage, stillbirth, premature delivery, and SIDS and is a cause of low birth weight in infants. A woman who stops smoking before pregnancy or during her first trimester (three months) of pregnancy significantly reduces her chances of having a low birth weight baby. According to the 2014 surgeon general's report *Health Consequences of Smoking—50 Years of Progress*, government policies aimed at curbing tobacco use have proven effective in helping pregnant smokers quit. For example, an additional $1 tax on each package of cigarettes resulted in a 44.1% to 48.9% increase in the rate of pregnant women who quit smoking.

Complaints about Quitting

A major side effect of smoking cessation is nicotine withdrawal. The short-term consequences of nicotine withdrawal may include anxiety, irritability, frustration, anger, difficulty concentrating, and restlessness. Possible long-term consequences are urges to smoke and increased appetite. Nicotine withdrawal symptoms peak in the first few days after quitting and subside during the following weeks. Improved self-esteem and an increased sense of control often accompany long-term abstinence.

One of the most common complaints among former smokers is that they gain weight when they stop smoking. Many reasons explain this weight gain, but two primary reasons are the metabolism changes associated with nicotine withdrawal and the change in food habits by many former smokers as a result of their attempts to manage withdrawal cravings. To combat weight gain, some former smokers start exercise programs.

Ways to Stop Smoking

Nicotine replacement treatments can be effective for many smokers. Nicotine patches and gum are two types of nicotine replacement therapy (NRT). The nicotine in a patch is absorbed through the skin, and the nicotine in the gum is absorbed through the mouth and throat. NRT helps a smoker cope with nicotine withdrawal symptoms that discourage many smokers from trying to stop. Nicotine patches and gum are available over the counter. Other NRT products are a nicotine nasal spray and a nicotine inhaler, which are available by prescription. Mila Kofman, Katie Dunton, and Mary Beth Senkewicz report in *Implementation of Tobacco Cessation Coverage under the Affordable Care Act: Understanding How Private Health Insurance Policies Cover Tobacco Cessation Treatments* (November 26, 2012, http://www.tobacco freekids.org/pressoffice/2012/georgetown/coveragereport .pdf) that the Affordable Care Act of 2010 mandated that health insurers provide coverage for smoking cessation treatments, including NRTs.

The non-nicotine therapy bupropion (an antidepressant drug) is also available by prescription for the relief of nicotine withdrawal symptoms. In addition, behavioral treatments, such as smoking-cessation programs, are useful for some smokers who want to quit. Behavioral methods are designed to create an aversion to smoking, develop self-monitoring of smoking behavior, and establish alternative coping responses.

Besides smoking-cessation therapies, a number of organizations offer programs and support groups that are aimed at helping smokers quit. Notable among these are the Smoking Cessation Program at Cedars-Sinai Medical Center in Los Angeles, California, and the American Academy of Family Physicians "Ask and Act" Tobacco Cessation Program. Furthermore, the Employee Assistance Program sponsors a number of smoking-cessation services and programs throughout the country. The website Smokefree.gov, a joint venture of the National Cancer Institute, the National Institutes of Health, the U.S. Department of Health and Human Services, and USA.gov, provides online information and resources that are designed to help people quit smoking.

ELECTRONIC CIGARETTES AND VAPING

Another product marketed to combat the use of cigarettes is the electronic cigarette (e-cigarette), which is a plastic device that is fashioned to look like an actual cigarette. E-cigarettes contain liquid nicotine. When the user inhales through the device, a battery heats up the nicotine into a vapor. Other electronic nicotine delivery systems (ENDS) include vaporizers, e-pipes, and vape pens. The use of ENDS to consume nicotine is generally referred to as vaping.

In September 2010 the FDA sent warning letters to five e-cigarette distributors for violations of the federal Food, Drug, and Cosmetic Act. The violations included poor manufacturing practices and unsubstantiated claims that the devices can help smokers quit their addiction. In the press release "FDA Acts against 5 Electronic Cigarette Distributors" (September 9, 2010, https://www.fda .gov/NewsEvents/Newsroom/PressAnnouncements/ucm 225224.htm), the FDA states, "A company cannot claim that its drug can treat or mitigate a disease, such as nicotine addiction, unless the drug's safety and effectiveness have been proven. Yet all five companies claim without FDA review of relevant evidence that the products help users quit smoking cigarettes." In April 2014 the FDA proposed a range of new regulations concerning the selling and marketing of e-cigarettes. Notable among these regulations was a provision that prohibited e-cigarette companies from claiming any health benefits associated with the use of their products. In 2016 the FDA formalized

TABLE 3.7

Attitudes among Americans toward health impact of e-cigarettes, by cigarette smoking and e-cigarette smoking status, December 2015

WHICH OF THE FOLLOWING BEST DESCRIBES YOUR OPINION REGARDING E-CIGARETTES AND A PERSON'S HEALTH?

	U.S. adults	Currently smoke tobacco cigarettes	Have tried e-cigarettes
	%	%	%
Just as bad as tobacco cigarettes	33	23	17
Not as bad as tobacco cigarettes, but still harmful	48	52	58
Not harmful	11	20	23
Don't know/refused	8	5	2

SOURCE: Alyssa Davis and Diana Liu, "Americans' Views on How E-Cigarettes Affect Personal Health," in *Americans Say E-Cigs Should Be Regulated Like Tobacco Cigs*, Gallup, Inc., March 2, 2016, http://www.gallup.com/poll/189716/americans-say-cigs-regulated-tobacco-cigs.aspx?g_source=cigarettes&g_medium=search&g_campaign=tiles (accessed January 9, 2017). Copyright © 2017. Republished with permission of Gallup, Inc.; permission conveyed through Copyright Clearance Center, Inc.

TABLE 3.8

Attitudes among Americans toward regulating e-cigarettes, by cigarette smoking and e-cigarette smoking status, December 2015

IN YOUR OPINION, WHICH OF THE FOLLOWING BEST DESCRIBES HOW E-CIGARETTES SHOULD BE REGULATED?

	U.S. adults	Current tobacco cigarette smokers	Have tried e-cigarettes
	%	%	%
Regulated as much as cigarettes	60	50	50
Regulated less than cigarettes	19	23	31
Not regulated at all	17	26	18
Don't know/refused	4	2	1

SOURCE: Alyssa Davis and Diana Liu, "Americans' Views on Regulating E-Cigarettes," in *Americans Say E-Cigs Should Be Regulated Like Tobacco Cigs*, Gallup, Inc., March 2, 2016, http://www.gallup.com/poll/189716/americans-say-cigs-regulated-tobacco-cigs.aspx?g_source=cigarettes&g_medium=search&g_campaign=tiles (accessed January 9, 2017). Copyright © 2017. Republished with permission of Gallup, Inc.; permission conveyed through Copyright Clearance Center, Inc.

TABLE 3.9

Attitudes among Americans toward banning of e-cigarette use in public places, by type of venue, December 2015

SHOULD THEY SET ASIDE CERTAIN AREAS, SHOULD THEY TOTALLY BAN E-CIGARETTES OR SHOULD THERE BE NO RESTRICTIONS ON USING E-CIGARETTES IN THE FOLLOWING VENUES?

	Totally ban	Set aside certain areas	No restrictions
	%	%	%
Restaurants	48	34	16
Workplaces	41	41	16
Hotels and motels	34	41	23
Bars	31	36	31
Public parks	29	30	39

SOURCE: Alyssa Davis and Diana Liu, "Americans' Views on Banning E-Cigarettes," in *Americans Say E-Cigs Should Be Regulated Like Tobacco Cigs*, Gallup, Inc., March 2, 2016, http://www.gallup.com/poll/189716/americans-say-cigs-regulated-tobacco-cigs.aspx?g_source=cigarettes&g_medium=search&g_campaign=tiles (accessed January 9, 2017). Copyright © 2017. Republished with permission of Gallup, Inc.; permission conveyed through Copyright Clearance Center, Inc.

a new rule that required ENDS manufacturers to include a warning about the addictive qualities of nicotine on their products by 2018.

Overall, a majority of Americans recognize the potentially harmful effects of using e-cigarettes. As Table 3.7 shows, in 2015 one-third (33%) of U.S. adults believed that e-cigarettes were as harmful as regular tobacco cigarettes; nearly half (48%) believed that, while not as harmful as tobacco cigarettes, e-cigarettes still posed a health risk. Sixty percent of U.S. adults said e-cigarettes should be regulated in the same way as tobacco cigarettes, while 50% of all current tobacco cigarette smokers felt they should be regulated the same way. (See Table 3.8.) Meanwhile, nearly half (48%) of all U.S. adults supported a complete ban on the use of e-cigarettes in restaurants in 2015. (See Table 3.9.)

CHAPTER 4
ILLICIT DRUGS

Illegal drugs are those with no currently accepted medical use in the United States, such as heroin, lysergic acid diethylamide (LSD), and marijuana. (Some states and local jurisdictions have decriminalized certain uses of specific amounts of marijuana, but federal laws supersede these state and local marijuana decriminalization laws. For a more detailed discussion on the legalization of marijuana, see Chapter 9.) Controlled substances are legal drugs whose sale, possession, and use are restricted because they are psychoactive (mood- or mind-altering) drugs that have the potential for abuse. These drugs are medications, such as certain narcotics, depressants, and stimulants, that physicians prescribe for various conditions. The term *illicit drugs* is used by the Substance Abuse and Mental Health Services Administration (SAMHSA) to mean both illegal drugs and controlled substances that are used illegally.

WHO USES ILLICIT DRUGS?

The National Survey on Drug Use and Health is an annual survey that is conducted by SAMHSA, and its 2015 survey results are published in *Key Substance Use and Mental Health Indicators in the United States: Results from the 2015 National Survey on Drug Use and Health* (September 2016, https://www.samhsa.gov/data/sites/default/files/NSDUH-FFR1-2015/NSDUH-FFR1-2015/NSDUH-FFR1-2015.pdf). SAMHSA reveals that an estimated 27.1 million Americans aged 12 years and older were current illicit drug users in 2015. By "current" SAMHSA means the people who were surveyed about their drug use and who had taken an illicit drug during the month before participating in the survey. (Current users are "past month" users.) This figure represented 10.1% of the U.S. population in 2015.

Figure 4.1 presents a demographic profile of this population of drug users. In 2015, 22.3% of those aged 18 to 25 years and 8.8% of those aged 12 to 17 years were current illicit drug users. By contrast, only 8.2% of those aged 26 years and older were current illicit drug users.

Table 4.1 provides a more detailed look at the demographics of illicit drug use. It shows that a higher proportion of males than females were current, past-year, or lifetime illicit drug users in 2015. (Past-year users took a specific drug during the 12 months before taking the SAMHSA survey and lifetime users took a specific drug at least once during their lifetime.) Individuals of two or more races had the highest percentage of current illicit drug users in their population in 2015 (17.2%). Native Americans or Alaskan Natives were the next highest (14.2%), followed by African Americans (12.5%) and whites (10.2%). Asian Americans (4%) had the lowest percentage of current illicit drug users in their population.

Table 4.2 shows drug use statistics by military veteran status for 2003–05, 2006–08, 2009–11, and 2012–14. Among adults aged 18 years and older, veterans (6.3%) were less likely than nonveterans (10%) to use illicit drugs in 2012–14. By contrast, veterans were more likely to use alcohol (58.2%) than nonveterans (56.4%) during this same period.

WHICH ILLICIT DRUGS ARE USED MOST FREQUENTLY?

Figure 4.2 shows the types of illicit drugs that were used in 2015 and how many people used those drugs during the past month. Overall, 27.1 million Americans aged 12 years and older were current illicit drug users in 2015. Of these, 22.2 million (82%) used marijuana. Another 7.8 million misused some form of prescription drug such as pain relievers, tranquilizers, stimulants, or sedatives. Of the 27.1 million current drug users in 2015, 300,000 had used heroin during the past month.

DRUG-RELATED DEATHS

Sherry L. Murphy of the Centers for Disease Control and Prevention (CDC) reports in "Deaths: Final Data for 1998" (*National Vital Statistics Reports*, vol. 48, no. 11, July 24, 2000) that there were 16,926 drug-related deaths in 1998, or 6.3 deaths per 100,000 population. According to Kenneth D. Kochanek et al. of the CDC, in "Deaths: Final Data for 2014" (*National Vital Statistics Reports*, vol. 65, no. 4, June 30, 2016), by 2014 the number of drug-related deaths nearly tripled, to 49,714. The rate more than doubled during this span as well, reaching 15.6 deaths per 100,000 population.

CANNABIS AND MARIJUANA

Cannabis sativa and *Cannabis indica*, the hemp plants from which marijuana is made, grow wild throughout most of the world's tropic and temperate regions, including Mexico, the Middle East, Africa, and India. For centuries its therapeutic potential has been explored, including uses as an analgesic (painkiller) and anticonvulsant. However, with the advent of new, synthetic drugs and the passage of the Marijuana Tax Act of 1937, interest in marijuana—even for medicinal purposes—faded. In 1970 the Controlled Substances Act (CSA) classified marijuana as a Schedule I drug because it has "no currently accepted medical use in treatment in the United States," although this classification is debated by those in favor of using it for medical and recreational purposes. (See Chapter 9.)

Besides regular marijuana, there is also sinsemilla. Both are tobacco-like substances that are produced by

FIGURE 4.1

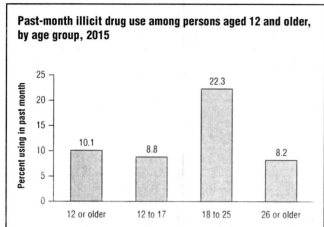

Past-month illicit drug use among persons aged 12 and older, by age group, 2015

SOURCE: "Figure 2. Past Month Illicit Drug Use among People Aged 12 or Older, by Age Group: Percentages, 2015," in *Key Substance Use and Mental Health Indicators in the United States: Results from the 2015 National Survey on Drug Use and Health*, U.S. Department of Health and Human Services, Substance Abuse and Mental Health Services Administration, September 2016, https://www.samhsa.gov/data/sites/default-files/NSDUH-FFR1-2015/NSDUH-FFR1-2015/NSDUH-FFR1-2015.pdf (accessed January 9, 2017)

TABLE 4.1

Use of illicit drugs among persons aged 12 and older, by age, sex, and race and Hispanic origin, 2014 and 2015

Demographic characteristic	Lifetime (2014)	Lifetime (2015)	Past year (2014)	Past year (2015)	Past month (2014)	Past month (2015)
Total	nc	48.8	nc	17.8	nc	10.1
Age						
12–17	nc	25.3	nc	17.5	nc	8.8
18 or older	nc	51.2	nc	17.9	nc	10.2
18–25	nc	57.5	nc	37.5	nc	22.3
26 or older	nc	50.1	nc	14.6	nc	8.2
Gender						
Male	nc	53.8	nc	20.5	nc	12.5
Female	nc	44.1	nc	15.3	nc	7.9
Hispanic origin and race						
Not Hispanic or Latino	nc	50.7	nc	18.0	nc	10.3
White	nc	53.4	nc	17.9	nc	10.2
Black or African American	nc	47.7	nc	20.7	nc	12.5
American Indian or Alaska Native	nc	54.3	nc	22.9	nc	14.2
Native Hawaiian or other Pacific Islander	nc	48.1	nc	20.5	nc	9.8
Asian	nc	24.1	nc	9.2	nc	4.0
Two or more races	nc	57.7	nc	27.1	nc	17.2
Hispanic or Latino	nc	38.8	nc	17.2	nc	9.2

nc = not comparable due to methodological changes

Notes: Illicit drug use includes the misuse of prescription psychotherapeutics or the use of marijuana, cocaine (including crack), heroin, hallucinogens, inhalants, or methamphetamine. Misuse of prescription drugs is defined as use in any way not directed by a doctor, including use without a prescription of one's own medication; use in greater amounts, more often, or longer than told to take a drug; or use in any other way not directed by a doctor. Prescription drugs do not include over-the-counter drugs.

SOURCE: "Table 1.28B. Illicit Drug Use in Lifetime, Past Year, and Past Month among Persons Aged 12 or Older, by Demographic Characteristics: Percentages, 2014 and 2015," in *2015 National Survey on Drug Use and Health: Detailed Tables*, U.S. Department of Health and Human Services, Substance Abuse and Mental Health Services Administration, September 8, 2016, https://www.samhsa.gov/data/sites/default/files/NSDUH-Det-Tabs-2015/NSDUH-DetTabs-2015/NSDUH-DetTabs-2015.pdf (accessed January 9, 2017)

TABLE 4.2

Past-month substance use among military veterans, by substance type, 2002–14

	Number of users (thousands)				Percentage who used			
	2003–2005	2006–2008	2009–2011	2012–2014	2003–2005	2006–2008	2009–2011	2012–2014
Veteran								
Any illicit drug[a]	1,200	1,342	1,198	1,486	4.5	5.4	5.1	6.3
Marijuana	905	1,025	964	1,247	3.4	4.1	4.1	5.3
Cocaine	194	155	101	89	0.7	0.6	0.4	0.4
Heroin	4	30	7	10	0.0	0.1	0.0	0.0
Methamphetamine	43	36	11	28	0.2	0.1	0.0	0.1
Nonmedical use of any psychotherapeutic drug[b]	355	374	331	293	1.3	1.5	1.4	1.2
Cigarettes	6,536	5,763	5,160	5,058	24.7	23.2	22.1	21.4
Alcohol	15,508	14,266	13,578	13,751	58.5	57.4	58.3	58.2
Non-veteran								
Any illicit drug[a]	15,553	16,386	18,649	21,349	8.2	8.3	9.0	10.0
Marijuana	11,836	12,151	14,605	17,238	6.3	6.1	7.1	8.1
Cocaine	1,899	1,864	1,328	1,450	1.0	0.9	0.6	0.7
Heroin	120	197	219	333	0.1	0.1	0.1	0.2
Methamphetamine	577	451	388	474	0.3	0.2	0.2	0.2
Nonmedical use of any psychotherapeutic drug[b]	5,079	5,568	5,627	5,692	2.7	2.8	2.7	2.7
Cigarettes	50,806	52,284	50,733	49,706	26.9	26.4	24.6	23.2
Alcohol	102,106	108,762	114,757	120,597	54.1	55.0	55.6	56.4

[a]Any illicit drug includes marijuana/hashish, cocaine (including crack), heroin, hallucinogens, inhalants, or any prescription-type psychotherapeutic drugs used nonmedically.
[b]Nonmedical use of prescription-type psychotherapeutics includes the nonmedical use of pain relievers, tranquilizers, stimulants, or sedatives and does not include over-the-counter drugs.

SOURCE: "Table 36. Substance Use in the Past Month by Veteran Status, Aged 18 or Older: Annual Averages for 2002–2004 to 2012–2014," in *National Drug Control Strategy: Data Supplement 2016*, Executive Office of the President, Office of National Drug Control Policy, 2016, https://obamawhitehouse.archives .gov/sites/default/files/ondcp/policy-and-research/2016_ndcs_data_supplement_20170110.pdf (accessed March 13, 2017)

FIGURE 4.2

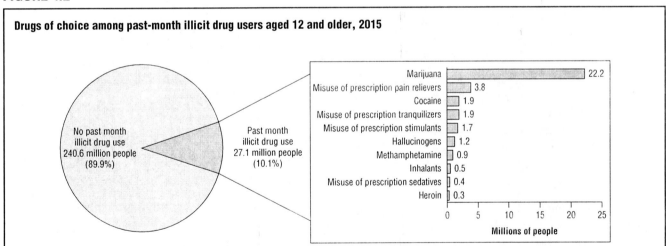

Drugs of choice among past-month illicit drug users aged 12 and older, 2015

No past month illicit drug use
240.6 million people
(89.9%)

Past month illicit drug use
27.1 million people
(10.1%)

	Millions of people
Marijuana	22.2
Misuse of prescription pain relievers	3.8
Cocaine	1.9
Misuse of prescription tranquilizers	1.9
Misuse of prescription stimulants	1.7
Hallucinogens	1.2
Methamphetamine	0.9
Inhalants	0.5
Misuse of prescription sedatives	0.4
Heroin	0.3

Note: Estimated numbers of people refer to people aged 12 or older in the civilian, noninstitutionalized population in the United States. The numbers do not sum to the total population of the United States because the population for NSDUH does not include people aged 11 years old or younger, people with no fixed household address (e.g., homeless or transient people not in shelters), active-duty military personnel, and residents of institutional group quarters, such as correctional facilities, nursing homes, mental institutions, and long-term care hospitals. The estimated numbers of current users of different illicit drugs are not mutually exclusive because people could have used more than one type of illicit drug in the past month.

SOURCE: "Figure 1. Numbers of Past Month Illicit Drug Users among People Aged 12 or Older: 2015," in *Key Substance Use and Mental Health Indicators in the United States: Results from the 2015 National Survey on Drug Use and Health*, U.S. Department of Health and Human Services, Substance Abuse and Mental Health Services Administration, September 2016, https://www.samhsa.gov/data/sites/default/files/NSDUH-FFR1-2015/NSDUH-FFR1-2015/ NSDUH-FFR1-2015.pdf (accessed January 9, 2017)

drying the leaves and flowery tops of cannabis plants. The Office of National Drug Control Policy (ONDCP) explains in *National Drug Control Strategy: Data Supplement 2015* (2015, https://obamawhitehouse.archives .gov/sites/default/files/ondcp/policy-and-research/2015_data _supplement_final.pdf) that potency varies considerably between the two. The potency of the drug depends on how much of the chemical THC (delta-9-tetrahydrocannabinol) is present. Sinsemilla is the most potent form of marijuana. The name is Spanish for "without seed" and refers to the unpollinated, and therefore seedless, female cannabis plant. Generally, marijuana cultivated in the United States has a THC content of about 2% to 3%, whereas the marijuana from other countries has a higher potency, in recent years ranging from about 6% to 7%. By contrast, the potency of sinsemilla is roughly between 7% to 14% THC.

Effects of Marijuana

Marijuana is usually smoked in the form of loosely rolled cigarettes called joints, in hollowed-out commercial cigars called blunts, in pipes made of glass, metal, or wood, or in water pipes called bongs. Sometimes it is ingested. The effects are felt within minutes, usually peaking in 10 to 30 minutes and lingering for two to three hours. Low doses induce restlessness and an increasing sense of well-being, followed by a dreamy state of relaxation and, frequently, hunger. Changes in sensory perception—a more vivid sense of sight, smell, touch, taste, and hearing—may occur, with subtle alterations in thought formation and expression. However, the National Institute on Drug Abuse reports in "DrugFacts: Marijuana" (February 2017, https://www.drugabuse.gov/publications/drugfacts/marijuana) that along with the pleasant side effects of smoking marijuana come some not-so-pleasant effects, including short-term memory loss, possible abnormalities in heart rhythm and an increased risk of heart attack, and lung damage.

The immediate physical effects of marijuana include a faster heartbeat (by as much as 50%), bloodshot eyes, and a dry mouth and throat. It can alter one's sense of time and reduce concentration and coordination. Some users experience lightheadedness and giddiness, whereas others feel depressed and sad. Many users have also reported experiencing severe anxiety attacks.

Although the immediate effects of marijuana usually disappear in about four to six hours, it takes about three days for 50% of the drug to be broken down and eliminated from the body. It takes three weeks to completely excrete the THC from one marijuana cigarette. If a user smokes two joints per week, it takes months for all traces of the THC to disappear from the body.

Hashish and Hash Oil

Two other drugs besides marijuana come from the cannabis plant: hashish and hash oil. Hashish is made from the THC-rich, tar-like material that can be collected from the cannabis plant. This resin is dried and compressed into a variety of forms, including balls and cakes. Larger pieces are broken into smaller pieces and smoked.

Most hashish comes from the Middle East, North Africa, Pakistan, and Afghanistan. Demand in the United States is limited.

Despite its name, hash oil is not directly related to hashish. It is produced by extracting the cannabinoids from the cannabis plant with a solvent. The color and odor of hash oil depend on the solvent that is used. Hash oil ranges from amber to dark brown and has a potency of about 15% THC. In terms of effect, a drop or two of hash oil on a cigarette is equal to a single marijuana joint.

Prevalence of Use of Marijuana

Figure 4.3 shows the lifetime, annual, and 30-day (current) use of marijuana among 18- to 55-year-olds in 2015. Current and annual use generally drops with age—younger people are more likely to have used marijuana during the past month or past year than older people. By the age of 55, however, 81% of Americans in 2015 had tried marijuana at some point during their lifetime.

In 2015, 21% of 18-year-olds were current users of marijuana. (See Figure 4.3.) Use rates rose to 23% for 19- to 20-year-olds and 21- to 22-year-olds. By the age of 35, 13% were current users of marijuana, and by the age of 50 this figure dropped to 8%.

Between 2002 and 2015 the percentage of current marijuana users aged 12 years and older rose from 6.2% to 8.3%. (See Figure 4.4.) During this period current marijuana use among adults aged 18 to 25 years rose from 17.3% to 19.8%, while use among adults aged 26 years and older rose from 4% to 6.5%. Meanwhile, the rate of current marijuana use among individuals between the ages of 12 and 17 years decreased over this span, falling from 8.2% in 2002 to 7% in 2015.

PSYCHOTHERAPEUTICS

Psychotherapeutics are drugs that include pain relievers, tranquilizers, stimulants (including methamphetamine), and sedatives. Although many of these drugs are available through prescription, they are also frequently abused. According to SAMHSA, approximately 6.4 million Americans aged 12 years and older were current users of psychotherapeutic drugs for nonprescription purposes in 2015. This figure represented 2.4% of the U.S. population in that age group.

Pain Relievers

Table 4.3 shows the percentages of people aged 12 years and older who used prescription pain relievers for both medical and nonmedical reasons in 2015. Overall, more than one-third (36.4%) of Americans aged 12 years and older used prescription painkillers at some point in 2015. Approximately 4.7% of people aged 12 years and older used painkillers for nonmedical reasons at some

FIGURE 4.3

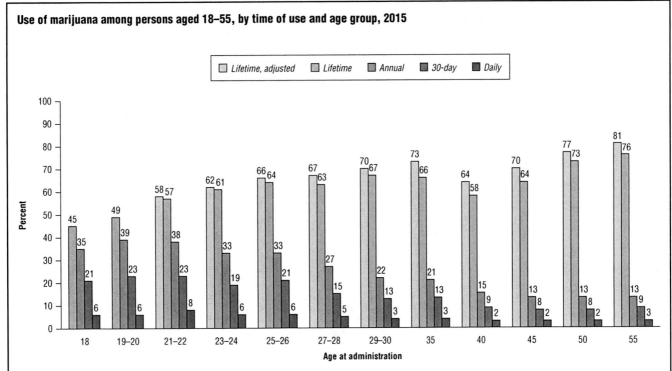

Use of marijuana among persons aged 18–55, by time of use and age group, 2015

Notes: Lifetime prevalence estimates were adjusted for inconsistency in self-reports of drug use over time. Due to rounding some bars with the same number may have uneven height.

SOURCE: Lloyd D. Johnston et al., "Figure 4-3. Marijuana: Lifetime, Annual, 30-Day, and Daily Prevalence among Respondents of Modal Ages 18 through 55 by Age Group, 2015," in *Monitoring the Future National Survey Results on Drug Use, 1975–2015: Volume 2, College Students and Adults Ages 19–55,* University of Michigan, Ann Arbor, Institute for Social Research, July 2016, http://www.monitoringthefuture.org//pubs/monographs/mtf-vol2_2015.pdf (accessed January 9, 2017)

point that year, while 1.4% were current abusers of prescription pain relievers.

Most current users of pain relievers for nonprescription purposes in 2015 were young adults aged 18 to 25 years (2.4%). (See Table 4.3.) Those aged 26 years and older were the next most likely to abuse these drugs (1.3%), while those aged 12 to 17 years (1.1%) were the least likely to misuse prescription pain relievers in 2015.

The percentage of current abusers of prescription pain relievers among Hispanics was 1.6% in 2015, the highest rate of any single race or ethnicity. (See Table 4.3.) In contrast, Asian Americans had a very low current rate of use, at 0.4%.

NARCOTICS: OXYCODONE, HYDROCODONE, AND MORPHINE. Two prescription pain relievers that have been popular with users of illicit prescription drugs are oxycodone and hydrocodone, both of which are strong narcotic pain relievers. Narcotics are addictive drugs, such as morphine, codeine, and opium, and they reduce pain, alter mood and behavior, and usually induce sleep. Whereas morphine, codeine, and opium are natural narcotics extracted from the juice of the opium poppy, oxycodone and hydrocodone are semisynthetic narcotics; that is, they are made in the laboratory from codeine.

Oxycodone and hydrocodone are two of the most commonly prescribed narcotic painkillers in the United States. Although they are designed to have a less euphoric effect than morphine, they are still highly sought after by recreational users and addicts. Like morphine, these drugs have enough potential for abuse that they are classified as Schedule II substances.

Oxycodone is the active ingredient in many narcotic pain relievers, including those manufactured as time-release caplets or those containing other pain relievers such as aspirin and acetaminophen. Illicit users of oxycodone crush, chew, or dissolve and inject the drug so that they receive all the oxycodone at once, giving them a heroin-like high. Emergency departments report serious injuries and deaths from the abuse of oxycodone, often by teenagers and young adults. One of the most prevalent forms of oxycodone in the early 21st century was the prescription drug OxyContin. In *Monitoring the Future National Survey Results on Drug Use, 1975–2015: Volume 1, Secondary School Students* (June 2016, http://www.monitoringthefuture.org/pubs/monographs/mtf-vol1_2015.pdf), Richard A. Miech et al. of the Institute for Social Research at the University of Michigan, Ann Arbor, report that 3.7% of high school seniors had tried oxycodone at least once during the past year in 2015.

FIGURE 4.4

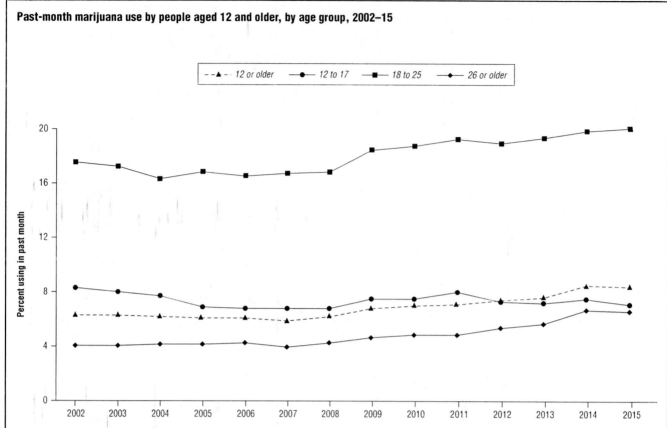

Past-month marijuana use by people aged 12 and older, by age group, 2002–15

Legend: ·–▲–· 12 or older —●— 12 to 17 —■— 18 to 25 —◆— 26 or older

SOURCE: "Figure 3. Past Month Marijuana Use among People Aged 12 or Older, by Age Group: Percentages, 2002–2015," in *Key Substance Use and Mental Health Indicators inn the United States: Results from the 2015 National Survey on Drug Use and Health,* U.S. Department of Health and Human Services, Substance Abuse and Mental Health Services Administration, September 2016, https://www.samhsa.gov/data/sites/default/files/NSDUH-FFR1-2015/NSDUH-FFR1-2015/NSDUH-FFR1-2015.pdf (accessed January 9, 2017)

TABLE 4.3

Use of pain relievers among persons aged 12 and older, by type of use, time of use, and select demographic characteristics, 2015

Demographic characteristic	Any use in past year	Misuse in past year	Misuse in past month
Total	36.4	4.7	1.4
Age			
12–17	22.7	3.9	1.1
18 or older	37.8	4.7	1.4
18–25	34.8	8.5	2.4
26 or older	38.3	4.1	1.3
Gender			
Male	33.9	5.3	1.6
Female	38.8	4.0	1.2
Hispanic origin and race			
Not Hispanic or Latino	37.6	4.6	1.4
White	38.7	4.8	1.4
Black or African American	38.3	4.4	1.3
American Indian or Alaska Native	38.7	5.6	1.1
Native Hawaiian or other Pacific Islander	32.7	5.4	0.9
Asian	22.0	1.8	0.4
Two or more races	44.8	8.4	3.0
Hispanic or Latino	30.2	5.0	1.6

Notes: Any use of prescription drugs is defined as (a) the use of one's own prescription medication as directed by a doctor or (b) misuse of prescription drugs. Misuse of prescription drugs is defined as use in any way not directed by a doctor, including use without a prescription of one's own medication; use in greater amounts, more often, or longer than told to take a drug; or use in any other way not directed by a doctor. Prescription drugs do not include over-the-counter drugs.

SOURCE: Adapted from "Table 1.68B. Any Use of Pain Relievers in Past Year and Misuse of Pain Relievers in Past Year and Past Month among Persons Aged 12 or Older, by Demographic Characteristics: Percentages, 2014 and 2015," in *2015 National Survey on Drug Use and Health: Detailed Tables,* U.S. Department of Health and Human Services, Substance Abuse and Mental Health Services Administration, September 8, 2016, https://www.samhsa.gov/data/sites/default/files/NSDUH-DetTabs-2015/NSDUH-DetTabs-2015/NSDUH-DetTabs-2015.pdf (accessed January 9, 2017)

Morphine is extracted from opium and is one of the most effective drugs known for pain relief. It is marketed in the form of oral solutions, sustained-release tablets, and injectable preparations. Morphine is used legally only in hospitals or hospice care, usually to control the severe pain that results from illnesses such as cancer. Tolerance and dependence develop rapidly in the morphine abuser. According to Miech et al., the annual prevalence rate of morphine use for high school seniors in 2015 was 1.3%.

Tranquilizers

A tranquilizer is a calming medication that relieves tension and anxiety. Tranquilizers are central nervous system depressants and include a group of drugs called benzodiazepines. They are also known as sleeping pills, downers, or tranks. Benzodiazepines have a relatively slow onset but long duration of action. They also have a greater margin of safety than other depressants.

Miech et al. note that most illicit tranquilizer use reported in recent years involved the drugs Valium and Xanax. The percentage of high school seniors who had taken Valium during the past year fell slightly between 2014 and 2015, from 1% to 0.9%, while the percentage of high school seniors who used Xanax fell from 3.4% to 2.5%.

Prolonged use of excessive doses of tranquilizers may result in physical and psychological dependence. Because benzodiazepines are eliminated from the body slowly, withdrawal symptoms generally develop gradually, usually seven to 10 days after continued high doses are stopped. When these drugs are used illicitly, they are often taken with alcohol or marijuana to achieve a euphoric high.

ROHYPNOL: THE DATE RAPE DRUG. Rohypnol, another benzodiazepine, has become increasingly popular among young people. Manufactured as a short-term treatment for severe sleeping disorders, the drug is not marketed legally in the United States and must be smuggled in. It is widely known as a date rape drug because would-be rapists have been known to drop it secretly into a victim's drink to facilitate sexual assault. In a sufficiently large dose it can leave a victim physically incapacitated and cause amnesia that may prevent him or her from recalling an assault. Responding to pressure from the U.S. government, Roche, the Mexican producer of Rohypnol, began putting a blue dye in the pill so that it can be seen when dissolved in a drink. Miech et al. indicate that in 2015, 1% of high school seniors used Rohypnol at least once during the previous year.

Synthetic Stimulants

Stimulants (uppers) are drugs that produce a sense of euphoria or wakefulness. They are used to increase alertness, boost endurance and productivity, and suppress the appetite. Examples of stimulants are caffeine, nicotine, amphetamine, methamphetamine, and cocaine.

Potent stimulants, such as amphetamine and methamphetamine, make users feel stronger, more decisive, and self-possessed. Chronic users often develop a pattern of using uppers in the morning and depressants (downers), such as alcohol or sleeping pills, at night. Such manipulation interferes with normal body processes and can lead to mental and physical illness.

Large doses of stimulants can produce paranoia and auditory and visual hallucinations. Overdoses can also produce dizziness, tremors, agitation, hostility, panic, headaches, flushed skin, chest pain with palpitations, excessive sweating, vomiting, and abdominal cramps. When withdrawing from stimulants, chronic high-dose users exhibit depression, apathy, fatigue, and disturbed sleep.

AMPHETAMINE AND METHAMPHETAMINE. Amphetamine has been used to treat sleeping disorders and during World War II (1939–1945) it was used to keep soldiers awake. Abuse of amphetamine was noticed during the 1960s. It was used by truck drivers to help them stay alert during long hauls, by athletes to help them train longer, and by many people to lose weight. An injectable form of amphetamine, methamphetamine, was abused by a subculture of people dubbed "speed freaks."

In 1965 the federal government realized that amphetamine products had tremendous potential for abuse, so it amended food and drug laws to place stricter controls on their distribution and use. All amphetamines are now Schedule II drugs, in the same category as morphine and cocaine.

Methamphetamine is a powerful stimulant that is relatively easy for drug traffickers to synthesize in homemade labs, so its illegal synthesis, distribution, and sale developed after new laws made amphetamine more difficult to get. Two products that come out of these clandestine labs are the injectable form of methamphetamine (meth) and the crystallized form (crystal meth or ice) that is smoked. Both forms are highly addictive and toxic. Chronic abuse results in a schizophrenic-like mental illness that is characterized by paranoia, picking at the skin, and hallucinations.

According to SAMHSA, there were approximately 897,000 current methamphetamine users aged 12 years and older in 2015. Lloyd D. Johnston et al. of the Institute for Social Research at the University of Michigan, Ann Arbor, note in *Monitoring the Future National Survey Results on Drug Use, 1975–2015: Volume 2, College Students and Adults Ages 19–55* (July 2016, http://www.monitoringthefuture.org/pubs/monographs/mtf-vol2_2015.pdf) that in 2015 annual methamphetamine use was approximately 1% for all age subgroups within the 18- to 30-year-old span. (See Figure 4.5.)

FIGURE 4.5

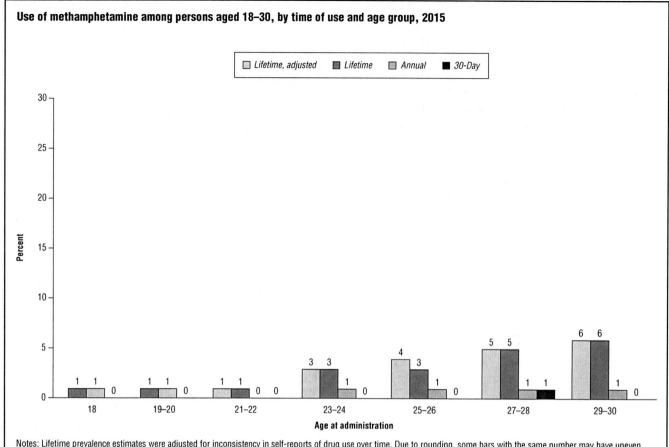

Use of methamphetamine among persons aged 18–30, by time of use and age group, 2015

Legend: ☐ Lifetime, adjusted ▨ Lifetime ▨ Annual ■ 30-Day

Notes: Lifetime prevalence estimates were adjusted for inconsistency in self-reports of drug use over time. Due to rounding, some bars with the same number may have uneven height. Questions about the use of methamphetamines were not included in the questionnaires for 35-, 40-, 45-, and 50-year-olds.

SOURCE: Lloyd D. Johnston et al., "Figure 4-5. Methamphetamine: Lifetime, Annual, and 30-Day Prevalence among Respondents of Modal Ages 18 through 30 by Age Group, 2015," in *Monitoring the Future National Survey Results on Drug Use, 1975–2015: Volume 2, College Students and Adults Ages 19–55*, University of Michigan, Ann Arbor, Institute for Social Research, July 2016, http://www.monitoringthefuture.org/pubs/monographs/mtf-vol2_2015.pdf (accessed January 9, 2017)

Sedatives

Like tranquilizers, sedatives are calming, soothing drugs. They relieve tension and anxiety. Also, like tranquilizers, sedatives are central nervous system depressants, but they include a group of drugs called barbiturates, which are generally stronger than tranquilizers. Barbiturates have many street names, including barbs, yellows, and reds.

Small therapeutic doses of sedatives calm nervous conditions; larger doses cause sleep within a short period. A feeling of excitement precedes the sedation. The primary danger of sedatives is that too large a dose can bring a person through stages of sedation, sleep, and coma and ultimately cause death via respiratory failure and cardiovascular complications. According to Miech et al., the past-year use of sedatives by high school seniors gradually rose from 2.8% in 1992 to 7.2% in 2005, before eventually falling to 3.6% in 2015.

COCAINE

Cocaine, a powerful stimulant, is extracted from the leaves of the coca plant (*Erythroxylon coca*). The plant has been cultivated in the Andean highlands of South America since prehistoric times. In these regions of South America, coca leaves are frequently chewed for refreshment and relief from fatigue—in much the same way some North Americans chew tobacco.

Pure cocaine was first used during the 1880s as a local anesthetic in eye, nose, and throat surgeries. It was also used in dental procedures. Since then, other drugs, such as lidocaine and novocaine, have replaced it as an anesthetic.

Illicit cocaine is distributed as a white crystalline powder and is often contaminated (cut) with sugars or local anesthetics. The drug is commonly snorted. Less commonly, it is mixed with water and injected, which brings a more intense high because the drug reaches the brain more rapidly.

Cocaine produces a short but extremely powerful rush of energy and confidence. Because the pleasurable effects are so intense, cocaine can lead to severe mental dependency, destroying a person's life as the need for the drug supersedes any other considerations. Physically, cocaine users risk permanent damage to their nose by exposing the cartilage and dissolving the nasal septum (membrane), resulting in a collapsed nose. Cocaine significantly increases the risk of a heart attack in the first hour after use. Heavy use (0.1 ounces [2 g] or more per week) impairs memory, decision making, and manual dexterity.

Freebasing is the smoking of purified cocaine prepared using a method that frees the cocaine base from impurities. Freebase is prepared by mixing cocaine with ether and sodium hydroxide or baking powder (sodium bicarbonate). The salt base dissolves, leaving granules of pure cocaine. Next, these granules are collected, dried, and heated in a pipe that is filled with water or rum until they vaporize. The vapor is inhaled directly into the lungs, causing an immediate high that lasts about 10 minutes.

There is a danger of being badly burned if the open flame gets too close to the ether or the rum, causing it to flare up as it burns. After the actor-comedian Richard Pryor (1940–2005) set himself on fire while freebasing in 1980, many users began searching for a safer way to achieve the same high. The dangers inherent in freebasing may have been the catalyst for the development of crack cocaine.

Crack Cocaine

Cocaine hydrochloride, the powdered form of cocaine, is soluble in water, can be injected, and is fairly insensitive to heat. Crack cocaine is processed by mixing cocaine with baking soda and heating it to remove the hydrochloride. The resultant chips or rocks of pure cocaine are usually smoked in a pipe or added to a cigarette or marijuana joint. The name comes from the crackling sound that is made when the mixture is smoked.

Inhaling the cocaine fumes produces a rapid, intense, and short-lived high. This incredible intensity is followed within minutes by an abnormally disconcerting and anxious crash, which leads almost inevitably to the need for more of the drug—and a great likelihood of addiction.

Prevalence of Cocaine Use

Figure 4.6 shows that in 2015 between 1% and 3% of 18- to 30-year-olds were current users and between 3% and 7% were annual users. For 35- to 55-year-olds, between 0% and 2% were current users and 1% to 5% were annual users.

HALLUCINOGENS

Hallucinogens, also known as psychedelics, are natural or synthetic substances that distort the perceptions of

FIGURE 4.6

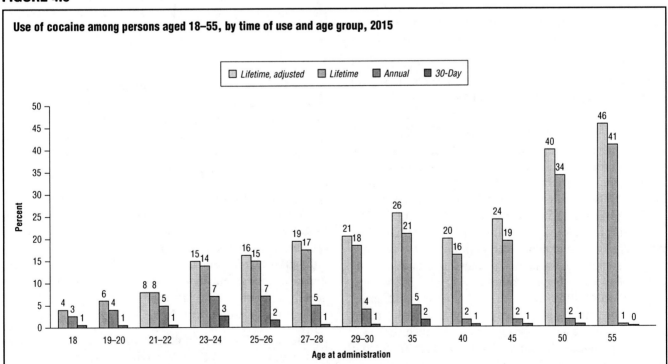

Use of cocaine among persons aged 18–55, by time of use and age group, 2015

Notes: Lifetime prevalence estimates were adjusted for inconsistency in self-reports of drug use over time. Due to rounding some bars with the same number may have uneven height.

SOURCE: Lloyd D. Johnston et al., "Figure 4-7. Cocaine: Lifetime, Annual, and 30-Day Prevalence among Respondents of Modal Ages 18 through 55 by Age Group, 2015," in *Monitoring the Future National Survey Results on Drug Use, 1975–2015: Volume 2, College Students and Adults Ages 19–55*, University of Michigan, Ann Arbor, Institute for Social Research, July 2016, http://www.monitoringthefuture.org/pubs/monographs/mtf-vol2_2015.pdf (accessed January 9, 2017)

reality. They cause excitation, which can vary from a sense of well-being to severe depression. Time may appear to stand still, and forms and colors seem to change and take on new meaning. Typically, the heart rate increases, the blood pressure rises, and the pupils dilate. The experience may be pleasurable or extremely frightening. The effects of hallucinogens vary from use to use and cannot be predicted.

The most common danger of using hallucinogens is impaired judgment, which can lead to rash decisions and accidents. Long after hallucinogens have been eliminated from the body, users may experience flashbacks, in the form of perceived intensity of color, the apparent motion of fixed objects, or illusions that present one object when another one is present. Some hallucinogens are present in plants (e.g., mescaline in the peyote cactus), whereas others (e.g., LSD) are synthetic.

Mescaline and Peyote

Mescaline is a psychoactive alkaloid, or chemical compound, known for its hallucinogenic properties. Mescaline is found naturally in several species of cacti, notably the peyote cactus (*Lophophora williamsii*), which is a small, spineless plant native to Mexico and the U.S. Southwest. The top of the cactus, often called the crown, consists of disk-shaped buttons that can be cut off and dried. These buttons are generally chewed or soaked in water to produce an intoxicating liquid. A dose of 0.01 to 0.02 ounces (350 to 500 mg) produces hallucinations that last from five to 12 hours. Mescaline can be extracted from peyote or other cacti or produced synthetically.

Peyote has long been used by Native Americans in religious ceremonies. The legality of the use of peyote in these ceremonies is decided by individual states.

MDMA and Other Designer Drugs

Designer drugs are those that are produced in a laboratory by making minor modifications to the chemical structure of existing drugs, resulting in new substances with similar effects. DOM (4-methyl-2,5-dimethoxyamphetamine), DOB (4-bromo-2,5-dimethoxyamphetamine), MDA (3,4-methylenedioxyamphetamine), MDMA (3,4-methylenedioxy-methamphetamine), and other designer drugs are chemical variations of mescaline and amphetamine that have been synthesized in the laboratory. Designer drugs differ from one another in speed of onset, duration of action, and potency. They are usually taken orally, but they can also be snorted or injected. Because they are produced illegally, designer drugs are seldom pure. Dosage quantity and quality vary considerably.

The most noted designer drug is MDMA (also called ecstasy). It acts as both a stimulant and a psychedelic and is known for enhancing a user's sense of touch. It was first banned by the U.S. Drug Enforcement Administration in 1985. The Anti-drug Abuse Act of 1986 made all designer drugs illegal. Widespread abuse placed MDMA in Schedule I of the CSA.

Designer drugs such as MDMA are often used at raves (large, all-night dance parties that are held in unusual places such as warehouses or railroad yards). Although many raves have become mainstream events that are professionally organized and held at public venues, the underground culture of raves remains an alluring draw to many teenagers. Part of the allure is drug use. For this reason, such drugs are also called club drugs. (Club drugs include MDMA, Rohypnol, LSD, and methamphetamine, among others.)

Users of MDMA have been known to suffer serious psychological effects—including confusion, depression, sleep problems, drug craving, severe anxiety, and paranoia—both during and sometimes weeks after taking the drug. Physical symptoms include muscle tension, involuntary teeth clenching, nausea, blurred vision, rapid eye movement, faintness, and chills or sweating. MDMA can also interfere with the body's ability to regulate temperature, and severe dehydration, particularly among users who dance for hours while under the drug's influence, is a serious hazard.

According to Miech et al., past-year MDMA use by high school seniors plummeted during the first half of the first decade of the 21st century, from 9.2% in 2001 to 3% in 2005. MDMA use among high school seniors then began a steady climb, reaching 5.3% in 2011, before dropping to 3.6% in 2015.

LSD

LSD is one of the most potent mood-changing chemicals in existence. Odorless, colorless, and tasteless, it is produced from a substance derived from ergot fungus or from a chemical found in morning glory seeds. Both chemicals are found in Schedule III of the CSA, whereas LSD itself is a Schedule I substance.

LSD is usually sold in tablets, thin squares of gelatin, or impregnated paper. It can also be taken in a liquid form that is dropped on the tongue or in the eyes with an eye dropper. The effects of doses higher than 30 to 50 micrograms can persist for 10 to 12 hours, severely impairing judgment and decision making. Tolerance develops rapidly, and more of the drug is needed to achieve the desired effect. It is, however, nonaddictive.

Because of its structural similarity to a chemical that is present in the brain, LSD was originally used as a research tool to study the mechanism of mental illness. It was later adopted by the drug culture of the 1960s. LSD use decreased during the 1980s, showed a resurgence during the 1990s, and then fell after 2001. Miech et al. note that the past-year use of LSD in 2015 was 2.9% for high school seniors.

Phencyclidine and Related Drugs

Many drug-treatment professionals believe that phencyclidine (PCP) poses greater risks to the user than any other drug. In the United States most PCP is manufactured in clandestine laboratories and sold on the black market. This drug is sold under at least 50 different names, many of which reflect its bizarre and volatile effects. It is often sold to users who think they are buying mescaline or LSD.

PCP is an anesthetic, so it produces an inability to feel pain, which can lead to serious bodily injury. Unlike other hallucinogens, PCP produces depression in some individuals. Regular use often impairs memory, perception, concentration, motor movement, and judgment. PCP can also produce a psychotic state that is in many ways indistinguishable from schizophrenia, or it can lead to hallucinations, mood swings, paranoia, and amnesia.

Because of the extreme psychic disorders that are associated with repeated use, or even with one dose, of PCP and related drugs, Congress passed the Psychotropic Substances Act of 1978. The penalties imposed for the manufacture or possession of these chemicals are the stiffest of any nonnarcotic violation under the CSA.

In its pure form PCP is a white crystalline powder that readily dissolves in water. It can be taken in tablet or capsule form. It can also be swallowed, snorted, smoked, or injected. It is commonly applied to a leafy material, such as parsley, mint, oregano, or marijuana, and smoked. According to Miech et al., the past-year use of PCP in 2015 was 1.4% for high school seniors, up from 0.8% in 2014.

Prevalence of Hallucinogen Use

According to SAMHSA, roughly 1.2 million people aged 12 years and older used hallucinogens during the past month in 2015. (See Figure 4.2.) In 2015 current users were primarily concentrated among 18- to 35-year-olds, while annual use persisted through age 40. (See Figure 4.7.) Johnston et al. indicate that the annual prevalence for hallucinogen use other than LSD in 2015 was 2.9% among high school seniors.

INHALANTS

Inhalants are volatile liquids, such as cleaning fluids, glue, gasoline, paint, and turpentine, the vapors of which are inhaled. Sometimes the sprays of aerosols are inhaled, such as those of spray paints, spray deodorants, hair spray, or fabric protector spray. According to SAMHSA, inhalants were among the least used group of illicit drugs in 2015, with roughly 527,000 current users aged 12 years and older. (See Figure 4.2.) Roughly one-third (175,000, or 33%) of this group was younger than 18 years old.

FIGURE 4.7

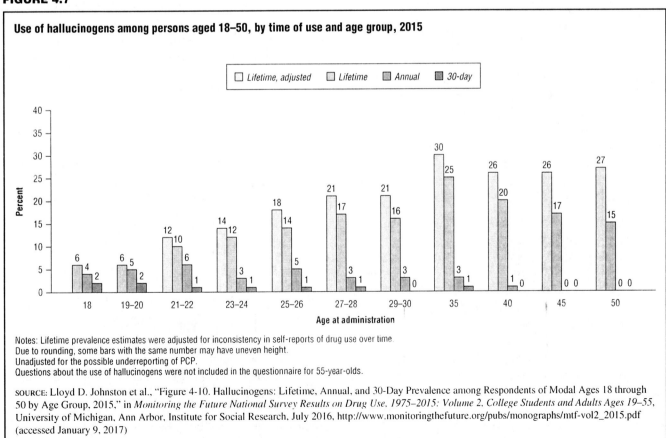

Use of hallucinogens among persons aged 18–50, by time of use and age group, 2015

Notes: Lifetime prevalence estimates were adjusted for inconsistency in self-reports of drug use over time.
Due to rounding, some bars with the same number may have uneven height.
Unadjusted for the possible underreporting of PCP.
Questions about the use of hallucinogens were not included in the questionnaire for 55-year-olds.

SOURCE: Lloyd D. Johnston et al., "Figure 4-10. Hallucinogens: Lifetime, Annual, and 30-Day Prevalence among Respondents of Modal Ages 18 through 50 by Age Group, 2015," in *Monitoring the Future National Survey Results on Drug Use, 1975–2015: Volume 2, College Students and Adults Ages 19–55*, University of Michigan, Ann Arbor, Institute for Social Research, July 2016, http://www.monitoringthefuture.org/pubs/monographs/mtf-vol2_2015.pdf (accessed January 9, 2017)

OTHER ILLICIT DRUGS

Heroin

Heroin is a narcotic, as are oxycodone, hydrocodone, and morphine. Heroin, however, is not used as a medicine, so it is not included with the psychotherapeutics.

Heroin is extracted from morphine, which is extracted from opium. This drug was not used extensively until the Bayer Company of Elberfeld, Germany, began commercial production in 1898. It was widely used as a cough remedy and painkiller for years, with the medical profession largely unaware of its potential for addiction. By 1914, however, the Harrison Narcotic Act established control of heroin in the United States.

Pure heroin, a bitter white powder, is usually dissolved and injected. Street-quality heroin may vary in color from white to dark brown, depending on the amount of impurities left from the extraction process or the presence of additives, such as food coloring, cocoa, or brown sugar.

Black tar heroin is popular in the western United States. A crudely processed form of heroin, black tar is manufactured illegally in Mexico and derives its name from its sticky, dark brown or black appearance. Black tar is often sold on the street in its tar-like state and can be diluted with substances such as burned cornstarch or converted into a powder.

In the past heroin was usually injected—intravenously (the preferred method), subcutaneously (directly under the skin), or intramuscularly (directly into the muscle). However, the increased availability of high-purity heroin meant that users could snort or smoke the drug, which contributed to an increase in heroin use. Snorting or smoking is more appealing to users who fear contracting the human immunodeficiency virus and hepatitis through needles that are shared with potentially infected users. Users who smoke or snort heroin also avoid the stigma that is attached to heroin use: the needle marks that are left on the user's skin. Once hooked, however, many abusers who started snorting or smoking heroin eventually shift to injecting it.

Symptoms and signs of heroin use include euphoria, drowsiness, respiratory depression, constricted pupils, and nausea. Withdrawal symptoms include watery eyes, runny nose, yawning, loss of appetite, tremors, panic, chills, sweating, nausea, diarrhea, muscle cramps, and insomnia. Elevations in blood pressure, pulse, respiratory rate, and temperature occur as withdrawal progresses. Because heroin abusers are often unaware of the actual strength of the drug and its true contents, they are at risk of overdose. Symptoms of overdose, which may result in death, include shallow breathing, clammy skin, convulsions, and coma. SAMHSA reports that 329,000 Americans aged 12 years and older were current heroin users in 2015. (See Figure 4.2.)

Anabolic Steroids

Anabolic steroids are drugs that are derived from the male sex hormone testosterone. They are used illegally by some athletes, including weight lifters, bodybuilders, long-distance runners, and cyclists, who believe these drugs can give them a competitive advantage or improve their physical appearance. When used in combination with exercise training and a high-protein diet, anabolic steroids can lead to increased muscle size and strength, improved endurance, and shorter recovery time between workouts.

Steroids are taken orally or by intramuscular injection. Most are smuggled into the United States and sold at gyms and competitions or sold by mail-order companies. In 1991 concerns about anabolic steroids led Congress to place them into Schedule III of the CSA.

There is growing evidence that using anabolic steroids can result in serious health problems, including cardiovascular and liver damage and harm to reproductive organs. The U.S. Department of Justice and the Drug Enforcement Administration's Diversion Control Program list the effects of anabolic steroids in "Anabolic Steroids: Hidden Dangers" (March 2008, https://www.deadiversion.usdoj.gov/pubs/brochures/steroids/hidden/hiddendangers.pdf). There are many types of physical side effects, including elevated LDL (bad) cholesterol levels and reduced HDL (good) cholesterol levels, severe acne, premature balding, mood swings, and atrophying of the testicles. Males may develop breasts, whereas females may experience a deepening of the voice, increased body-hair growth, fewer menstrual cycles, and diminished breast size. Some of these effects are irreversible. In adolescents, bone development may stop, causing stunted growth. Some users become violently aggressive.

By the turn of the 21st century a few professional sports agencies had begun to acknowledge that widespread steroid use was taking place in their ranks. For example, in 2005 Major League Baseball (MLB) initiated regular testing of players for steroid use. In 2009 the New York Yankees third baseman Alex Rodriguez (1975–) was accused of using steroids back in 2003, when he played shortstop for the Texas Rangers. Rodriguez joined a long list of other record-breaking, award-winning MLB players who have been implicated in the use of performance-enhancing drugs, including Roger Clemens (1962–), Mark McGwire (1963–), and Barry Bonds (1964–).

Among the most high-profile drug scandals in the history of international sports broke in 2012, when it was discovered that the celebrated American cyclist Lance Armstrong (1971–) had used a number of banned substances over the course of his career, including corticosteroids, testosterone, human growth hormone, and erythropoietin. In addition, the U.S. Anti-Doping Agency revealed that Armstrong had also coerced several of his teammates on the U.S. Postal Service cycling team to use performance-enhancing drugs. As a result, Armstrong was stripped of all seven of his Tour de France titles, in addition to being permanently banned from competitive cycling.

According to Amy Brittain and Mark Mueller, in "N.J. Doctor Supplied Steroids to Hundreds of Law Enforcement Officers, Firefighters" (NJ.com, December 12, 2010), a seven-month-long investigation by the *Star-Ledger* of Newark, New Jersey, revealed in December 2010 that more than 200 police officers and firefighters had been using steroids. Brittain and Mueller note that the investigation implicated Joseph Colao, a Jersey City, New Jersey, physician, who died in 2007, and state that "in just over a year, records show, at least 248 officers and firefighters from 53 agencies used Colao's fraudulent practice to obtain muscle-building drugs, some of which have been linked to increased aggression, confusion and reckless behavior." Taxpayer dollars were allegedly used to fill the prescriptions.

The most far-reaching steroid scandal in the history of athletic competition came to light in 2016, when a report issued by the World Anti-Doping Agency (WADA) revealed that Russian officials had overseen an extensive state-sponsored doping program between 2011 and 2015. Max Blau, Ashley Fantz, and Rob Hodgetts report in "Russian Official Disputes NYT Doping Story; NYT Stands behind Reporting" (CNN.com, December 28, 2016) that the program involved more than 1,000 athletes competing in 30 sports and was perpetrated with the direct involvement of the Russian Federal Security Service. The article "Russian Doping: McLaren Report Says More Than 1,000 Athletes Implicated" (BBC.com, December 9, 2016) notes that Russian athletes provided officials with clean urine samples prior to engaging in the doping program. These clean samples were later switched with contaminated urine samples prior to being tested by the WADA, allowing the athletes to elude detection. According to the article, dozens of Russian medal winners from both the 2012 Summer Olympic games in London and the 2014 Winter Olympics in Sochi, Russia, were implicated in the scandal.

Steroid use is not limited to professional athletes and other public figures, however. Laura Kann et al. report in "Youth Risk Behavior Surveillance—United States, 2015" (*Morbidity and Mortality Weekly Report*, vol. 65, no. 6, June 10, 2016) that in 2015, 4% of male high school students and 2.7% of female students had used illegal steroids. Kann et al. determine that overall steroid use among students rose from 2.7% to 5% between 1991 and 2001, before dropping to 3.5% in 2015.

ILLICIT DRUG USE DURING PREGNANCY

Illicit drug use during pregnancy places both the mother and the fetus (unborn child) at risk for serious health problems. For example, a fetus may become addicted to heroin in its mother's womb—provided the fetus reaches full term and is born (fetal death is a possibility). Cocaine use by the pregnant mother carries similar risks to the fetus and may kill the mother as well. LSD use may lead to birth defects. PCP use may result in smaller-than-normal babies who later turn out to have poor muscle control. Learning disabilities are associated with children born to women using cocaine and MDMA while pregnant. Smoking marijuana may prevent an embryo from attaching to the uterine wall and halt pregnancy.

SAMHSA surveyed women regarding their illicit drug use. A smaller percentage of pregnant women took illicit drugs than did women who were not pregnant. However, illicit drug use among pregnant women did occur. In 2015, 4.7% of pregnant women took illicit drugs. (See Table 4.4.) The most prevalent illicit drug used by pregnant women that year was marijuana, at 3.4%. Although smoking marijuana may seem safe to some pregnant women, it is not. In "Neurobiological Consequences of Maternal Cannabis on Human Fetal Development and Its Neuropsychiatric Outcome" (*European Archives of Psychiatry and Clinical Neuroscience*, vol. 259, no. 7, October 2009), Didier Jutras-Aswad et al. note that there is growing scientific evidence that smoking marijuana during pregnancy has a long-term influence on the developing brain and other parts of the nervous system of the fetus, which affects behavior and mental health.

The next most used illicit drugs during pregnancy were psychotherapeutics, which were taken for nonmedical reasons. (See Table 4.4.) In 2015, 1% of pregnant women took prescription drugs such as pain relievers, tranquilizers, stimulants, and sedatives. Of the psychotherapeutics, pain relievers were taken the most often. The percentage of pregnant women who used heroin, hallucinogens, or inhalants during their pregnancy was low.

ILLICIT DRUG USE IN THE WORKPLACE

The use of illicit drugs in the workplace presents a range of potential problems, both to employers and employees. Drug use can impair an employee's motor skills and judgment, leading to a decline in productivity and efficiency. In certain industries, such as those involving the use of heavy machinery, on-site drug use can create serious safety hazards, increasing the potential for injury or death. The National Council on Alcoholism and Drug Dependence indicates in "Drugs and Alcohol in the Workplace" (April 26, 2015, https://www.ncadd.org/about-addiction/addiction-update/drugs-and-alcohol-in-the-workplace) that drug use by employees can also lead to higher incidences of tardiness and absenteeism, while exerting a negative impact on workplace morale.

TABLE 4.4

Percentage of past-month illicit drug use among females aged 15–44, by pregnancy status, 2014 and 2015

	Total[a]		Pregnancy status			
			Pregnant		Not pregnant	
Drug	2014	2015	2014	2015	2014	2015
Illicit drugs[b]	c	12.1	c	4.7	c	12.5
Marijuana	9.7	10.1	3.6	3.4	10.0	10.3
Cocaine	0.7	0.7	0.4	0.0	0.7	0.7
Crack	0.1	0.1	0.2	d	0.1	0.1
Heroin	0.2	0.1	0.2	d	0.2	0.1
Hallucinogens	c	0.5	c	0.1	c	0.5
LSD	0.1	0.1	d	d	0.2	0.1
PCP	0.0	0.0	d	d	0.0	0.0
Ecstasy	c	0.3	c	d	c	0.3
Inhalants	c	0.2	c	0.1	c	0.2
Methamphetamine	c	0.3	c	d	c	0.3
Misuse of psychotherapeutics[e]	c	3.2	c	1.0	c	3.2
Pain relievers	c	1.6	c	0.8	c	1.7
Tranquilizers	c	1.0	c	0.1	c	1.0
Stimulants	c	1.0	c	0.1	c	1.0
Sedatives	c	0.3	c	d	c	0.3
Illicit drugs other than marijuana[b]	c	4.2	c	1.8	c	4.3

[a]Estimates in the total column represent all females aged 15 to 44, including those with unknown pregnancy status.
[b]Illicit drug use includes the misuse of prescription psychotherapeutics or the use of marijuana, cocaine (including crack), heroin, hallucinogens, inhalants, or methamphetamine. Illicit drug use other than marijuana use includes the misuse of prescription psychotherapeutics or the use of cocaine (including crack), heroin, hallucinogens, inhalants, or methamphetamine.
[c]Not comparable due to methological changes.
[d]Low precision.
[e]Prescription psychotherapeutics include pain relievers, tranquilizers, stimulants, or sedatives and do not include over-the-counter drugs.
Note: Misuse of prescription drugs is defined as use in any way not directed by a doctor, including use without a prescription of one's own medication; use in greater amounts, more often, or longer than told to take a drug; or use in any other way not directed by a doctor. Prescription drugs do not include over-the-counter drugs. The difference between this estimate and the 2015 estimate is statistically significant at the 0.05 level. Rounding may make the estimates appear identical. The difference between this estimate and the 2015 estimate is statistically significant at the 0.01 level. Rounding may make th e estimates appear identical.

SOURCE: "Table 6.71B. Types of Illicit Drug Use in Past Month Among Females Aged 15 to 44, by Pregnancy Status: Percentages, 2014 and 2015," in *Results from the 2015 National Survey on Drug Use and Health: Detailed Tables*, U.S. Department of Health and Human Services, Substance Abuse and Mental Health Services Administration, September 8, 2016, https://www.samhsa.gov/data/sites/default/files/NSDUH-DetTabs-2015/NSDUH-DetTabs-2015/NSDUH-DetTabs-2015.pdf (accessed January 9, 2017)

In "Greater Share of U.S. Workers Testing Positive for Illicit Drugs" (WSJ.com, September 14, 2016), Lauren Weber reports that the percentage of the U.S. labor force that tested positive for drug use in the workplace fell dramatically between the late 1980s and the first decade of the 21st century. In 1988, 13.6% of all employee drug tests came back positive for drug use; by 2010 this figure fell to 3.5%. Rates of workplace drug use remained steady through 2012, before eventually rising to 4% in 2015. According to Weber, roughly half of all positive drug tests that year involved the use of marijuana.

DRUG ABUSE ARRESTS

The ONDCP reports in *National Drug Control Strategy* that there were more than 1.5 million arrests for drug abuse violations in 2013. As Table 4.5 shows, the estimated number of arrests for drug abuse violations gradually increased beginning in the early 1990s, peaked at nearly 1.9 million in 2006, before steadily decreasing over the next seven years. The ONDCP also indicates that drug arrests as a proportion of all arrests peaked at 13.3% in 2013; by comparison, drug arrests accounted for only 7.1% of all arrests in 1991. During this span, the distribution of arrests for specific drug infractions shifted dramatically. For example, in 1989 arrests for heroin and cocaine possession represented more than one-third (34.7%) of all drug arrests; by 2013 this figure had dropped to 16.4%. By contrast, marijuana possession accounted for less than a quarter (23.1%) of all drug arrests in 1989. By 2010 this figure had nearly doubled to 45.8%, before gradually falling to 40.6% in 2013.

Most people arrested for drug offenses are charged with possession (carrying some kind of drug) rather than with trafficking (the sale or manufacture of drugs). As Table 4.5 shows, in 2013 more than four-fifths (82.3%) of those arrested for drug law violations were for possession.

ARRESTEE DRUG USE

The National Institute of Justice operated the Arrestee Drug Abuse Monitoring (ADAM) Program from 1987 to 2004 and published an annual report that summarized the previous year's data. The ADAM Program ended in 2004 in response to budgetary considerations and resumed in 2007 under the ONDCP.

In 2013 the ADAM Program surveyed arrestees in five urban sites about drug use during the past year and conducted urinalyses to determine if any of 10 drugs

TABLE 4.5

Drug arrests as percentage of total arrests, by drug category, 1989–2013

Year	Total arrests[a]	Arrests for all drug abuse violations Number	Percent of all arrests	Percent of all drug violations	Heroin/cocaine[c] Sale[d]	Heroin/cocaine[c] Possession	Marijuana Sale[d]	Marijuana Possession	Synthetics Sale[d]	Synthetics Possession	Other drugs Sale[d]	Other drugs Possession
1989	14,340,900	1,361,700	9.4	100	19.1	34.7	6.2	23.1	0.7	1.4	6.3	8.4
1990	14,195,100	1,089,500	7.6	100	21.0	33.3	6.1	23.9	0.6	1.5	3.9	9.7
1991	14,211,900	1,010,000	7.1	100	22.5	32.8	6.1	22.4	0.8	1.4	4.0	10.1
1992	14,075,100	1,066,400	7.5	100	20.6	32.4	6.6	25.5	0.7	1.2	3.9	9.2
1993	14,036,300	1,126,300	8.0	100	19.2	31.1	6.2	27.6	0.6	1.2	3.7	10.4
1994	14,648,700	1,351,400	9.2	100	16.8	30.3	5.8	29.8	0.5	1.2	3.6	12.0
1995	15,119,800	1,476,100	9.7	100	14.7	27.8	5.8	34.1	0.7	1.5	3.7	11.8
1996	15,168,100	1,506,200	9.9	100	14.2	25.6	6.3	36.3	0.6	1.4	3.7	11.9
1997	15,284,300	1,583,600	10.3	100	10.3	25.4	5.6	38.3	0.8	1.8	3.9	14.0
1998	14,528,300	1,559,100	10.7	100	11.0	25.6	5.4	38.4	1.0	1.9	3.8	12.9
1999	14,031,070	1,532,200	10.9	100	10.0	24.5	5.5	40.5	1.2	1.9	2.9	13.5
2000	13,980,297	1,579,566	10.9	100	9.3	24.2	5.6	40.9	1.1	2.2	3.0	13.6
2001	13,699,254	1,586,902	11.5	100	9.7	23.1	5.2	40.4	1.4	2.7	3.1	14.4
2002	13,741,438	1,538,813	11.2	100	8.8	21.3	5.4	39.9	1.4	3.0	4.0	16.0
2003	13,639,479	1,678,192	12.3	100	8.8	21.5	5.5	39.5	1.5	3.1	3.6	16.6
2004	13,938,071	1,746,670	12.5	100	8.3	22.0	5.0	39.3	1.6	3.5	3.3	17.0
2005	14,094,186	1,846,351	13.1	100	8.0	22.2	4.9	37.7	1.4	3.4	4.0	18.3
2006	14,380,370	1,889,810	13.1	100	8.0	22.8	4.8	39.1	1.5	3.4	3.2	17.2
2007	14,209,365	1,841,182	13.0	100	7.9	21.5	5.3	42.1	1.5	3.3	2.8	15.6
2008	14,005,615	1,702,537	12.2	100	7.7	20.1	5.5	44.3	1.5	3.3	3.0	14.6
2009	13,687,241	1,663,582	12.2	100	7.1	17.7	6.0	45.6	1.7	3.7	3.5	14.6
2010	13,120,947	1,638,846	12.5	100	6.2	16.4	6.3	45.8	1.8	4.1	3.7	15.7
2011	12,408,899	1,531,251	12.3	100	6.3	16.7	6.2	43.3	1.8	4.6	4.0	17.2
2012	12,196,959	1,552,432	12.7	100	6.1	16.5	5.9	42.4	1.9	4.5	4.0	18.7
2013	11,302,102	1,501,043	13.3	100	6.0	16.4	5.6	40.6	1.9	4.6	4.2	20.7

[a]Arrest totals are based on all reporting agencies and estimates for unreported areas from table entitled "Estimated Number of Arrests, United States."
[b]Percentages may not add to 100 because of rounding.
[c]Includes heroin or cocaine and their derivatives.
[d]Includes sale/manufacture of drugs.

SOURCE: "Table 58. Total Estimated Arrests and Drug Arrests, 1989–2013," in *National Drug Control Strategy: Data Supplement 2015*, Executive Office of the President, Office of National Drug Control Policy, 2015, https://obamawhitehouse.archives.gov/sites/default/files/ondcp/policy-and-research/2015_data_supplement_final.pdf (accessed January 23, 2017)

(amphetamine/methamphetamine, barbiturates, benzodiazepines, cocaine, marijuana, methadone, opiates, oxycodone, PCP, and propoxyphene) had been used recently. According to the *ADAM II 2013 Annual Report* (January 2014, https://obamawhitehouse.archives.gov/sites/default/files/ondcp/policy-and-research/adam_ii_2013_annual_report.pdf), in the sites surveyed, urinalysis revealed that 62% or more of adult male arrestees in 2013 had used at least one of the 10 drugs. Over all sites, use ranged from a low of 62.9% of arrestees in Atlanta, Georgia, to a high of 83% in Sacramento, California. Many had used multiple drugs, ranging from 11.9% in Atlanta to 49.8% in Sacramento.

Arrests and Race

Enforcing the official public policy on drugs has a significant impact on the nation's justice system: the law enforcement agencies, the courts, and the state and federal corrections systems. A relatively small percentage of total users are arrested, but at increasing rates. Sentencing policies have changed to require mandatory incarceration of those who possess, not just those who sell, drugs. As a consequence, prison populations have swollen, thereby putting pressure on prison capacities. The number of people in state and federal correctional facilities for drug offenses escalated from 682,563 in 1989 to nearly 1.6 million in 2014. (See Table 4.6.) Table 4.7 shows the sentenced prisoners by offense under state jurisdiction in 2014. The 206,700 people who were incarcerated for drug offenses made up 15.7% of the total state prison population of just over 1.3 million. The proportion of state prison inmates incarcerated on drug charges was similar for whites, African Americans, and Hispanics. In 2014, 15% (67,700 out of 451,100) of state drug offense arrestees were white, 14.9% (68,000 out of 456,600) were African American, and 14.6% (38,100 out of 261,000) were Hispanic. However, the actual percentages of white, African American, and Hispanic state prison inmates convicted of drug offenses in relation to the total prison population differed. Specifically, 33% (67,700 out of 206,300) of inmates serving drug offense sentences were white, 33% (68,000 out of 206,300) were African American, and 18% (38,100 out of 206,300) were Hispanic. The remainder were people of other races and ethnicities.

E. Ann Carson and Elizabeth Anderson of the Bureau of Justice Statistics (BJS) report in *Prisoners in 2015* (December 2016, https://www.bjs.gov/content/pub/pdf/p15.pdf) that nearly half (49.5%) of all federal prisoners

TABLE 4.6

Drug offenders in state and federal prisons, 1989–2014

| Year | Inmates in custody | | | Estimated inmates in custody with drug offense as the most serious offense | | | |
| | State | Federal | Total | Number | | Percent of Inmates | |
				State[a]	Federal[b]	State[a]	Federal[b]
1989	629,995	52,568	682,563	120,100	25,300	19.1	48.1
1990	684,544	56,989	741,533	148,600	30,500	21.7	53.5
1991	728,605	63,930	792,535	155,200	36,800	21.3	57.6
1992	778,245	72,071	850,316	168,100	42,900	21.6	59.5
1993	828,400	80,815	909,215	177,000	49,000	21.4	60.6
1994	904,647	85,500	990,147	193,500	49,500	21.4	57.9
1995	989,005	88,101	1,077,106	212,800	51,700	21.5	58.7
1996	1,032,676	92,672	1,125,348	216,900	55,200	21.0	59.6
1997	1,075,167	98,944	1,174,111	222,100	58,600	20.7	59.2
1998	1,113,676	110,793	1,224,469	230,500	64,000	20.7	57.8
1999	1,161,490	125,682	1,287,172	245,100	72,100	21.1	57.4
2000	1,248,815	145,416	1,394,231	258,100	70,500	20.7	48.5
2001	1,247,039	156,993	1,404,032	240,800	77,000	19.3	49.0
2002	1,276,616	163,528	1,440,144	258,800	80,600	20.3	49.3
2003	1,295,542	173,059	1,468,601	244,400	85,300	18.9	49.3
2004	1,316,772	180,328	1,497,100	243,800	85,300	18.5	47.3
2005	1,338,292	187,618	1,525,910	246,100	87,800	18.4	46.8
2006	1,375,628	193,046	1,568,674	264,300	91,500	19.2	47.4
2007	1,397,217	199,618	1,596,835	273,600	95,200	19.6	47.7
2008	1,407,002	201,280	1,608,282	258,000	94,300	18.3	46.9
2009	1,407,369	208,118	1,615,487	247,900	97,700	17.6	46.9
2010	1,404,032	209,771	1,613,803	237,000	97,800	16.9	46.6
2011	1,382,606	216,362	1,598,968	225,242	99,900	16.8	46.2
2012	1,352,582	217,815	1,570,397	210,200	98,900	16.0	45.4
2013	1,361,084	215,866	1,576,950	208,000	98,200	15.3	45.5
2014	1,350,958	210,567	1,561,525	—	96,500	—	45.8

[a]From 1989 to 1999, estimates for state prisoners held for drug offenses as the most serious crime were made using the Survey of Inmates in State Correctional Facilities, and adjusted up to the custody population collected in the National Prisoner Statistics. After 1999, estimates for state prisoners held for drug offenses as the most serious crime were made using the National Correctional Reporting Program and the National Prisoner Statistics.

[b]Percent of federal drug offenders calculated using the Federal Justice Statistics Resource Center query system and applied to the federal custody count and rounded for an estimated number of federal drug offenders.

Note: These estimates may not match previously published data. State and federal drug offender counts will differ from previous publications because custody rather than jurisdiction counts are used as denominators to enhance comparability to the 1989 to 1999 estimates.

SOURCE: "Table 60. Adult Drug Offenders in State or Federal Prisons, 1989–2013," in *National Drug Control Strategy: Data Supplement 2016*, Executive Office of the President, Office of National Drug Control Policy, 2016, https://obamawhitehouse.archives.gov/sites/default/files/ondcp/policy-and-research/2016_ndcs_data_supplement_20170110.pdf (accessed March 13, 2017)

were serving time for drug offenses in September 2015. (See Table 4.8.) However, in contrast to the proportion of state prison inmates serving drug offense sentences, a larger proportion of Hispanic (57.7%) and African American (51%) federal prison inmates were serving time for drug offenses than white (39.6%) federal prison inmates.

SENTENCING TRENDS

As noted earlier, 33% state prison inmates incarcerated on drug charges in 2014 were African American. According to the U.S. Census Bureau (2017, https://factfinder.census.gov), in 2014 the overall population of the United States was 314.1 million. Of this total, 73.8% was white, whereas 12.6% was African American. These figures reveal that a disproportionate number of African Americans were serving time for drug offenses, relative to their proportion of the overall population.

This racial discrepancy has prompted activists to seek ways to reform state sentencing laws for drug offenses. A breakthrough in these efforts came in November 2014, when California voters passed Proposition 47. Under the new law, the charge for possession of small amounts of heroin, cocaine, and other illegal drugs was downgraded from felony to misdemeanor status. Hayley Munguia reports in "What to Expect Now That California Passed Prop 47" (FiveThirtyEight.com, November 6, 2014) that the passage of Proposition 47 was expected to affect more than 16,000 of the state's 65,355 inmates serving time on dangerous drug charges in 2014.

THE BROADER RELATIONSHIP BETWEEN ILLICIT DRUGS AND CRIME

The relationship between illicit drugs and crime goes beyond the fact that illicit drug use is illegal. There are strong correlations between drug use and a variety of nondrug crimes. There are usually three reasons given for this correlation:

• Drugs may reduce inhibitions or stimulate aggression and interfere with the ability to earn a legitimate income.

TABLE 4.7

Percentages of offenders in state prisons, by type of offense, sex, and race and Hispanic origin, December 31, 2014

Most serious offense	All prisoners[a]	Male	Female	White[b]	Black[b]	Hispanic
Total	100%	100%	100%	100%	100%	100%
Violent	52.9%	54.3%	35.8%	46.6%	57.8%	58.7%
Murder[c]	13.0	13.2	11.0	10.2	14.9	14.7
Manslaughter	1.3	1.2	2.3	1.4	0.8	1.0
Rape/sexual assault	12.4	13.2	2.2	15.9	8.0	13.1
Robbery	12.8	13.2	8.0	7.4	19.4	12.9
Aggravated/simple assault	10.2	10.4	8.3	8.6	11.2	13.2
Other	3.2	3.1	4.0	3.1	3.4	3.9
Property	19.0%	18.3%	27.8%	24.8%	16.0%	13.6%
Burglary	10.1	10.3	7.2	11.9	9.7	8.0
Larceny-theft	3.6	3.2	8.0	5.2	2.8	2.4
Motor vehicle theft	0.8	0.8	0.9	1.0	0.5	0.9
Fraud	2.3	1.8	8.6	3.4	1.6	1.1
Other	2.2	2.2	3.2	3.3	1.3	1.3
Drug	15.7%	14.9%	25.1%	15.0%	14.9%	14.6%
Drug possession	3.5	3.3	6.5	3.9	3.5	3.5
Other[d]	12.2	11.7	18.5	11.2	11.3	11.1
Public order[e]	11.6%	11.7%	10.2%	12.8%	11.0%	12.6%
Weapons	3.9	4.0	1.8	2.5	5.2	5.1
Driving under the influence	2.1	2.1	2.9	3.0	0.7	2.7
Other[e]	5.6	5.6	5.5	7.2	5.1	4.8
Other/unspecified[f]	0.8%	0.8%	1.1%	0.8%	0.4%	0.4%
Total number of sentenced prisoners[g]	1,316,409	1,222,873	93,536	451,100	456,600	261,000

[a]Includes American Indians and Alaska natives; Asians, native Hawaiians, and other Pacific Islanders; and persons of two or more races.
[b]Excludes persons of Hispanic or Latino origins and persons of two or more races.
[c]Includes nonnegligent manslaughter.
[d]Includes trafficking and other drug offenses.
[e]Includes court offenses; commercialized vice, morals, and decency offenses; and liquor violations and other public order offenses.
[f]Includes juvenile offenses and other unspecfied offense categories.
[g]Race and Hispanic origin totals are rounded to the nearest 100 to accommodate differences in data collection techniques between jurisdictions.
Note: Jurisdiction refers to the legal authority of state correctional officials over a prisoner, regardless of where the prisoner is held. Counts are based on prisoners with a sentence of more than 1 year. Detail may not sum to total due to rounding and missing offense data.

SOURCE: E. Anne Carson and Elizabeth Anderson, "Table 9. Percent of Sentenced Prisoners under the Jurisdiction of State Correctional Authority, by Most Serious Offense, Sex, Race, and Hispanic Origin, December 31, 2014," in *Prisoners in 2015*, U.S. Department of Justice, Office of Justice Programs, Bureau of Justice Statistics, December 2016, https://www.bjs.gov/content/pub/pdf/p15.pdf (accessed January 9, 2017)

- People who develop a dependence on an illegal drug need a substantial income to pay for it and may commit crimes to fund their habit.

- Drug trafficking may lead to crimes such as extortion, aggravated assault, and homicide.

In *Drug Use and Dependence, State and Federal Prisoners, 2004* (October 2006, https://www.bjs.gov/content/pub/pdf/dudsfp04.pdf), the most recent report on this topic as of March 2017, Christopher J. Mumola and Jennifer C. Karberg of the BJS discuss the drug use of state and federal prisoners by the type of offense they committed in 2004. Overall, more than half of state and federal prisoners (56% and 50.2%, respectively) reported using illicit drugs in the month before their offense. Unsurprisingly, a high percentage of those in state prison for drug offenses (71.9%) had used drugs in the month before their offense. The correlation between drug use and nondrug crimes can be seen, however, in the fact that 64% of state prisoners who committed property offenses and 49.6% of those who committed violent offenses had used drugs in the month before their offense. The percentages for

federal prisoners were lower but still substantial, with 57.3% of drug offenders, 49.1% of violent offenders, and 27.7% of property offenders reporting drug use in the month before their offense. Furthermore, more than a quarter of state and federal prisoners (32.1% and 26.4%, respectively) reported they were using illicit drugs at the time of their offense.

For state prisoners, the likelihood that they used drugs in the month before the offense stayed the same between 1997 and 2004, at approximately 56%. The likelihood that federal prisoners used drugs in the month before their offense rose from 44.8% in 1997 to 50.2% in 2004. For state prisoners, women were more likely than men to have used drugs in the month before their offense in both years. Federal prisoners showed the opposite trend—men were more likely than women to have used drugs in the month before their offense in both years.

For both state and federal prisoners, people aged 24 years and younger were the most likely to have used drugs in the month before the offense in both years. The likelihood of drug use fell with age in both years and for both sets of prisoners. In general, whites were

TABLE 4.8

Percentages of offenders in federal prisons, by type of offense, sex, and race and Hispanic origin, September 30, 2015

Most serious offense	All prisoners[a]	Male	Female	White[b]	Black[b]	Hispanic
Total	100%	100%	100%	100%	100%	100%
Violent	7.4%	7.6%	4.1%	7.0%	10.0%	2.1%
Homicide[c]	1.5	1.5	1.3	0.7	2.4	0.3
Robbery	3.7	3.9	1.6	4.7	5.6	0.9
Other	2.1	2.2	1.2	1.6	2.0	0.9
Property	6.0%	5.2%	18.2%	9.6%	6.1%	2.8%
Burglary	0.2	0.2	0.1	0.1	0.4	0.0
Fraud	4.7	4.0	15.4	7.6	4.6	2.3
Other	1.1	1.0	2.7	1.9	1.1	0.4
Drug[d]	49.5%	48.9%	58.6%	39.6%	51.0%	57.7%
Public order	36.3%	37.6%	18.3%	42.4%	32.4%	37.0%
Immigration	8.0	8.4	3.3	0.9	0.3	23.4
Weapons	16.3	17.1	4.3	14.8	25.2	7.7
Other	12.0	12.1	10.7	26.7	6.9	5.9
Other/unspecified[e]	0.8%	0.8%	0.7%	1.5%	0.5%	0.4%
Total number of sentenced prisoners	185,917	173,857	12,060	50,300	69,000	60,800

[a]Includes American Indians and Alaska natives; Asians, native Hawaiians, and other Pacific Islanders; and persons of two or more races.
[b]Excludes persons of Hispanic or Latino origins and persons of two or more races.
[c]Includes murder, negligent manslaughter, and nonnegligent manslaughter.
[d]Includes trafficking, possession, and other drug offenses.
[e]Includes offenses not classified.
Note: Jurisdiction refers to the legal authority of federal correctional officials over a prisoner, regardless of where the prisoner is held. Counts are based on sentenced prisoners of all sentence lengths under federal jurisdiction on September 30, 2015. Detail may not sum to total due to rounding and missing offense data.

SOURCE: E. Anne Carson and Elizabeth Anderson, "Table 10. Percent of Sentenced Prisoners under the Jurisdiction of Federal Correctional Authority, by Most Serious Offense, Sex, Race, and Hispanic Origin, September 30, 2015," in *Prisoners in 2015*, U.S. Department of Justice, Office of Justice Programs, Bureau of Justice Statistics, December 2016, https://www.bjs.gov/content/pub/pdf/p15.pdf (accessed January 9, 2017)

slightly more likely than African Americans to have used drugs in the month before their offense in both years. Hispanics were the least likely of the three racial groups to have used drugs in the month before their offense. In 2004 the incidence of drug use was more than half for whites (58.2%) and African Americans (52.7%) in federal prison. Only 38.4% of Hispanic federal prisoners used drugs in the month before their offense.

CHAPTER 5
ALCOHOL, TOBACCO, ILLICIT DRUGS, AND YOUTH

In 2012, when teens were asked, "What is the most important problem facing people your age?" the most frequent answer was "drugs," which included tobacco and alcohol. The National Center on Addiction and Substance Abuse (CASA) at Columbia University has been asking this question in its national survey for many years. In *National Survey of American Attitudes on Substance Abuse XVII: Teens* (August 2012, http://www.center onaddiction.org/addiction-research/reports/national-survey -american-attitudes-substance-abuse-teens-2012), CASA states that "every year, including this year, teens tell us that tobacco, alcohol and other drugs are the biggest problem facing teens their age."

According to CASA, 26% of teen respondents said drugs (including alcohol and tobacco) are the most important problem facing them. The second-most important problem was social pressures (18%). These social pressures often include the pressure to drink, smoke, or use drugs. Furthermore, social networking sites such as Facebook, Instagram, and Snapchat can play a key role in influencing a teenager's decision whether to take drugs, drink alcohol, or smoke cigarettes. According to CASA, 75% of teens surveyed believed that viewing photos on social networking sites of teens drinking alcohol or smoking marijuana encourages other teens to want to emulate that behavior. Almost half (47%) of teens surveyed reported that "it generally seems like the teens in the picture are having a good time."

PROBLEM BEHAVIORS BEGIN EARLY IN LIFE
Risk and Protective Factors

Figure 5.1 shows the risk factors that are associated with drug addiction. The figure points out that drug addiction is not due to a single factor but to a variety of interacting factors. A person's heredity and environment act together to influence his or her behavior. More specifically, the National Institute on Drug Abuse (NIDA) explains in *Drugs, Brains, and Behavior: The Science of Addiction* (July 2014, https://www.drugabuse.gov/sites/ default/files/soa_2014.pdf) that genetic factors account for about half of an individual's risk for addiction. In addition, certain environmental factors, such as having parents or close friends who use drugs, being a victim of abuse, or being an underachiever in school, raise the risk that an individual will use and become addicted to drugs. Figure 5.1 notes that early use of drugs is also a risk factor for drug addiction.

Protective factors are those that lower the risk for drug addiction. According to the NIDA, these factors include positive relationships with peers and parents, success in schoolwork, self-control, and a strong neighborhood attachment.

Early Use of Alcohol, Tobacco, and Marijuana

Laura Kann et al. of the Centers for Disease Control and Prevention indicate in "Youth Risk Behavior Surveillance—United States, 2015" (*Morbidity and Mortality Weekly Report*, vol. 65, no. 6, June 10, 2016) that high school students were asked if they had drunk alcohol, smoked a whole cigarette, or tried marijuana before the age of 13 years. The results are shown in Table 5.1, Table 5.2, and Table 5.3.

As Table 5.1 and Table 5.3 reveal, in 2015 a higher percentage of younger students than older students reported having initiated alcohol or marijuana use before the age of 13 years. In contrast, 10th graders were more likely than any other age group to have smoked a whole cigarette before the age of 13 years in 2015. (See Table 5.2.) The most frequently reported behavior in 2015 was drinking alcohol before the age of 13 years. Roughly one out of five (20.3%) ninth graders reported they had done so, as had almost one-fifth (18.6%) of 10th graders, nearly one-sixth (15.2%) of 11th graders, and nearly one-seventh (13.5%) of 12th graders. (See Table 5.1.)

Males (19.7%) throughout all grades were more likely to report having had a drink before the age of 13 years than females (14.6%). Of the groups surveyed, Hispanics (21.3%) were the most likely ethnic group to report having an alcoholic drink before the age of 13 years, followed by non-Hispanic African Americans (18%) and non-Hispanic whites (14.5%).

Table 5.3 shows that the next most frequently reported behavior among high school students in 2015 was using marijuana before the age of 13 years. Once again, males (9.2%) throughout all grades were more likely than females (5.6%) to report having used marijuana before the age of 13 years. In 2015, 10th-grade girls (7.2%) were nearly twice as likely as 12th-grade girls (3.7%) to have used marijuana before the age of 13 years. Hispanics (10.9%) and non-Hispanic African Americans (10.6%) were considerably more likely than non-Hispanic whites (5.4%) to have used marijuana before turning 13 years old.

The same pattern between males (8%) and females (5%) emerged among high school students who reported having smoked a whole cigarette before the age of 13 years in 2015. (See Table 5.2.) Hispanics (7.1%) and non-Hispanic African Americans (7%) were the most likely to report this early behavior, followed by non-Hispanic whites (6%).

ALCOHOL AND YOUTH

Age of First Use

The Substance Abuse and Mental Health Services Administration (SAMHSA) conducts the annual National Survey on Drug Use and Health, and its 2015 survey results are published in *Key Substance Use and Mental Health Indicators in the United States: Results from the 2015 National Survey on Drug Use and Health* (September 2016, https://www.samhsa.gov/data/sites/default/files/NSDUH-FFR1-2015/NSDUH-FFR1-2015/NSDUH-FFR1-2015.pdf). According to SAMHSA, 2.4 million adolescents between the ages of 12 and 17 years were current alcohol users in 2015. This figure represented nearly one out of 10 (9.6%) of all people in that age group. SAMHSA also indicates that there were approximately 7.7 million current alcohol users who were under the legal drinking age in 2015.

FIGURE 5.1

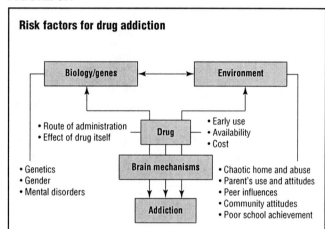

Risk factors for drug addiction

SOURCE: "Risk Factors," in *Drugs, Brains, and Behavior: The Science of Addiction*, National Institute of Health, U.S. Department of Health and Human Services, National Institute on Drug Abuse, July 2014, https://www.drugabuse.gov/publications/drugs-brains-behavior-science-addiction/drug-abuse-addiction (accessed January 9, 2017)

TABLE 5.1

Percentage of high school students who ever drank alcohol, and who drank alcohol before aged 13 years, by gender, ethnicity, and grade, 2015

	Ever drank alcohol			Drank alcohol before age 13 years		
	Female	Male	Total	Female	Male	Total
Category	%	%	%	%	%	%
Race/ethnicity						
White*	66.7	64.0	65.3	11.7	17.3	14.5
Black*	57.9	51.0	54.4	16.9	18.7	18.0
Hispanic	68.6	63.4	65.9	19.0	23.6	21.3
Grade						
9	53.0	48.9	50.8	18.8	21.5	20.3
10	62.7	58.8	60.8	15.8	21.3	18.6
11	72.1	68.7	70.3	12.9	17.5	15.2
12	75.2	71.5	73.3	9.9	17.0	13.5
Total	**65.3**	**61.4**	**63.2**	**14.6**	**19.7**	**17.2**

*Non-Hispanic.
Note: "Ever drank alcohol" means at least one drink of alcohol on at least one day during the student's life; "who drank alcohol" means other than a few sips.

SOURCE: Adapted from Laura Kann et al., "Table 47. Percentage of High School Students Who Ever Drank Alcohol and Who Drank Alcohol for the First Time before Age 13 Years, by Sex, Race/Ethnicity, and Grade—United States, Youth Risk Behavior Survey, 2015," in "Youth Risk Behavior Surveillance—United States, 2015," *MMWR*, vol. 65, no. 6, ne 10, 2016, https://www.cdc.gov/healthyyouth/data/yrbs/pdf/2015/ss6506_updated.pdf (accessed January 10, 2017)

TABLE 5.2

Percentage of high school students who ever smoked cigarettes, and who smoked a whole cigarette by the age of 13, by gender, ethnicity, and grade, 2015

	Ever tried cigarette smoking			Smoked a whole cigarette before age 13 years		
	Female	Male	Total	Female	Male	Total
Category	%	%	%	%	%	%
Race/ethnicity						
White*	30.4	33.2	31.8	5.3	6.6	6.0
Black*	29.5	30.6	30.1	3.8	10.1	7.0
Hispanic	32.7	37.8	35.2	4.9	9.2	7.1
Grade						
9	24.5	25.8	25.1	6.1	8.2	7.2
10	28.2	30.0	29.1	6.0	9.1	7.6
11	34.4	40.5	37.5	4.5	6.8	5.6
12	36.3	40.4	38.3	3.0	7.3	5.2
Total	**30.7**	**33.8**	**32.3**	**5.0**	**8.0**	**6.6**

*Non-Hispanic.
Note: "Ever smoked cigarettes means even one or two puffs.

SOURCE: Adapted from Laura Kann et al., "Table 29. Percentage of High School Students Who Ever Tried Cigarette Smoking and Who Smoked a Whole Cigarette for the First Time before Age 13 Years, by Sex, Race/Ethnicity, and Grade—United States, Youth Risk Behavior Survey, 2015," in "Youth Risk Behavior Surveillance—United States, 2015," *MMWR*, vol. 65, no. 6, June 10, 2016, https://www.cdc.gov/healthyyouth/data/yrbs/pdf/2015/ss6506_updated.pdf (accessed January 10, 2017)

TABLE 5.3

Percentage of high school students who ever used marijuana, and who used marijuana before aged 13 years, by gender, ethnicity, and grade, 2015

	Ever used marijuana			Tried marijuana before age 13 years		
	Female	Male	Total	Female	Male	Total
Category	%	%	%	%	%	%
Race/ethnicity						
White*	34.3	36.2	35.2	4.2	6.7	5.4
Black*	40.5	49.7	45.5	7.4	13.0	10.6
Hispanic	45.3	46.0	45.6	8.2	13.6	10.9
Grade						
9	25.3	26.5	25.9	6.8	9.9	8.5
10	33.8	37.1	35.5	7.2	9.4	8.3
11	43.6	46.9	45.2	4.5	8.9	6.7
12	48.8	50.9	49.8	3.7	8.5	6.1
Total	**37.5**	**39.8**	**38.6**	**5.6**	**9.2**	**7.5**

*Non-Hispanic.
Note: "Ever used marijuana" means one or more times during their life.

SOURCE: Adapted from Laura Kann et al., "Table 53. Percentage of High School Students Who Ever Used Marijuana and Who Tried Marijuana for the First Time before Age 13 Years, by Sex, Race/Ethnicity, and Grade—United States, Youth Risk Behavior Survey, 2015," in "Youth Risk Behavior Surveillance—United States, 2015," *MMWR*, vol. 65, no. 6, June 10, 2016, https://www.cdc.gov/healthyyouth/data/yrbs/pdf/2015/ss6506_updated.pdf (accessed January 10, 2017)

How Do Adolescents Obtain Alcohol?

In "Youth Risk Behavior Surveillance—United States, 2015," Kann et al. indicate that of high school students who drank alcohol in 2015, 44.1% were given the alcohol. CASA notes in *National Survey of American Attitudes on Substance Abuse XVII: Teens* that it supports the idea that alcohol is easy for youth to obtain. When asked by researchers "Which is easiest to *get*: cigarettes, marijuana, beer or prescription drugs?," more than a quarter (27%) of teens responded that cigarettes were easiest to obtain, but alcohol was a close second, cited by nearly a quarter (24%) of teens.

According to the Century Council, in "We Don't Serve Teens" (2017, http://www.centurycouncil.org/underage-drinking/we-dont-serve-teens), 96% of parents do not think it is acceptable for another adult to provide alcohol to their teens. However, in *Key Substance Use and Mental Health Indicators in the United States: Results from the 2015 National Survey on Drug Use and Health*, SAMHSA indicates that 23.7% of underage drinkers acquired alcohol through parents, guardians, or other adult family members in 2015. Indeed, many adults do not know that they can be held liable if they serve alcohol to a minor and if the minor is then killed or injured or kills or injures another person while under the influence of the alcohol that they served. Such laws are called social liability laws. The National Conference of State Legislatures explains in "Social Host Liability for Underage Drinking Statutes" (March 27, 2014, http://www.ncsl.org/research/financial-services-and-commerce/social-host-liability-for-underage-drinking-statutes.aspx) that social liability laws vary from state to state. For example, offenders in Alaska face felony charges in incidents involving significant bodily harm or death. By contrast, adults who provide alcohol to minors face misdemeanor charges in a number of states, including Alabama, Arizona, California, Ohio, and Oklahoma. In some states, such as Arkansas, Florida, and Illinois, the state provides exemptions from social liability statutes for alcohol consumed in religious ceremonies.

Current Use of Alcohol by High School Students

It is illegal for high school students to purchase alcoholic beverages, yet Richard A. Miech et al. of the Institute for Social Research at the University of Michigan, Ann Arbor, report in *Monitoring the Future National Survey Results on Drug Use, 1975–2015: Volume 1, Secondary School Students* (June 2016, http://www.monitoringthefuture.org/pubs/monographs/mtf-vol1_2015.pdf) that in 2015, 9.7% of eighth graders, 21.5% of 10th graders, and 35.3% of 12th graders had consumed alcohol at least once in the 30 days before being surveyed. These students are considered to be current users. In addition, 17.7% of high school students had engaged in binge drinking—that is, consumed five or more drinks in the space of a couple of hours—at least once within the past 30 days. (See Table 5.4.)

In *Results from the 2015 National Survey on Drug Use and Health: Detailed Tables* (September 8, 2016, https://www.samhsa.gov/data/sites/default/files/NSDUH-DetTabs-2015/NSDUH-DetTabs-2015/NSDUH-DetTabs-2015.pdf), SAMHSA also provides data on alcohol use. It reports that an estimated 2.4 million people aged 12 to 17 years (9.6% of this age group) used alcohol in the month before the survey. SAMHSA presents rates of current alcohol use in 2015 by age: 0.8% among 12-year-olds, 1.8% among 13-year-olds, 4.9% among 14-year-olds, 9.9% among 15-year-olds, 16.4% among 16-year-olds, and 23% among 17-year-olds.

Taken separately or together, data from these surveys present a picture of a high percentage of teens who use alcohol, which can cause bodily harm, diseases, and possibly death. Studies also show that binge drinking can inflict serious damage on the adolescent brain, which is particularly vulnerable because it is still in the process of developing. Michelle Trudeau reports in "Teen Drinking May Cause Irreversible Brain Damage" (NPR.org, January 25, 2010) that binge drinking has been shown to cause cognitive problems in high school students. Citing a study conducted by Susan Tapert of the University of California, San Diego, Trudeau reveals that binge drinking was linked to shorter attention spans in high school boys and to an inability to process spatial relationships in high school girls. In addition, brain scans revealed that binge drinking can cause damage to the nerve tissue, or

TABLE 5.4

Percentage of high school students who ever consumed five drinks in a row, and who ever consumed 10 or more drinks in a row, by gender, ethnicity, and grade, 2015

	Five or more drinks in a row			Largest number of drinks in a row was 10 or more		
	Female	Male	Total	Female	Male	Total
Category	%	%	%	%	%	%
Race/ethnicity						
White*	18.6	21.0	19.7	2.4	6.6	4.5
Black*	9.9	12.8	11.4	1.0	3.2	2.1
Hispanic	17.9	17.5	17.7	3.6	6.5	5.1
Grade						
9	10.5	10.2	10.4	2.3	2.4	2.4
10	14.1	16.2	15.1	2.2	6.3	4.2
11	19.6	24.4	22.1	2.5	7.3	5.0
12	23.8	25.6	24.6	3.0	8.8	5.9
Total	**16.8**	**18.6**	**17.7**	**2.5**	**6.1**	**4.3**

*Non-Hispanic.

Notes: "Drank five or more drinks of alcohol in a row" means within a couple of hours on at least 1 day during the 30 days before the survey. "Drinks in a row was 10 or more" means within a couple of hours during the 30 days before the survey.

SOURCE: Adapted from Laura Kann et al., "Table 51. Percentage of High School Students Who Drank Five or More Drinks of Alcohol in a Row and Whose Largest Number of Drinks in a Row Was 10 or More, by Sex, Race/Ethnicity, and Grade—United States, Youth Risk Behavior Survey, 2015," in "Youth Risk Behavior Surveillance—United States, 2015," *MMWR*, vol. 65, no. 6, June 10, 2016, https://www.cdc.gov/healthyyouth/data/yrbs/pdf/2015/ss6506_updated.pdf (accessed January 10, 2017)

"white matter," of the brain, which is responsible for relaying information between individual brain cells. Underage binge drinkers were also shown to have poor functioning in the hippocampus, the area of the brain responsible for storing memory.

Underage drinking can lead to other long-term negative consequences. In "Effects and Consequences of Underage Drinking" (*Juvenile Justice Bulletin*, September 2012), the Office of Justice Programs (OJP) of the U.S. Department of Justice indicates that drinking alcohol to excess can significantly compromise adolescents' decision making, leading them to engage in risky activities such as unprotected sex or driving under the influence. Furthermore, many teens have little understanding of the limits of their body when it comes to binge drinking, putting them at risk for alcohol poisoning. According to the OJP, underage binge drinkers are also more likely to develop problems with alcoholism as adults.

Unfortunately, the tendency to binge drink comes all too naturally to adolescents. Ron Dahl, a brain specialist and pediatrician at the University of Pittsburgh, told Trudeau that the adolescent brain is wired to become "passionate about a particular activity, a particular sport, passionate about literature or changing the world or a particular religion." Dahl warned that "those same tendencies ... may also increase the likelihood of starting on negative pathways."

Alcohol Use among College Students and Other Young Adults

In *Monitoring the Future National Survey Results on Drug Use, 1975–2015: Volume 2, College Students and Adults Ages 19–55* (July 2016, http://www.monitoringthe future.org/pubs/monographs/mtf-vol2_2015.pdf), Lloyd D. Johnston et al. of the Institute for Social Research at the University of Michigan, Ann Arbor, report the drug use results for college students and adults. Table 5.5 shows the annual prevalence of alcohol use by college students and other young adults who are one to four years beyond high school. The results indicate that both groups had a high annual prevalence of alcohol use in 2015: 79% for full-time college students and 70.7% for other young adults of the same age. Female college students (79.2%) were slightly more likely to have consumed alcohol during the past year than male college students (78.7%). The same was true for other young adults one to four years beyond high school; females (72.1%) were more likely than males (69.1%) to have consumed alcohol during the past year.

Table 5.6 shows the trend of lifetime prevalence of alcohol use between 1995 and 2015 among those aged 19 to 28 years. In 1995 the annual prevalence of alcohol use for this group was 91.6%. Throughout the rest of the 1990s the annual prevalence fell slightly; by 1999 the annual prevalence of alcohol use for this group was 90.2%. In 2015 the lifetime prevalence reached a low of 85.7%, which was a slight decrease from the rate of 86.3% in 2014. The lifetime prevalence of drinking flavored alcoholic beverages (the data for which did not begin being gathered until the first decade of the 21st century) among 19- to 28-year-olds was 84.6% in 2005 and eventually dropped to 81% by 2015.

Table 5.7 shows the trend of lifetime prevalence of alcohol use among college students one to four years beyond high school. The lifetime prevalence of alcohol use in this group (81.4% in 2015) was lower than that for the 19- to 28-year-old group (85.7% in 2015). (See Table 5.6.)

Heavy Drinking, Binge Drinking, and Drunkenness

Merriam-Webster (2017, https://www.merriam-web ster.com/dictionary/drunk) defines the term *drunk* as "having the faculties impaired by alcohol." According

TABLE 5.5

Annual prevalence of alcohol use by full-time college students vs. other adults one to four years beyond high school, by gender, 2015

[Entries are percentages]

	Total		Males		Females	
	Full-time college	Others	Full-time college	Others	Full-time college	Others
Alcohol	**79.0**	**70.7**	**78.7**	**69.1**	**79.2**	**72.1**
Been drunk[a]	61.6	51.4	64.1	55.1	60.0	48.2
Flavored alcoholic beverages[b]	64.5	54.2	50.3	49.2	72.7	57.7
Alcoholic beverages containing caffeine[c]	34.1	32.5	38.4	36.0	31.3	29.5
Approximate weighted population =	1,020	570	380	260	640	310

[a]This drug was asked about in three of the six questionnaire forms. Total population in 2015 for college students is approximately 510.
[b]This drug was asked about in one of the six questionnaire forms. Total population in 2015 for college students is approximately 170.
[c]This drug was asked about in two of the six questionnaire forms. Total population in 2015 for college students is approximately 340.

SOURCE: Adapted from Lloyd D. Johnston et al., "Table 8-2. Annual Prevalence of Use for Various Types of Drugs, 2015: Full-Time College Students vs. Others among Respondents 1 to 4 Years beyond High School by Gender," in *Monitoring the Future National Survey Results on Drug Use, 1975–2015: Volume 2, College Students and Adults Ages 19–55,* University of Michigan, Ann Arbor, Institute for Social Research, July 2016, http://www.monitoringthefuture.org/pubs/monographs/mtf-vol2_2015.pdf (accessed January 10, 2017)

TABLE 5.6

Trends in lifetime prevalence of alcohol use among adults aged 19–28, selected years 1995–2015

	1995	1997	1999	2001	2003	2005	2007	2009	2010	2011	2012	2013	2014	2015	2014–2015 change
Approximate weighted population =	6,400	6,400	6,000	5,800	5300	5,400	4,800	4,900	4,900	4,600	4,600	4,400	4,200	4,000	
Alcohol[a]	91.6	90.7	90.2	89.9	89.3	89.1	87.9	87.9	87.5	87.4	86.5	86.2	86.3	85.7	−0.7
Been drunk[b]	82.1	81.4	81.6	81.1	80.9	79.9	80.1	78.2	79.0	78.9	78.9	77.4	78.3	76.4	−1.9
Flavored alcoholic beverages[c]	—	—	—	—	—	84.6	84.0	83.5	81.4	82.2	82.4	80.9	80.6	81.0	+0.5

[a]In 1993 and 1994, the question text was changed slightly in three of the six questionnaire forms to indicate that a drink meant more than just a few sips. Because this revision resulted in rather little change in reported prevalence in the surveys of high school graduates, the data for all forms combined are used in order to provide the most reliable estimate of change. After 1994 the new question text was used in all six of the questionnaire forms.

[b]This drug was asked about in three of the six questionnaire forms; population is three sixths of population indicated. For small cigars only, beginning in 2014 question asked on two of the six questionnaire forms; population is two sixths of population indicated.

[c]This drug was asked about in one of the six questionnaire forms; population is one sixth of population indicated.

SOURCE: Adapted from Lloyd D. Johnston et al., "Table 5-1. Trends in Lifetime Prevalence of Various Types of Drugs among Respondents of Modal Ages 19–28," in *Monitoring the Future National Survey Results on Drug Use, 1975–2015: Volume 2, College Students and Adults Ages 19–55*, University of Michigan, Ann Arbor, Institute for Social Research, July 2016, http://www.monitoringthefuture.org/pubs/mono- graphs/mtf-vol2_2015.pdf (accessed January 10, 2017)

TABLE 5.7

Trends in lifetime prevalence of alcohol use among college students one to four years beyond high school, selected years 1995–2015

[Entries are percentages]

	1995	1997	1999	2001	2003	2005	2007	2009	2011	2012	2013	2014	2015	2014–2015 change
Approximate weighted population =	1,450	1,480	1,440	1,340	1,270	1,360	1,250	1,320	1,230	1,150	1,090	1,030	1,020	
Alcohol[a]	88.5	87.3	88.0	86.1	86.2	86.6	83.1	82.6	80.5	81.0	78.0	79.4	81.4	+2.0
Been drunk[b]			74.7	76.1	74.9	72.9	71.6	69.1	67.9	70.0	66.5	68.8	68.6	−0.3
Flavored alcoholic beverages[c]	—	—	—	—	—	84.5	80.6	78.1	76.7	76.6	67.5	72.7	74.8	+2.1
			—	—	—	—	—	—	—	—	—	—	—	—
			0.6	1.5	1.2	1.0	0.6	1.3	1.1	0.4	0.8	0.9	0.6	−0.1

Note: ' — ' indicates data not available.

[a]In 1993 and 1994, the question text was changed slightly in three of the six questionnaire forms to indicate that a drink meant more than just a few sips. Because this revision resulted in rather little change in reported prevalence in the surveys of high school graduates, the data for all forms combined are used in order to provide the most reliable estimate of change. After 1994 the new question text was used in all six of the questionnaire forms.

[b]This drug was asked about in three of the six questionnaire forms. Total population in 2015 is approximately 510.

[c]This drug was asked about in one of the six questionnaire forms. Total population in 2015 is approximately 170.

SOURCE: Adapted from Lloyd D. Johnston et al., "Table 9-1. Trends in Lifetime Prevalence of Various Types of Drugs among College Students 1 to 4 Years beyond High School," in *Monitoring the Future National Survey Results on Drug Use, 1975–2015: Volume 2, College Students and Adults Ages 19–55*, University of Michigan, Ann Arbor, Institute for Social Research, July 2016, http://www.monitoringthefuture.org/pubs/monographs/mtf-vol2_2015.pdf (accessed January 10, 2017)

to Miech et al., the rate of occurrences of drunkenness within the past 30 days among high school students rose considerably between eighth and 12th grade. Specifically, 3.1% of eighth graders reported being drunk within the 30 days prior to being surveyed. This figure rose to 10.3% among 10th graders and to 20.6% among 12th graders.

The National Institute on Alcohol Abuse and Alcoholism defines binge drinking as the consumption of five or more drinks (for men), or four or more drinks (for women), of alcoholic beverages in about two hours. Heavy drinking is an average of more than one drink per day for women and more than two drinks per day for men. (There is a male–female difference because the same amount of alcohol affects women more than it does men. Women's bodies have less water than men's bodies, so a given amount of alcohol becomes more highly concentrated in a woman's body than in a man's.)

According to Kann et al., in "Youth Risk Behavior Surveillance—United States, 2015," 17.7% of high school students were current binge drinkers in 2015. (See Table 5.4.) The incidence of binge drinking increased with grade level: 10.4% in ninth grade, 15.1% in 10th grade, 22.1% in 11th grade, and 24.6% in 12th grade.

Demographic Factors in Youth Alcohol Use

GENDER, RACIAL, AND ETHNIC DIFFERENCES. Miech et al. note that in 2015 male high school seniors (36%) were more likely to be current alcohol users than female high school seniors (35%). By contrast, a higher proportion of female high school sophomores (22.5%) were current alcohol users than male high school sophomores (20.6%) that year. Female eighth graders (9.9%) were also more likely than male eighth graders (9.1%) to be current alcohol users in 2015. However, male high school students (18.6%) were more likely than female high school students (16.8%) to engage in binge drinking. (See Table 5.4.)

Johnston et al. also provide annual prevalence rates for males and females among full-time college students and other young adults one to four years beyond high school. In 2015 full-time college males (64.1%) were more likely than full-time college females (60%) to have been drunk. (See Table 5.5.) Similarly, among young adults not attending college, males (55.1%) were more likely than females (48.2%) to have been drunk. In contrast, full-time college females (72.7%) and young female adults not attending college (57.7%) were considerably more likely than full-time college males (50.3%) and males not attending school (49.2%) to drink flavored alcoholic beverages in 2015.

Miech et al. also report that in 2015 Hispanic eighth graders were more likely to have consumed alcohol during their lifetime than non-Hispanic white or non-Hispanic African American eighth graders and high school students. In 2015, 12.7% of Hispanic eighth graders reported having drunk alcohol at some point during their lifetime, compared with 10.3% of non-Hispanic whites and 8.6% of non-Hispanic African Americans. By 12th grade, however, non-Hispanic whites (53.3%) were more likely than Hispanics (44.8%) to have drunk alcohol at some point during their lifetime. Among male high school students, non-Hispanic whites (21%) were more likely to have engaged in binge drinking than Hispanics (17.5%); both groups were considerably more likely to have done so than male non-Hispanic African Americans (12.8%). (See Table 5.4.)

WHERE STUDENTS LIVE. Miech et al. look at population density as a factor in student drinking patterns. They use the category metropolitan statistical area (MSA), which means the area contains at least one town that has more than 50,000 inhabitants. Large MSAs are the biggest cities in the United States, such as New York, New York; Los Angeles, California; Chicago, Illinois; Philadelphia, Pennsylvania; and Boston, Massachusetts. In 2015 a smaller proportion of eighth graders who lived in large MSAs were current drinkers (9.2%) than were eighth graders who lived in other MSAs (9.6%) or non-MSAs (10.4%). Comparable discrepancies were found among 10th graders, with students from large MSAs (21.2%) being less likely than those from other MSAs (21.4%) and non-MSAs (22.4%) to be current alcohol drinkers in 2015. By contrast, 12th graders in large MSAs (38.5%) had the greatest proportion of current drinkers, followed by those in non-MSAs (35%) and those in other MSAs (33.4%). Tenth- and 12th-grade high school students who lived in the Northeast were more likely to be current alcohol users than same-aged students who lived in other parts of the country, while eighth graders who lived in the South were more likely to be current alcohol users than their peers in other parts of the country.

PARENTAL EDUCATION. Miech et al. show an inverse relationship between current alcohol use among eighth graders and parental education: for the most part, the less parental education, the more likely eighth graders were to drink. For 10th and 12th graders these statistics vary somewhat. Among 10th graders, students whose parents had attained the third-highest education level (23.6%) were the most likely to drink, and students whose parents had reached the fourth-highest education level (19.9%) were the least likely to be current alcohol users. Among 12th graders, those whose parents had attained the lowest education level were the least likely to be current alcohol users, at 32.5%. This percentage rose to 36.5% among 12th graders whose parents were in the middle level of educational attainment, fell to 36.1% for 12th graders whose parents had attained the fourth-highest education level, before rising slightly to 36.3% for 12th graders whose parents had attained the highest education level.

Perception of Harmfulness of Alcohol Use

Miech et al. report that in 2015 more than half of all eighth graders (53.9%) and 10th graders (54.5%) and nearly half of all 12th graders (46.5%) viewed binge drinking on the weekend as dangerous. The proportion of eighth, 10th, and 12th graders who disapproved of weekend binge drinking was substantially higher. As Miech et al. note, 85.4% of eighth graders, 79.6% of 10th graders, and 65.1% of 12th graders had a negative view of weekend binge drinking in 2015.

Easy access to alcohol increases the probability that adolescents and teenagers will drink. Kann et al. show in "Youth Risk Behavior Surveillance—United States, 2015" that female high school students (48.5%) were considerably more likely than male high school students (39.9%) to drink alcohol that was given to them by someone else. (See Table 5.8.) Among gender and ethnic groups, white female high school students (50.7%) were the most likely to drink alcohol given to them by someone else, while male Hispanic high school students (36.5%) were the least likely to consume alcohol obtained for them by someone else.

Drinking and Young Drivers

In *Traffic Safety Facts, 2014 Data: Young Drivers* (May 2016, https://crashstats.nhtsa.dot.gov/Api/Public/ViewPublication/812278), the National Highway Traffic Safety Administration (NHTSA) reports that a total of 1,717 drivers aged 15 to 20 years were involved in fatal crashes in 2014, which was a 1% increase over the 1,697 drivers in that age group who were involved in fatal crashes in 2013. Overall, traffic fatalities among drivers aged 15 to 20 years old fell 48% between 2005 and 2014. In 2014, 17% of the drivers aged 15 to 20 years who were killed in crashes were intoxicated (had a blood alcohol level of 0.08 grams per deciliter [g/dL] or higher).

TABLE 5.8

Percentage of high school students who drank alcohol and who usually obtained their alcohol by someone giving it to them, by gender, ethnicity, and grade, 2015

	Current alcohol use			Someone gave alcohol to them		
	Female	Male	Total	Female	Male	Total
Category	%	%	%	%	%	%
Race/ethnicity						
White*	35.3	35.2	35.2	50.7	41.6	46.1
Black*	25.9	22.1	23.8	46.2	40.2	43.3
Hispanic	35.6	33.4	34.4	45.9	36.5	41.3
Grade						
9	24.9	22.1	23.4	50.4	39.4	44.9
10	28.8	29.3	29.0	50.0	34.5	42.3
11	38.3	37.7	38.0	49.7	39.3	44.3
12	43.2	41.6	42.4	45.3	44.9	45.1
Total	**33.5**	**32.2**	**32.8**	**48.5**	**39.9**	**44.1**

*Non-Hispanic.

Notes: "Currently drank alcohol" means drinking at least one drink of alcohol on at least 1 day during the 30 days before the survey. "By someone giving it to them" means during the 30 days before the survey, amonth the 32.8% of students nationwide who currently drank alcohol.

SOURCE: Laura Kann et al., "Table 49. Percentage of High School Students Who Currently Drank Alcohol and Who Usually Obtained the Alcohol They Drank by Someone Giving It to Them, by Sex, Race/Ethnicity, and Grade—United States, Youth Risk Behavior Survey, 2015," in "Youth Risk Behavior Surveillance—United States, 2015," *MMWR*, vol. 65, no. 6, June 10, 2016, https://www.cdc.gov/healthyyouth/data/yrbs/pdf/2015/ss6506_updated.pdf (accessed January 10, 2017)

As of July 2004, all 50 states, the District of Columbia, and Puerto Rico had lowered the legal blood alcohol concentration (BAC) limit for driving to 0.08 g/dL. The NHTSA estimates that between 1975 and 2014 the minimum drinking age laws saved approximately 30,323 lives. All 50 states and the District of Columbia have zero-tolerance laws for drinking drivers under the age of 21 years. It is illegal for drivers under the age of 21 years to drive with BAC levels of 0.02 g/dL or greater.

TOBACCO AND YOUTH

Health Consequences of Early Tobacco Use

Andrea Várkonyi et al. indicate in "Polyphenol Associated-DNA Adducts in Lung and Blood Mononuclear Cells from Lung Cancer Patients" (*Cancer Letters*, vol. 236, no. 1, May 8, 2006) that the age at which smoking is initiated is a significant factor in the risk of developing lung cancer. Smoking during the teen years appears to cause permanent genetic changes in the lungs, increasing the risk of lung cancer—even if the smoker quits. The younger a person starts smoking, the more lasting damage is done to his or her lungs. Such damage is less likely among smokers who start in their 20s.

In *Preventing Tobacco Use among Young People: A Report of the Surgeon General* (1994, https://profiles.nlm.nih.gov/NN/B/C/L/Q/_/nnbclq.pdf), the U.S. surgeon general indicates that cigarette smoking during adolescence seems to retard lung growth and reduce maximum lung function. As a result, young smokers are less likely than their nonsmoking peers to be physically fit and more likely to experience shortness of breath, coughing spells, wheezing, and overall poorer health. These health problems pose a clear risk for developing other chronic conditions in adulthood, such as chronic obstructive pulmonary disease, including emphysema and chronic bronchitis. Early smoking is also linked to an increased risk of cardiovascular diseases, such as high cholesterol and triglyceride levels, atherosclerosis (a hardening of the walls of the arteries caused by the buildup of fatty deposits on the inner walls of the arteries that interferes with blood flow), and early onset of heart disease.

The surgeon general also points out that the use of smokeless tobacco has undesirable health effects on young users. Adolescent use is linked to the development of periodontal disease, soft-tissue damage, and oral cancers. In addition, young people who use smokeless tobacco are more likely than their nonusing peers to become cigarette smokers.

Tobacco Regulation and Youth

In June 2009 President Barack Obama (1961–) signed the Family Smoking Prevention and Tobacco Control Act, which granted the U.S. Food and Drug Administration (FDA) the power to regulate the production and marketing of tobacco products. The FDA outlines in "Overview of the Family Smoking Prevention and Tobacco Control Act" (November 2015, https://www.fda.gov/downloads/TobaccoProducts/Labeling/RulesRegulationsGuidance/UCM336940.pdf) key points of the law. Under the law, cigarette manufacturers were no longer allowed to produce flavored cigarettes (with the exception of menthol and tobacco), which appealed to adolescents and teens. In June 2010 provisions went into effect that banned marketing tactics that appealed to young

TABLE 5.9

Percentage of high school students who smoked cigars and who used smokeless tobacco, by gender, ethnicity, and grade, 2015

	Current smokeless tobacco use			Current cigar use		
	Female	Male	Total	Female	Male	Total
Category	%	%	%	%	%	%
Race/ethnicity						
White*	2.5	15.9	9.3	6.0	14.8	10.4
Black*	1.1	5.6	3.7	8.5	12.9	11.0
Hispanic	2.5	6.4	4.5	6.5	12.4	9.5
Grade						
9	2.4	8.8	5.9	4.1	8.5	6.6
10	2.0	10.6	6.3	6.6	12.5	9.6
11	2.9	15.0	9.3	6.3	15.1	11.0
12	1.7	13.1	7.5	8.1	20.4	14.3
Total	**2.3**	**11.9**	**7.3**	**6.3**	**14.0**	**10.3**

*Non-Hispanic.
Notes: "Currently used smokeless tobacco" means chewing tobacco, snuff, or dip on at least 1 day during the 30 days before the survey. "Currently smoked cigars" means cigars, cigarillos, or little cigards on at least 1 day during the 30 days before the survey.

SOURCE: Laura Kann et al., "Table 39. Percentage of High School Students Who Currently Used Smokeless Tobacco and Who Currently Smoked Cigars, by Sex, Race/Ethnicity, and Grade—United States, Youth Risk Behavior Survey, 2015," in "Youth Risk Behavior Surveillance—United States, 2015," *MMWR*, vol. 65, no. 6, June 10, 2016, https://www.cdc.gov/healthyyouth/data/yrbs/pdf/2015/ss6506_updated.pdf (accessed January 10, 2017)

smokers, such as advertising cigarettes at sporting events, giving away clothing with cigarette company logos, and distributing free samples of tobacco products to youth. The law also called for "revised and strengthened" warning labels to appear on all tobacco products by July 2011; however, this requirement was successfully challenged by the tobacco industry in federal court. (See Chapter 3.)

Age of First Use

Although the health effects of early tobacco use are known, most cigarette smokers begin their habit early in life. According to Miech et al., 3.8% of the eighth graders surveyed in 2015 said they had their first cigarette by the fifth grade, and 6.6% said they had their first cigarette by the sixth grade. In contrast, just 3.3% of the 12th graders who were surveyed said they had their first cigarette by the sixth grade.

Miech et al. reveal that smokeless tobacco use begins early in life as well. Smokeless tobacco is chewing tobacco or finer-cut tobacco that is inhaled (snuff). The highest rates of initiation in smokeless tobacco use are in grades seven to 11. In 2015, 3.7% of the eighth graders surveyed reported they began using smokeless tobacco by the sixth grade, and another 4.9% started by the eighth grade.

Current Use of Tobacco by High School Students

According to SAMHSA, in *Key Substance Use and Mental Health Indicators in the United States: Results from the 2015 National Survey on Drug Use and Health*, 4.2% of students aged 12 to 17 years smoked cigarettes in the month before the survey in 2015. The use of cigarettes among this age group declined from 13% in 2002. The rates of monthly cigar use among 12- to 17-year-olds also fell during this span, from 4.5% in 2002 to 2.1% in 2015.

In "Youth Risk Behavior Surveillance—United States, 2015," Kann et al. focus on students in grades nine to 12. The researchers note that 10.8% of high school students in 2015 reported being current cigarette smokers. They also find that among of high school students in 2015, 10.3% were current cigar smokers and 7.3% were current smokeless tobacco users. (See Table 5.9).

Trends in Prevalence of Cigarette Use by High School Students

In "Youth Risk Behavior Surveillance—United States, 2015," Kann et al. look for trends in the prevalence of cigarette smoking by high school students between 1991 and 2015. Their results reveal that in 2015, 10.8% of high school students were current cigarette smokers. This rate was down from 27.5% in 1991. Current cigarette smoking rates rose from 1991 to 1997, however, to a high of 36.4% in 1997 before falling in the ensuing years to the 2015 level. In 2015, 12.6% of high school students bought cigarettes in a store or gas station. (See Table 5.10.) Male high school students (16.5%) were considerably more likely than female high school students (7.7%) to purchase cigarettes in a store or gas station.

What are the causes of the general decrease in current smoking rates among high school students after 1997? Miech et al. provide a possible answer to this question:

A series of public events, such as highly visible lawsuits against the tobacco industry, brought considerable adverse publicity to the product and the industry, eventually leading to the widely publicized Tobacco Master Settlement Agreement in November 1998 between the

TABLE 5.10

Percentage of high school students who purchased their own cigarettes from a store or gas station or over the Internet, by gender, ethnicity, and grade, 2015

	Bought cigarettes in a store or gas station			Bought cigarettes on the Internet		
	Female	Male	Total	Female	Male	Total
Category	%	%	%	%	%	%
Race/ethnicity						
White[a]	6.6	12.8	**9.7**	0.1	0.2	**0.1**
Black[a]	b	b	b	b	b	b
Hispanic	9.8	21.9	**17.5**	0.6	0.9	**0.8**
Grade						
9	6.4	6.2	**6.3**	0.0	0.3	**0.2**
10	5.6	6.7	**6.1**	0.4	2.5	**1.3**
11	8.8	27.1	**20.2**	0.0	0.5	**0.5**
12	10.7	22.8	**16.5**	0.9	3.8	**2.3**
Total	**7.7**	**16.5**	**12.6**	**0.3**	**1.4**	**1.0**

[a]Non-Hispanic.
[b]Not available.
Note: The buying of cigarettes at a store or a gas station occurs during the 30 days before the survey, among the 8.5% of students nationwide who currently smoked cigarettes and who were aged <18 years.

SOURCE: Laura Kann et al., "Table 35. Percentage of High School Students Who Usually Obtained Their Own Cigarettes by Buying Them in a Store or Gas Station and Who Usually Obtained Their Own Cigarettes by Buying Them on the Internet, by Sex, Race/Ethnicity, and Grade—United States, Youth Risk Behavior Survey, 2015," in "Youth Risk Behavior Surveillance—United States, 2015," *MMWR*, vol. 65, no. 6, June 10, 2016, https://www.cdc.gov/healthyyouth/data/yrbs/pdf/2015/ss6506_updated.pdf (accessed January 10, 2017)

states' Attorneys General and the major tobacco companies. Additional deterrents included increased cigarette prices, increased tobacco taxes, substantial tobacco prevention efforts in several large states, antismoking ad campaigns (the largest of which was funded by the American Legacy Foundation—an entity created and funded under the tobacco settlement), the withdrawal of advertising from billboards, and the elimination of the Joe Camel ads (that we believe may have been particularly successful with adolescent boys from the upper end of the socioeconomic spectrum).

According to Kann et al., lifetime cigarette use among high school students was also lower in 2015 (32.3%) than in 1991. In 1991, 70.1% of all high school students had tried smoking. The lifetime rates did not begin to fall, however, until 2000. The percentage of high school students who were current, frequent users of cigarettes in 2015 (3.4%) was also down from 1991 (12.7%), as was the percentage of students who smoked more than 10 cigarettes per day (7.9% in 2015 versus 18% in 1991).

Tobacco Use among College Students and Other Young Adults

Johnston et al. report on the prevalence of cigarette use for college students and young adults. In 2015 the rates of current cigarette smoking for young adults was lowest for 18-year-olds (11.4%) and 19- to 20-year-olds (14.8%). Figures for current smokers were slightly higher for the 21- to 24-year-old range—17% to 18.1%. Johnston et al. note that beginning in around 2004 smoking rates began to fall steadily among both college students and young adults. The decline was slightly more notable among college students. In 2004, 24.3% of college students were current smokers; by 2015 this figure had dropped to 11.3%. By comparison, current smoking rates among all young adults aged 19 to 20 years fell from 27.9% to 14.8% during this same span; among all young adults aged 21 to 22 years, smoking rates fell from 31.3% in 2004 to 17% in 2015.

Demographic Factors in Youth Tobacco Use

GENDER, RACIAL, AND ETHNIC DIFFERENCES. According to Kann et al., in "Youth Risk Behavior Surveillance—United States, 2015," male high school students were much more likely to be current cigar smokers (14% for males versus 6.3% for females) and current smokeless tobacco users (11.9% for males versus 2.3% for females). (See Table 5.9.) According to Miech et al., there were similar differences in current smokeless tobacco use in 2015 between males and females in grades eight (4% for males versus 2.3% for females), 10 (7.9% versus 1.8%), and 12 (10.7% versus 1.6%).

Looking at current cigarette use alone, Miech et al. indicate that whereas female rates of cigarette smoking were slightly higher than that of males in the eighth grade (3.7% for females versus 3.3% for males) and 10th grade (6.3% for females versus 6.1% for males), rates were substantially higher for males than females in the 12th grade (13% versus 9.1%).

Johnston et al. note that in 2015 male college students (15.5%) had a higher rate of current cigarette smoking than females (8.8%), but it has not always been that way. From 1980 to 1994 female college students were more likely to be current smokers than male college students. In 1994 their current rates of smoking were roughly the same—just under 25%. The rates for both increased during the mid- to late 1990s, with males generally leading females, but then both rates dropped to the 1994 level again in 2005, and dropped even further by 2011. Current smoking rates among male college students subsequently rose in both 2012 and 2013, before falling in 2014 and 2015. At the same time, the percentage of female college students who were current smokers dropped sharply between 2011 and 2012, then rose slightly in 2013 before declining steadily in 2014 and 2015.

Kann et al. note that non-Hispanic white (12.4%) high school students were more likely than Hispanic (9.2%) and non-Hispanic African American (6.5%) high school students to be current cigarette smokers in 2015. They also report that this pattern persisted with current smokeless tobacco use (9.3% of non-Hispanic whites, 4.5% of Hispanics, and 3.7% of non-Hispanic African Americans). (See Table 5.9.) Non-Hispanic African American (11%) high school students had a higher prevalence of current cigar smoking than non-Hispanic white (10.4%) and Hispanic (9.5%) high school students.

WHERE STUDENTS LIVE. Miech et al. look at population density as a factor in student patterns of tobacco use. Eighth, 10th, and 12th graders who lived in the largest cities in the United States in 2015 (large MSAs such as Boston, Los Angeles, and New York) were the least likely to be current cigarette smokers. Those who lived in smaller cities (other MSAs) were somewhat more likely to be current smokers, and those who lived in rural areas (non-MSAs) were the most likely to be current smokers. The American Lung Association cites in *Cutting Tobacco's Rural Roots: Tobacco Use in Rural Communities* (2012, http://www.lung.org/assets/documents/research/cutting-tobaccos-rural-roots.pdf) a number of factors that might explain higher smoking rates among rural adolescents, such as "poverty, stress and targeting by the tobacco industry," as well as a "greater level of social acceptance of smoking." Meanwhile, the association indicates that a number of rural communities in the South are economically dependent on the tobacco industry, which may also contribute to an increased prevalence of smoking. It also notes that numerous studies have identified a correlation between lower levels of income and education and increased smoking rates. Because residents of rural areas tend to be poorer and less educated than those living in suburban and urban areas, the higher prevalence of smoking among rural high school students is not unusual.

PARENTAL EDUCATION. Miech et al. note an inverse relationship between current daily cigarette use among high school students and parental education: the less parental education, the more likely eighth, 10th, and 12th graders were to be current daily smokers in 2015. In addition, students in all three grades who had no college plans or had plans to complete less than four years of college were much more likely to be current smokers and to have used smokeless tobacco than those students who had plans to complete four years of college.

Perception of Harmfulness of Tobacco Use

According to Pride Surveys, a private company that measures adolescent drug use in the United States, in *Pride Surveys: Questionnaire Report for Grades 6 to 12, National Summary Statistics for 2011–12* (April 26, 2014, http://www.pridesurveys.com/customercenter/us11ns.pdf), 71.3% of sixth graders perceived the use of tobacco as "very harmful." Between 64.5% and 66.4% of ninth, 10th, 11th, and 12th graders perceived tobacco use as being very harmful. Although the perception of risk of tobacco use stayed relatively steady in grades nine to 12, the use of tobacco increased in these grades as the grade level increased, as noted by Kann et al. in "Youth Risk Behavior Surveillance—United States, 2015."

ILLICIT DRUGS AND YOUTH
Age of First Use

The use of alcohol and tobacco often begins early in life; the initiation data are presented previously in this chapter. Regarding the initiation of other drugs, Miech et al. reveal that inhalants and marijuana are the drugs next most likely to be initiated early in life. Peak initiation rates for illicit drugs other than marijuana generally do not occur until grades nine to 11 in high school, and initiation rates for hallucinogens, amphetamines, and tranquilizers tend to be in grades 10 to 12. Miech et al. state:

Of all 12th graders who reported prior use of each drug, the proportions reporting their initial use of that drug *by the end of grade 9* are presented below:

- inhalants (68%)
- cigarettes (55%)
- crack (53%)
- heroin (50%)
- alcohol (48%)
- smokeless tobacco (48%)
- marijuana (45%)
- sedatives (barbiturates) (41%)
- been drunk (36%)
- narcotics other than heroin (33%)
- steroids (30%)
- amphetamines (30%)
- cocaine (30%)
- hallucinogens other than LSD (29%)
- tranquilizers (26%)

- cocaine powder (24%)

- hallucinogens (23%)

- LSD (19%)

Trends in Annual Prevalence of Drug Use in Youth

TRENDS ACROSS FIVE POPULATIONS. Annual prevalence means that a person has tried a particular drug at least once during the year before being surveyed about its use. Figure 5.2 compares trends in the annual prevalence of drug use across five populations: eighth-, 10th-, and 12th-grade students; full-time college students aged 19 to 22 years; and all young adults through the age of 28 years who are high school graduates (a group that includes college students). During the early to mid-1980s the rates of drug use decreased, and college students had roughly the same rate of drug use as high school seniors. During the late 1980s, when data for young adults were added, the annual prevalence rates of drug use in all three groups declined dramatically. The annual prevalence of drug use by college students and 12th graders was about the same during those years, and the annual prevalence of drug use by young adults was slightly lower.

In 1991 data for eighth and 10th graders were added. The annual prevalence of drug use rose dramatically for high school students for several years, peaking during the second half of the 1990s. The increase was somewhat less dramatic for college students. The annual prevalence of drug use increase for young adults was also relatively minor. Indeed, by 1997 the annual prevalence of drug use for 10th and 12th graders was higher than the annual prevalence for college students and young adults. Around 1998, however, the annual prevalence of drug use for 12th graders began to slowly decline. It dropped, then rose, then dropped again for 10th graders, and it dropped dramatically for eighth graders. Nevertheless, the annual prevalence rates continued to slowly climb for young adults and eventually dropped somewhat for college students. In 2005 the annual prevalence rate of drug use was the highest for 12th graders at nearly 40%, followed by college students at about 38%, young adults at about 33%, 10th graders at about 30%, and eighth graders at about 17%. By 2009 the rates for all three groups of high school students had dropped somewhat from the 2005 rates, whereas the rates for college students and young adults had increased slightly. Between 2009 and 2015

FIGURE 5.2

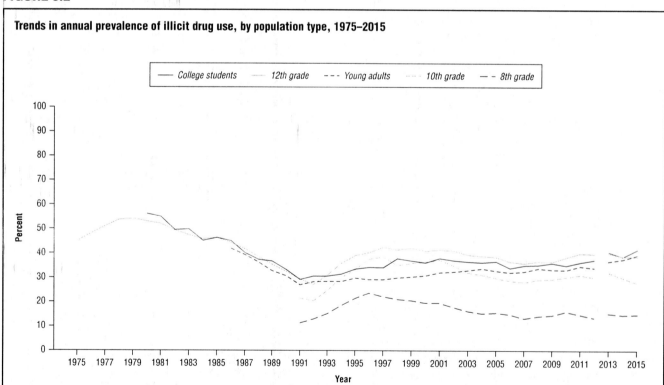

Trends in annual prevalence of illicit drug use, by population type, 1975–2015

Notes: Illicit drug use index includes any use of marijuana, LSD, other hallucinogens, crack, other cocaine, or heroin; or any use of narcotics other than heroin which is not under a doctor's orders, stimulants, sedatives (barbiturates), methaqualone (excluded since 1990), or tranquilizers. Beginning in 1982, the question about stimulant use (i.e., amphetamines) was revised to get respondents to exclude the inappropriate reporting of nonprescription stimulants. The prevalence rate dropped slightly as a result of this methodological change. In 2013, the question on use of amphetamines was changed such that "amphetamines" was replaced with "amphetamines and other stimulant drugs." Data for any illicit drug were affected by this change.

SOURCE: Lloyd D. Johnston et al., "Figure 2-1. Trends in Annual Prevalence of an Illicit Drug Use Index across 5 Populations," in *Monitoring the Future National Survey Results on Drug Use, 1975–2015: Volume 2, College Students and Adults Ages 19–55*, University of Michigan, Ann Arbor, Institute for Social Research, July 2016, http://www.monitoringthefuture.org/pubs/monographs/mtf-vol2_2015.pdf (accessed January 10, 2017)

annual prevalence of drug use among college students and young adults rose. Drug use among eighth graders and 10th graders rose slightly until 2010 and then declined, while drug use among 12th graders increased until 2011 and then fell.

TRENDS IN INHALANT USE IN HIGH SCHOOL STUDENTS. Inhalants are volatile liquids, such as cleaning fluids, glue, gasoline, paint, and turpentine, the vapors of which are inhaled. Sometimes the sprays of aerosols are inhaled, such as those of spray paints, spray deodorants, hair spray, or fabric protector spray. These products may be purchased legally and are easily accessible.

Figure 5.3 shows trends in annual prevalence of inhalant use for eighth, 10th, and 12th graders. Since 1991, when data collection began for all three of these grade levels, eighth graders have had the highest annual prevalence of inhalant use, followed by 10th graders and then 12th graders. Between 1991 and 1995 the annual prevalence of inhalant use rose by more than one-third among eighth graders to reach 12.8% and among 10th graders to reach 9.6%, and rose by about one-fifth among 12th graders to reach 8%. The annual prevalence rates for inhalant use then fell through 2002 for eighth graders to 7.7%, and through 2003 for 10th graders to 5.4% and for 12th graders to 3.9%. Rates rose quite steeply for eighth graders from 2002 until 2004, reaching 9.6%, then dropping to 4.6% by 2015. Rates rose relatively less dramatically through 2007 for 10th graders to 6.6% and through 2005 for 12th graders to 5%. Rates overall fell for both grades between 2007 and 2015. The decline was more dramatic for 10th graders, which saw rates of annual

inhalant use fall from 6.6% in 2007 to 2.9% in 2015; in contrast, annual prevalence of inhalant use among 12th graders experienced a more modest decline, from 3.7% in 2007 to 1.9% in 2015.

TRENDS IN MARIJUANA USE IN HIGH SCHOOL STUDENTS. Besides inhalants, marijuana is one of the first drugs tried by high school students. Miech et al. note that perceptions concerning the risks involved with marijuana use drop considerably as high school students become older. In 2015, 36.8% of eighth graders viewed even occasional marijuana use to pose a "great risk of harm"; this figure dropped to 24.7% of 10th graders and to 15.8% of 12th graders.

Figure 5.4 shows trends in annual prevalence rates of marijuana use for eighth, 10th, and 12th graders. Since 1991, when data collection began for all three of these grade levels, 12th graders have had the highest annual prevalence of marijuana use, followed by 10th graders and then eighth graders. The annual prevalence rate of marijuana use for eighth graders rose from 1991 to 1996, reaching 18.3%. The rate then dropped steadily to 11.8% in 2004 and to 10.3% in 2007. Annual marijuana use rates among eighth graders fluctuated over the next several years, peaking at 13.7% in 2010 before eventually falling to 11.8% in 2015. For 10th graders the annual prevalence rates of marijuana use rose to 34.8% between 1992 and 1997, and for 12th graders in the same period the annual prevalence rates of marijuana use rose to 38.5%. The rates for both groups held relatively steady from 1998 to 2001 and then dropped to the 2007 levels of 24.6% and 31.7%, respectively. After 2008 the annual

FIGURE 5.3

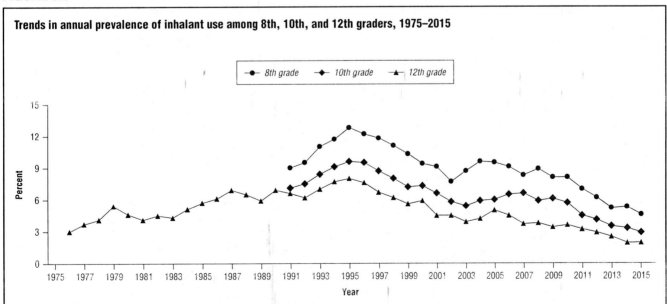

Trends in annual prevalence of inhalant use among 8th, 10th, and 12th graders, 1975–2015

SOURCE: Richard A. Miech et al., "Figure 5-4c. Inhalants: Trends in Annual Prevalence in Grades 8, 10, and 12," in *Monitoring the Future National Survey Results on Drug Use, 1975–2015: Volume 1, Secondary School Students*, University of Michigan, Ann Arbor, Institute for Social Research, June 2016, http://www.monitoringthefuture.org/pubs/monographs/mtf-vol1_2015.pdf (accessed January 10, 2017)

FIGURE 5.4

Trends in annual and 30-day prevalence of daily marijuana use among 8th, 10th, and 12th graders, 1975–2015

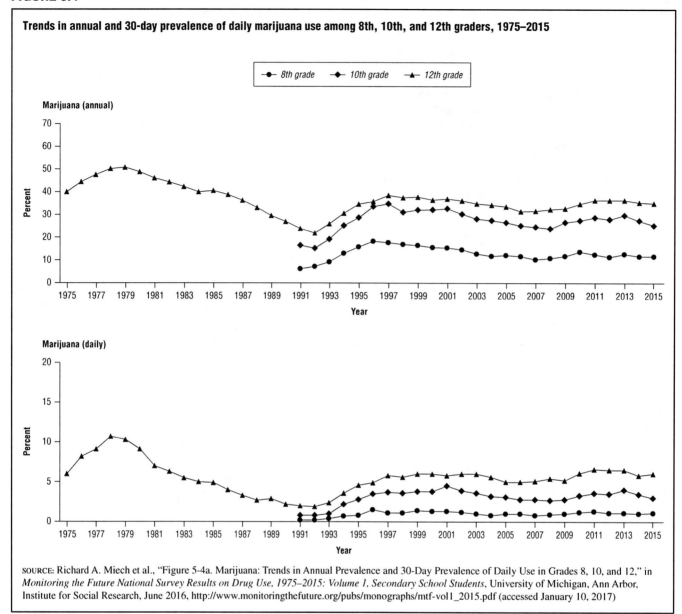

SOURCE: Richard A. Miech et al., "Figure 5-4a. Marijuana: Trends in Annual Prevalence and 30-Day Prevalence of Daily Use in Grades 8, 10, and 12," in *Monitoring the Future National Survey Results on Drug Use, 1975–2015: Volume 1, Secondary School Students,* University of Michigan, Ann Arbor, Institute for Social Research, June 2016, http://www.monitoringthefuture.org/pubs/monographs/mtf-vol1_2015.pdf (accessed January 10, 2017)

prevalence rates for marijuana use began to rise steadily for both groups, reaching 29.8% for 10th graders and 36.4% for 12th graders in 2013. Thereafter, the rates for both grades declined slightly over the next two years, dropping to 25.4% for 10th graders and to 34.9% for 12th graders in 2015.

TRENDS IN TRANQUILIZER USE IN HIGH SCHOOL STUDENTS. Tranquilizers are drugs that are prescribed by a physician to relieve a patient's tension and anxiety. Drugs such as diazepam, chlordiazepoxide, and alprazolam are tranquilizers. This type of drug does not have a high rate of early initiation as inhalants and marijuana do.

Figure 5.5 shows trends in annual prevalence rates of tranquilizer use for eighth, 10th, and 12th graders. Since 1991, when data collection began for all three of these grade levels, 10th and 12th graders have had the highest prevalence of use. Eighth graders have had a lower annual prevalence rate of tranquilizer use. The annual prevalence rate for eighth graders rose slowly from 1.8% in 1991 to 3.3% in 1996. The rate declined slightly to 2.9% in 1997 and then leveled off. The 2015 annual prevalence rate for tranquilizer use by eighth graders was 1.7%.

For 10th graders the annual prevalence rate remained fairly steady between 1991 and 1994. (See Figure 5.5.) The rate proceeded to rise steadily from 3.3% in 1994 to 7.3% in 2001, then declined to 4.8% in 2005. The annual prevalence rate of tranquilizer use among 10th graders continued to fall over the next decade, dropping to 3.9% in 2015. For 12th graders the annual prevalence rate fell from 3.6%

FIGURE 5.5

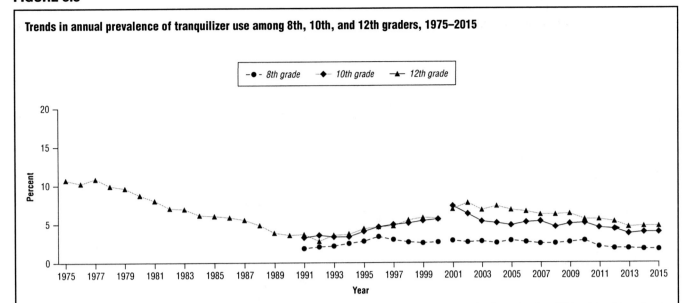

Trends in annual prevalence of tranquilizer use among 8th, 10th, and 12th graders, 1975–2015

- ● - 8th grade   ◆ 10th grade   ▲ 12th grade

Note: Beginning in 2001, a revised set of questions on tranquilizer use was introduced in which Xanax replaced Miltown in the list of examples. From 2001 on data points are based on the revised question.

SOURCE: Richard A. Miech et al., "Figure 5-4m. Tranquilizers: Trends in Annual Prevalence in Grades 8, 10, and 12," in *Monitoring the Future National Survey Results on Drug Use, 1975–2015: Volume 1, Secondary School Students*, University of Michigan, Ann Arbor, Institute for Social Research, June 2016, http://www.monitoringthefuture.org/pubs/monographs/mtf-vol1_2015.pdf (accessed January 10, 2017)

in 1991 to 2.8% in 1992. The rate then rose steadily, reaching 7.7% in 2002. It declined in 2003, rose in 2004, and declined again in 2005. The 2015 annual prevalence rate of tranquilizer use in 12th graders was 4.7%.

TRENDS IN AMPHETAMINE AND METHAMPHETAMINE USE IN HIGH SCHOOL STUDENTS. Amphetamines are stimulants (uppers), drugs that act on the brain and central nervous system to produce a sense of euphoria or wakefulness. They are used to increase alertness, boost endurance and productivity, and suppress the appetite. A derivative of amphetamine, methamphetamine shares many of the same qualities, but with greater potency, longer-lasting effects, and a higher potential for addiction.

Figure 5.6 shows trends in annual prevalence rates of amphetamine use for eighth, 10th, and 12th graders. Since 1991, when data collection began for all three of these grade levels, 10th and 12th graders have had the highest rate of use. From 1992 to 2001, 10th-grade annual prevalence rates were higher than 12th-grade rates. From 1991 to 2015, eighth-grade annual prevalence rates were consistently lower than those of their older classmates.

The annual prevalence rate of amphetamine use for eighth graders rose from 6.2% in 1991 to 9.1% in 1996. (See Figure 5.6.) The rate then declined to 6.9% in 1999 and then declined in short plateaus to 4.1% in 2015. For 10th graders the annual prevalence rate rose from 8.2% in 1991 to 11.7% in 2001, and then declined to 6.8% in 2015. For 12th graders the annual prevalence rate of amphetamine use generally rose throughout the 1990s

and after 2000 in a slight up-and-down fashion, from 8.2% in 1991 to 11.1% in 2002. After 2002 the annual prevalence rate of amphetamine use in 12th graders declined to 6.6% in 2009, before rising to 9.2% in 2013. Annual amphetamine use among 12th graders proceeded to decline over the next two years, falling to 7.7% in 2015.

Annual prevalence for methamphetamine use among high school students has declined steadily since 1999, the first year Monitoring the Future began monitoring use of the drug. (See Figure 5.7.) Among eighth graders the annual prevalence of methamphetamine use fell from 3.2% in 1999 to 0.5% in 2015. The annual prevalence of methamphetamine use dropped even more dramatically among 10th and 12th graders during this span. In 1999, 4.6% of 10th graders and 4.7% of 12th graders had used methamphetamine during the previous year; by 2015 these rates fell to 0.8% and 0.6%, respectively.

TRENDS IN HALLUCINOGEN USE IN HIGH SCHOOL STUDENTS. Hallucinogens, also known as psychedelics, distort the perception of reality. They cause excitation, which can vary from a sense of well-being to severe depression. The experience may be pleasurable or quite frightening. The effects of hallucinogens vary from use to use and cannot be predicted.

Figure 5.8 shows trends in the annual prevalence rates of hallucinogen use for eighth, 10th, and 12th graders. Since 1991, when data collection began for all three of these grade levels, 12th graders have had the

FIGURE 5.6

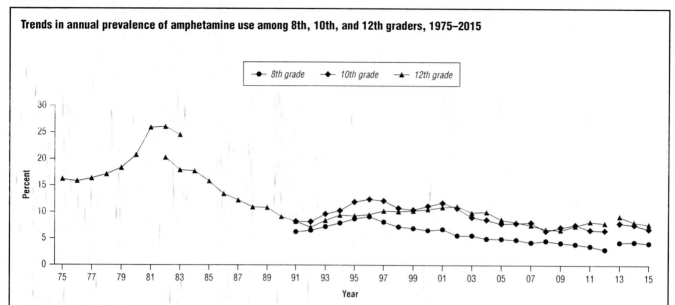

Trends in annual prevalence of amphetamine use among 8th, 10th, and 12th graders, 1975–2015

Note: Beginning in 1982, the lines connect percentages that result if nonprescription stimulants are excluded. In 2013, the text was changed on some of the questionnaire forms for all three grades, with the remaining forms changed in 2014. Data presented here include only the changed forms.

SOURCE: Richard A. Miech et al., "Figure 5-4j. Amphetamines: Trends in Annual Prevalence in Grades 8, 10, and 12," in *Monitoring the Future National Survey Results on Drug Use, 1975–2015: Volume 1, Secondary School Students*, University of Michigan, Ann Arbor, Institute for Social Research, June 2016, http://www.monitoringthefuture.org/pubs/monographs/mtf-vol1_2015.pdf (accessed January 10, 2017)

highest annual prevalence of hallucinogen use, followed by 10th graders and then eighth graders.

The annual prevalence rate of hallucinogen use for eighth graders rose from 1.9% in 1991 to 4.1% in 1996. (See Figure 5.8.) The rate declined to 2.2% in 2004 and then rose slightly to 2.4% in 2005. The rate then remained relatively steady, hovering around 2% through 2011, before falling to 1.3% in 2015. The trend patterns of annual prevalence rates of hallucinogen use for 10th and 12th graders were similar to that of eighth graders and to each other. The annual prevalence rates rose from 4% in 1991 to 7.8% in 1996 for 10th graders and from 5.8% in 1991 to 10.1% in 1996 for 12th graders. The rates for both grades then declined through 2003 to 4.1% for 10th graders and to 5.9% for 12th graders. For 10th graders the rate stayed relatively steady until 2012, when it dropped to 3.5%; this rate fell further in 2015, to 3.1%. For 12th graders the rate rose slightly in 2004 and then dipped to its lowest rate, 4.7%, in 2009. The rate of annual prevalence of hallucinogen use among 12th graders then rose to 5.5% in 2010, before gradually dropping to 4.2% in 2015.

TRENDS IN MDMA USE IN HIGH SCHOOL STUDENTS.
MDMA (3,4-methylenedioxy-methamphetamine), or ecstasy, is a mind-altering drug with hallucinogenic properties. It is related to amphetamine and is created in laboratories by making minor modifications in the chemical structure of this drug. Thus, it is called a designer drug and is one of the most popular of this type of drug.

Figure 5.9 shows trends in the annual prevalence rates of ecstasy use for eighth, 10th, and 12th graders. Since 1996, when data collection began for this drug, 12th graders have had the highest annual prevalence of ecstasy use, followed by 10th graders and then eighth graders.

The annual prevalence rate of MDMA use for eighth graders declined initially from 2.3% in 1996 and 1997 to 1.7% in 1999. (See Figure 5.8.) The rate then peaked in 2001 at 3.5% but then dropped significantly through 2006 to 1.4%, and rose to 1.7% in 2008. In 2009 the rate dropped to 1.3%, before rising again to 2.4% in 2010. By 2015 the rate declined to 1.4%. The trend patterns of annual prevalence rates of MDMA use for 10th and 12th graders were similar to that of eighth graders and to each other, with an initial drop, a sharp peak in 2001, a drop through 2004 and 2005, and then an increase through 2007. After a drop in 2008, the rate for 10th graders was 2.4% in 2015 and for 12th graders was 3.6%. The peak annual prevalence rate for MDMA use for 10th graders was 6.2% and for 12th graders was 9.2%, both in 2001.

ABUSE OF NONPRESCRIPTION COUGH AND COLD MEDICINES. In 2006 Monitoring the Future added dextromethorphan to its questionnaires for eighth, 10th, and 12th graders. Dextromethorphan is a cough suppressant that is found in over-the-counter (nonprescription) cough and cold remedies. Students were asked how often they took cough or cold medicines to get high. Miech et al. note that 4.2% of eighth graders, 5.3% of 10th graders, and 6.9% of 12th graders were current abusers of this drug in 2006. In 2015

FIGURE 5.7

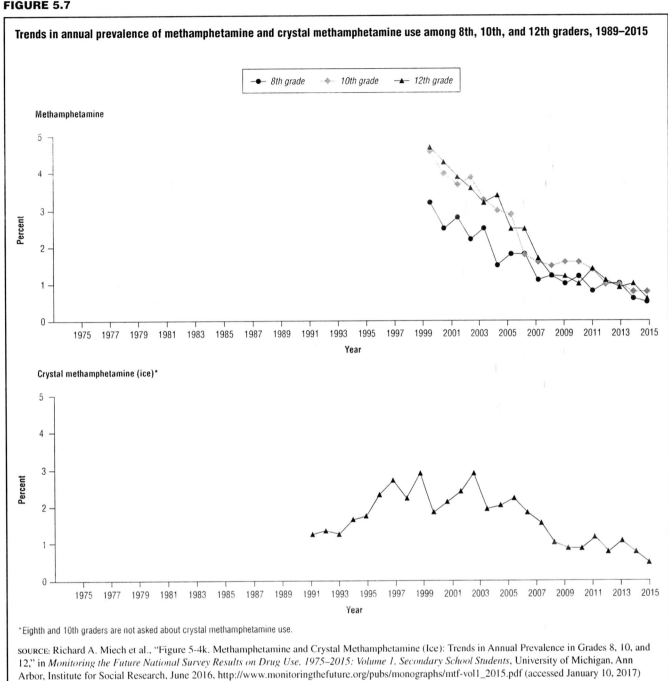

Trends in annual prevalence of methamphetamine and crystal methamphetamine use among 8th, 10th, and 12th graders, 1989–2015

*Eighth and 10th graders are not asked about crystal methamphetamine use.

SOURCE: Richard A. Miech et al., "Figure 5-4k. Methamphetamine and Crystal Methamphetamine (Ice): Trends in Annual Prevalence in Grades 8, 10, and 12," in *Monitoring the Future National Survey Results on Drug Use, 1975–2015: Volume 1, Secondary School Students*, University of Michigan, Ann Arbor, Institute for Social Research, June 2016, http://www.monitoringthefuture.org/pubs/monographs/mtf-vol1_2015.pdf (accessed January 10, 2017)

the rates were substantially lower for all three grades, at 1.6%, 3.3%, and 4.6%, respectively.

NEW DRUGS. Each decade, new and potentially harmful drugs gain popularity among young people. As data about use of these drugs emerge, Monitoring the Future includes this information in its annual surveys. For instance, Adderall, a stimulant that is used in the treatment of attention-deficit/hyperactivity disorder, is sometimes used for nonprescription purposes among high school students. Monitoring the Future first began surveying high school students concerning annual prevalence of Adderall use in 2009. Miech et al. indicate that in that year 10th graders (5.7%) were the most likely to have taken Adderall in the previous year, followed by 12th graders (5.4%) and eighth graders (2%). In 2015 annual prevalence of Adderall use had risen to 7.5% among 12th graders, while dropping among both 10th (5.2%) and eighth (1%) graders.

The NIDA notes in "DrugFacts: Hallucinogens" (January 2016, https://www.drugabuse.gov/publications/drugfacts/hallucinogens) that salvia is an herb, indigenous to southern Mexico and Central and South America, and is known to induce hallucinations, sensory disorientation, and in some cases psychotic episodes when

FIGURE 5.8

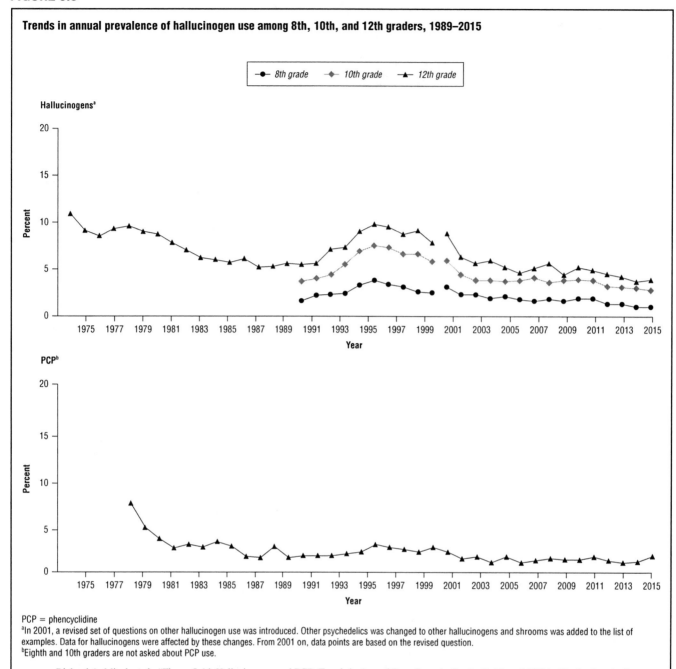

Trends in annual prevalence of hallucinogen use among 8th, 10th, and 12th graders, 1989–2015

— ●— 8th grade   — ◆— 10th grade   — ▲— 12th grade

Hallucinogens[a]

PCP[b]

PCP = phencyclidine

[a] In 2001, a revised set of questions on other hallucinogen use was introduced. Other psychedelics was changed to other hallucinogens and shrooms was added to the list of examples. Data for hallucinogens were affected by these changes. From 2001 on, data points are based on the revised question.
[b] Eighth and 10th graders are not asked about PCP use.

SOURCE: Richard A. Miech et al., "Figure 5-4d. Hallucinogens and PCP: Trends in Annual Prevalence in Grades 8, 10, and 12," in *Monitoring the Future National Survey Results on Drug Use, 1975–2015: Volume 1, Secondary School Students*, University of Michigan, Ann Arbor, Institute for Social Research, June 2016, http://www.monitoringthefuture.org/pubs/monographs/mtf-vol1_2015.pdf (accessed January 10, 2017)

chewed or smoked. Monitoring the Future began tracking salvia use among 12th graders in 2009, and among eighth and 10th graders the following year. According to Miech et al., in 2015 annual prevalence of salvia use among eighth, 10th, and 12th graders was 0.7%, 1.2%, and 1.9%, respectively. In 2011 Monitoring the Future also began tracking annual prevalence of synthetic marijuana use among 12th graders, which Miech et al. note was 11.4% that year. Synthetic marijuana consists of natural herbs that are sprayed with synthetic cannabinoids, and then are legally marketed as "herbal incense" or "herbal smoke."

In 2012 annual prevalence of synthetic marijuana use was 4.4% among eighth graders, 8.8% among 10th graders, and 11.3% among 12th graders. These rates fell for all three grades over the next three years, to 3.1%, 4.3%, and 5.2%, respectively, by 2015.

Another potentially dangerous drug, generally known as "bath salts," first began gaining popularity around 2010. Bath salts, which are legally marketed under brand names such as Cloud Nine and Drone, have been known to cause hallucinations, panic attacks, and in some cases

FIGURE 5.9

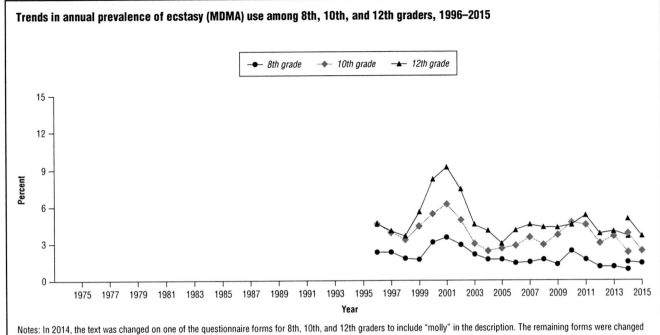

Trends in annual prevalence of ecstasy (MDMA) use among 8th, 10th, and 12th graders, 1996–2015

Notes: In 2014, the text was changed on one of the questionnaire forms for 8th, 10th, and 12th graders to include "molly" in the description. The remaining forms were changed in 2015. Data for both versions of the question are presented here.

SOURCE: Richard A. Miech et al., "Figure 5-4f. Ecstasy (MDMA): Trends in Annual Prevalence in Grades 8, 10, and 12," in *Monitoring the Future National Survey Results on Drug Use, 1975–2015: Volume 1, Secondary School Students*, University of Michigan, Ann Arbor, Institute for Social Research, June 2016, http://www.monitoringthefuture.org/pubs/monographs/mtf-vol1_2015.pdf (accessed January 10, 2017)

heart failure. In spite of these hazards, high school students remain particularly at risk for experimenting with bath salts. Monitoring the Future began adding data concerning the use of bath salts in its 2012 survey. Miech et al. indicated that in that year 0.8% of eighth graders, 0.6% of 10th graders, and 1.3% of 12th graders admitted to using bath salts during the past year. These rates rose for eighth and 10th graders in 2013, to 1% and 0.9%, respectively, while falling to 0.9% for 12th graders. In 2015 rates of annual prevalence of bath salts use were 0.4% among eighth graders, 0.7% among 10th graders, and 1% among 12th graders.

A Youth Phenomenon

Miech et al. sum up the situation of drugs and youth quite well: "Young people are often at the leading edge of social change, and this has been particularly true of drug use. The massive upsurge in illicit drug use during the last 50 or so years has proven to be largely a youth phenomenon, and Monitoring the Future documented that the relapse in the drug epidemic in the early 1990s initially occurred almost exclusively among adolescents. Adolescents and adults in their 20s fall into the age groups at highest risk for illicit drug use. Moreover, for some drug users, use that begins in adolescence continues well into adulthood."

CHAPTER 6
DRUG TREATMENT

DRUG ABUSE AND ADDICTION

Psychiatric Definition

Although not all experts agree on a single definition of drug addiction, the American Psychiatric Association's (APA) *Diagnostic and Statistical Manual of Mental Disorders-5* (*DSM-5*; 2013) is the most widely used reference for diagnosing and treating mental illness and substance-related disorders. In the *DSM-5*, the APA classifies all issues relating to substance abuse and dependence into a single category, substance use disorder, which is measured along a spectrum from mild to severe, depending on the number of symptoms.

As is mentioned in Chapter 1, the *DSM-5* lists 11 symptoms related to substance use disorder. Common symptoms include:

- The person has repeatedly failed to live up to major obligations, such as on the job, at school, or in the family, because of drug use

- The person has used the substance in dangerous situations, such as before driving

- The person has had multiple legal problems because of drug use

- The person continues to use drugs in the face of interpersonal problems, such as arguments or fights caused by substance use

The *DSM-5* requires that at least two to three of the 11 symptoms be present before an individual is diagnosed with mild substance abuse disorder; the presence of four to five symptoms indicates a moderate disorder, while six or more symptoms are associated with severe substance use disorder.

The National Institute on Drug Abuse Definition

In *Drugs, Brains, and Behavior: The Science of Addiction* (July 2014, https://www.drugabuse.gov/sites/default/files/soa_2014.pdf), the National Institute on Drug Abuse (NIDA) answers the question "What is drug addiction?" the following way: "Addiction is defined as a chronic, relapsing brain disease that is characterized by compulsive drug seeking and use, despite harmful consequences. It is considered a brain disease because drugs change the brain—they change its structure and how it works. These brain changes can be long lasting, and can lead to the harmful behaviors seen in people who abuse drugs.... Addiction is a lot like other diseases, such as heart disease. Both disrupt the normal, healthy functioning of the underlying organ, have serious harmful consequences, and are preventable and treatable, but if left untreated, can last a lifetime."

Disease Model of Addiction

Beginning in the 1980s advances in neuroscience led to a new understanding of how people become addicted to drugs and why they stay that way. As reflected in the NIDA definition, most psychiatric and medical researchers espouse the disease model of addiction. Addicts, they say, respond to drugs differently than people who are not addicted. Much of the difference is associated with differences in brain functioning and can be linked to genetic factors. According to George R. Uhl et al., in "Molecular Genetics of Addiction and Related Heritable Phenotypes" (*Annals of the New York Academy of Sciences*, vol. 1141, October 2008), drug addiction is a disease that is linked to the effects of many genes as well as to environmental factors. Approaches to treatment emphasize that addiction must be treated in the same way as other chronic diseases.

In "Evidence-Based Treatments of Addiction" (*Philosophical Transactions of the Royal Society*, vol. 363, no. 1507, October 12, 2008), Charles P. O'Brien of the University of Pennsylvania points out that modern definitions of addiction (such as the NIDA definition) emphasize "uncontrolled drug use rather than tolerance and physiological dependence as essential features of the disorder." He adds that "it is generally recognized that addiction has strong hereditary influences and once established, it behaves as a chronic brain disorder with relapses and remissions over the long term." To help understand this pattern of compulsive behavior and its importance, O'Brien suggests that one only need to think of a friend, relative, or acquaintance who has tried to give up smoking only to relapse at some later time, and probably multiple times, into compulsive smoking behavior while knowing full well the health consequences of his or her actions.

An Integrated Approach to Treatment

The modern approach to treatment has come to reflect the complexity of the drug abuse–addiction spectrum and combines medical approaches, behavior modification, education, and social support functions that are intended to redress imbalances in the patient's total environment. The components of a comprehensive drug treatment approach are shown in Figure 6.1. Arrayed in the

center are categories of treatment used alone or in combination and, on the periphery, social service functions that may have to be deployed to solve some of the patient's problems that led to drug use or addiction in the first place.

TREATMENT FACILITIES
National Survey of Substance Abuse Treatment Services Data

The Substance Abuse and Mental Health Services Administration (SAMHSA) has been collecting data on substance abuse facilities since 1976. One of its current programs is the National Survey of Substance Abuse Treatment Services (N-SSATS). The N-SSATS numbers represent a snapshot of the treatment units on a particular day and do not indicate how many people are being treated over the course of an entire year.

SAMHSA reports in *National Survey of Substance Abuse Treatment Services (N-SSATS): 2014* (March 2016, https://www.samhsa.gov/data/sites/default/files/2014 _National_Survey_of_Substance_Abuse_Treatment_Services/ 2014_National_Survey_of_Substance_Abuse_Treatment

FIGURE 6.1

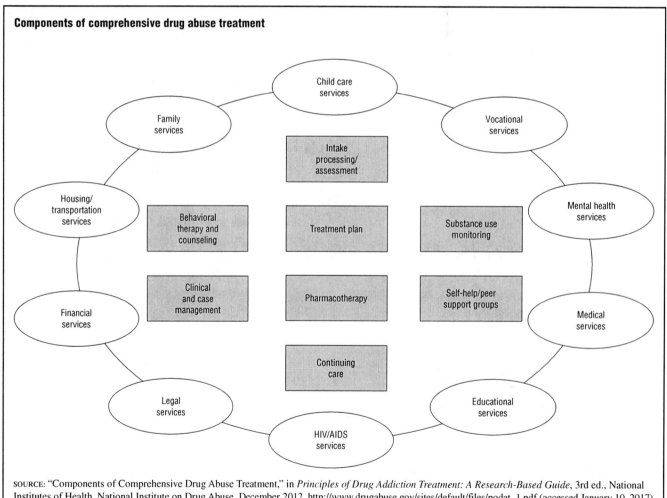

Components of comprehensive drug abuse treatment

SOURCE: "Components of Comprehensive Drug Abuse Treatment," in *Principles of Drug Addiction Treatment: A Research-Based Guide*, 3rd ed., National Institutes of Health, National Institute on Drug Abuse, December 2012, http://www.drugabuse.gov/sites/default/files/podat_1.pdf (accessed January 10, 2017)

_Services/2014_National_Survey_of_Substance_Abuse_Treatment_Services.pdf) that as of 2014, the number of treatment facilities that responded to the N-SSATS stood at 14,152. (See Table 6.1.) More than one-tenth (1,454) of these facilities were in California.

Of the 14,152 facilities offering substance abuse treatment in 2014, 11,618 (82.1%) offered outpatient care. (See Table 6.1.) Nearly a quarter (3,473, or 24.5%) offered nonhospital residential care, while 762 (5.4%) provided hospital inpatient treatment.

Overall, there were 1,312 facilities certified by SAMHSA to provide opioid addiction treatment in 2014. Of these, 1,184 (90.2%) offered outpatient care. An additional 125 facilities (9.5%) provided hospital inpatient services for people receiving treatment for opioid addiction in 2014, while 112 facilities (8.5%) offered nonhospital residential treatment for opioid addiction.

HOW MANY PEOPLE ARE BEING TREATED?
National Survey on Drug Use and Health Data

To collect data from people who seek and receive substance abuse treatment, SAMHSA included questions about treatment in its 2015 National Survey on Drug Use and Health and published its findings in *Key Substance Use and Mental Health Indicators in the United States: Results from the 2015 National Survey on Drug Use and Health* (September 2016, https://www.samhsa.gov/data/sites/default/files/NSDUH-FFR1-2015/NSDUH-FFR1-2015/NSDUH-FFR1-2015.pdf). Figure 6.2 shows the results of a survey asking recipients whether or not they needed treatment for substance use during the past year. SAMHSA defines individuals needing treatment as those who either suffered from substance use disorder or received treatment for substance use disorder at a specialized facility at some point during the past year. As Figure 6.2 shows, 21.7 million individuals aged 12 years and older needed substance abuse treatment in 2015; this figure represented 8.1% of all people in that age group. Among young adults between the ages of 18 and 25 years, more than 5.4 million (15.5%) needed substance abuse treatment in 2015. In addition, 1.3 million (5.1%) adolescents between the ages of 12 and 17 years needed substance abuse treatment that year.

SAMHSA also asked substance abusers whether or not they received treatment in 2015. Of the 21.7 million individuals aged 12 years and older who needed treatment that year, only 3 million (14%) actually received treatment for substance abuse. (See Figure 6.3.) Among individuals needing treatment for substance abuse, those aged 26 years and older (2.3 million, or 15.5%) were the most likely to receive treatment; by contrast, young people between the ages of 18 and 25 years (563,000, or 10.4%) who needed treatment for substance abuse were the least likely to receive treatment that year.

According to SAMHSA, 20.8 million people aged 12 years and older suffered from substance use disorder in 2015. This figure represented 7.8% of all individuals in that age group. Incidences of substance abuse disorder were typically higher among adults suffering from mental illness. As Figure 6.4 shows, nearly one out of five (8.1 million, or 18.7%) adults aged 18 years and older who struggled with mental illness also struggled with substance use disorder in 2015.

Treatment Episode Data Set Data

Another source of data for the drug-treatment population comes from SAMHSA's Treatment Episode Data Set (TEDS). This program counts admissions over the period of a year rather than the number of people in treatment on a particular day during the year. When the same person is admitted two or more times during the same year, he or she is counted for each of those admissions, whereas the N-SSATS counts individuals only once. SAMHSA reports in *Treatment Episode Data Set (TEDS) 2003–2013: National Admissions to Substance Abuse Treatment Services* (December 2015, https://www.samhsa.gov/data/sites/default/files/2003_2013_TEDS_National/2003_2013_Treatment_Episode_Data_Set_National.pdf) that there were nearly 1.7 million TEDS admissions in 2013.

CHARACTERISTICS OF THOSE ADMITTED

TEDS data from 2003 to 2013 on admissions by sex, age, race, and ethnicity are presented in Table 6.2 and Table 6.3.

Gender

In *Treatment Episode Data Set (TEDS) 2003–2013*, SAMHSA indicates that males represented most of those who were admitted for drug and/or alcohol treatment, although the percentage of men dropped slightly between 2003 and 2013 (from 69.1% to 66.3%) and that of women increased (from 30.9% to 33.7%). The number of males admitted for treatment in 2013 was more than 1.1 million versus 565,906 female admissions. (See Table 6.2.) These results and data reflect that a greater proportion of men than women abuse drugs in the United States. According to Table 4.1 in Chapter 4, 12.5% of males were past-month (current) users in 2015, compared with 7.9% of females.

Age

In 2003, 35- to 39-year-olds accounted for 282,422 of the nearly 1.9 million people receiving substance abuse treatment, the largest number out of any age group; this age demographic was followed by those aged 40 to 44 years (280,378). (See Table 6.2.) Ten years later, of the nearly 1.7 million people receiving treatment for substance

TABLE 6.1

Type of care offered at substance abuse treatment facilities, by state, 2014

		Number of facilities[b]												
		Type of care offered												
		Outpatient							Residential (non-hospital)			Hospital inpatient		
State or jurisdiction[a]	Total	Any out-patient	Regular	Intensive	Day treatment or partial hospitalization	Detox	Methadone/ buprenorphine maintenance or injectable naltrexone[d] treatment	Any residential	Short-term	Long-term	Detox	Any hospital inpatient	Treatment	Detox
Total	**14,152**	**11,618**	**10,826**	**6,409**	**1,759**	**1,422**	**2,498**	**3,473**	**1,785**	**2,845**	**914**	**762**	**550**	**664**
Alabama	144	113	83	67	14	18	29	31	17	20	3	10	7	9
Alaska	91	78	78	50	10	7	8	24	9	20	3	2	—	2
Arizona	317	263	234	167	31	33	59	80	41	69	19	23	18	21
Arkansas	81	73	71	41	24	3	9	25	18	23	14	8	5	7
California	1,454	1,041	924	592	242	219	200	547	313	501	176	46	38	41
Colorado	452	415	407	230	23	19	34	61	29	46	18	12	10	10
Connecticut	204	153	131	92	28	29	47	56	25	40	3	14	10	13
Delaware	39	33	31	17	6	7	14	7	3	6	—	2	2	1
District of Columbia	35	27	26	19	4	2	9	10	8	6	3	4	4	3
Florida	657	544	495	250	137	75	93	199	104	158	59	44	33	38
Georgia	353	293	261	119	62	68	68	80	36	63	17	23	18	22
Hawaii	177	170	170	60	15	9	9	15	9	13	6	—	—	—
Idaho	125	119	117	110	12	8	15	15	11	12	6	3	2	2
Illinois	682	614	602	430	82	65	104	109	60	74	25	31	14	28
Indiana	269	247	239	136	29	25	28	35	16	30	7	31	18	27
Iowa	152	136	132	85	20	8	11	33	25	27	7	8	4	8
Kansas	204	195	194	96	8	13	21	27	20	21	13	3	2	1
Kentucky	347	306	295	113	25	29	38	49	18	40	18	18	12	17
Louisiana	159	123	105	79	20	19	25	49	24	37	13	15	13	14
Maine	225	205	199	40	9	19	36	24	9	20	2	7	4	6
Maryland	375	323	298	181	23	55	128	76	20	66	15	14	10	14
Massachusetts	339	213	190	64	31	44	95	128	35	98	13	31	20	28
Michigan	478	431	426	160	36	46	77	86	64	69	30	12	8	10
Minnesota	369	290	256	226	56	10	33	137	86	111	22	5	4	3
Mississippi	96	68	62	35	21	4	7	33	20	30	12	15	9	14
Missouri	267	250	242	173	82	21	47	62	51	26	25	6	4	5
Montana	69	60	58	37	7	10	12	18	10	11	4	4	4	4
Nebraska	113	97	94	43	7	4	8	36	15	30	8	—	—	—
Nevada	77	65	59	38	5	18	16	17	6	15	4	6	5	6
New Hampshire	48	37	34	16	5	11	11	18	12	14	7	3	1	3
New Jersey	362	326	311	224	76	37	66	56	23	51	11	12	8	11
New Mexico	124	106	99	51	4	10	18	20	9	15	8	5	5	4
New York	935	635	576	254	83	74	347	259	64	211	40	81	67	54
North Carolina	436	362	338	174	62	38	98	84	30	62	19	22	16	19
North Dakota	67	59	57	32	19	6	2	24	19	21	11	5	4	5
Ohio	378	335	320	202	43	40	98	84	38	75	13	16	11	15
Oklahoma	214	184	181	69	13	15	16	50	22	40	13	7	4	6
Oregon	239	213	204	173	31	24	23	47	34	42	25	5	2	4
Pennsylvania	544	424	401	261	75	34	116	136	68	109	40	26	19	24
Puerto Rico	150	60	50	29	22	17	19	96	20	94	25	18	14	15
Rhode Island	61	52	50	29	9	14	21	17	15	15	1	3	3	3
South Carolina	110	88	83	46	10	15	23	19	12	8	2	18	12	17
South Dakota	70	56	54	44	9	—	4	24	16	17	4	8	7	1
Tennessee	213	177	148	99	32	17	19	72	46	63	27	15	13	15
Texas	480	388	318	243	62	54	90	130	89	115	41	46	38	44
Utah	178	144	139	97	44	23	34	52	37	50	15	7	5	5
Vermont	47	38	37	13	3	4	18	9	4	7	4	4	4	4
Virginia	223	190	173	82	29	27	50	42	25	33	12	15	12	14
Washington	442	395	389	340	21	21	49	63	42	40	21	8	8	7
West Virginia	105	83	80	33	5	20	30	27	12	20	8	7	3	7
Wisconsin	307	264	250	100	26	25	57	54	32	42	7	28	12	27
Wyoming	60	48	46	43	6	6	7	17	10	15	13	4	3	4
Other jurisdictions[c]	9	9	9	5	1	3	2	4	4	4	2	2	1	2

abuse, the two largest groups were those aged 25 to 29 years (273,508) and 20 to 24 years (244,501).

Race and Ethnicity

Most of those admitted to substance abuse treatment facilities in 2013 were non-Hispanic white, who accounted for more than 1 million of the nearly 1.7 million people receiving treatment that year. (See Table 6.3.) They were followed by non-Hispanic African Americans (313,771) and Hispanics (225,753). As Table 6.3 shows, the total number of individuals admitted for substance abuse treatment declined for all three racial groups between 2003 and

TABLE 6.1

Type of care offered at substance abuse treatment facilities, by state, 2014 [CONTINUED]

— = Quantity is zero
[a]Facilities operated by federal agencies are included in the states in which the facilities are located.
[b]Numbers of facilities sum to more than the *Total* column because a facility could provide more than one type of care.
[c]Includes the territory of Guam, the Federated States of Micronesia, the Republic of Palau, and the Virgin Islands of the United States.
[d]Injectable naltrexone = extended release, injectable naltrexone/Vivitrol®.

SOURCE: "Table 4.5a. Type of Care Offered, by State or Jurisdiction: Number, 2014," in *National Survey of Substance Abuse Treatment Services (N-SSATS): 2014*, U.S. Department of Health and Human Services, Substance Abuse and Mental Health Services Administration, March 2016, https://www.samhsa.gov/data/sites/default/files/2014_National_Survey_of_Substance_Abuse_Treatment_Services/2014_National_Survey_of_Substance_Abuse_Treatment_Services/2014_National_Survey_of_Substance_Abuse_Treatment_Services.pdf (accessed March 14, 2017)

FIGURE 6.2

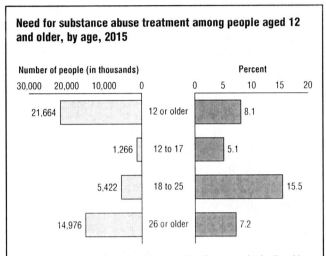

Need for substance abuse treatment among people aged 12 and older, by age, 2015

SOURCE: "Figure 36. Need for Substance Use Treatment in the Past Year among People Aged 12 or Older, by Age Group: 2015," in *Key Substance Use and Mental Health Indicators in the United States: Results from the 2015 National Survey on Drug Use and Health*, U.S. Department of Health and Human Services, Substance Abuse and Mental Health Services Administration, September 2016, https://www.samhsa.gov/data/sites/default/files/NSDUH-FFR1-2015/NSDUH-FFR1-2015/NSDUH-FFR1-2015.pdf (accessed January 10, 2017)

FIGURE 6.3

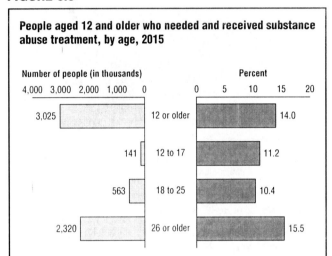

People aged 12 and older who needed and received substance abuse treatment, by age, 2015

SOURCE: "Figure 37. Received Substance Use Treatment in the Past Year among People Aged 12 or Older Who Needed Substance Use Treatment in the Past Year, by Age Group: 2015," in *Key Substance Use and Mental Health Indicators in the United States: Results from the 2015 National Survey on Drug Use and Health*, U.S. Department of Health and Human Services, Substance Abuse and Mental Health Services Administration, September 2016, https://www.samhsa.gov/data/sites/default/files/NSDUH-FFR1-2015/NSDUH-FFR1-2015/NSDUH-FFR1-2015.pdf (accessed January 10, 2017)

2013. In contrast, the number of Native Americans or Alaskan Natives receiving substance abuse treatment rose from 35,486 to 41,953 during this period.

TYPES OF TREATMENT

The disease model of addiction described at the beginning of this chapter, which views drug addiction as a chronic disease, considers long-term treatment as necessary. O'Brien notes that "as is the case with other chronic diseases, when the treatment is ended, relapse eventually occurs in most cases."

Detoxification is usually a precursor to rehabilitation because that process cannot begin until the individual's body has been cleared of the drug and a certain physiological equilibrium has been established. Drug rehabilitation refers to processes that assist a drug-addicted person in discontinuing drug use and returning to a drug-free life.

Detoxification

Drug-addicted individuals must usually undergo medical detoxification (detox) in an outpatient facility, a residential center, or a hospital. Medical help, including sedation, is provided to manage the painful physical and psychological symptoms of withdrawal. The detox of many drugs can be achieved with minimal discomfort by replacing the drug of dependence with a less risky drug in the same pharmacological category (e.g., replacing heroin with methadone) and gradually reducing the dose. People addicted to nicotine can accomplish detox on their own by using gradually decreasing doses of nicotine patches. Rehabilitation usually follows detox.

Rehabilitation

Rehabilitation (rehab) has many forms, but it is always designed to change the behavior of the drug abuser. Changed behavior (achieving independence of drugs or alcohol) requires understanding the circumstances that led to dependence, building the confidence that the individual can succeed, and changing the individual's lifestyle so that

he or she avoids occasions that produce drug-using behavior. Individual counseling, interaction with support groups, and formal education are used in combination with close supervision, incentives, and disincentives. Certain individuals require a new socialization that is achieved by living for an extended period in a structured and supportive environment in which new life skills can be acquired. Treatment may involve guiding the individual to seek help from other social agencies to reorder his or her life. (See Figure 6.1.)

Some individuals may be mentally ill and will then receive, as part of drug rehab, mental health services in outpatient or hospital settings. Most treatment takes place in outpatient settings, with the individual reporting daily, weekly, or less frequently for periodic treatment and assessment.

STATISTICS ON ADMITTED PATIENTS
Admissions by Substance

Data on admissions by the primary substance of abuse provided by TEDS for 2013 are shown in Table 6.4. In that year alcohol alone or in combination with a secondary substance accounted for the largest number of people receiving treatment (631,578, or 37.5% of all admissions), followed by opiates (471,575, or 28%, mainly heroin), marijuana (281,991, or 16.8%), methamphetamine/amphetamines (138,514, or 8.2%), and cocaine (102,387, or 6.1%).

FIGURE 6.4

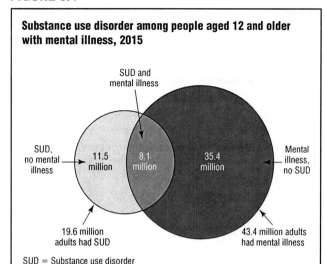

Substance use disorder among people aged 12 and older with mental illness, 2015

SUD = Substance use disorder

SOURCE: "Figure 46. Past Year Substance Use Disorder (SUD) and Mental Illness among Adults Aged 18 or Older: 2015," in *Key Substance Use and Mental Health Indicators in the United States: Results from the 2015 National Survey on Drug Use and Health*, U.S. Department of Health and Human Services, Substance Abuse and Mental Health Services Administration, September 2016, https://www.samhsa.gov/data/sites/default/files/NSDUH-FFR1-2015/NSDUH-FFR1-2015/NSDUH-FFR1-2015.pdf (accessed January 10, 2017)

TABLE 6.2

Number of persons admitted into substance abuse treatment, by gender and age of admission, 2003–13

Gender and age at admission	2003	2004	2005	2006	2007	2008	2009	2010	2011	2012	2013
Total	1,861,401	1,805,560	1,893,058	1,958,126	1,962,274	2,059,445	2,044,628	1,928,464	1,926,226	1,798,295	1,680,402
Gender											
Male	1,286,354	1,235,802	1,291,300	1,327,560	1,325,325	1,390,745	1,385,252	1,292,724	1,281,418	1,194,665	1,114,128
Female	574,657	569,046	601,270	630,154	636,409	668,317	657,937	633,314	642,601	602,551	565,906
No. of admissions	1,861,011	1,804,848	1,892,570	1,957,714	1,961,734	2,059,062	2,043,189	1,926,038	1,924,019	1,797,216	1,680,034
Age at admission											
12 to 17 years	157,181	146,406	144,994	146,712	145,980	157,873	156,869	141,688	145,082	124,111	101,404
18 to 19 years	76,584	75,553	77,669	78,707	78,444	84,218	85,971	78,631	72,497	64,072	54,397
20 to 24 years	249,783	254,119	272,101	281,396	280,004	296,584	303,782	292,606	287,107	264,700	244,501
25 to 29 years	216,707	223,594	250,852	274,343	283,320	304,063	310,847	299,636	300,718	284,749	273,508
30 to 34 years	244,920	225,388	224,781	222,139	219,463	232,839	238,464	237,651	249,931	245,562	240,364
35 to 39 years	282,422	257,210	257,255	255,895	244,443	239,282	221,779	198,418	187,548	175,480	170,645
40 to 44 years	280,378	268,660	274,892	272,859	261,798	257,150	236,878	211,624	204,417	183,368	163,183
45 to 49 years	188,544	186,864	202,814	218,045	225,385	236,636	231,162	211,881	205,423	185,474	166,166
50 to 54 years	95,955	98,644	110,631	121,966	131,232	146,077	149,141	144,862	152,704	146,997	141,337
55 to 59 years	41,127	41,825	47,402	55,001	58,653	67,272	69,960	71,305	77,326	78,092	77,824
60 to 64 years	16,648	16,526	18,182	19,335	21,464	24,242	26,132	26,830	29,986	31,163	32,240
65 years and older	11,152	10,771	11,485	11,728	12,088	13,209	13,643	13,332	13,487	14,527	14,833
No. of admissions	1,861,401	1,805,560	1,893,058	1,958,126	1,962,274	2,059,445	2,044,628	1,928,464	1,926,226	1,798,295	1,680,402
Average age at admission	34.0 yrs	34.0 yrs	34.1 yrs	34.2 yrs	34.4 yrs	34.4 yrs	34.2 yrs	34.3 yrs	34.4 yrs	34.7 yrs	35.0 yrs

Note: Based on administrative data reported to Treatment Episode Data Set (TEDS) by all reporting states and jurisdictions (excluding Puerto Rico).

SOURCE: "Table 1.3a. Admissions Aged 12 and Older, by Gender and Age at Admission: Number and Average Age at Admission, 2003–2013," in *Treatment Episode Data Set (TEDS) 2003–2013: National Admissions to Substance Abuse Treatment Services*, U.S. Department of Health and Human Services, Substance Abuse and Mental Health Services Administration, December 2015, https://www.samhsa.gov/data/sites/default/files/2003_2013_TEDS_National/2003_2013_Treatment_Episode_Data_Set_National.pdf (accessed January 10, 2017)

TABLE 6.3

Number and percentage distribution of persons admitted into substance abuse treatment, by race/ethnicity, 2003–13

Race/ethnicity	Treatment Episode Data Set (TEDS) admissions											U.S. pop. aged 12 and older (000s)
	2003	2004	2005	2006	2007	2008	2009	2010	2011	2012	2013	2013
	Number											
Total	1,861,401	1,805,560	1,893,058	1,958,126	1,962,274	2,059,445	2,044,628	1,928,464	1,926,226	1,798,295	1,680,402	256,339
White (non-Hispanic)	1,082,946	1,068,444	1,107,204	1,165,446	1,168,732	1,215,105	1,195,406	1,162,351	1,164,572	1,095,823	1,024,421	176,254
Black (non-Hispanic)	444,097	409,440	419,339	421,205	410,569	428,873	417,929	394,413	393,960	349,819	313,771	30,985
Hispanic origin	236,857	230,198	254,467	259,467	255,859	265,947	259,682	243,395	242,807	235,666	225,753	33,290
Mexican	95,179	95,304	100,236	106,355	108,319	111,538	106,335	81,611	76,436	79,072	77,261	n/a
Puerto Rican	76,563	69,398	74,199	70,335	67,983	71,259	69,414	65,595	67,677	63,670	59,988	n/a
Cuban	7,070	5,563	9,483	8,155	3,790	4,287	4,328	4,026	6,229	4,944	3,446	n/a
Other/not specified	58,045	59,933	70,549	74,622	75,767	78,863	79,605	92,163	92,465	87,980	85,058	n/a
Other	83,867	85,506	90,541	100,927	107,191	112,554	110,684	115,168	113,985	108,312	108,157	15,809
American Indian/Alaska Native	35,486	35,837	39,043	42,252	44,339	45,327	44,474	43,636	43,258	42,299	41,953	1,899
Asian/Pacific Islander	17,724	16,055	19,021	18,646	17,951	19,062	18,595	19,181	19,325	17,773	17,029	12,809
Other	30,657	33,614	32,477	40,029	44,901	48,165	47,615	52,351	51,402	48,240	49,175	1,101
No. of admissions	1,847,767	1,793,588	1,871,551	1,947,045	1,942,351	2,022,479	1,983,701	1,915,327	1,915,324	1,789,620	1,672,102	
	Percent distribution											
White (non-Hispanic)	58.6	59.6	59.2	59.9	60.2	60.1	60.3	60.7	60.8	61.2	61.3	68.8
Black (non-Hispanic)	24.0	22.8	22.4	21.6	21.1	21.2	21.1	20.6	20.6	19.5	18.8	12.1
Hispanic origin	12.8	12.8	13.6	13.3	13.2	13.1	13.1	12.7	12.7	13.2	13.5	13.0
Mexican	5.2	5.3	5.4	5.5	5.6	5.5	5.4	4.3	4.0	4.4	4.6	n/a
Puerto Rican	4.1	3.9	4.0	3.6	3.5	3.5	3.5	3.4	3.5	3.6	3.6	n/a
Cuban	0.4	0.3	0.5	0.4	0.2	0.2	0.2	0.2	0.3	0.3	0.2	n/a
Other/not specified	3.1	3.3	3.8	3.8	3.9	3.9	4.0	4.8	4.8	4.9	5.1	n/a
Other	4.5	4.8	4.8	5.2	5.5	5.6	5.6	6.0	6.0	6.1	6.5	6.2
American Indian/Alaska Native	1.9	2.0	2.1	2.2	2.3	2.2	2.2	2.3	2.3	2.4	2.5	0.7
Asian/Pacific Islander	1.0	0.9	1.0	1.0	0.9	0.9	0.9	1.0	1.0	1.0	1.0	5.0
Other	1.7	1.9	1.7	2.1	2.3	2.4	2.4	2.7	2.7	2.7	2.9	0.4
Total	100.0	100.0	100.0	100.0	100.0	100.0	100.0	100.0	100.0	100.0	100.0	100.0

n/a = not applicable
Note: Based on administrative data reported to Treatment Episode Data Set (TEDS) by all reporting states and jurisdictions (excluding Puerto Rico).

SOURCE: "Table 1.4. Admissions Aged 12 and Older, by Race/Ethnicity: Number and Percent Distribution, 2003–2013 and 2013 U.S. Population Aged 12 and Older," in *Treatment Episode Data Set (TEDS) 2003–2013: National Admissions to Substance Abuse Treatment Services*, U.S. Department of Health and Human Services, Substance Abuse and Mental Health Services Administration, December 2015, https://www.samhsa.gov/data/sites/default/files/2003_2013_TEDS_National/2003_2013_Treatment_Episode_Data_Set_National.pdf (accessed January 10, 2017)

The 2013 admissions for alcohol abuse (either alone or in combination with a secondary substance) of 37.5% were down from 41.6% reported by TEDS in 2003, when 776,369 of nearly 1.9 million total admissions for substance abuse treatment were for alcohol abuse. Total alcohol-related admissions declined annually through 2004, when it fell to 729,192 of 1.8 million (40.3%). The total number of alcohol-related admissions then climbed steadily over the next four years, peaking at 854,471 out of 2.1 million (41.4%) in 2008, before falling gradually to the 2013 figure.

Demographics by Substance

A detailed examination of admissions in 2013 is provided in Table 6.4, which shows the distribution of people at admission by major drug categories: gender, race, and ethnicity.

GENDER. As noted earlier, the total male admissions (66.3%) were higher than the total female admissions (33.7%) in 2013. This trend held in all but two substance categories: sedatives (52.5% females versus 40.5% males; the total does not add to 100% because the "all other" category does not show gender) and tranquilizers (47% females versus 46.5% males). (See Table 6.4.) The greatest male–female differences were noted in hallucinogens admissions (67.1% males versus 25.1% females), alcohol admissions with a secondary drug (66.7% males versus 25.8% females), alcohol-only admissions (65.2% males versus 26.6% females), marijuana-related admissions (65.1% males versus 24.4% females), and heroin admissions (60.8% males versus 32.1% females).

RACE AND ETHNICITY. In 2013 non-Hispanic whites made up 61.1% of the substance abuse treatment admissions; non-Hispanic African Americans, 18.7%; Hispanics, 8.4%; Native Americans or Alaskan Natives, 2.5%; and Asians or Pacific Islanders, 1%. (See Table 6.4.) Non-Hispanic whites had the highest admission rates for all drug categories except smoked cocaine and phencyclidine (PCP). Non-Hispanic African Americans had the highest PCP-related admissions (63.8%) and smoked-cocaine admissions (56.5%). Non-Hispanic

TABLE 6.4

Percentage of persons admitted into substance abuse treatment, by gender, ethnicity, and primary substance abused, 2013

Primary substance at admission

Selected race/ethnicity/gender/age group	All admissions	Alcohol		Opiates		Cocaine		Marijuana/hashish	Methamphetamine/amphetamines	Tranquilizers	Sedatives	Hallucinogens	PCP	Inhalants	Other/none specified
		Alcohol only	With secondary drug	Heroin	Other opiates	Smoked cocaine	Other route								
Total	1,683,451	355,366	276,212	316,797	154,778	69,629	32,758	281,991	138,514	15,384	3,307	2,088	5,109	913	30,605
White (non-Hispanic) male	38.7	45.4	40.4	42.1	45.2	16.2	27.6	31.0	35.7	39.2	33.9	50.5	7.2	44.4	38.5
White (non-Hispanic) female	22.4	20.3	17.3	25.4	40.1	15.1	15.7	13.1	32.8	42.2	47.6	18.5	4.7	26.8	28.0
Black (non-Hispanic) male	13.5	10.1	17.7	8.8	2.4	35.4	24.0	24.3	2.5	3.0	3.8	10.3	38.2	5.1	11.7
Black (non-Hispanic) female	5.2	3.3	5.5	3.9	2.2	21.1	9.5	7.7	1.3	2.6	2.4	4.4	25.6	2.1	6.6
Mexican-origin male	3.3	4.1	2.9	2.2	0.8	0.7	2.3	5.0	6.5	0.5	1.0	1.5	1.6	2.9	0.8
Mexican-origin female	1.3	1.0	0.9	0.8	0.8	0.5	0.6	1.6	5.1	0.5	0.8	0.6	1.2	1.9	0.4
Puerto Rican-origin male	3.0	1.8	2.8	6.9	0.8	2.3	5.8	2.7	0.2	3.1	0.9	2.3	7.1	1.2	2.6
Puerto Rican-origin female	0.8	0.4	0.6	1.3	0.5	1.1	1.4	0.9	0.1	1.1	0.5	0.8	3.9	0.7	0.8
American Indian/Alaska Native male	1.5	3.0	2.3	0.4	0.8	0.3	0.5	1.2	1.1	0.3	0.6	1.6	0.4	2.1	1.0
American Indian/Alaska Native female	1.0	1.3	1.3	0.5	1.2	0.5	0.4	0.7	1.6	0.4	0.9	0.4	0.3	3.1	0.9
Asian/Pacific Islander male	0.7	0.8	0.6	0.4	0.4	0.5	0.6	0.9	1.8	0.4	0.3	0.9	0.2	0.9	0.7
Asian/Pacific Islander female	0.3	0.3	0.2	0.2	0.2	0.2	0.2	0.4	0.9	0.2	0.3	0.4	0.2	1.0	0.6
All other	8.2	8.2	7.3	7.3	4.7	6.1	11.4	11.4	10.4	6.5	7.0	7.8	9.3	7.9	7.4
Total	100.0	100.0	100.0	100.0	100.0	100.0	100.0	100.0	100.0	100.0	100.0	100.0	100.0	100.0	100.0
No. of admissions	1,674,801	353,841	275,002	315,525	153,838	69,346	32,610	280,230	137,976	15,312	3,290	2,072	5,085	907	29,767

PCP = phencyclidine

Note: Based on administrative data reported to Treatment Episode Data Set (TEDS) by all reporting states and jurisdictions.

SOURCE: Adapted from "Table 2.3a. Selected Race/Ethnicity/Gender/Age Group among Admissions Aged 12 and Older, by Primary Substance of Abuse: Column Percent Distribution, 2013," in *Treatment Episode Data Set (TEDS) 2003–2013: National Admissions to Substance Abuse Treatment Services*, U.S. Department of Health and Human Services, Substance Abuse and Mental Health Services Administration, December 2015, https://www.samhsa.gov/data/sites/default/files/2003_2013_TEDS_National/2003_2013_TEDS_National/2003_2013_Treatment_Episode_Data_Set_National.pdf (accessed January 10, 2017)

African Americans were second in admission rates for alcohol only, alcohol with a secondary drug, heroin, other opiates, cocaine other than smoked, marijuana, sedatives, hallucinogens, inhalants, and other. Hispanics were second in admission rates for methamphetamine/amphetamines. It should be noted that the Hispanics category is treated as an ethnicity rather than as a race and includes both white and African American individuals of Hispanic origin.

It is important, however, to consider these rates of substance abuse treatment by race in the context of the overall racial composition of the United States. The 2013 TEDS data indicate that the total U.S. population consisted of 68.8% non-Hispanic whites, 13% Hispanics, and 12.1% non-Hispanic African Americans. (See Table 6.3.) When substance abuse treatment rates for 2013 are compared with these population statistics, non-Hispanic whites were underrepresented in treatment (61% in treatment versus 68.8% of the U.S. population), the proportion of Hispanics in treatment was comparable to Hispanics in the population (13.4% in treatment versus 13% of the U.S. population), and non-Hispanic African Americans were disproportionately admitted for treatment (18.7% in treatment versus 12.1% of the U.S. population).

Type of Treatment

In 2013, 61.3% of those admitted to treatment were admitted into ambulatory (nonresidential) treatment facilities; of the remainder, 21.8% went into 24-hour detox (both residential-type and hospital inpatient) and 16.9% went into residential facilities. (See Table 6.5.)

Among those going into detox, the largest percentages were admitted for tranquilizers (40.8%), heroin (32.7%), and alcohol only (30.7%). (See Table 6.5.) Those using marijuana had the highest percentage entering ambulatory care (86%).

Referring Source

Table 6.6 shows the source of referral of patients to substance abuse treatment in 2013. More than one-third (36.8%) of all people admitted came to get treatment on their own volition. The largest referral source (sending 33.7% of individuals) was the criminal justice system. Much of the remaining one-third of all referrals came from substance abuse care providers and other health care providers (9.1% and 7.3% of referrals, respectively). Other referrals came from schools, employers, and community agencies.

Regarding the source of referral based on the drug of abuse, most heroin users (58.4%) and other opiate users (50%) sought treatment on their own accord. (See Table 6.6.) The criminal justice system sent more than half of marijuana users (51.9%) and nearly half of methamphetamine/amphetamine users (46.6%) to treatment.

HOW EFFECTIVE IS TREATMENT?

During the 1960s there was an opioid epidemic in the United States, and the federal government released substantial funds to substance abuse treatment programs. This funding has continued over the decades and is supplemented by state governments and private sources. According to the Office of National Drug Control Policy, in *FY 2017 Budget and Performance Summary: Companion to the National Drug Control Strategy* (December 2016, https://obamawhitehouse.archives.gov/sites/default/files/ondcp/policy-and-research/fy2017_budget_summary -final.pdf), the fiscal year 2017 federal budget request for drug abuse treatment and prevention was $15.8 billion, up from $14.7 billion enacted in fiscal year 2016.

With so much money devoted to substance abuse treatment, there has been considerable research conducted on the effectiveness of the programs. The bulk of this research began during the late 1960s and extended into the 1990s.

In the press release "New Research Documents Success of Drug Abuse Treatments" (December 16, 1997, http:// drugfree.org/learn/drug-and-alcohol-news/new-research-docu ments-success-of-drug-abuse-treatments/), the National Institutes of Health notes that the first major study of drug-treatment effectiveness was the Drug Abuse Reporting Program (DARP), which studied more than 44,000 clients in 52 treatment centers between 1969 and 1973. Program staff then studied a smaller group of these clients six and 12 years after their treatment. A second important study was the Treatment Outcome Prospective Study (TOPS), which followed 11,000 clients admitted to 41 treatment centers between 1979 and 1981. Both DARP and TOPS found major reductions in both drug abuse and criminal activity after treatment.

Services Research Outcomes Study

SAMHSA's Services Research Outcomes Study (SROS; September 1998, http://archive.samhsa.gov/data/Sros/toc.htm) confirmed that both drug use and criminal behavior are reduced after drug treatment. The SROS provided the first nationally representative data to answer the question: Does treatment work? This study, although now nearly 20 years old and reporting on even older data, has not been repeated.

In this nationally representative sample, alcohol use decreased by 14% and drug use declined by 21%. Decreases varied from drug to drug, with heroin use decreasing the least.

Results by type of treatment were variable. On average, the best results for decreasing use of all drugs, especially cocaine and marijuana, were achieved with treatment that lasted six months or more. Long-term drug treatment appears to be necessary due to the chronic nature of addiction and its tendency to recur when treatment is stopped.

TABLE 6.5

Percentage of persons admitted into substance abuse treatment, by primary substance of abuse and type of care received, 2013

Type of service at admission and planned medication-assisted opioid therapy	All admissions	Alcohol		Opiates		Cocaine		Marijuana/ hashish	Metham- phetamine/ amphetamines	Tranquilizers	Sedatives	Hallucinogens	PCP	Inhalants	Other/none specified
		Alcohol only	With secondary drug	Heroin	Other opiates	Smoked cocaine	Other route								
Total	**1,683,451**	**355,366**	**276,212**	**316,797**	**154,778**	**69,629**	**32,758**	**281,991**	**138,514**	**15,384**	**3,307**	**2,088**	**5,109**	**913**	**30,605**
Type of service at admission															
Ambulatory	61.3	57.5	56.5	48.8	60.4	53.4	67.9	86.0	61.5	38.4	63.3	63.9	66.4	61.3	78.2
Outpatient	48.5	46.0	44.1	37.3	47.6	40.3	55.2	70.6	46.2	29.7	45.9	44.9	40.7	48.6	67.5
Intensive outpatient	11.6	10.0	12.0	8.4	10.6	13.0	12.6	15.4	15.2	8.0	9.4	18.9	25.7	12.3	10.4
Detoxification	1.2	1.5	0.4	3.2	2.2	0.1	0.1	*	0.1	0.6	8.0	0.2	*	0.4	0.3
Rehabilitation/residential	16.9	11.9	17.9	18.5	16.9	30.3	21.8	11.2	27.4	20.9	15.4	26.4	28.4	25.6	13.5
Short-term (<31 days)	9.2	7.3	10.6	9.7	10.5	16.0	11.6	5.4	12.0	14.6	8.8	15.5	16.5	15.7	7.3
Long-term (31+ days)	7.4	4.2	6.9	8.5	6.1	14.0	9.9	5.7	15.3	5.5	5.5	10.5	11.6	9.7	5.9
Hospital (non-detox)	0.3	0.4	0.4	0.3	0.3	0.3	0.3	0.1	0.2	0.8	1.1	0.4	0.2	0.2	0.3
Detoxification (24-hour service)	21.8	30.7	25.6	32.7	22.7	16.3	10.2	2.8	11.1	40.8	21.3	9.7	5.2	13.0	8.2
Free-standing residential	18.6	26.5	20.2	28.0	20.2	15.0	8.8	2.4	10.8	30.7	18.1	9.3	5.0	12.3	6.9
Hospital inpatient	3.2	4.2	5.4	4.6	2.5	1.3	1.5	0.3	0.3	10.0	3.1	0.4	0.2	0.8	1.3
Total	**100.0**	**100.0**	**100.0**	**100.0**	**100.0**	**100.0**	**100.0**	**100.0**	**100.0**	**100.0**	**100.0**	**100.0**	**100.0**	**100.0**	**100.0**
No. of admissions	**1,683,445**	**355,366**	**276,208**	**316,797**	**154,778**	**69,628**	**32,758**	**281,991**	**138,514**	**15,384**	**3,307**	**2,088**	**5,109**	**913**	**30,604**
Planned medication-assisted opioid therapy															
Yes	7.3	0.3	0.8	26.8	18.0	1.0	1.5	0.3	0.4	4.2	3.3	1.8	1.3	1.6	6.2
No	92.7	99.7	99.2	73.2	82.0	99.0	98.5	99.7	99.6	95.8	96.7	98.2	98.7	98.4	93.8
Total	**100.0**	**100.0**	**100.0**	**100.0**	**100.0**	**100.0**	**100.0**	**100.0**	**100.0**	**100.0**	**100.0**	**100.0**	**100.0**	**100.0**	**100.0**
No. of admissions	**1,604,304**	**339,861**	**261,189**	**307,180**	**147,990**	**65,807**	**31,049**	**268,016**	**133,095**	**14,100**	**3,058**	**2,014**	**5,019**	**865**	**25,061**

PCP = phencyclidine

Notes: Planned medication-assisted opioid therapy is therapy with methadone or buprenorphine is part of client's treatment plan. Information is based on administrative data reported to Treatment Episode Data Set (TEDS) by all reporting states and jurisdictions.

SOURCE: "Table 2.7. Type of Service at Admission and Planned Medication-Assisted Opioid Therapy among Admissions Aged 12 and Older, by Primary Substance of Abuse: Percent Distribution, 2013," in *Treatment Episode Data Set (TEDS) 2003–2013: National Admissions to Substance Abuse Treatment Services*, U.S. Department of Health and Human Services, Substance Abuse and Mental Health Services Administration, December 2015. https://www.samhsa.gov/data/sites/default/files/2003_2013_TEDS_National/2003_2013_TEDS_National/2003_2013_Treatment_Episode_Data_Set_National.pdf (accessed January 10, 2017)

TABLE 6.6

Percentage of persons admitted into substance abuse treatment, by primary substance of abuse and source of referral, 2013

| | | Alcohol | | Opiates | | Cocaine | | | Metham- | | | | | | | |
Treatment referral source and detailed criminal justice referral	All admissions	Alcohol only	With secondary drug	Heroin	Other opiates	Smoked cocaine	Other route	Marijuana/ hashish	phetamine/ amphetamines	Tranquilizers	Sedatives	Hallucinogens	PCP	Inhalants	Other/none specified
Total	1,683,451	355,366	276,212	316,797	154,778	69,629	32,758	281,991	138,514	15,384	3,307	2,088	5,109	913	30,605
Treatment referral source															
Self or individual	36.8	32.2	33.8	58.4	50.0	40.5	30.2	18.1	27.2	46.9	46.1	29.9	26.8	31.1	36.1
Criminal justice referral	33.7	38.3	33.3	16.1	20.4	25.9	37.3	51.9	46.6	18.8	19.6	36.4	43.2	28.3	28.3
Other community referral (see detail below)	11.7	11.0	13.1	6.6	9.3	12.3	14.3	15.9	14.8	9.0	9.2	13.1	17.9	13.0	14.3
Substance abuse care provider	9.1	7.6	9.9	14.3	10.4	12.4	9.4	4.5	6.0	12.2	14.1	9.6	8.5	8.8	6.5
Other health care provider	7.3	9.7	8.9	4.5	9.4	8.6	7.6	4.7	4.9	12.3	9.9	9.8	3.2	16.1	12.0
School (educational)	1.0	0.5	0.5	*	0.1	0.1	0.1	4.3	0.2	0.3	0.5	0.9	0.1	2.4	2.5
Employer/EAP	0.4	0.7	0.5	0.1	0.4	0.2	0.9	0.6	0.2	0.4	0.7	0.2	0.3	0.2	0.3
Total	100.0	100.0	100.0	100.0	100.0	100.0	100.0	100.0	100.0	100.0	100.0	100.0	100.0	100.0	100.0
No. of admissions	1,652,719	349,486	270,828	311,684	152,524	68,514	32,062	277,017	136,417	15,183	3,255	2,044	5,026	899	27,780
Detailed criminal justice referral															
Total	557,178	133,979	90,224	50,192	31,118	17,730	11,975	143,826	63,612	2,851	638	745	2,172	254	7,862
Probation/parole	33.7	16.6	28.9	37.1	34.3	41.3	41.7	44.1	45.0	33.5	31.1	36.1	46.0	30.1	32.3
State/federal court	14.7	10.9	15.9	17.7	20.4	17.7	18.8	16.2	11.8	16.9	18.8	19.2	12.9	15.0	13.6
Formal adjudication	13.8	14.5	13.2	13.6	18.0	12.3	9.7	11.5	16.4	21.0	29.0	17.9	12.4	20.2	16.1
DUI/DWI	10.5	27.9	16.0	1.5	3.2	1.0	1.6	2.8	0.6	6.5	5.4	2.0	2.0	3.5	4.3
Other legal entity	8.4	12.9	6.9	6.8	6.7	7.5	7.2	8.9	2.7	9.3	6.6	8.9	7.6	16.2	17.1
Diversionary program	2.9	0.9	2.2	9.4	5.8	4.9	4.2	3.0	0.7	4.6	0.9	2.0	7.2	1.7	4.0
Prison	2.3	1.1	2.3	4.4	3.0	3.6	4.1	2.2	2.0	1.6	1.4	1.8	4.5	1.7	1.1
Other	13.8	15.2	14.6	9.5	8.6	11.7	12.6	11.4	20.7	6.6	6.8	12.1	7.3	11.6	11.5
Total	100.0	100.0	100.0	100.0	100.0	100.0	100.0	100.0	100.0	100.0	100.0	100.0	100.0	100.0	100.0
No. of admissions	401,693	97,405	63,812	38,300	20,022	11,995	8,270	99,125	54,320	2,105	441	504	1,614	173	3,607

DUI = driving under the influence
DWI = driving while intoxicated
PCP = phencyclidine
EAP = employee assistance program

Notes: Detailed criminal justice referral is a supplemental data set item. Individual supplement data set items are reported at each state's option. Information is based on administrative data reported to Treatment Episode Data Set (TEDS) by all reporting states and jurisdictions.

SOURCE: "Table 2.6. Treatment Referral Source and Detailed Criminal Justice Referral among Admissions Aged 12 and Older, by Primary Substance of Abuse: Percent Distribution, 2013," in *Treatment Episode Data Set (TEDS) 2003–2013: National Admissions to Substance Abuse Treatment Services*, U.S. Department of Health and Human Services, Substance Abuse and Mental Health Services Administration, December 2015, https://www.samhsa.gov/data/sites/default/files/2003_2013_TEDS_National/2003_2013_TEDS_National_2003_2013_Treatment_Episode_Data_Set_National.pdf (accessed January 10, 2017)

The SROS also showed that treatment for substance abuse can significantly reduce crime. Criminal activities such as breaking and entering, drug sales, prostitution, driving under the influence, and theft/larceny decreased between 23% and 38% after drug treatment.

Current Principles of Effective Treatment

Although no comprehensive research survey to rival the scope of the SROS has emerged, a number of important studies that evaluate the effectiveness of certain substance abuse treatment and prevention programs have been published since the late 1990s. For example, Ted R. Miller and Delia Hendrie provide in *Substance Abuse Prevention Dollars and Cents: A Cost-Benefit Analysis* (2008, http://store.samhsa.gov/shin/content/SMA07-4298/SMA07-4298.pdf) a detailed analysis of existing substance abuse treatment programs (including school-based programs for minors) and of the various social and economic costs that are associated with addiction. The NIDA offers an overview of some recent findings in "DrugFacts: Lessons from Prevention Research" (March 2014, https://www.drugabuse.gov/publications/drugfacts/lessons-prevention-research). Drawing from a range of scholarly papers, the NIDA outlines 16 key "principles" of effective treatment methods, including the role of "protective factors" (such as family and community support) in sustaining effective substance abuse treatment and the importance of tailoring prevention programs to address the unique needs of particular communities and social groups. The NIDA cites several valuable research studies concerning the efficacy (the ability of an intervention to produce the intended diagnostic or therapeutic effect in optimal circumstances) of certain approaches to drug treatment, among them E. Michael Foster, Allison E. Olchowski, and Carolyn H. Webster-Stratton's "Is Stacking Intervention Components Cost-Effective? An Analysis of the Incredible Years Program" (*Journal of the American Academy of Child and Adolescent Psychology*, vol. 46, no. 11, November 2007) and J. David Hawkins et al.'s "Results of a Type 2 Translational Research Trial to Prevent Adolescent Drug Use and Delinquency: A Test of Communities That Care" (*Archives of Pediatrics and Adolescent Medicine*, vol. 163, no. 9, September 2009).

Additionally, the NIDA notes that treatment should be readily available and address issues in a person's life—not just the addiction. According to the NIDA principles, effective treatment should include counseling, behavioral therapies, appropriate medications, and drug use monitoring. Drug-addicted individuals often have other illnesses, such as mental illnesses or infectious diseases that were contracted by needle-sharing or other risky practices, and the NIDA suggests that these illnesses should also be treated. It adds that one single treatment is not appropriate for everyone and that any drug treatment plan should be periodically reevaluated and adjusted, depending on a patient's progress and needs.

In the third edition of *Principles of Drug Addiction Treatment: A Research-Based Guide* (December 2012, https://www.drugabuse.gov/sites/default/files/podat_1.pdf), the NIDA breaks down the broader economic benefits of drug treatment programs. Every dollar spent on addiction treatment saves an estimated $12 in costs related to drug-related crime (including the prosecution of these crimes), as well as drug-related health care expenses. From the perspective of health benefits related to addiction treatment, the NIDA notes that the likelihood of relapse among addicts who have received treatment ranges from between 40% and 60%. This range is slightly higher than that of individuals recovering from type 1 diabetes, who suffer relapses at a rate of between 30% to 50%, but lower than the relapse rates for hypertension and asthma, both of which range from 50% to 70%.

The Development of Antidrug Vaccines

Medications can help drug-addicted individuals not only by suppressing drug withdrawal symptoms but also by helping reestablish proper brain function and reducing drug cravings during treatment. Antidrug vaccines, which were under development as of March 2017, may help drug-addicted individuals in the future. In "Anti-drug Vaccines to Treat Substance Abuse" (*Immunology and Cell Biology*, vol. 87, no. 4, May–June 2009), Berma M. Kinsey, David C. Jackson, and Frank M. Orson review the status of the development of these vaccines for treating addictions. The researchers explain that antidrug vaccines work by triggering the development of antibodies against particular drugs in vaccinated individuals. The antibodies bind to the drug in the bloodstream before it is able to get to the brain. Thus, the vaccinated individual receives no drug effects by taking a drug, such as cocaine or methamphetamine—that is, the pleasure centers of the brain are not stimulated because the drug never reaches the brain. Because the person does not experience any "reward" for taking the drug, the craving sensations for the drug eventually subside.

In reality, however, antidrug vaccines do not work perfectly. For example, if an individual's body does not respond well to the vaccine by developing a substantial amount of antibodies, then only some of the drug is bound in the bloodstream and some enters the brain. To get a desired drug effect, a drug addict will have to increase the doses of a drug. Thus, Kinsey, Jackson, and Orson suggest that counseling and behavior therapy will also be needed for antidrug vaccines to be effective.

Kinsey, Jackson, and Orson surmise that antinicotine vaccines are the ones most likely to be available first to the public because their development is the furthest along. Nicholas T. Jacob et al. of the Scripps Research Institute reveal in "Investigations of Enantiopure Nicotine Haptens Using an Adjuvanting Carrier in Anti-nicotine Vaccine Development" (*Journal of Medicinal Chemistry*, vol. 59, no. 6, March 2016) that vaccines containing high numbers of antinicotine antibodies helped delay the physiological effects of nicotine on mice during testing. According to the researchers, mice given the antinicotine vaccine were also revealed to have lower concentrations of nicotine in their brain, the area of the body where the drug has its most powerful addictive effects.

As of March 2017, vaccines were also under development for cocaine, morphine, and methamphetamine addictions. In "Scientists Working to Create a Vaccine for Drug Addiction" (DrugRehab.com, March 14, 2016), Chris Elkins reports that one promising treatment is TA-CD, a vaccine that helped cocaine addicts refrain from using the drug during clinical trials. In addition, Elkins notes that vaccines under development for methamphetamine and PCP addiction were proven to reduce levels of the drug in the brains of animals undergoing laboratory testing.

DRUG COURTS

Drug courts are programs that use the court's authority to offer certain drug-addicted offenders to have their charges dismissed or their sentences reduced if they participate in drug court substance abuse treatment programs. Drug court programs vary across the nation, but most programs offer a range of treatment options and generally require one year of commitment from the defendant.

Randall T. Brown of the University of Wisconsin School of Medicine and Public Health describes drug courts and reviews their effect in "Systematic Review of the Impact of Adult Drug-Treatment Courts" (*Translational Research*, vol. 155, no. 6, June 2010). Brown notes that drug courts vary in the number of individuals they serve annually, with the typical range being between 80 and 120. Courts in large urban areas often serve hundreds more. He explains that drug courts use rewards and sanctions to motivate individuals to comply with their treatment. Rewards include praise from the judge, fewer court appearances, and gift cards to local stores.

Those who adhere to the rules and remain drug free for a sustained period (48% on average) graduate from treatment and are provided with a ceremony that is attended by family and friends. Sanctions include admonitions from the judge, community service, increased drug screening, and incarceration. Brown's review of the literature on the effect of drug courts "points toward benefit versus traditional adjudication in averting future criminal behavior and in reducing future substance use, at least in the short term."

The National Drug Court Institute, which is supported by the Office of National Drug Control Policy and the U.S. Department of Justice's Office of Justice Programs, studied its own drug court system, and its findings were reported by West Huddleston and Douglas B. Marlowe in *Painting the Current Picture: A National Report on Drug Courts and Other Problem-Solving Court Programs in the United States* (July 2011, http://www.ndci.org/sites/default/files/nadcp/PCP%20Report%20FINAL.PDF). Huddleston and Marlowe indicate that drug courts decrease criminal recidivism (relapse into criminal activity), save money, increase retention in treatment, and provide affordable treatment. The researchers note that between 2005 and 2009 the total number of drug courts in the United States rose from 1,756 to 2,459, an increase of 40%.

WHERE TO GO FOR HELP

Many organizations provide assistance for addicts, their families, and their friends. Most of the self-help groups are based on the Twelve Step program of Alcoholics Anonymous (AA). Whereas AA is a support group for problem drinkers, Al-Anon/Alateen is for friends and families of alcoholics. Families Anonymous provides support for family members and friends who are concerned about a loved one's problems with drugs and/or alcohol. Other organizations include Adult Children of Alcoholics, Cocaine Anonymous, and Narcotics Anonymous. For an addict, many of these organizations can provide immediate help. For families and friends, they can provide knowledge, understanding, and support. For contact information for some of these organizations, see the Important Names and Addresses section at the back of this book.

CHAPTER 7
HOW ALCOHOL, TOBACCO, AND ILLICIT DRUG USE AFFECT ECONOMICS AND GOVERNMENT

The alcohol and tobacco industries play large roles in the U.S. economy. Both industries not only provide jobs and income for those involved in growing, manufacturing, and selling these products but also contribute significant tax revenues to the federal, state, and local governments. The U.S. economy also feels the effects of alcohol, tobacco, and illicit drug use in other, less beneficial, ways. All these drugs can have significant health consequences, with associated health care costs. There are also costs in the form of loss of productivity, including work that was never performed because of poor health, death, or imprisonment. The cost of enforcing drug laws and incarcerating those convicted of breaking such laws are also significant.

U.S. ALCOHOL SALES AND CONSUMPTION

Retail sales of alcoholic beverages are divided into three groups: beer, wine, and distilled spirits (hard liquor). According to the Economic Research Service (January 26, 2016, https://www.ers.usda.gov/webdocs/DataFiles/Food_Expenditures__17981/FoodExpenditures_table4.xls?v=42395), Americans spent $176.1 billion on alcoholic beverages in 2014. (See Table 2.1 in Chapter 2.) More than half ($92.8 billion, or 52.7%) of this money was spent on alcoholic beverages to be consumed at home, and more than one-third ($66.9 billion, or 38%) of all alcoholic beverage expenditures were made at restaurants and bars.

Beer

According to the National Beer Wholesalers Association, in "The U.S. Beer Industry" (2017, https://www.nbwa.org/resources/industry-fast-facts), beer consumption among Americans of legal drinking age topped 27.5 gallons (104.1 L) per capita (per person) in 2015. Samuel Stebbins and Michael B. Sauter report in "States Drinking the Most Beer" (247wallst.com, June 5, 2016) that New Hampshire was the state with the highest per capita beer consumption in 2015, at 43 gallons (162.8 L)

per person, followed by North Dakota (40 gallons [151.4 L]) and Montana (39.7 gallons [150.3 L]).

The early 21st century saw a dramatic rise in the popularity of craft beer in the United States. The Brewers Association states in "Craft Brewer Defined" (2017, https://www.brewersassociation.org/statistics/craft-brewer-defined/) that a craft brewery is defined by its limited production capacity (no more than 6 million barrels of beer annually), its independent ownership, and its commitment to traditional brewing techniques. At the same time, the Brewers Association notes that craft brewers are distinguished by a commitment to innovation, both in developing new interpretations of traditional beers and inventing original new styles. The increased popularity of craft beer has led to a rapid proliferation of breweries in the United States. The National Beer Wholesalers Association reports in "The U.S. Beer Industry" that the total number of U.S. breweries rose from 4,475 in 2015 to 7,190 in 2016, an increase of more than 60%. California had the most breweries in 2016, with 927, followed by Washington (424), New York (394), Colorado (386), and Michigan (379).

Wine

The Wine Institute reports in "Wine Consumption in the U.S." (July 8, 2016, https://www.wineinstitute.org/resources/statistics/article86) that Americans consumed 913 million gallons (3.5 billion L) of wine in 2015. This figure encompasses a range of wine products, including table wine, sparkling wine, dessert wine, and vermouth. The Wine Institute indicates that wine consumption rose steadily during the first decade of the 21st century, from 2 gallons (7.6 L) per capita in 2000 to 2.8 gallons (10.7 L) per capita in 2015. In "2015 California Wine Sales in U.S. Hit $31.9 Billion Retail Value" (July 8, 2016, https://www.wineinstitute.org/resources/statistics/article86), the Wine Institute states that 384 million cases of wine were sold in the

United States in 2015, with a total retail value of $55.8 billion. This volume of wine sales represented an increase of 2% over the previous year. Of these sales, California accounted for 229 million cases sold domestically, or 60% of total U.S. wine sales in 2013. In addition, California wines accounted for 90% of the nation's wine exports, with 51.2 million cases of California wines sold to foreign markets in 2015.

Besides California, the top-10 wine-producing states in 2014, as identified by WineAmerica, the national association of American wineries (December 15, 2014, http://wineamerica.org/policy/by-the-numbers), included Washington, New York, Pennsylvania, Oregon, Vermont, Ohio, Michigan, Kentucky, and Texas. Andy Kiersz reports in "The States That Love Wine the Most" (BusinessInsider.com, March 6, 2014) that a study by the Beverage Information Group in 2013 found per capita wine consumption in the United States was greatest in the District of Columbia at 6.8 gallons (25.7 L) per person, followed by New Hampshire (5.2 gallons [19.6 L]), Vermont (4.6 gallons [17.5 L]), Massachusetts (4.5 gallons [16.9 L]), New Jersey (3.93 gallons [14.9 L]), and Nevada (3.88 gallons [14.7 L]). As indicated by the study, wine consumption per capita in 2013 was lowest in West Virginia at 0.6 gallons (2.4 L) per person, Mississippi (0.7 gallons [2.8 L]) Kansas (0.8 gallons [3.2 L]), Utah (0.8 gallons [3.2 L]), and Kentucky (1 gallon [3.9 L]).

Distilled Spirits

The Distilled Spirits Council of the United States (DISCUS) indicates in "Apparent Consumption of Distilled Spirits by State, in Wine Gallons" (December 2015, http://www.discus.org/assets/1/7/December_2015 _Preliminary.pdf) that Americans drank 531.2 million gallons (2 billion L) of distilled spirits in 2015. This figure represented 3% growth over 2014 totals, when 515.5 million gallons (1.95 billion L) of spirits were consumed in the United States. Among the states, California was the leading consumer of distilled spirits in 2015, at 59.2 million gallons (224.1 million L), followed by Florida (42.1 million gallons [159.4 million L]), Texas (35.9 million gallons [135.9 million L]), and New York (31.1 million gallons [117.7 million L]). DISCUS reports in "Distilled Spirits Sector Growth Accelerates in 2016 Gains Market Share for Seventh Consecutive Year" (February 7, 2017, http://www.discus.org/2016AnnualEconomicBriefing/) that sales of distilled spirits in the United States topped $25.2 billion in 2016, a 4.5% increase over the previous year. According to the Alcohol and Tobacco Tax and Trade Bureau (TTB), a part of the U.S. Department of the Treasury, in "Distilled Spirits Producers and Bottlers" (March 5, 2017, https://www .ttb.gov/foia/xls/frl-spirits-producers-and-bottlers.htm), there were 2,231 licensed producers and bottlers of distilled spirits in the United States in 2017. Leading states included California with 291 operators, New York (165), Washington (154), Texas (120), Michigan (99), Colorado (97), Oregon (88), and Pennsylvania (76). The fewest licensed producers and bottlers of distilled spirits in 2017 were in Rhode Island (2), Mississippi (4), North Dakota (4), Arkansas (7), Delaware (7), Oklahoma (8), District of Columbia (9), and South Dakota (9).

U.S. TOBACCO PRODUCTION AND CONSUMPTION
Farming Trends

In 1881 James A. Bonsack (1859–1924) invented the cigarette-making machine, which made cigarettes cheaper and faster to manufacture. Tom Capehart of the Economic Research Service notes in "Trends in U.S. Tobacco Farming" (November 2004, http://usda.mannlib .cornell.edu/usda/ers/TBS/2000s/2004/TBS-11-08-2004 _Special_Report.pdf) that tobacco production in the United States grew from 300 million pounds (136,000 t) annually during the mid-1860s to more than 1 billion pounds (454,000 t) in 1909. In 1946, at the end of World War II (1939–1945), tobacco production was greater than 2 billion pounds (907,000 t).

During the 1960s changes in tobacco preparation and the introduction of new machinery increased the amount of tobacco production per acre. Nonetheless, the number of tobacco farms dropped dramatically from about 512,000 in 1954 to 56,977 in 2002. In general, the amount of land devoted to cultivating tobacco, the value of production, and the production of tobacco decreased as well. By 2005, acres devoted to cultivating tobacco reached a low of 297,080 acres (120,224 ha). (See Table 7.1.) Tobacco crop acreage increased again beginning in 2006, reaching 356,000 acres (144,068 ha) in 2007, before falling to 325,040 acres (131,539 ha) in 2011. The total land devoted to tobacco farming subsequently increased over the next three years, to 378,360 acres (153,117 ha) in 2014. The value of production declined by almost $1 billion between 2001 and 2005, then climbed steadily to $1.5 billion in 2009. As shown in Table 7.1, the value of production dropped to $1.3 billion in 2010 and $1.1 billion in 2011 before eventually rising to $1.8 billion in 2014. The overall production of tobacco also fell at decade's end, from 822.6 million pounds (373,100 t) in 2009 to 598.3 million pounds (271,400 t) in 2011, before rising again to 876.4 million pounds (438,200 t) by 2014. (See Table 7.1.) As reported by the Centers for Disease Control and Prevention (CDC), in "Economic Trends in Tobacco" (December 19, 2016, https://www.cdc.gov/tobacco/data_statistics/ fact_sheets/economics/econ_facts/), three states—North Carolina, Kentucky, and Georgia—account for nearly 80% of all tobacco production in the United States.

Manufacturing

The CDC reports in "Economic Trends in Tobacco" that more than 258 billion cigarettes were sold in the

TABLE 7.1

Tobacco crops by area, yield, production, price, and value, 2005–14

Year	Area harvested	Yield per acre	Production	Marketing year average price per pound received by farmers	Value of production
	Acres	Pounds	1,000 pounds	Dollars	1,000 dollars
2005	297,080	2,171	645,015	1.642	1,059,324
2006	339,000	2,147	727,897	1.665	1,211,885
2007	356,000	2,213	787,653	1.693	1,329,235
2008	354,490	2,258	800,504	1.859	1,488,069
2009	354,040	2,323	822,581	1.837	1,511,196
2010	337,500	2,128	718,190	1.782	1,279,920
2011	325,040	1,841	598,252	1.857	1,110,737
2012	336,245	2,268	762,709	2.027	1,579,964
2013	355,675	2,034	723,579	2.177	1,574,982
2014	378,360	2,316	876,415	2.094	1,835,308

*Production figures are on farm-sales-weight basis.

SOURCE: "Table 2-37. Tobacco: Area, Yield, Production, Price, and Value, United States, 2005–2014," in *Agricultural Statistics 2015*, U.S. Department of Agriculture, National Agricultural Statistics Service, 2015, https://www.nass.usda.gov/Publications/Ag_Statistics/2015/Ag_Stats_2015_complete%20 publication.pdf (accessed January 10, 2017)

United States in 2016, a decrease of 2.5% from the previous year, when cigarette sales surpassed 264 billion. Four companies (Philip Morris USA Inc., Reynolds American Inc., ITG Brands, and Liggett) accounted for roughly 92% of total sales in 2016. The CDC also notes that 13 billion cigars were sold in the United States in 2014 and that 128 million pounds (64,000 t) of smokeless tobacco were sold in 2013.

Consumer Spending on Tobacco

Table 7.2 shows that the average U.S. family (or other consumer unit) spent $351 on tobacco products and smoking supplies in 2011, $332 in 2012, $330 in 2013, and $319 in 2014. According to the U.S. Bureau of Labor Statistics, in *Consumer Expenditures in 2014* (October 2016, https://www.bls.gov/opub/reports/consumer-expenditures/2014/pdf/home.pdf), the $319 spent per family on tobacco products and supplies in 2014 represented 0.6% of the $53,495 average annual expenditures by a U.S. household.

The Bureau of Labor Statistics indicates in *Consumer Expenditures in 2014* that the amount spent on tobacco products and smoking supplies varied in 2014, depending on the characteristics of the household. On average, households without at least one member who had graduated from college spent $417. By contrast, households with members who had earned at least a bachelor's degree devoted an average of $168 to tobacco products and supplies in 2014.

WORLD TOBACCO MARKETS

Michael Eriksen et al. report in the fifth edition of *The Tobacco Atlas* (2015, http://3pk43x313ggr4cy0lh3tctjh .wpengine.netdna-cdn.com/wp-content/uploads/2015/03/TA5 _2015_WEB.pdf), that global tobacco production approached 8.3 million tons (7.5 million t) in 2012. That year China harvested nearly 3.5 million tons (3.2 million t) of tobacco, accounting for more than 42% of global production. The world's other leading tobacco producers in 2012 included Brazil, India, the United States, and Argentina. According to Eriksen et al., tobacco cultivation accounted for 10.6 million acres (4.3 million ha) of arable land, and was grown in 124 countries worldwide in 2012.

Eriksen et al. note that 5.8 trillion cigarettes were consumed worldwide in 2014. That year, nearly 2.5 trillion cigarettes were smoked in China, more than the total number of cigarettes smoked in the next 29 leading cigarette-consuming countries combined. Other leading cigarette-consuming nations in 2014 included Russia, the United States, Indonesia, Japan, Germany, India, and Turkey.

World Tobacco Control Treaty

On February 27, 2005, the world's first tobacco control treaty, the WHO Framework Convention on Tobacco Control (2005, http://www.who.int/tobacco/framework/ WHO_FCTC_english.pdf), became law in the 40 countries that ratified it (became bound by it). According to the World Health Organization (WHO), in "Parties to the WHO Framework Convention on Tobacco Control" (http://www.who.int/fctc/signatories_parties/en/), the United States signed the measure in May 2004, but as of March 2017 it had not ratified the treaty. The goal of the treaty is to improve global health by reducing tobacco consumption. Nations that ratified the treaty obligated themselves to raise taxes on tobacco products, ban tobacco advertising, pass laws requiring smoke-free workplaces and public places, and provide stronger health warnings about the dangers of smoking to their

TABLE 7.2

Average annual consumer spending and percentage changes, by category, 2011–14

Item	2011	2012	2013	2014	Percent change 2011–2012	2012–2013	2013–2014
Number of consumer units (in thousands)	122,287	124,416	125,670	127,006	—	—	—
Consumer unit characteristics:							
Income before taxes	$63,685	$65,596	$63,784	$66,877	3.0	−2.8	4.8
Age of reference person	49.7	50.0	50.1	50.3	—	—	—
Average number in consumer unit:							
People	2.5	2.5	2.5	2.5	—	—	—
Children under 18	0.6	0.6	0.6	0.6	—	—	—
Adults 65 and older	0.3	0.3	0.3	0.4	—	—	—
Earners	1.3	1.3	1.3	1.3	—	—	—
Vehicles	1.9	1.9	1.9	1.9	—	—	—
Percent homeowner	65	64	64	63	—	—	—
Average annual expenditures	$49,705	$51,442	$51,100	$53,495	3.5	−0.7	4.7
Food	6,458	6,599	6,602	6,759	2.2	0.0	2.4
Food at home	3,838	3,921	3,977	3,971	2.2	1.4	−0.2
Cereals and bakery products	531	538	544	519	1.3	1.1	−4.6
Meats, poultry, fish, and eggs	832	852	856	892	2.4	0.5	4.2
Dairy products	407	419	414	423	2.9	−1.2	2.2
Fruits and vegetables	715	731	751	756	2.2	2.7	0.7
Other food at home	1,353	1,380	1,412	1,382	2.0	2.3	−2.1
Food away from home	2,620	2,678	2,625	2,787	2.2	−2.0	6.2
Alcoholic beverages	456	451	445	463	−1.1	−1.3	4.0
Housing	16,803	16,887	17,148	17,798	0.5	1.5	3.8
Shelter	9,825	9,891	10,080	10,491	0.7	1.9	4.1
Owned dwellings	6,148	6,056	6,108	6,149	−1.5	0.9	0.7
Rented dwellings	3,029	3,186	3,324	3,631	5.2	4.3	9.2
Other lodging	648	649	649	710	0.2	0.0	9.4
Utilities, fuels, and public services	3,727	3,648	3,737	3,921	−2.1	2.4	4.9
Household operations	1,122	1,159	1,144	1,174	3.3	−1.3	2.6
Housekeeping supplies	615	610	645	632	−0.8	5.7	−2.0
Household furnishings and equipment	1,514	1,580	1,542	1,581	4.4	−2.4	2.5
Apparel and services	1,740	1,736	1,604	1,786	−0.2	−7.6	11.3
Transportation	8,293	8,998	9,004	9,073	8.5	0.1	0.8
Vehicle purchases (net outlay)	2,669	3,210	3,271	3,301	20.3	1.9	0.9
Gasoline and motor oil	2,655	2,756	2,611	2,468	3.8	−5.3	−5.5
Other vehicle expenses	2,454	2,490	2,584	2,723	1.5	3.8	5.4
Public and other transportation	516	542	537	581	5.0	−0.9	8.2
Healthcare	3,313	3,556	3,631	4,290	7.3	2.1	18.1
Entertainment	2,572	2,605	2,482	2,728	1.3	−4.7	9.9
Personal care products and services	634	628	608	645	−0.9	−3.2	6.1
Reading	115	109	102	103	−5.2	−6.4	1.0
Education	1,051	1,207	1,138	1,236	14.8	−5.7	8.6
Tobacco products and smoking supplies	351	332	330	319	−5.4	−0.6	−3.3
Miscellaneous	775	829	645	782	7.0	−22.2	21.2
Cash contributions	1,721	1,913	1,834	1,788	11.2	−4.1	−2.5
Personal insurance and pensions	5,424	5,591	5,528	5,726	3.1	−1.1	3.6
Life and other personal insurance	317	353	319	327	11.4	−9.6	2.5
Pensions and Social Security	5,106	5,238	5,209	5,399	2.6	−0.6	3.6

SOURCE: "Table A. Average Annual Expenditures by Major Category of All Consumer Units and Percent Changes, Consumer Expenditure Survey, 2011–14," in *Consumer Expenditures in 2014*, U.S. Department of Labor, Bureau of Labor Statistics, October 2016, https://www.bls.gov/opub/reports/consumer-expenditures/2014/pdf/home.pdf (accessed January 10, 2017)

residents. (For further information on this effort and its progress, see Chapter 3.)

ALCOHOL AND TOBACCO ADVERTISING
Alcohol Advertising

The Federal Trade Commission (FTC) reports in *Self-Regulation in the Alcohol Industry* (March 2014, https://www.ftc.gov/system/files/documents/reports/self -regulation-alcohol-industry-report-federal-trade-com mission/140320alcoholreport.pdf) that the alcohol indus try spent $3.5 billion on marketing in 2011. Of this total, nearly one-third ($1.1 billion, or 31.9%) was spent on advertising through traditional media outlets, a category

that includes national and local television, radio, magazines, and newspapers. Advertising on national television accounted for the largest proportion of the alcohol industry's expenditures on traditional media in 2011, with $778.8 million, or 22.5% of the industry's total marketing budget, devoted to national television ads that year. Over a quarter ($987.1 million, or 28.6%) of alcohol marketing was devoted to point-of-sale advertis ing and promotions in 2011, whereas $397.3 million (11.5%) was allocated toward sponsorship of sporting events or individual athletes.

A turning point in the history of alcohol advertising came in 1996, when the distilled spirits industry removed a self-imposed ban on television advertising. Stuart Elliott reports in "Thanks to Cable, Liquor Ads Find a TV Audience" (NYTimes.com, December 15, 2003) that by the end of 2003 hard liquor was being advertised on two dozen national cable networks, 140 local cable systems, and 420 local broadcast stations. In "In a First, CNN Runs a Liquor Commercial" (NYTimes.com, March 2, 2005), Elliott notes that in March 2005 CNN became the first national cable news network to air advertisements for hard liquor, with a commercial for Grey Goose vodka. DISCUS reports in *Distilled Spirits Council 2012 Industry Review* (February 6, 2013, http://www.discus.org/assets/1/7/Distilled_Spirits_Industry_Briefing_Feb_6.pdf) that television accounted for $5.7 million (1.1%) of the $502.8 million the liquor industry spent on marketing in 2000. By 2012 television advertising accounted for well over one-third ($192.4 million of $490.4 million, or 39.2%) of the liquor industry's total marketing budget.

ALCOHOL ADVERTISING AND YOUTH. Matthis Morgenstern et al. examine in "Exposure to Alcohol Advertising and Teen Drinking" (*Preventive Medicine*, vol. 52, no. 2, February 1, 2011) whether there is an association between exposure to alcohol advertisements and the use of alcohol in adolescents. The researchers acknowledge that the results of many studies show that exposure to alcohol advertisements encourages youth to drink alcoholic beverages, to drink more if they already drink, and to develop favorable attitudes toward drinking. However, Morgenstern et al. go a step further by testing whether an association exists between youth drinking and alcohol advertisements or between youth drinking and any type of advertisements in general. The researchers conclude that a positive association exists between exposure to alcohol advertising and certain youth drinking behaviors, such as current and binge drinking, but that no association exists between these behaviors and advertisements in general. These findings suggest that attempts to reduce youth drinking must involve limiting or changing alcohol advertising to lessen its effect on youth and/or countering alcohol advertising with public health campaigns to reduce youth drinking.

Is alcohol advertising targeted to youth or do young people just happen to watch advertising that is aimed at those aged 21 years and older? In "Association between Adolescent Viewership and Alcohol Advertising on Cable Television" (*American Journal of Public Health*, vol. 100, no. 3, March 2010), Paul J. Chung et al. research this question and conclude that "across the vast majority of time slots, adolescent viewers, especially girls, were exposed to more beer, spirits, and alcopop [flavored alcoholic beverage] ads on cable television than would be expected through incidental exposure." The researchers comment that "the underage viewership threshold of 30% adopted by the various industries has

been ineffective in reducing adolescent exposure to advertisements. Moreover, the wine industry's relative success in reaching young adults while avoiding adolescents suggests that more-careful discrimination between the two groups may be possible."

The CDC indicates in "Youth Exposure to Alcohol Advertising on Television—25 Markets, United States, 2010" (*Morbidity and Mortality Weekly Report*, vol. 62, no. 44, November 8, 2013) that in 2010 roughly one out of four alcohol advertisements in the nation's 25 largest television markets were seen by audiences in which the proportion of viewers between the ages of 12 and 20 years exceeded the 30% threshold. Furthermore, the CDC notes that the "increase in spirits advertising on cable television also coincides with an observed increase in consumption of spirits by high school students, particularly among those who binge drink." At the same time, the degree of exposure to alcohol advertising can influence the amount of alcohol that young people consume. In "Amount of Televised Advertising Exposure and the Quantity of Alcohol Consumed by Youth" (*Journal of Studies on Alcohol and Drugs*, vol. 77, no. 5, September 2016), Timothy S. Naimi et al. identify a direct correlation between increased exposure to brand-specific alcohol advertising and increased consumption of those brands of alcoholic beverages among underage drinkers.

Tobacco Advertising

According to the FTC, in *Cigarette Report for 2013* (March 2016, https://www.ftc.gov/system/files/documents/reports/federal-trade-commission-cigarette-report-2013/2013cigarettept.pdf), U.S. cigarette sales fell 4.1% between 2012 and 2013, from 267.7 billion cigarettes to 256.7 billion cigarettes. Advertising expenditures also fell slightly during this span, from $9.2 billion in 2012 to $8.9 billion in 2013.

The tobacco industry is forbidden by law to advertise on radio, television, and billboards. Where do the industry's advertising dollars go? In 2013 the largest share ($7.6 billion, or 85.4%) of the $8.9 billion spent was used for price discounts, which are paid to cigarette retailers and wholesalers to discount the price of the cigarettes to consumers. Approximately $688.5 million was paid in promotional allowances to retailers and wholesalers involved in the distribution of cigarettes, and $248.8 million was devoted to coupons. These were all considered promotional activities and were the primary ways in which cigarettes were advertised.

TOBACCO ADVERTISING AND YOUTH. In March 2010 the U.S. Food and Drug Administration (FDA) announced that it would restrict tobacco companies' marketing practices (especially the ones that targeted youth) using the power given it under a new tobacco control law that was passed in 2009. Lyndsey Layton explains in "New FDA Rules Will Greatly Restrict Tobacco Advertising and Sales" (WashingtonPost.com, March 19, 2010) that tobacco companies will no longer be able to sell cigarettes to people under the age of 18 years; sponsor sporting and entertainment events; give away cigarettes or other items with the purchase of tobacco products, such as tiny purses, wristbands, and cell phone jewelry for women and girls; offer fewer than 20 cigarettes per package (larger packages are less affordable and less likely to be purchased by youth); or sell cigarettes in vending machines to which young people have access. These new rules went into effect in June 2010.

ALCOHOL AND TOBACCO TAXATION

Taxation is an age-old method by which the government raises money. Alcoholic beverages have been taxed since colonial times, and tobacco products have been taxed since 1863. The alcohol and tobacco industries contribute a great deal of tax money to federal, state, and local governments.

Alcohol Taxes

According to DISCUS, in "Increasing Alcohol Taxes Punishes the Entire Hospitality Industry" (2017, http://www.discus.org/policy/taxes), "Beverage alcohol products rank among the highest taxed consumer items available today in the United States." DISCUS estimates that direct and indirect local, state, and federal taxes and fees account for 54% of the retail price of a typical 750-milliliter (1.6 pints) bottle of 80 proof spirits. Although the beer and wine industries are taxed at lower levels, they still contribute a significant amount of tax revenue.

In fiscal year (FY) 2016 the federal government collected nearly $10.7 billion in excise taxes (monies paid on purchases of specific goods) on alcoholic beverages. (See Table 7.3.) Federal excise taxes on distilled spirits amounted to more than half (55.1%) of that total—about $5.9 billion, which included taxes on both domestic and imported distilled spirits. Distilled spirits are taxed by the proof gallon, which is a standard U.S. gallon of 231 cubic inches (3.8 L) containing 50% ethyl alcohol by volume, or 100 proof.

TABLE 7.3

Federal government tax collections on alcohol and tobacco, fiscal year 2016

[In thousands of dollars]

Revenue source	1st quarter	2nd quarter	3rd quarter	4th quarter	Cumulative 2016	2015
Excise tax, total	$5,719,433	$5,934,001	$6,549,886	$7,321,072	$25,524,392	$25,461,969
Alcohol tax, total	$2,388,180	$2,516,262	$2,733,959	$3,031,571	$10,669,972	$10,370,140
Distilled spirits tax, total	$1,367,616	$1,406,469	$1,507,534	$1,624,806	$5,906,425	$5,714,903
Domestic	$1,048,270	$932,339	$1,147,085	$1,160,051	$4,287,745	$4,219,879
Imported*	$319,346	$474,130	$360,449	$464,755	$1,618,680	$1,495,024
Wine tax, total	$285,107	$266,874	$273,915	$297,583	$1,123,479	$1,074,672
Domestic	$201,087	$175,360	$187,742	$205,534	$768,723	$738,723
Imported*	$84,020	$91,514	$86,173	$93,049	$354,756	$335,949
Beer tax, total	$735,457	$842,919	$,952,510	$1,109,182	$3,640,068	$3,580,565
Domestic	$641,305	$666,839	$802,931	$908,961	$3,020,036	$3,038,238
Imported*	$94,152	$176,080	$149,579	$200,221	$620,032	$542,327
Tobacco tax, total	$3,168,025	$3,234,745	$3,611,225	$4,089,241	$14,103,236	$14,453,285
Domestic						
Regular	$2,958,882	$3,053,025	$3,395,131	$3,866,316	$13,273,354	$13,621,410
Floor stocks	$2	$4	$237	$2	$245	$2,444
Imported*	$209,141	$181,716	$215,857	$222,923	$829,637	$829,431
Unclassified alcohol and tobacco tax, (domestic) total	$200	$305	$0	$867	$1,372	$26
Firearms and ammunition tax, total	$163,028	$182,689	$204,702	$199,393	$749,812	$638,518
Special (occupational) tax, total	$4	$7	$146	$101	$258	$289
Total imports (U.S. Customs)*	**$706,659**	**$923,440**	**$812,058**	**$980,948**	**$3,423,105**	**$3,202,731**
Total TTB tax collections	**$5,012,778**	**$5,010,568**	**$5,737,974**	**$6,340,225**	**$22,101,545**	**$22,259,527**
Total tax collections	**$5,719,437**	**$5,934,008**	**$6,550,032**	**$7,321,173**	**$25,524,650**	**$25,462,258**

TTB = Alcohol and Tobacco Tax and Trade Bureau
*All "imported" tax collection figures are obtained from U.S. Customs data.
Notes: This is an unofficial report. Official revenue collection figures are stated in the TTB Chief Financial Officer Annual Report. Addition of current fiscal year prior quarter figures year may not agree with cumulative figures reported on this report for current fiscal year due to rounding. Cumulative figures for current fiscal year adjusted to reflect classification of unclassified alcohol and tobacco tax collections previously reported and to reflect collection adjustments for prior tax periods. Source for other tax collection figures on this report is a TTB database that records tax collection data by tax return period. This data is summarized on this report by the quarter in which an incurred tax liability is satisfied. Unclassified Alcohol and Tobacco Tax is tax collected, but not yet posted to a taxpaper account due to missing Employer Identification Number (EIN), permit number, and/or other taxpayer identity information.

SOURCE: "Tax Collections TTB S 5630-FY-2016 Cumulative Summary Fiscal Year 2016 Final," in *Alcohol and Tobacco Tax and Trade Bureau Statistical Release*, U.S. Department of the Treasury, Alcohol and Tobacco Tax and Trade Bureau, December 1, 2016, https://www.ttb.gov/statistics/final16.pdf (accessed January 10, 2017)

Excise taxes on wine and beer made up the other half of the excise taxes that were collected on alcoholic beverages in FY 2016. The calculation of wine taxes depends on several variables, such as alcohol content and the size of the winery. In FY 2016 federal excise taxes on wine totaled just over $1.1 billion. (See Table 7.3.) Total beer excise taxes were much higher, at $3.6 billion. According to the TTB, in "Common Compliance and Tax Issues Found during Brewery Audits" (February 13, 2017, https://www.ttb.gov/beer/beer-tutor ial.shtml), brewers that produce fewer than 2 million barrels (1 barrel equals 31 gallons [117.3 L]) get a reduced excise tax rate of $7 per barrel on the first 60,000 barrels, and pay $18 per barrel on all subsequent barrels produced. Those that produce more than 2 million barrels pay an excise tax of $18 per barrel on all barrels produced.

Besides the federal excise taxes, the states levy sales taxes on alcohol. According to the U.S. Census Bureau, in *State Government Tax Collections: 2015* (September 23, 2016, https://factfinder.census.gov/), state sales taxes collected on alcoholic beverages totaled $6.4 billion in FY 2015. This amounted to about 0.7% of all state taxes collected that fiscal year ($916.5 billion).

Tobacco Taxes

The Census Bureau reports in *State Government Tax Collections: 2015* that state sales taxes on tobacco products amounted to $17.7 billion in FY 2015. States have raised their excise taxes on cigarettes to help defray health care costs that are associated with tobacco, to discourage young people from starting to smoke, and to motivate smokers to stop. Figure 7.1 shows state cigarette excise tax rates in 2017. New York had the highest state excise tax on cigarettes at $4.35 per pack. Connecticut was second with $3.90 per pack. Missouri had the lowest excise tax of $0.17 per pack. Ann Boonn of the Campaign for Tobacco-Free Kids indicates in the fact sheet "State Cigarette Excise Tax Rates and Rankings" (January 3, 2017, https://www.tobaccofreekids.org/research/factsheets/pdf/0097.pdf) that the average cigarette tax in 2017 was $1.69 per pack nationwide. Rates were considerably lower in the major tobacco-producing states, where the average tax was $0.485 per pack.

Besides state taxes on tobacco, the federal government imposes taxes on cigarettes and other tobacco products. In February 2009 President Barack Obama (1961–) signed into law the State Children's Health Insurance Plan bill, which included an increase in the federal tobacco tax. As of April 1, 2009, the federal excise tax on cigarettes increased to just under $1.01 per pack.

GOVERNMENT REGULATION OF ALCOHOL AND TOBACCO

Besides taxation, the alcohol and tobacco industries are subject to federal and state laws that regulate factors such as sales, advertising, and shipping.

Alcohol Regulation

The best-known pieces of legislation regarding alcohol are the 18th and 21st Amendments to the U.S. Constitution. The 18th Amendment prohibited the manufacture, sale, and importation of alcoholic beverages. Ratified in 1919, it took effect in 1920 and ushered in a period in U.S. history known as Prohibition. After 13 years, during which it failed to stop the manufacture and sale of alcohol, Prohibition was repealed in 1933 by the 21st Amendment.

Most interpretations of the 21st Amendment hold that the amendment gives individual states the power to regulate and control alcoholic beverages within their own borders. Consequently, every state has its own alcohol administration and enforcement agency. "Control states" directly control the sale and distribution of alcoholic beverages within their borders. According to the TTB, in "Alcohol Beverage Authorities in United States, Canada, and Puerto Rico" (December 16, 2016, https://www.ttb.gov/wine/state-ABC.shtml), there were 18 control states in 2016: Alabama, Idaho, Iowa, Maine, Michigan, Mississippi, Montana, New Hampshire, North Carolina, Ohio, Oregon, Pennsylvania, Utah, Vermont, Virginia, Washington, West Virginia, and Wyoming. Montgomery County in Maryland acted as a control state as well. Some critics of this policy question whether such state monopolies violate antitrust laws. The other 32 states were licensure states and allowed only licensed businesses to operate as wholesalers and retailers.

DIRECT SHIPMENTS: RECIPROCITY OR FELONY? Controversy has developed over the direct shipment of alcoholic beverages from one state directly to consumers or retailers in another state. Under the U.S. Constitution's interstate commerce clause, Congress has the power to regulate trade between states. Nevertheless, the 21st Amendment gives states the authority to regulate the sale and distribution of alcoholic beverages. Furthermore, it allows states to set their own laws governing the sale of alcohol within their borders.

Because the laws of the states are not uniform, several states have passed reciprocity legislation that allows specific states to exchange direct shipments, thus eliminating the state-licensed wholesalers from the exchange. Wholesalers and retailers charge that reciprocity and direct shipment are violations of the 21st Amendment. They fear being bypassed in the exchange, as do states that prohibit direct shipments of alcohol. Other stakeholders in this issue are consumers and wine producers who want the right to deal directly with each other.

ALCOHOL SALES AND THE INTERNET. In January 2001 the 21st Amendment Enforcement Act became law. This legislation makes it difficult for companies to sell alcohol over the Internet or through mail-order services. It allows attorneys general in states that ban direct

FIGURE 7.1

State cigarette tax rates, 2017

Average state cigarette tax: $1.69 per pack.
Average cigarette tax in major tobacco states: 48.5 cents per pack.
Average cigarette tax in non-tobacco states: $1,85 per pack.

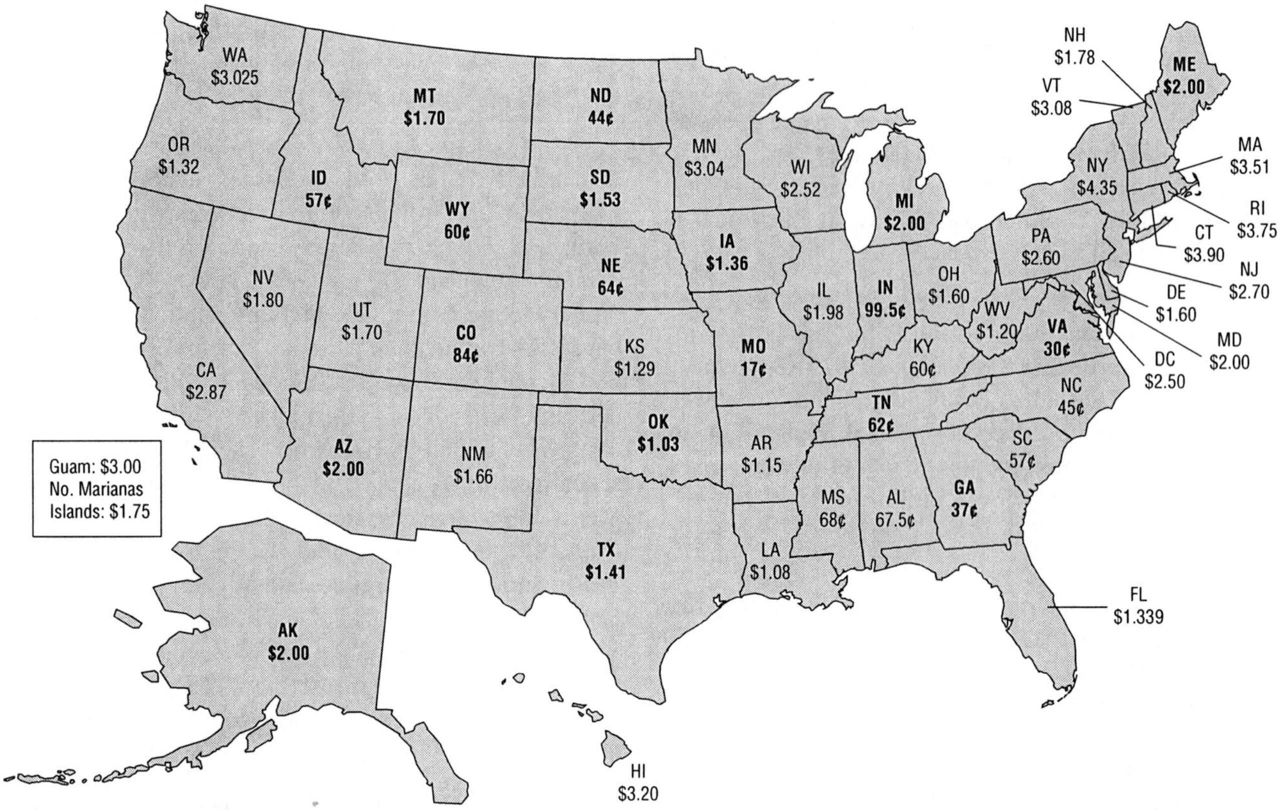

State	Tax
WA	$3.025
MT	$1.70
ND	44¢
NH	$1.78
ME	$2.00
OR	$1.32
ID	57¢
MN	$3.04
WI	$2.52
VT	$3.08
NY	$4.35
MA	$3.51
SD	$1.53
MI	$2.00
RI	$3.75
WY	60¢
PA	$2.60
CT	$3.90
NV	$1.80
NE	64¢
IA	$1.36
OH	$1.60
NJ	$2.70
UT	$1.70
IL	$1.98
IN	99.5¢
WV	$1.20
DE	$1.60
CO	84¢
KS	$1.29
MO	17¢
KY	60¢
VA	30¢
MD	$2.00
CA	$2.87
OK	$1.03
AR	$1.15
TN	62¢
DC	$2.50
NC	45¢
AZ	$2.00
NM	$1.66
SC	57¢
MS	68¢
AL	67.5¢
GA	37¢
TX	$1.41
LA	$1.08
FL	$1.339
AK	$2.00
HI	$3.20

Guam: $3.00
No. Marianas
Islands: $1.75

Notes: Map shows state cigarette tax rates in effect as of April 1, 2017 (CA effective 4/1/17). The states in bold have not increased their tax for at least 10 years (since 2007 or earlier). Currently, 35 states, DC, Puerto Rico, the Northern Marianas, and Guam have cigarette tax rates of $1.00 per pack or higher; 17 states, DC, Puerto Rico, and Guam have cigarette tax rates of $2.00 per pack or higher; eight states, Puerto Rico, and Guam have cigarette tax rates of $3.00 per pack or higher; and one state (NY) has a cigarette tax rate more than $4.00 per pack. The state averages listed above do not include Puerto Rico (with a population larger than those in more than 20 states and DC) or any of the U.S. territories (such as Guam). The major tobacco states with extensive tobacco farming and, often, cigarette manufacturing, are NC, KY, VA, SC, TN, & GA. Federal cigarette tax is $1.01 per pack. Not shown are the special taxes or fees some states place on cigarettes made by Non-Participating Manufacturers (NPMs), the companies that have not joined the Master Settlement Agreement (MSA) between the states and the major cigarette companies. Some local governments also have their own cigarette taxes, such as Chicago ($1.18), Cook County, IL ($3.00), New York City ($1.50), Philadelphia ($2.00), and Juneau, AK ($3.00). Nationally, estimated smoking-caused health costs and lost productivity totals $19.16 per pack.

SOURCE: Ann Boonn, "Map of State Cigarette Tax Rates," Campaign for Tobacco-Free Kids, January 3, 2017, https://www.tobaccofreekids.org/research/factsheets/pdf/0222.pdf (accessed January 10, 2017)

alcohol sales to seek federal injunctions against companies that violate their liquor sales laws.

Within a month of the passage of this act, the high-tech community voiced its concern regarding such legislation, suggesting that if states could ban Internet alcohol sales they might restrict other electronic commerce as well. The U.S. senator Orrin G. Hatch (1934–; R-UT) said he crafted the bill to take other e-commerce concerns into account and insisted that the measure is narrowly tailored to deal only with alcohol.

In May 2005 the U.S. Supreme Court ruled on three cases that had been consolidated under the name *Granholm v. Heald* (544 U.S. 460). At issue were state laws in

Michigan and New York that prohibited out-of-state wineries from selling their products over the Internet directly to Michigan and New York residents but that allowed in-state wineries to make such sales. The Michigan and New York state governments argued that these laws were permissible under the 21st Amendment. A group of wineries and business advocates argued that the state laws were unconstitutional restrictions of interstate trade. In a 5–4 decision, the court agreed that the state laws were unconstitutional, stating, "States have broad power to regulate liquor under §2 of the Twenty-First Amendment. This power, however, does not allow States to ban, or severely limit, the direct shipment of out-of-state wine while simultaneously authorizing direct shipment by in-state producers. If a State chooses to allow direct shipment of wine, it must do so on even-handed terms." It should be noted that this ruling only applies to state laws that prohibit out-of-state Internet alcohol sales and not to the 21st Amendment Enforcement Act.

Tobacco Regulation and Legislation

Federal tobacco legislation has covered everything from unproved advertising claims and warning-label requirements to the development of fire-safe cigarettes and little cigars that self-extinguish if left unattended in order to reduce the likelihood of fire. In the past the FDA prohibited the claim that Fairfax cigarettes prevented respiratory and other diseases (1953) and denied the claim that tartaric acid, which was added to Trim Reducing-Aid cigarettes, helped promote weight loss (1959).

The FTC has also been given jurisdiction over tobacco issues in several areas. As early as 1942 the commission issued a cease-and-desist order in reference to Kool cigarettes' claim that smoking Kools gave extra protection against or cured colds. In January 1964 the FTC proposed a rule to strictly regulate cigarette advertisements and to prohibit explicit or implicit health claims by cigarette companies.

The tobacco industry had avoided some other forms of federal regulation by being exempted from many federal health and safety laws. For example, in the Hazardous Substances Act of 1960, the term *hazardous substance* does not include tobacco and tobacco products, nor does the term *consumer product* in the Consumer Product Safety Act of 1972. Tobacco was similarly exempted from regulation under the Fair Packaging and Labeling Act of 1966 and the Toxic Substance Control Act of 1976.

Some of the legislation of the late 1980s included requiring four alternating health warnings to be printed on tobacco packaging, prohibiting smokeless tobacco advertising on television and radio, and banning smoking on domestic airline flights. In 1992 the Synar Amendment was passed. The amendment said that states must have laws that ban the sale of tobacco products to people under 18 years of age.

In 1993 the U.S. Environmental Protection Agency released its final risk assessment on secondhand smoke and classified it as a known human carcinogen (cancer-causing agent). In 1994 the Occupational Safety and Health Administration proposed regulations that would prohibit smoking in workplaces, except in smoking rooms that are separately ventilated. As of March 2015, the United States did not have federal smoking control legislation, but many states and municipalities did have legislation that banned smoking in a variety of public places and workplaces. Nevertheless, the Family Smoking Prevention and Tobacco Control Act of 2009 did give the FDA the authority to regulate the production and marketing of tobacco products within limits, such as banning certain flavored cigarettes that appealed to youth and strengthening the warnings on cigarette packages.

TOBACCO SALES AND THE INTERNET. In the early 21st century it became apparent that some online tobacco vendors were not following the same rules as conventional tobacco retailers. For example, some vendors did not indicate that sales to minors were prohibited on their site. Many required that a user simply state that he or she was of legal age, making no attempt to verify the information. In addition, many did not collect and pay cigarette sales taxes.

Congress responded to these problems by passing the Prevent All Cigarette Trafficking (PACT) Act of 2009. The law affects Internet sales of tobacco products in that it ensures the collection of federal, state, and local taxes on cigarettes and smokeless tobacco by requiring online vendors of tobacco products to register with the states in which their customers reside and by imposing strong penalties against those who do not comply. Paying these taxes is important not only for government revenues but also to ensure that the price of cigarettes remains high to discourage their use, especially by youth.

To further safeguard illegal sales to youth, the PACT Act also bars Internet vendors of tobacco products from shipping these products via the U.S. Postal Service (USPS). The USPS does not have the means to verify the age and identification of the person receiving the products. According to Brian Hickey of the Campaign for Tobacco-Free Kids, in the fact sheet "The PACT Act: Preventing Illegal Internet Sales of Cigarettes & Smokeless Tobacco" (April 22, 2016, http://www.tobaccofree kids.org/research/factsheets/pdf/0361.pdf), "The PACT Act will stop such Internet sales of cigarettes and smokeless tobacco to kids by requiring the sellers to verify the age of their customers prior to sale by checking against available government and commercial ID databases, and by requiring sellers to use a method of delivery that will verify the age and ID of the person accepting the final delivery of the cigarettes or smokeless tobacco prior to handing them over."

FDA REGULATION OF TOBACCO PRODUCTS. In 1994 the FDA investigated the tobacco industry to determine whether nicotine is an addictive drug that should be regulated like other addictive drugs. Weeks of testimony before Congress indicated that tobacco companies may have been aware of the addictive effects of nicotine and the likely connection between smoking and cancer as early as the mid-1950s.

In August 1995 the FDA ruled that the nicotine in tobacco products is a drug and, therefore, is liable to FDA regulation. However, the tobacco, advertising, and convenience store industries filed a lawsuit against the FDA, claiming it did not have the authority to regulate tobacco as an addictive drug. After conflicting decisions in the lower courts, the Supreme Court ruled 5–4 in *FDA v. Brown and Williamson Tobacco Corp.* (529 U.S. 120 [2000]) that the FDA lacked this authority. Although the ruling did not allow the FDA to regulate tobacco, state laws regarding selling cigarettes to minors were not affected.

In March 2005 bipartisan bills were introduced in the U.S. House of Representatives and the U.S. Senate to grant the FDA the authority to regulate tobacco products. The bills never became law during that session of Congress, but similar legislation was introduced again in 2009. The Family Smoking Prevention and Tobacco Control Act was passed by the House and the Senate and was subsequently signed into law by President Obama in June 2009. This law gives the FDA the authority to control tobacco advertising and sales to children, require changes in tobacco products to make them less harmful, prohibit health claims that have no scientific backing, and require the contents and health dangers of tobacco products to be listed on the packaging.

GOVERNMENT REGULATION OF MARIJUANA

As of 2017, marijuana remained illegal under federal law in the United States. Despite this prohibition, during the early 21st century a number of state laws were enacted that allowed for the legal cultivation, sale, and use of marijuana, either for medical or recreational purposes. As a result of these laws, marijuana became a new source of tax revenue in states where the drug had been legalized. In the *World Drug Report: 2016* (2016, https://www.unodc.org/doc/wdr2016/WORLD_DRUG_REPORT_2016_web.pdf), the United Nations Office on Drugs and Crime (UNODC) provides information on revenues generated by marijuana sales in Colorado and Washington. In 2014 sales of recreational marijuana in Colorado generated $56 million in tax revenues; a year later, marijuana tax revenues in Colorado topped $114 million, an increase of more than 100%. In Washington marijuana sales generated $256 million in FY 2015, resulting in $65 million in tax revenues. The UNODC notes that data relating to marijuana sales in other states remained unavailable at the time the *World Drug Report: 2016* was published.

Additional information relating to marijuana legalization appears in Chapters 8 and 9.

THE SOCIETAL COSTS OF SUBSTANCE USE

Few reports are available on the economic costs of alcohol, tobacco, and illicit drug use, and many are outdated. In the most recent report on the subject from the

CDC, "Excessive Drinking Costs U.S. $223.5 Billion" (April 17, 2014, https://www.cdc.gov/features/alcohol consumption/), the agency estimates that costs related to alcohol abuse and dependence were approximately $223.5 billion in 2006. More research has followed in subsequent years on the costs of drug abuse and tobacco use.

Costs of Illicit Drug Use

The U.S. Department of Justice's National Drug Intelligence Center discusses the costs that are associated with illicit drug use in *The Economic Impact of Illicit Drug Use on American Society, 2011* (April 2011, https://www.justice.gov/archive/ndic/pubs44/44731/44731p.pdf). In 2007 illicit drug use resulted in total economic losses of $193.1 billion.

The National Drug Intelligence Center divides the costs of illicit drug use into three major cost components: crime, health, and productivity. The largest cost component in 2007 was productivity. In this case, productivity means lost productivity. It is an indirect cost that reflects losses such as work that was never performed because of poor health, premature death, or incarceration. In 2007 lost productivity accounted for $120.3 billion (62%) of the total costs associated with illicit drug use that year.

The second-largest cost component was crime, which includes drug-related crime costs such as the operation of prisons, state and local police protection, and victim costs. These costs totaled $61.4 billion in 2007.

The third-largest cost component associated with illicit drug use in 2007 was health care. These costs include expenses associated with specialty treatment, hospital care, and other costs. In 2007 these costs totaled $11.4 billion.

As Figure 7.2 shows, death rates related to drug poisoning and opioid poisoning rose steadily between 2000 and 2014. Table 7.4 provides an overview of drug-related death rates in the United States for select years between 1999 and 2014, by age, sex, geographical region, and race and ethnicity. In 1999, there were 6.1 drug-related deaths per 100,000 population; by 2014, this rate had more than doubled, to 14.7 drug-related deaths per 100,000 population. The drug-related death rate in 2014 was highest among non-Hispanic white males, at 23.2 deaths per 100,000 population. The lowest rate of drug-related deaths in 2014 was among Asian or Pacific Islander females, with 1.7 deaths per 100,000 population.

Between 1999 and 2014, the rate of drug-related deaths linked to opioid abuse more than quadrupled, from 1.4 deaths per 100,000 population in 1999 to 5.9 deaths per 100,000 population in 2014. (See Table 7.4.) The largest percentage increase in opioid-related deaths during this span occurred among non-Hispanic white females. In 1999 the opioid-related death rate among

FIGURE 7.2

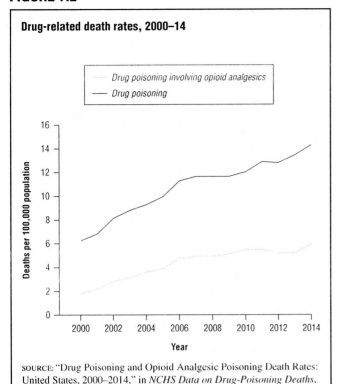

Drug-related death rates, 2000–14

SOURCE: "Drug Poisoning and Opioid Analgesic Poisoning Death Rates: United States, 2000–2014," in *NCHS Data on Drug-Poisoning Deaths*, Centers for Disease Control and Prevention, National Center for Health Statistics, March 2016, https://www.cdc.gov/nchs/data/factsheets/factsheet_drug_poisoning.pdf (accessed January 10, 2017)

non-Hispanic white women was 1.1 deaths per 100,000 population; by 2014 this rate had climbed to 6.5 deaths per 100,000 population, an increase of more than 590%. (See Table 7.4.) Over this span, the opioid-related death rate dropped slightly among Hispanic males, from 2.9 deaths per 100,000 population in 1999 to 2.7 deaths per 100,000 population in 2014. By contrast, the opioid-related death rate among Hispanic females tripled during these years, rising from 0.5 deaths per 100,000 population in 1999 to 1.6 deaths per 100,000 population in 2014. (See Table 7.4.)

Table 7.4 also provides data on heroin-related death rates for select years between 1999 and 2014. Non-Hispanic white males experienced the largest increase in heroin-related deaths during this span, rising from 1.1 deaths per 100,000 population in 1999 to 6.7 deaths per 100,000 population in 2014. In 2014 Asian or Pacific Islander males had the lowest recorded rate of heroin-related deaths, with 0.6 deaths per 100,000 population that year. Because there were fewer than 20 heroin-related deaths among Asian or Pacific Islander females in any given year between 1999 and 2014, there were no heroin-related death rates recorded for this group during this span. (See Table 7.4.)

Figure 7.3 provides an overview of drug-related death rates by state. In 2014, 26 of 50 states recorded

drug-related death rates that were between 14.8 and 36.3 deaths per 100,000 population. North Dakota recorded the lowest drug-related death rate in 2014, with fewer than 6.8 drug-related deaths per 100,000 population that year.

Figure 7.4 breaks down drug-related death rates in 2014 by age group. Adults between the ages of 45 and 54 years experienced the highest rate of drug-related deaths that year, with 28.2 deaths per 100,000 population. This rate was more than double the rate of 11.5 deaths per 100,000 population experienced by adults aged 18 to 24 years. Among individuals under the age of 18 years, the drug-related death rate was 0.4 deaths per 100,000 population in 2014. (See Figure 7.4.)

In 2009 Rosalie Liccardo Pacula et al. published *Issues in Estimating the Economic Cost of Drug Abuse in Consuming Nations* (http://www.rand.org/content/dam/rand/pubs/technical_reports/2009/RAND_TR709.pdf), which was developed for the European Commission by the Rand Corporation. The researchers analyze studies undertaken in various developed countries to try to quantify the economic costs of drug abuse and observe that they use a range of approaches and methods, which makes it impossible to compare results across countries. Pacula et al. also note that "the pitfalls and assumptions necessary to construct a comparable estimate across countries are quite significant and described in detail throughout this report. We conclude that it is not possible at this time to develop a meaningful comparative estimate of the cost of drug use across countries or to aggregate these costs to the regional or global level."

Despite these challenges, a number of studies have attempted to explore the broader economic and social costs of substance abuse. For example, in *World Drug Report: 2016*, the UNODC estimates that, among the countries surveyed, costs related to drug abuse account for between 0.7% and 1.7% of gross domestic product (GDP) each year. The UNODC further reports that abuse of opioids, cocaine, amphetamines, and cannabis resulted in approximately 12 million years of lives lost in 2013 alone. Of these, roughly two-thirds (8 million) were related to opioid abuse.

The International Narcotics Control Board (INCB) monitors compliance with global drug treaties throughout the world. In *Report of the International Narcotics Control Board for 2013* (2014, https://www.incb.org/documents/Publications/AnnualReports/AR2013/English/AR_2013_E.pdf), the INCB reports that each year approximately 4.5 million people receive drug treatment worldwide, at an overall cost of $35 billion. The INCB notes that this figure represents only one-sixth of the total number of drug users needing treatment. According to INCB estimates, if all individuals struggling with drug dependency received the treatment they needed, the total cost would range from $200 billion to $250 billion.

TABLE 7.4

Drug-induced deaths by age, sex, and race/ethnicity, selected years, 1999–2014

[Data are based on death certificates]

Sex, age, race, and Hispanic origin	1999	2000	2004	2005	2010	2011	2012	2013	2014
All persons	Drug poisoning deaths per 100,000 resident population[a]								
All ages, age-adjusted[b]	6.1	6.2	9.4	10.1	12.3	13.2	13.1	13.8	14.7
All ages, crude	6.0	6.2	9.4	10.1	12.4	13.3	13.2	13.9	14.8
Under 15 years	0.1	0.1	0.2	0.2	0.2	0.2	0.2	0.2	0.2
15–24 years	3.2	3.7	6.6	6.9	8.2	8.6	8.0	8.3	8.6
25–34 years	8.1	7.9	11.9	13.6	18.4	20.2	20.1	20.9	23.1
35–44 years	14.0	14.3	19.3	19.6	20.8	22.5	22.1	23.0	25.0
45–54 years	11.1	11.6	19.3	21.1	25.1	26.7	26.9	27.5	28.2
55–64 years	4.2	4.2	7.8	9.0	15.0	15.9	16.6	19.2	20.3
65–74 years	2.4	2.0	2.9	3.2	4.7	5.4	5.8	6.4	6.9
75–84 years	2.8	2.4	2.9	3.1	3.4	3.4	3.4	3.6	3.6
85 years and over	3.8	4.4	4.0	4.1	4.7	4.2	4.3	4.3	4.1
Male									
All ages, age-adjusted[b]	8.2	8.3	11.8	12.8	15.0	16.1	16.1	17.0	18.3
All ages, crude	8.2	8.4	11.9	12.9	15.2	16.3	16.3	17.2	18.4
Under 15 years	0.1	0.2	0.2	0.2	0.3	0.2	0.2	0.2	0.2
15–24 years	4.5	5.3	9.6	10.0	11.6	12.4	11.4	11.7	12.1
25–34 years	11.5	11.3	16.6	18.7	25.0	27.5	27.0	28.6	31.9
35–44 years	19.2	19.5	23.8	24.4	24.9	26.8	27.1	28.1	30.8
45–54 years	15.2	15.7	23.8	25.8	28.5	30.4	30.4	31.5	32.9
55–64 years	4.9	4.4	8.6	10.6	17.3	18.5	19.4	22.7	23.5
65–74 years	2.7	2.1	2.9	3.3	4.5	5.4	6.2	6.9	7.3
75–84 years	2.5	2.5	2.8	3.4	3.6	3.4	3.2	3.7	3.8
85 years and over	4.4	5.9	4.8	5.2	5.1	4.3	5.3	5.9	4.3
Female									
All ages, age-adjusted[b]	3.9	4.1	6.9	7.3	9.6	10.2	10.2	10.6	11.1
All ages, crude	3.9	4.1	6.9	7.4	9.8	10.3	10.3	10.7	11.3
Under 15 years	0.1	0.1	0.2	0.2	0.2	0.2	0.2	0.2	0.2
15–24 years	1.8	1.9	3.3	3.5	4.6	4.6	4.4	4.8	5.0
25–34 years	4.6	4.6	7.2	8.5	11.9	12.8	13.1	13.0	14.1
35–44 years	8.7	9.2	14.8	14.8	16.8	18.2	17.1	18.0	19.2
45–54 years	7.2	7.7	15.0	16.5	21.8	23.1	23.4	23.6	23.7
55–64 years	3.5	3.9	7.0	7.5	12.9	13.5	14.0	15.9	17.2
65–74 years	2.1	2.0	3.0	3.1	4.8	5.3	5.5	5.9	6.5
75–84 years	3.0	2.3	2.9	2.9	3.3	3.4	3.5	3.4	3.5
85 years and over	3.5	3.9	3.7	3.7	4.5	4.2	3.8	3.5	4.0
All ages, age-adjusted[b, c]									
Male:									
White	8.1	8.4	12.6	13.6	16.8	18.1	18.1	19.0	20.4
Black or African American	11.5	10.8	11.1	12.8	10.1	10.1	11.3	12.9	13.8
American Indian or Alaska Native	5.7	6.1	11.2	10.8	11.8	12.9	12.8	12.9	15.9
Asian or Pacific Islander	1.5	1.4	2.1	2.2	2.5	3.2	3.1	3.2	3.3
Hispanic or Latino	8.6	7.1	7.5	8.4	7.6	8.1	8.5	9.2	9.3
White, not Hispanic or Latino	8.0	8.6	13.7	14.7	19.0	20.5	20.4	21.4	23.2
Female:									
White	4.0	4.3	7.5	8.0	10.9	11.7	11.6	12.1	12.7
Black or African American	3.9	4.1	5.5	6.0	5.7	5.9	6.0	6.3	7.0
American Indian or Alaska Native	4.6	3.7	7.9	8.6	9.7	10.7	12.2	11.6	11.2
Asian or Pacific Islander	1.0	0.8	1.1	1.3	1.5	1.6	1.4	1.5	1.7
Hispanic or Latino	2.2	2.0	2.9	3.0	3.6	4.0	4.0	4.1	4.1
White, not Hispanic or Latino	4.3	4.5	8.3	8.8	12.5	13.3	13.2	13.8	14.6
All persons	Drug poisoning deaths involving opioid analgesics per 100,000 resident population[d]								
All ages, age-adjusted[b]	1.4	1.5	3.4	3.7	5.4	5.4	5.1	5.1	5.9
All ages, crude	1.4	1.6	3.4	3.7	5.4	5.4	5.1	5.1	5.9
Under 15 years	*	0.0	0.1	0.1	0.1	0.1	0.1	0.1	0.1
15–24 years	0.7	0.8	2.7	2.7	3.9	3.6	2.8	2.6	3.1
25–34 years	1.9	1.9	4.4	5.3	8.5	8.5	7.7	7.5	9.0
35–44 years	3.5	3.7	6.8	6.9	9.1	9.3	8.8	8.6	10.3
45–54 years	2.9	3.2	7.1	7.9	10.9	11.2	10.6	10.6	11.7
55–64 years	1.0	1.1	2.6	3.1	6.2	6.3	6.6	7.5	8.5
65–74 years	0.4	0.4	0.8	1.0	1.5	1.8	2.0	2.3	2.7
75–84 years	0.3	0.2	0.5	0.6	0.7	0.7	0.9	0.8	0.9
85 years and over	*	*	0.5	0.9	1.1	0.8	0.8	0.9	0.9

Investment in drug treatment programs can play a significant role in reducing other costs related to illicit drug use. According to the INCB, in *Report of the International Narcotics Control Board for 2013*, studies show that every $1 devoted to treatment can save between $4 and $12 in legal and health care costs related to drug abuse. At the same time, every $1 invested in effective drug-prevention programs can result in roughly $10 saved in costs stemming from substance use.

TABLE 7.4

Drug-induced deaths by age, sex, and race/ethnicity, selected years, 1999–2014 [CONTINUED]

[Data are based on death certificates]

Sex, age, race, and Hispanic origin	1999	2000	2004	2005	2010	2011	2012	2013	2014
Male	Drug poisoning deaths involving opioid analgesics per 100,000 resident population[d]								
All ages, age-adjusted[b]	2.0	2.0	4.2	4.6	6.5	6.5	6.0	5.9	6.9
All ages, crude	2.0	2.1	4.2	4.6	6.6	6.5	6.0	5.9	7.0
Under 15 years	*	*	0.1	0.1	0.2	0.1	0.1	0.1	0.1
15–24 years	1.0	1.2	4.2	4.2	5.6	5.3	4.2	3.9	4.4
25–34 years	2.7	2.7	6.1	7.2	11.7	11.4	10.0	10.0	12.2
35–44 years	5.0	4.9	8.2	8.3	10.9	10.9	10.3	9.6	11.9
45–54 years	3.9	4.3	8.3	9.4	12.0	12.1	11.1	11.1	12.5
55–64 years	1.1	1.0	2.8	3.5	7.0	6.9	7.3	8.0	9.2
65–74 years	0.5	0.3	0.7	0.7	1.2	1.7	2.0	2.2	2.5
75–84 years	*	*	0.4	0.6	0.7	0.7	0.7	0.9	0.8
85 years and over	*	*	*	*	1.3	*	1.0	1.3	*
Female									
All ages, age-adjusted[b]	0.9	1.1	2.5	2.8	4.2	4.3	4.2	4.3	4.9
All ages, crude	0.9	1.1	2.5	2.8	4.2	4.4	4.2	4.4	4.9
Under 15 years	*	*	0.1	*	0.1	0.1	0.1	0.1	0.1
15–24 years	0.3	0.4	1.1	1.2	2.1	1.9	1.5	1.4	1.7
25–34 years	1.1	1.2	2.8	3.4	5.3	5.5	5.3	5.0	5.7
35–44 years	2.1	2.5	5.4	5.6	7.3	7.8	7.3	7.6	8.7
45–54 years	1.9	2.2	5.9	6.5	9.8	10.2	10.1	10.1	10.9
55–64 years	0.8	1.1	2.4	2.8	5.5	5.7	6.0	6.9	7.8
65–74 years	0.3	0.4	0.9	1.2	1.7	1.8	2.0	2.4	2.9
75–84 years	0.4	*	0.6	0.6	0.7	0.7	0.9	0.7	1.0
85 years and over	*	*	*	0.8	1.1	0.8	0.7	0.8	1.0
All ages, age-adjusted[b, c]									
Male:									
White	2.2	2.3	4.8	5.3	7.7	7.6	7.0	6.8	8.0
Black or African American	1.2	1.2	1.8	2.1	2.2	2.4	2.3	2.7	3.9
American Indian or Alaska Native	*	1.9	4.5	4.4	5.3	5.5	5.8	4.8	6.4
Asian or Pacific Islander	*	*	0.4	0.5	0.8	1.0	0.7	0.9	0.9
Hispanic or Latino	2.9	1.7	2.1	2.2	2.4	2.6	2.5	2.7	2.7
White, not Hispanic or Latino	2.1	2.3	5.3	5.9	9.0	8.8	8.1	7.9	9.3
Female:									
White	1.0	1.2	2.9	3.2	4.8	5.1	4.9	5.0	5.6
Black or African American	0.6	0.6	1.2	1.4	2.0	2.0	2.0	2.2	2.6
American Indian or Alaska Native	*	*	2.7	3.8	4.9	4.6	5.4	5.4	4.6
Asian or Pacific Islander	*	*	*	0.4	0.5	0.4	0.4	0.3	0.5
Hispanic or Latino	0.5	0.5	1.0	1.0	1.3	1.4	1.5	1.5	1.6
White, not Hispanic or Latino	1.1	1.3	3.2	3.5	5.6	5.8	5.6	5.8	6.5
All persons	Drug poisoning deaths involving heroin per 100,000 resident population[d]								
All ages, age-adjusted[b]	0.7	0.7	0.6	0.7	1.0	1.4	1.9	2.7	3.4
All ages, crude	0.7	0.7	0.6	0.7	1.0	1.4	1.9	2.6	3.3
Under 15 years	*	*	*	*	*	*	*	*	*
15–24 years	0.5	0.6	0.6	0.7	1.2	1.8	2.2	2.9	3.3
25–34 years	1.0	1.0	1.1	1.2	2.2	3.4	4.6	6.3	8.0
35–44 years	1.8	1.5	1.2	1.2	1.6	2.2	3.1	4.4	5.9
45–54 years	1.3	1.2	1.2	1.4	1.4	2.0	2.8	3.7	4.7
55–64 years	0.3*	0.3	0.4	0.4	0.7	1.0	1.3	2.1	2.7
65–74 years	*	*	*	*	*	0.2	0.1	0.3	0.5
75–84 years	*	*	*	*	*	*	*	*	*
85 years and over	*	*	*	*	*	*	*	*	*
Male									
All ages, age-adjusted[b]	1.2	1.1	1.1	1.1	1.6	2.3	3.1	4.2	5.2
All ages, crude	1.2	1.1	1.1	1.1	1.6	2.3	3.0	4.2	5.2
Under 15 years	*	*	*	*	*	*	*	*	*
15–24 years	0.8	0.9	1.0	1.0	1.9	2.8	3.2	4.2	4.8
25–34 years	1.6	1.7	1.9	2.0	3.5	5.4	7.1	9.9	12.3
35–44 years	3.0	2.6	2.0	1.9	2.8	3.6	5.1	6.9	9.2
45–54 years	2.3	2.2	2.0	2.3	2.4	3.2	4.5	6.0	7.2
55–64 years	0.5	0.4	0.6	0.7	1.1	1.7	2.3	3.6	4.4
65–74 years	*	*	*	*	*	0.3	0.3	0.5	0.9
75–84 years	*	*	*	*	*	*	*	*	*
85 years and over	*	*	*	*	*	*	*	*	*

Lost productivity in the workplace represents the most substantial economic cost related to drug use. According to the INCB, drug-related nonparticipation in the work force cost the United States an estimated $120 billion in 2011. This figure represented nearly two-thirds (62%) of all costs related to drug use that year. In "Substance Use and Substance Use Disorder by Industry" (*The CBHSQ Report*, April 16, 2015, https://www.ncbi.nlm.nih.gov/books/NBK343542/pdf/Bookshelf_NBK 343542.pdf), Donna M. Bush and Rachel N. Lipari provide

TABLE 7.4

Drug-induced deaths by age, sex, and race/ethnicity, selected years, 1999–2014 [CONTINUED]

[Data are based on death certificates]

Sex, age, race, and Hispanic origin	1999	2000	2004	2005	2010	2011	2012	2013	2014
Female									
All ages, age-adjusted[b]	0.2	0.2	0.2	0.3	0.4	0.6	0.8	1.2	1.6
All ages, crude	0.2	0.2	0.2	0.3	0.4	0.6	0.8	1.1	1.5
Under 15 years	*	*	*	*	*	*	*	*	*
15–24 years	0.2	0.2	0.3	0.3	0.6	0.9	1.1	1.5	1.7
25–34 years	0.3	0.4	0.4	0.5	0.9	1.4	2.0	2.6	3.7
35–44 years	0.6	0.5	0.5	0.5	0.6	0.8	1.1	1.9	2.6
45–54 years	0.3	0.3	0.4	0.5	0.5	0.8	1.1	1.6	2.2
55–64 years	*	*	0.1	*	0.3	0.3	0.4	0.7	1.0
65–74 years	*	*	*	*	*	*	*	*	*
75–84 years	*	*	*	*	*	*	*	*	*
85 years and over	*	*	*	*	*	*	*	*	*
All ages, age-adjusted [b,c]									
Male:									
White	1.2	1.1	1.1	1.1	1.8	2.6	3.5	4.7	6.0
Black or African American	1.4	1.6	1.1	1.3	1.2	1.6	2.1	3.4	4.1
American Indian or Alaska Native	*	*	*	*	*	1.3	1.7	2.6	3.5
Asian or Pacific Islander	*	*	*	*	*	0.3	0.3	0.5	0.6
Hispanic or Latino	2.0	1.6	1.3	1.4	1.5	1.7	2.2	2.6	3.2
White, not Hispanic or Latino	1.1	1.0	1.1	1.1	1.9	2.9	3.9	5.3	6.7
Female:									
White	0.2	0.2	0.2	0.3	0.4	0.6	0.9	1.3	1.8
Black or African American	0.3	0.3	0.3	0.3	0.3	0.4	0.5	0.7	1.1
American Indian or Alaska Native	*	*	*	*	*	1.0	*	1.0	1.2
Asian or Pacific Islander	*	*	*	*	*	*	*	*	*
Hispanic or Latino	0.2	0.1	0.2	0.2	0.2	0.3	0.4	0.5	0.7
White, not Hispanic or Latino	0.2	0.2	0.3	0.3	0.5	0.7	1.1	1.5	2.1

* Rates based on fewer than 20 deaths are considered unreliable and are not shown.
0.0 Rate more than zero but less than 0.05.
[a]Drug poisoning was coded using underlying cause of death according to the 10th Revision of the *International Classification of Diseases* (ICD–10).
Drug poisoning deaths include those resulting from accidental or intentional overdoses of a drug, being given the wrong drug, taking thewrong drug in error, taking a drug inadvertently, or other misuses of drugs. These deaths are from all manners and intents, including unintentional, suicide, homicide,undetermined intent, legal intervention, and operations of war.
[b]Age-adjusted rates are calculated using the year 2000 standard population with unrounded population numbers.
[c]The race groups, white, black, Asian or Pacific Islander, and American Indian or Alaska Native, include persons of Hispanic and non-Hispanic origin. Persons of Hispanic origin may be of any race. Death rates for Hispanic, American Indian or Alaska Native, and Asian or Pacific Islander persons should be interpreted with caution because of inconsistencies in reporting Hispanic origin or race on the death certificate (death rate numerators) compared with population figures (death rate denominators). The net effect of misclassification is an underestimation of deaths and death rates for races other than white and black.
[d]Opioid analgesics include opioids such as hydrocodone, codeine, and methadone, and synthetic narcotics such as fentanyl, tramadol, and propoxyphene (removed from the market in 2010). Drug poisoning deaths involving opioid analgesics include those with an underlying cause of drug poisoning and with an opioid analgesic mentioned in the ICD–10 multiple causes of death. Drug poisoning deaths involving heroin include those with an underlying cause of drug poisoning and with heroin mentioned in the ICD–10 multiple causes of death. Drug-poisoning deaths may involve multiple drugs. Deaths involving both opioid analgesics and heroin are included in the death rate for opioid analgesics and the death rate for heroin. Opioid analgesic death rates include deaths involving fentanyl, a synthetic opioid. A sharp increase in deaths involving synthetic opioids, other than methadone, in 2014 coincided with law enforcement reports of increased availability of illicitly manufactured, or non-pharmaceutical,fentanyl. Illicitly manufactured fentanyl cannot be distinguished from pharmaceutical fentanyl in death certificate data.
Metabolic breakdown of heroin into morphine in the body can make it difficult to distinguish between deaths from heroin and deaths from morphine based on the information on the death certificate. Some deaths reported to involve morphine could be deaths from heroin. This may result in an undercount of heroin-related deaths.
In 1999–2014, 19%–25% of drug poisoning deaths did not include specific information on the death certificate on the type of drug that was involved. Some of these deaths could have potentially involved heroin or opioid analgesics.

Notes: Rates for 1999 were computed using intercensal population estimates based on the 1990 and 2000 censuses. Rates for 2000 were computed based on 2000 bridged-race April 1 census counts. Starting with *Health, United States, 2012*, rates for 2001–2009 were revised using intercensal population estimates based on the 2000 and 2010 censuses. Rates for 2010 were based on 2010 bridged-race April 1 census counts. Rates for 2011 and beyond were computed using 2010-based postcensal estimates. Age groups were selected to minimize the presentation of unstable age-specific death rates based on small numbers of deaths and for consistency among comparison groups.
Starting with 2003 data, some states allowed the reporting of more than one race on the death certificate. The multiple-race data for these states were bridged to the single-race categories of the 1977 Office of Management and Budget standards, for comparability with other states.

SOURCE: "Table 27. Death Rates for Drug Poisoning and Drug Poisoning Involving Opioid Analgesics and Heroin, by Sex, Age, Race, and Hispanic Origin: United States, Selected Years 1999–2014," in *Health, United States, 2015: With Special Feature on Racial and Ethnic Health Disparities*, U.S. Department of Health and Human Services, Centers for Disease Control and Prevention, National Center for Health Statistics, May 2016, https://www.cdc.gov/nchs/data/hus/hus15.pdf (accessed January 10, 2017)

an overview of illicit drug use among U.S. employees between 2008 and 2012, by industry. According to Bush and Lipari, people working in the accommodations and food services industry experienced the highest rate of illicit drug use during this span. Between 2008 and 2012, nearly one in five (19.1%) individuals employed in the accommodations and food services sector were current drug users.

This rate was nearly 40% higher than current drug use among employees in the arts, entertainment, and recreation sector (13.7%), which represented the industry with the second-highest proportion of employees who were current drug users. Of the professions surveyed, public administrators (4.3%) had the lowest rate of current drug use between 2008 and 2012.

FIGURE 7.3

Drug-related death rates, by state, 2014

[Age-adjusted death rate per 100,000 population]

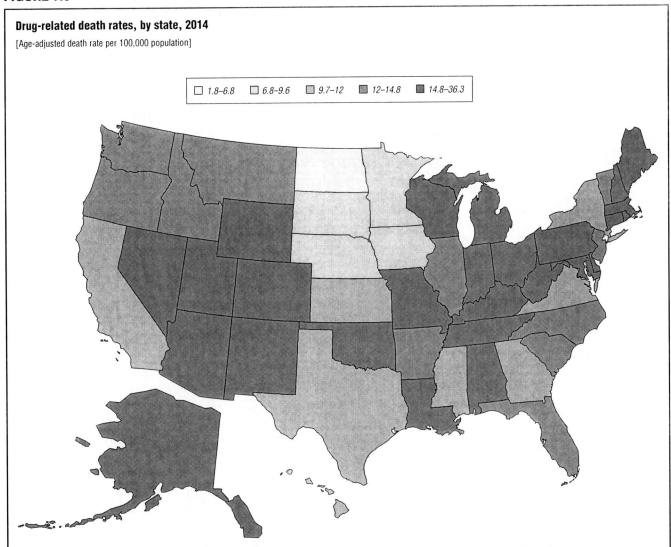

SOURCE: Adapted from "Age-Adjusted Death Rates for Drug Poisoning by State, 2014," in *Drug Poisoning Mortality: United States, 1999–2014*, Centers for Disease Control and Prevention, National Center for Health Statistics, January 19, 2016, https://blogs.cdc.gov/nchs-data-visualization/drug-poisoning-mortality/ (accessed January 10, 2017)

In *Report of the International Narcotics Control Board for 2013*, the INCB reports that costs associated with drug-related crime in the United States approach $61 billion annually. A sizable proportion of these costs are related to crimes committed in order to support an addict's drug habit. The INCB notes that 17% of all inmates held in state prisons in the United States in 2013, as well as 18% of all inmates in U.S. federal prisons, reported that they had committed the crime for which they were imprisoned in order to acquire the money they needed to purchase drugs.

Costs of Tobacco Use

In *The Health Consequences of Smoking—50 Years of Progress: A Report of the Surgeon General* (2014, https://www.surgeongeneral.gov/library/reports/50-years-of-progress/full-report.pdf), the U.S. surgeon general estimates that from 2009 to 2012 economic losses related to smoking came to between $289 billion and $332.5 billion. Of this total, roughly $132.5 billion to $175.9 billion was related to medical expenses; $151 billion was attributed to lost productivity incurred by smoking-related deaths that occurred between 2005 and 2009; and $5.6 billion was related to lost productivity due to exposure to secondhand smoke in 2006. Furthermore, the surgeon general states that smoking resulted in an average of 480,320 premature deaths annually between 2005 and 2009. On average, men (278,540) suffered more annual premature deaths related to smoking than women (201,770) during this span. Likewise, secondhand smoke resulted in an average of 41,280 premature deaths each year between 2005 and 2009. The surgeon general also projects that roughly 5.6 million youths aged zero to 17 years in 2014 will eventually suffer premature deaths due to smoking-related causes.

FIGURE 7.4

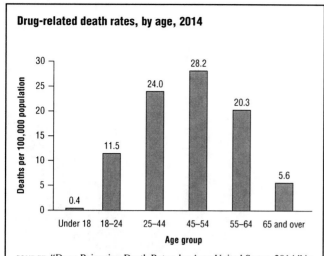

Drug-related death rates, by age, 2014

SOURCE: "Drug-Poisoning Death Rates, by Age: United States, 2014," in *NCHS Data on Drug-Poisoning Deaths*, Centers for Disease Control and Prevention, National Center for Health Statistics, March 2016, https://www.cdc.gov/nchs/data/factsheets/factsheet_drug_poisoning.pdf (accessed January 10, 2017)

TOBACCO COMPANIES AND RESPONSIBILITY FOR THE COSTS OF TOBACCO USE

Between 1960 and 1988 approximately 300 lawsuits sought damages from tobacco companies for smoking-related illnesses; however, courts consistently held that people who choose to smoke are responsible for the health consequences of that decision. This changed in 1988, when a tobacco company was ordered to pay damages for the first time. A federal jury in Newark, New Jersey, ordered Liggett Group, Inc., to pay $400,000 to the family of Rose Cipollone, a longtime smoker who died of lung cancer in 1984. The case was overturned on appeal, but the U.S. Supreme Court ruled in favor of the Cipollone family in *Cipollone v. Liggett Group, Inc.* (505 U.S. 504 [1992]). In a 7–2 ruling, the court broadened a smoker's right to sue cigarette makers in cancer cases. The justices decided that the Federal Cigarette Labeling and Advertising Act of 1965, which required warnings on tobacco products, did not preempt damage suits. Despite the warnings on tobacco packaging, people could still sue on the grounds that tobacco companies purposely concealed information about the risks of smoking.

The Master Settlement Agreement

Following the Supreme Court's decision, the tobacco industry was faced with the possibility of never-ending lawsuits and massive damage awards. Many state governments began lawsuits against major cigarette companies, seeking to recover the costs the states had incurred in caring for those with smoking-related health problems. The tobacco industry responded by negotiating with the states and offering money and changes in its business practices in exchange for an end to the lawsuits and protection from future lawsuits.

In November 1998 the attorneys general from 46 states (Florida, Minnesota, Mississippi, and Texas were excluded because they had already concluded previous settlements), five territories, and the District of Columbia signed an agreement with the five largest cigarette companies (Philip Morris, R. J. Reynolds, Brown and Williamson, Lorillard, and Liggett Group) to settle all the state lawsuits brought to recover the Medicaid costs of treating smokers. The Master Settlement Agreement (MSA; https://oag.ca.gov/tobacco/msa) required the tobacco companies to make annual payments totaling $206 billion over 25 years, beginning in 2000. It also placed restrictions on how the companies could advertise, market, and promote tobacco products. Since the original signing, more than 30 additional tobacco firms have signed the MSA, and Philip Morris has contributed more than half of the payments received by the states under the agreement. Although the MSA settles all the state and local government lawsuits, the tobacco industry is still subject to class-action and individual lawsuits.

The four states that negotiated their own lawsuit settlements began receiving payments from the tobacco companies in 1998. "Up-front" payments to other states began in 1999, prior to the beginning of the annual payments in 2000. In the fact sheet "Actual Tobacco Settlement Payments Received by the States, 2006–2015" (April 27, 2016, http://www.tobaccofreekids.org/research/factsheets/pdf/0365.pdf), the Campaign for Tobacco-Free Kids details the amount of money that the states received between 1998 and 2015. As of 2015, the states had received a total of $130.5 billion from the tobacco companies. According to the terms of the MSA, these payments were scheduled to continue through 2025.

HOW ARE STATES USING THE SETTLEMENT FUNDS? The MSA did not place any restrictions on how state governments are to use the funds they receive under the agreement. Antismoking and public health organizations argue that the most appropriate use for MSA money is to fund smoking prevention and cessation programs. Since the November 1998 tobacco settlement, the Campaign for Tobacco-Free Kids, the American Lung Association, the American Cancer Society, and the American Heart Association have published an annual report to monitor how states are handling the settlement funds. The FY 2015 report, *Broken Promises to Our Children: A State-by-State Look at the 1998 State Tobacco Settlement 18 Years Later* (December 14, 2016, http://www.tobaccofreekids.org/microsites/statereport2017/pdf/StateReport_FY2017.pdf), notes that states have fallen far short in their efforts to adequately fund tobacco prevention and cessation programs and that "there is conclusive evidence that tobacco prevention and cessation programs work to reduce smoking, save lives and save money by reducing tobacco-related health care costs, especially when part of a comprehensive strategy to reduce tobacco use."

TABLE 7.5

Rankings of funding for state tobacco-prevention programs, fiscal year 2017

State	FY2017 current annual funding (millions)	CDC annual recommendation (millions)[a]	FY2017 percent of CDC's recommendation	Current rank
North Dakota	$9.9	$9.8	100.9%	1
Alaska[b]	$9.5	$10.2	93.0%	2
Oklahoma	$23.5	$42.3	55.6%	3
Wyoming	$4.2	$8.5	49.4%	4
Maine	$7.8	$15.9	49.1%	5
Delaware	$6.4	$13.0	48.9%	6
Montana	$6.4	$14.6	44.1%	7
Colorado	$23.2	$52.9	43.8%	8
Minnesota	$22.0	$52.9	41.7%	9
Vermont	$3.4	$8.4	40.2%	10
Utah	$7.5	$19.3	38.9%	11
Hawaii	$5.3	$13.7	38.6%	12
South Dakota	$4.5	$11.7	38.5%	13
Florida	$67.8	$194.2	34.9%	14
Mississippi	$10.7	$36.5	29.4%	15
Arizona	$18.4	$64.4	28.6%	16
Oregon	$9.8	$39.3	25.0%	17
New Mexico	$5.7	$22.8	24.9%	18
Arkansas	$9.0	$36.7	24.5%	19
Maryland	$10.6	$48.0	22.0%	20
California	$75.7	$347.9	21.8%	21
New york	$39.3	$203.0	19.4%	22
Idaho	$2.9	$15.6	18.4%	23
Iowa	$5.2	$30.1	17.4%	24
Nebraska	$2.6	$20.8	12.4%	25
Louisiana	$7.0	$59.6	11.7%	26
West Virginia	$3.0	$27.4	11.1%	27
Ohio	$13.5	$132.0	10.3%	28
Pennsylvania	$13.9	$140.0	9.9%	29
South Carolina	$5.0	$51.0	9.8%	30
District of Columbia	$1.0	$10.7	9.3%	31
Wisconsin	$5.3	$57.5	9.2%	32
Virginia	$8.2	$91.6	9.0%	33
Indiana	$5.9	$73.5	8.0%	34
Illinois	$9.1	$136.7	6.7%	35
Massachusetts	$3.9	$66.9	5.8%	36
Kentucky	$2.4	$56.4	4.2%	37
Texas	$10.2	$264.1	3.9%	38
Washington	$2.3	$63.6	3.6%	39
Nevada	$1.0	$30.0	3.3%	40
Kansas	$847,041	$27.9	3.0%	41
Rhode Island	$375,622	$12.8	2.9%	42
Alabama	$1.5	$55.9	2.7%	43
Georgia	$1.8	$106.0	1.7%	44
Tennessee	$1.1	$75.6	1.5%	45
Michigan	$1.6	$110.6	1.4%	46
North Carolina	$1.1	$99.3	1.1%	47
New Hampshire	$125,000	$16.5	0.8%	48
Missouri	$109,341	$72.9	0.1%	49
Connecticut	$0.0	$32.0	0.0%	50
New Jersey	$0.0	$103.3	0.0%	50

FY = Fiscal year

CDC = Centers for Disease Control and Prevention

[a]CDC annual recommendations are based on CDC Best Practices for Comprehensive Tobacco Control Programs, 2014.

[b]Alaska funds tobacco prevention programs at the CDC-recommended levels if both state and federal funding are counted.

SOURCE: "FY2017 State Rankings: States Ranked by Percent of CDC-Recommended Funding Levels," in *Broken Promises to Our Children: A State-by-State Look at the 1998 State Tobacco Settlement 18 Years Later*, Campaign for Tobacco-Free Kids, December 14, 2016, http://www.tobaccofreekids.org/microsites/statereport2017/pdf/StateReport_FY2017.pdf (accessed January 10, 2017)

According to the report, in FY 2017 North Dakota (100.9%) was the only state to fund tobacco prevention and cessation programs at the minimum levels recommended by the CDC. (See Table 7.5.) Only two other states were funding these programs at half the recommended level or more: Alaska (93%) and Oklahoma (55.6%). The remaining 47 states and the District of Columbia funded tobacco prevention and cessation programs at less than half

the CDC-recommended amount. Overall, states dedicated $491.6 million to tobacco prevention initiatives in fiscal 2017, or 1.8% of all tobacco-related revenues generated that year. (See Table 7.6.)

What have states done with the tobacco settlement funds not allocated to tobacco prevention and cessation programs? The answer to this question varies with each state; in general,

TABLE 7.6

Tobacco-prevention spending, tobacco-related health costs, and tobacco revenues, by state, fiscal year 2017

[All amounts are in millions of dollars per year, except where otherwise indicated]

State	Annual smoking caused health costs	Fiscal year 2017 state tobacco prevention spending	Total annual state revenues from tobacco (est.)	Tobacco prevention spending % of tobacco revenue
States total	$170 bill.	$491.6	$26.6 bill.	1.8%
Alabama	$1.88 bill.	$1.5	$306.3	0.5%
Alaska	$438	$9.5	$98.0	9.7%
Arizona	$2.38 bill.	$18.4	$438.6	4.2%
Arkansas	$1.21 bill.	$9.0	$285.2	3.2%
California	$13.29 bill.	$75.7	$1.9 bill.	4.1%
Colorado	$1.89 bill.	$23.2	$296.3	7.8%
Connecticut	$2.03 bill.	$0.0	$519.7	0.0%
Delaware	$532	$6.4	$136.8	4.6%
DC	$391	$1.0	$69.9	1.4%
Florida	$8.64 bill.	$67.8	$1.6 bill.	4.3%
Georgia	$3.18 bill.	$1.8	$376.7	0.5%
Hawaii	$526	$5.3	$178.3	3.0%
Idaho	$508	$2.9	$77.5	3.7%
Illinois	$5.49 bill.	$9.1	$1.2 bill.	0.8%
Indiana	$2.93 bill.	$5.9	. $579.0	1.0%
Iowa	$1.28 bill.	$5.2	$300.3	1.7%
Kansas	$1.12 bill.	$0.8	$208.7	0.4%
Kentucky	$1.92 bill.	$2.4	$361.0	0.7%
Louisiana	$1.89 bill.	$7.0	$451.7	1.5%
Maine	$811	$7.8	$196.7	4.0%
Maryland	$2.71 bill.	$10.6	$553.9	1.9%
Massachusetts	$4.08 bill.	$3.9	$903.2	0.4%
Michigan	$4.59 bill.	$1.6	$1.2 bill.	0.1%
Minnesota	$2.51 bill.	$22.0	$746.2	3.0%
Mississippi	$1.23 bill.	$10.7	$249.9	4.3%
Missouri	$3.03 bill.	$0.1	$254.2	0.0%
Montana	$440	$6.4	$118.5	5.4%
Nebraska	$795	$2.6	$103.7	2.5%
Nevada	$1.08 bill.	$1.0	$207.7	0.5%
New Hampshire	$729	$0.1	$265.6	0.0%
New Jersey	$4.06 bill.	$0.0	$944.5	0.0%
New Mexico	$844	$5.7	$133.8	4.2%
New York	$10.39 bill.	$39.3	$2.0 bill.	2.0%
North Carolina	$3.81 bill.	$1.1	$435.6	0.3%
North Dakota	$326	$9.9	$66.8	14.8%
Ohio	$5.64 bill.	$13.5	$1.3 bill.	1.0%
Oklahoma	$1.62 bill.	$23.5	$396.6	5.9%
Oregon	$1.54 bill.	$9.8	$357.9	2.8%
Pennsylvania	$6.38 bill.	$13.9	$1.7 bill.	0.8%
Rhode Island	$640	$0.4	$194.4	0.2%
South Carolina	$1.90 bill.	$5.0	$240.5	2.1%
South Dakota	$373	$4.5	$88.3	5.1%
Tennessee	$2.67 bill.	$1.1	$418.3	0.3%
Texas	$8.85 bill.	$10.2	$1.9 bill.	0.5%
Utah	$542	$7.5	$150.9	5.0%
Vermont	$348	$3.4	$117.6	2.9%
Virginia	$3.11 bill.	$8.2	$307.6	2.7%
Washington	$2.81 bill.	$2.3	$595.9	0.4%
West Virginia	$1.00 bill.	$3.0	$259.2	1.2%
Wisconsin	$2.66 bill.	$5.3	$779.1	0.7%
Wyoming	$258	$4.2	$45.5	9.2%

Notes: Annual funding amounts only include state funds. Annual state health care costs and CDC annual spending targets are from CDC, Best Practices for Comprehensive Tobacco Control, January 2014. National health care costs are from Xu, Xin, "Annual Healthcare Spending Attributable to Cigarette Smoking," Am J Prev Med, published online: December 09, 2014. State settlement revenue estimates reflect base payments made to the states adjusted for inflation and volume as required by the Master Settlement Agreement. State tobacco tax revenue estimates are based on monthly and annual revenue reports from Orzechowski & Walker's Tax Burden on Tobacco [industry-funded reports], and account for on-going background declines in smoking as well as projected new revenues from recent tobacco tax increases. Despite receiving massive amounts of annual revenue from tobacco taxes and the state tobacco lawsuit settlements with the cigarette companies, the vast majority of states are still failing to invest the amounts recommended in the U.S. Centers for Disease Control and Prevention (CDC) to prevent and reduce tobacco use and minimize related health harms.

SOURCE: "State Tobacco-Prevention Spending vs. State Tobacco Revenues and Annual Smoking-Caused Health Costs," in *Broken Promises to Our Children: A State-by-State Look at the 1998 State Tobacco Settlement 18 Years Later*, Campaign for Tobacco-Free Kids, December 14, 2016, http://www.tobaccofreekids.org/microsites/statereport2017/pdf/StateReport_FY2017.pdf (accessed January 10, 2017)

states have used settlement monies to fund other health- and youth-related programs, capital projects (e.g., building hospitals), medical research, medical education, enforcement of tobacco control laws, and expansion of health clinics for low-income citizens. Some states also used part of the money to pay down their debt or to help balance their budgets.

CHAPTER 8
DRUG TRAFFICKING

Trafficking in drugs refers to commercial activity: the buying and selling of illegal and controlled substances without a permit to do so—a permit that, for example, a physician, pharmacist, or researcher would have. Illegal drugs are those with no currently accepted medical use in the United States, such as heroin, lysergic acid diethylamide (LSD), and marijuana. It is illegal to buy, sell, possess, and use these drugs except for research purposes. (Some states and local jurisdictions have decriminalized certain uses of specific amounts of marijuana, but federal laws supersede these state and local marijuana decriminalization laws.)

Legal drugs are those whose sale, possession, and use as intended are not forbidden by law. However, the use of legal psychoactive (mood- or mind-altering) drugs, which have the potential for abuse, is restricted. These drugs, which include narcotics, depressants, and stimulants, are available only with a prescription. They are called controlled substances. Drug trafficking includes all commercial activities that are integral to the buying and selling of illegal and controlled substances, including their manufacture, production, preparation, importation, exportation, supply, distribution, and transportation.

CRIMINAL PENALTIES FOR TRAFFICKING
Federal Penalties

The Controlled Substances Act of 1970 provides penalties for the unlawful trafficking in controlled substances, based on the schedule (rank) of the drug or substance. (For definitions of the schedules, see Table 1.3 in Chapter 1.) Generally, the more dangerous the drug and the larger the quantity involved, the stiffer the penalty. The trafficking of heroin, cocaine, LSD, and phencyclidine (PCP), all Schedule I or II drugs, includes mandatory jail time and fines. For example, a person caught selling at least 18 ounces (500 grams [g]) but less than 11 pounds (5 kg) of cocaine powder will receive a

minimum of five years in prison and may be fined up to $5 million for a first offense. (See Table 8.1.) The same penalty is imposed for the sale of between 1 ounce and 9.8 ounces (28 g and 279 g) of cocaine base (crack).

Following the second offense, penalties double to a minimum of 10 years in prison and up to $8 million in fines. When larger quantities are involved (11 pounds or more [5 kg or more] of cocaine powder, 9.8 ounces or more [280 g or more] of crack, and so on), penalties for the first offense are a minimum of 10 years in prison and fines up to $10 million. For the second offense, a minimum of 20 years and up to $20 million in fines are given, and the third offense results in mandatory life imprisonment. These examples are for an individual. Higher penalties apply if an organized group is involved or if a death or injury is associated with the arrest event.

These penalties also apply to the sale of fentanyl (a powerful pain medicine) or similar-acting drugs, heroin, LSD, methamphetamine, and PCP. The smallest amount, which can earn someone a minimum sentence of five years in prison and a fine of up to $2 million, involves trafficking in LSD, in which an amount of 0.03 ounces (1 g) carries a five-year-minimum sentence in prison.

Punishments for marijuana, hashish, and hashish oil are shown in Table 8.2. Special penalties exist for marijuana trafficking because it may be traded in large quantities or grown in substantial amounts. The lower the amounts sold or the fewer the plants grown, the lower the sentence. A person cultivating one to 49 plants or selling less than 110 pounds (50 kg) of marijuana mixture, 22 pounds (10 kg) or less of hashish, or 2.2 pounds (1 kg) or less of hashish oil may get a maximum sentence of five years in prison and a maximum fine of $250,000. Sentences for second offenses involving large amounts of marijuana may earn the trafficker up to life imprisonment.

TABLE 8.1

Federal drug trafficking penalties, excluding marijuana

Schedule	Substance/quantity	Penalty	Substance/quantity	Penalty
II	Cocaine 500–4,999 grams mixture	**First offense:** Not less than 5 yrs. and not more than 40 yrs. If death or serious bodily injury, not less than 20 yrs. or more than life. Fine of not more than $5 million if an individual, $25 million if not an individual.	Cocaine 5 kilograms or more mixture	**First offense:** Not less than 10 yrs. and not more than life. If death or serious bodily injury, not less than 20 yrs. or more than life. Fine of not more than $10 million if an individual, $50 million if not an individual.
II	Cocaine base 28–279 grams mixture		Cocaine base 280 grams or more mixture	
IV	Fentanyl 40–399 grams mixture		Fentanyl 400 grams or more mixture	
I	Fentanyl analogue 10–99 grams mixture		Fentanyl analogue 100 grams or more mixture	
I	Heroin 100–999 grams mixture	**Second offense:** Not less than 10 yrs. and not more than life. If death or serious bodily injury, life imprisonment. Fine of not more than $8 million if an individual, $50 million if not an individual.	Heroin 1 kilogram or more mixture	**Second offense:** Not less than 20 yrs, and not more than life. If death or serious bodily injury, life imprisonment. Fine of not more than $20 million if an individual, $75 million if not an individual.
I	LSD 1–9 grams mixture		LSD 10 grams or more mixture	
II	Methamphetamine 5–49 grams pure or 50–499 grams mixture		Methamphetamine 50 grams or more pure or 500 grams or more mixture	**2 or more prior offenses:** Life imprisonment. Fine of not more than $20 million if an individual, $75 million if not an individual.
II	PCP 10–99 grams pure or 100–999 grams mixture		PCP 100 grams or more pure or 1 kilogram or more mixture	

Substance/quantity	Penalty
Any amount of other Schedule I & II substances	**First offense:** Not more than 20 yrs. If death or serious bodily injury, not less than 20 yrs. or more than Life. Fine $1 million if an individual, $5 million if not an individual.
Any drug product containing gamma hydroxybutyric acid	
Flunitrazepam (Schedule IV) 1 gram	**Second offense:** Not more than 30 yrs. If death or serious bodily injury, life imprisonment. Fine $2 million if an individual, $10 million if not an individual.
Any amount of other Schedule III drugs	**First offense:** Not more than 10 yrs. If death or serious bodily injury, not more that 15 yrs. Fine not more than $500,000 if an individual, $2.5 million if not an individual.
	Second offense: Not more than 20 yrs. If death or serious injury, not more than 30 yrs. Fine not more than $1 million if an individual, $5 million if not an individual.
Any amount of all other Schedule IV drugs (other than one gram or more of Flunitrazepam)	**First offense:** Not more than 5 yrs. Fine not more than $250,000 if an individual, $1 million if not an individual.
	Second offense: Not more than 10 yrs. Fine not more than $500,000 if an individual, $2 million if other than an individual.
Any amount of all Schedule V drugs	**First offense:** Not more than 1 yr. Fine not more than $100,000 if an individual, $250,000 if not an individual.
	Second offense: Not more than 4 yrs. Fine not more than $200,000 if an individual, $500,000 if not an individual.

SOURCE: "Federal Trafficking Penalties for Schedules I, II, III, IV, and V (Except Marijuana)," U.S. Department of Justice, U.S. Drug Enforcement Administration, 2017, https://www.dea.gov/druginfo/ftp_chart1.pdf (accessed January 10, 2017)

TABLE 8.2

Federal marijuana trafficking penalties

Drug	Quantity	First offense	Second offense
Marijuana	1,000 kilograms or more marijuana mixture or 1,000 or more marijuana plants	• Not less than 10 yrs. or more than life • If death or serious bodily injury, not less than 20 yrs., or more than life • Fine not more than $10 million if an individual, $50 million if other than an individual	• Not less than 20 yrs. or more than life • If death or serious bodily injury, life imprisonment • Fine not more than $20 million if an individual $75 million if other than an individual
Marijuana	100 to 999 kilograms marijuana mixture or 100 to 999 marijuana plants	• Not less than 5 yrs. or more than 40 yrs. • If death or serious bodily injury, not less than 20 yrs. or more than life • Fine not more than $5 million if an individual, $25 million if other than an individual.	• Not less than 10 yrs. or more than life • If death or serious bodily injury, life imprisonment • Fine not more than $8 million if an individual, $50 million if other than an individual
Marijuana	50 to 99 kilograms marijuana mixture, 50 to 99 marijuana plants	• Not more than 20 yrs. • If death or serious bodily injury, not less than 20 yrs. or more than life • Fine $1 million if an individual, $5 million if other than an individual	• Not more than 30 yrs. • If death or serious bodily injury, life imprisonment • Fine $2 million if an individual, $10 million if other than an individual
Hashish	More than 10 kilograms		
Hashish oil	More than 1 kilogram		
Marijuana	Less than 50 kilograms marijuana (but does not include 50 or more marijuana plants regardless of weight) 1 to 49 marijuana plants	• Not more than 5 yrs. • Fine not more than $250,000, $1 million if other than an individual	• Not more than 10 yrs. • Fine $500,000 if an individual, $2 million if other than individual
Hashish	10 kilograms or less		
Hashish oil	1 kilogram or less		

SOURCE: "Federal Trafficking Penalties for Marijuana, Hashish and Hashish Oil, Schedule I Substances," U.S. Department of Justice, U.S. Drug Enforcement Administration, 2017, https://www.dea.gov/druginfo/ftp_chart2.pdf (accessed January 10, 2017)

State Laws

States have the discretionary power to make their own drug laws. The possession of marijuana may be a misdemeanor in one state but a felony in another. For example, in California there is no penalty whatsoever for possessing less than 1 ounce (28 g) of marijuana, but in neighboring Arizona, possession of any amount of marijuana is a felony with a potential prison sentence of up to two years and a fine up to $150,000. Prison sentences can also vary for the same charges in different states—the distribution of 18 ounces (500 g) of cocaine as a Class C felony may specify 10 years to 50 years in one state and 24 years to 40 years in another. Most states follow the model of the Controlled Substances Act and enforce laws that facilitate the seizure of drug trafficking profits, specify greater penalties for trafficking, and promote user accountability by punishing drug users.

During the first two decades of the 21st century, an increasing number of states passed legislation allowing for the legal use of marijuana. The National Conference of State Legislatures indicates in "State Medical Marijuana Laws" (March 1, 2017, http://www.ncsl.org/research/health/state-medical-marijuana-laws.aspx) that in 1996 California became the first state to legalize the use of marijuana for medical purposes. By March 2017, 27 more states, along with the District of Columbia, had passed legislation permitting the use of medical marijuana. An additional 17 states allow the use of marijuana containing low levels of THC (delta-9-tetrahydrocannabinol, the principle psychoactive ingredient in marijuana) for medical reasons. The National Conference of State Legislatures notes in "Marijuana Overview" (March 1, 2017, http://www.ncsl.org/research/civil-and-criminal-justice/marijuana-overview.aspx) that by March 2017 an additional eight states (Alaska, California, Colorado, Maine, Massachusetts, Nevada, Oregon, and Washington) and the District of Columbia, had passed legislation allowing businesses and individuals to cultivate, sell, and possess limited quantities of marijuana for recreational purposes.

IS THE PROFIT WORTH THE RISK?

Despite the possibility of long prison terms (up to life imprisonment), many drug dealers evidently consider the enormous potential profits of drug trafficking worth the risk. The media often report drug busts and indictments of people involved in multimillion- or billion-dollar operations. Paying fines of hundreds of thousands of dollars, or even millions of dollars, becomes part of doing business when the profits are so high.

THE WORLD'S POPULATION AND ILLICIT DRUGS

The United Nations Office on Drugs and Crime estimates in *World Drug Report: 2016* (2016, https://www.unodc.org/doc/wdr2016/WORLD_DRUG_REPORT_2016_web.pdf) that roughly 247 million people (5% of the world's population aged 15 to 64 years) were users of illicit drugs in 2014. An estimated 29 million of these people were classified as problem drug users, many of whom were addicted to drugs.

WORLD PRODUCTION OF PLANT-DERIVED (ORGANIC) DRUGS

In *International Narcotics Control Strategy Report: Volume I, Drug and Chemical Control* (March 2016, https://www.state.gov/documents/organization/253655.pdf), the Bureau for International Narcotics and Law Enforcement Affairs (INL), an element of the U.S. Department of State, provides data on the amount of land that is cultivated to raise opium poppy, the source of heroin and other opioids; coca leaf, from which cocaine is derived; and cannabis, the hemp plant from which marijuana and hashish are derived. The INL cautions that these are estimates, based on satellite observations and other sources of intelligence, and that there are countries and areas of countries that were not studied.

According to the INL, the largest amount of cultivated land used for illicit drug cultivation was dedicated to the production of opium poppy, followed by coca leaf and cannabis. (See Table 8.3.) In 2014, the most recent year for which data were complete, opium poppy was cultivated on 702,372 acres (284,240 ha). The largest producer was Afghanistan. Coca leaf was cultivated on 478,149 acres (193,500 ha) of land, more than half of which was cultivated in Colombia. Cannabis cultivation took place on 27,182 acres (11,000 ha) in 2014. (Cultivation within the United States was excluded from this calculation.) As Table 8.4 shows, overall production of opium and coca leaf declined between 2007 and 2014.

ILLICIT DRUG MOVEMENT INTO AND WITHIN THE UNITED STATES

Illicit drug cultivation takes place primarily outside the United States. Although each drug type has its own method and route of entering the United States, the most common method is overland smuggling and subsequent transportation via the interstate highway system. Table 8.5 provides a breakdown of drug seizures by federal, state, and local law enforcement agencies between 1989 and 2015.

The U.S. Drug Enforcement Administration (DEA) provides in *National Drug Threat Assessment Summary, 2016* (November 2016, https://www.dea.gov/resource-center/2016%20NDTA%20Summary.pdf) detailed data on drug seizures in the United States. As Figure 8.1 shows, the amount of heroin seized by U.S. law enforcement officials more than doubled between 2010 and 2015, from 6,091 pounds to 14,819 pounds (2,763 kg to 6,722 kg). During this same period the amount of heroin seized at the nation's southwestern border with Mexico rose at an even higher rate, from 2,240 pounds

TABLE 8.3

Illicit drug production worldwide, by crop and country, 2007–15

[All figures in hectares]

	2007	2008	2009	2010	2011	2012	2013	2014	2015
Poppy									
Afghanistan	202,000	157,000	131,000	119,000	115,000	180,000	198,000	211,000	201,000
Burma*	21,700	22,500	19,000	45,500	36,500		51,000	52,000	
Colombia	1,000		1,100					800	
Guatemala						220	310	640	
Laos	1,100	1,900	940	1,800	4,400				
Mexico					12,000	10,500	11,000	17,000	In process
Pakistan		700	705			755	4,300	2,800	In process
Coca									
Bolivia	24,000	26,500	29,000	29,000	25,500	25,000	27,000	35,000	In process
Colombia	167,000	119,000	116,000	100,000	83,000	78,000	80,500	112,000	In process
Peru	36,000	41,000	40,000	53,000	49,500	50,500	59,500	46,500	In process
Total coca	**227,000**	**186,500**	**185,000**	**182,000**	**158,000**	**153,500**	**167,000**	**193,500**	
Cannabis									
Mexico					12,000	11,500	13,000	11,000	In process

*Official name is Republic of the Union of Myanmar.
Note on Colombia poppy cultivation: No estimates in 2008 and 2010–2013 due to cloud cover.
Note on Guatemala poppy cultivation: 2012 survey limited to fall season in San Marcos and Huehuetenango only.
Note on Laos poppy cultivation: Estimates for 2009–2010 are for Phongsali only. Survey area for 2011 was significantly expanded to include parts of Louang Namtha.
Note on Mexico poppy cultivation: 2011 and later surveys incorporate a major methodological change; 2007–2010 estimates have therefore been removed.
Note on Pakistan poppy cultivation: 2008 and 2012 estimates are for Bara River Valley in Khyber Agency only. 2009 estimate is for Khyber, Mohmand, and Bajaur Agencies only. 2013 includes Khyber, Mohmand, Bajaur, and selected areas in Balochistan. 2014 includes Khyber and areas in Balochistan.

SOURCE: "Worldwide Illicit Drug Crop Cultivation, 2007–2015," in *International Narcotics Control Strategy Report: Volume 1, Drug and Chemical Control*, U.S. Department of State, Bureau of International Narcotics and Law Enforcement Affairs, March 2016, https://www.state.gov/documents/organization/253655.pdf (accessed January 10, 2017)

(1,016 kg) in 2010 to 5,565 pounds (2,524 kg) in 2015, an increase of 148%. (See Figure 8.2.) By 2014 roughly 95% of all heroin trafficked into the United States originated in either Mexico or South America. (See Figure 8.3.)

Greatest Drug Threat

The DEA surveyed state and local law enforcement agencies nationwide in 2016 to determine what they believed to be the greatest drug threat in the United States. As shown in Figure 8.4, methamphetamine was perceived to be the greatest drug threat among law enforcement agencies in the Pacific, southwest, west-central, and southeast regions. Marijuana was regarded as the biggest threat in Florida, whereas heroin was viewed as the most serious drug threat by law enforcement agencies in New England, New York and New Jersey, the mid-Atlantic, and Great Lakes regions.

As Figure 8.5 shows, in 2016 marijuana was the most readily available illegal drug in every region of the country. Methamphetamine was the second-most readily available drug in the Pacific and southwest regions, whereas heroin was the second-most readily available illicit substances in New England, New York and New Jersey, the mid-Atlantic, and Great Lakes regions. Controlled prescription drugs (CPDs) were the second-most readily available drug in the west-central region, whereas crack cocaine was the second-most readily available drug in Florida.

Federal Interdiction Efforts

As drug smuggling into the Southwest from Mexico increased, federal law enforcement agencies developed an aggressive interdiction strategy that was aimed at curbing the movement of illegal drugs across U.S. borders. Much of the responsibility for implementing this strategy lies with U.S. Customs and Border Protection (CBP), a law enforcement division that was founded as part of the Homeland Security Act of 2002. James F. Tomsheck of the CBP said in a statement before the U.S. Senate Committee on Homeland Security and Governmental Affairs, Ad Hoc Subcommittee on State, Local, and Private Sector Preparedness and Integration (March 11, 2010, https://www.gpo.gov/fdsys/pkg/CHRG-111shrg58385/html/CHRG-111shrg58385.htm) that by 2010 the CBP was the largest single law enforcement agency in the nation, with more than 58,000 employees, including 20,000 border patrol agents. The Office of National Drug Control Policy notes in *FY 2017 Budget and Performance Summary: Companion to the National Drug Control Strategy* (December 2016, https://obama whitehouse.archives.gov/sites/default/files/ondcp/policy-and-research/fy2017_budget_summary-final.pdf) that the federal government designated $4.1 billion toward interdiction efforts in fiscal year (FY) 2017. This amount was roughly comparable to interdiction budgets for FY 2015 and FY 2016.

TABLE 8.4

Potential illicit drug production worldwide, by crop and country, 2007–15

[All figures in metric tons]

	2007	2008	2009	2010	2011	2012	2013	2014	2015
Opium[a]									
Afghanistan	8,000	5,500	5,300	3,200	4,400	4,300	5,500	6,300	4,100
Burma[b]	270	340	305	530	450		795	900	
Colombia	15		17					13	
Guatemala						4	6	14	
Laos	6	17	12	23	57				
Mexico	150	325	425	300	250	220	225	360	In process
Pakistan		26	26			28	220	105	In process
Total potential L. America heroin production	20	38	52	36	30	26	26	44	In process
Coca leaf									
Bolivia	38,500	36,500	35,500	35,500	39,500	32,500	37,500	47,000	In process
Colombia	134,000	82,000	76,500	70,500	52,500	48,000	54,000	70,000	In process
Peru	38,000	38,000	40,000	57,500	52,500	50,500	54,500	58,500	In process
Total coca leaf	210,500	156,500	152,000	163,500	144,500	131,000	146,000	175,500	In process
Potential pure cocaine									
Bolivia	130	150	150	160	175	145	165	210	In process
Colombia	450	265	260	240	180	165	185	245	In process
Peru	185	185	195	280	260	250	265	285	In process
Total potential pure cocaine	765	600	605	680	615	560	615	740	
Potential export-quality cocaine									
Bolivia	140	165	170	175	195	165	210	280	In process
Colombia	540	335	345	330	240	215	245	315	In process
Peru	210	210	230	325	310	320	320	345	In process
Total potential export-quality cocaine	890	710	745	830	745	700	775	940	

[a]Opium reported at zero percent.
[b]Official name is Republic of the Union of Myanmar.

SOURCE: "Worldwide Potential Illicit Drug Production, 2007–2015," in *International Narcotics Control Strategy Report: Volume I, Drug and Chemical Control,* U.S. Department of State, Bureau of International Narcotics and Law Enforcement Affairs, March 2016, https://www.state.gov/documents/organization/253655.pdf (accessed January 10, 2017)

Although the federal government has made considerable investment in forceful interdiction measures to curtail drug trafficking, many people question its effectiveness in curbing the flow of illegal drugs into the United States. Writing for the Council on Foreign Relations, David A. Shirk of the University of San Diego states in *The Drug War in Mexico: Confronting a Shared Threat* (March 2011, http://i.cfr.org/content/publications/attachments/Mexico_CSR60.pdf) that U.S. interdiction activities along the Mexican border have ultimately proven "inconsequential" in stemming the activities of the Mexican drug cartels, while unintentionally resulting in "the expansion and increased sophistication of cross-border smuggling operations, and greater U.S. vulnerability to attacks and even infiltration by traffickers." (Federal drug interdiction efforts are discussed in further detail in Chapter 9.)

METHAMPHETAMINE

Methamphetamine (meth) is made in laboratories from precursor drugs rather than directly from plant material. The drug was first synthesized in 1919 and has been a factor on the drug market since the 1960s. The Substance Abuse and Mental Health Services Administration (SAMHSA) estimates in *Key Substance Use and Mental Health Indicators in the United States: Results from the 2015 National Survey on Drug Use and Health* (September 2016, https://www.samhsa.gov/data/sites/default/files/NSDUH-FFR1-2015/NSDUH-FFR1-2015/NSDUH-FFR1-2015.pdf) that 897,000 people were current users of methamphetamine in 2015.

Methamphetamine Production

Like other synthetics, such as LSD or MDMA (3,4-methylenedioxy-methamphetamine), methamphetamine appeals to small and large criminal enterprises alike because it frees them from dependence on vulnerable crops such as coca or opium poppy. Even a small organization can control the whole process, from manufacture to sale on the street, of methamphetamine. The drug can be made almost anywhere and can generate large profit margins. The DEA indicates in *National Drug Threat Assessment Summary, 2016* that in FY 2015 most methamphetamine in

TABLE 8.5

Cocaine, heroin, marijuana, and methamphetamine seizures, 1989–2015

Year	Cocaine (kilograms)	Heroin (kilograms)	Cannabis (metric tons)	Methamphetamine (kilograms)	Methamphetamine (dosage units)	Methamphetamine Liquid (milliliters)
1989	114,903	1,311	416	—	—	—
1990	96,085	687	241	—	—	—
1991	128,247	1,448	304	—	—	—
1992	120,175	1,251	345	—	—	—
1993	121,215	1,502	421	7	—	—
1994	129,378	1,285	475	178	—	—
1995	111,031	1,543	642	369	—	—
1996	128,555	1,362	677	136	—	—
1997	101,495	1,624	700	1,099	—	—
1998	118,436	1,458	827	2,559	—	—
1999	132,063	1,151	1,076	2,779	—	—
2000	106,619	1,674	1,247	3,470	—	—
2001	112,138	2,601	1,435	4,812	233,262	89,820,612
2002	91,509	2,783	1,400	4,433	90,460	9,926,204
2003	114,013	2,486	1,648	5,867	238,346	4,645,054
2004	147,622	1,893	1,352	5,772	25,125	18,281,781
2005	164,585	1,889	1,398	6,280	22,052	1,382,804
2006	164,922	2,027	1,392	7,063	5,635	334,303
2007	152,259	2,770	1,835	5,198	9,552	210,800
2008	133,581	2,118	1,681	6,570	47,061	5,088,277
2009	120,671	2,552	2,296	7,158	130,953	997,404
2010	84,582	3,242	2,280	11,968	133,359	1,586,698
2011	109,961	3,980	2,174	14,102	206,905	459,389
2012	122,380	4,974	1,976	30,383	11,407	2,931,982
2013	81,708	4,792	1,763	28,326	27,509	1,063,463
2014	85,304	7,030	1,243	30,467	9,305	4,957,141
2015	147,811	7,639	948	44,077	10,889	1,268,147

Notes: The black lines denote that there was no data. From 1989 to 2000, data include seizures by all federal agencies; 2001 and later include some state and local seizures; 2007 to 2014 includes seizures as reported by the U.S. Coast Guard.

SOURCE: "Table 78. Seizures of Cocaine, Heroin, Cannabis, and Methamphetamine, 1989–2015," in *National Drug Control Strategy: Data Supplement 2016*, Executive Office of the President, Office of National Drug Control Policy, 2016, https://obamawhitehouse.archives.gov/sites/default/files/ondcp/policy-and-research/2016_ndcs_data_supplement_20170110.pdf (accessed March 13, 2017)

FIGURE 8.1

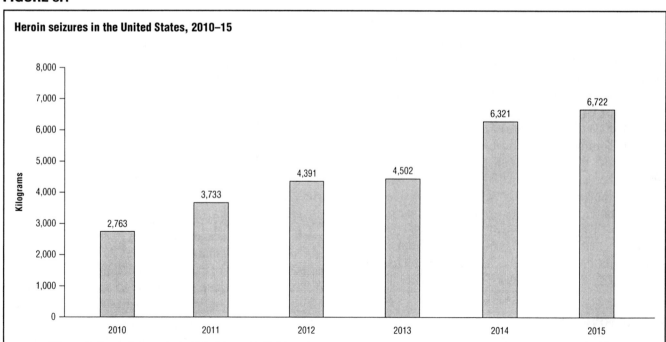

Heroin seizures in the United States, 2010–15

SOURCE: "Figure 48. Heroin Seizures in the United States, 2010–2015," in *National Drug Threat Assessment Summary, 2016*, U.S. Department of Justice, Drug Enforcement Administration, November 2016, https://www.dea.gov/resource-center/2016%20NDTA%20Summary.pdf (accessed January 10, 2017)

FIGURE 8.2

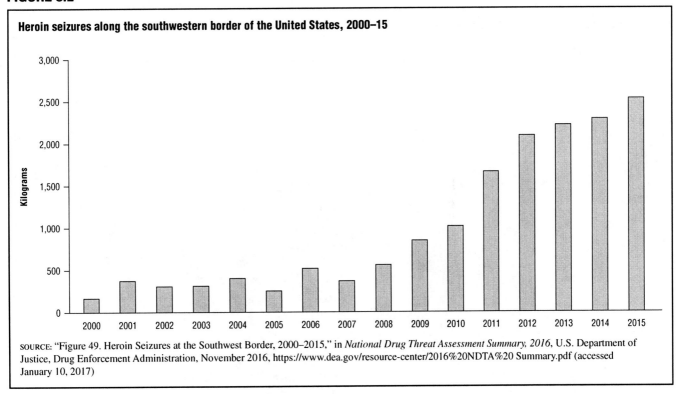

Heroin seizures along the southwestern border of the United States, 2000–15

SOURCE: "Figure 49. Heroin Seizures at the Southwest Border, 2000–2015," in *National Drug Threat Assessment Summary, 2016*, U.S. Department of Justice, Drug Enforcement Administration, November 2016, https://www.dea.gov/resource-center/2016%20NDTA%20 Summary.pdf (accessed January 10, 2017)

FIGURE 8.3

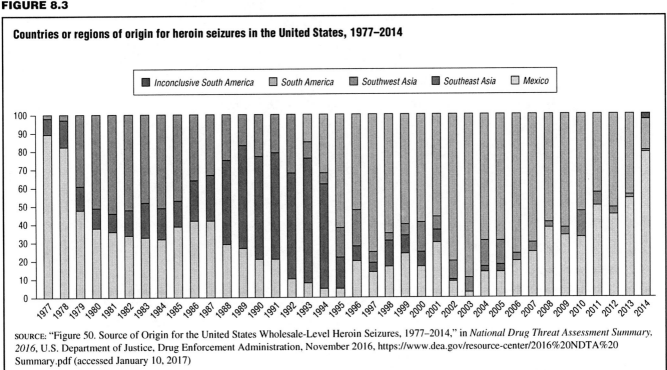

Countries or regions of origin for heroin seizures in the United States, 1977–2014

SOURCE: "Figure 50. Source of Origin for the United States Wholesale-Level Heroin Seizures, 1977–2014," in *National Drug Threat Assessment Summary, 2016*, U.S. Department of Justice, Drug Enforcement Administration, November 2016, https://www.dea.gov/resource-center/2016%20NDTA%20 Summary.pdf (accessed January 10, 2017)

the United States was produced in Mexico. According to the DEA, methamphetamine seizures along the nation's southwestern border with Mexico increased from 8,871 pounds (4,024 kg) in 2010 to 35,898 pounds (16,283 kg) in 2015, an increase of more than 300%. As Figure 8.6 shows, between 2014 and 2016 the largest increases in methamphetamine seizures along the southwestern border with Mexico occurred in the El Centro and San Diego regions of California, and in the Del Rio region of Texas.

FIGURE 8.4

Drugs perceived by state and local agencies as greatest threat to population, by region, 2016

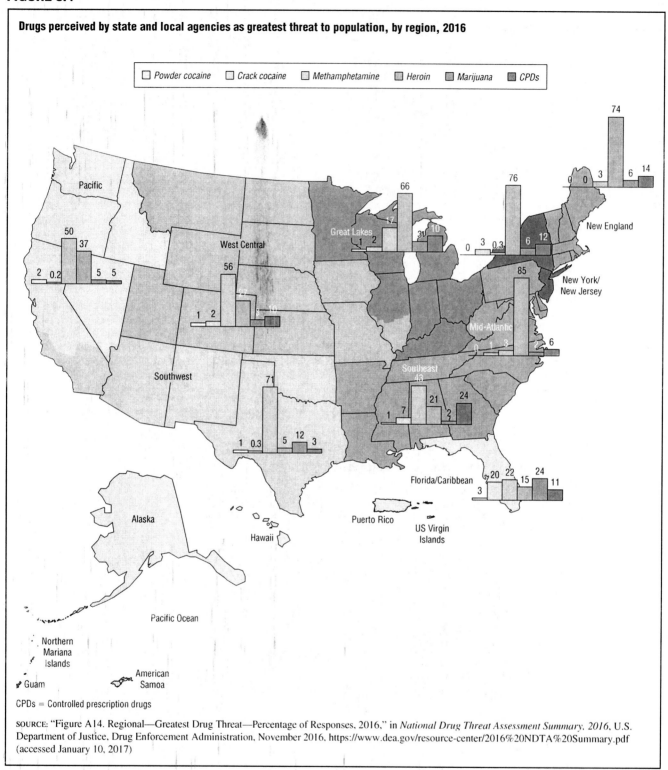

CPDs = Controlled prescription drugs

SOURCE: "Figure A14. Regional—Greatest Drug Threat—Percentage of Responses, 2016," in *National Drug Threat Assessment Summary, 2016*, U.S. Department of Justice, Drug Enforcement Administration, November 2016, https://www.dea.gov/resource-center/2016%20NDTA%20Summary.pdf (accessed January 10, 2017)

The ingredients for making methamphetamine are lithium (available from batteries), acetone (e.g., from paint thinner), lye (a widely used chemical), and ephedrine/pseudoephedrine (found in cold medicines). Anhydrous ammonia, which is used as a fertilizer, can be used to dry the drug and cut the production cycle by 10 hours. Making methamphetamine creates a horrible odor, forcing producers into remote areas to avoid arousing the suspicion of those living downwind; explosions and fires are also common.

Ephedrine, a stimulant, appetite suppressant, and decongestant, is the key ingredient for making methamphetamine. In 1989 the Chemical Diversion and Trafficking Act gave the DEA authority to regulate the bulk sales of ephedrine, but over-the-counter (without a prescription)

FIGURE 8.5

Drug availability by region, as reported by state and local agencies, 2016

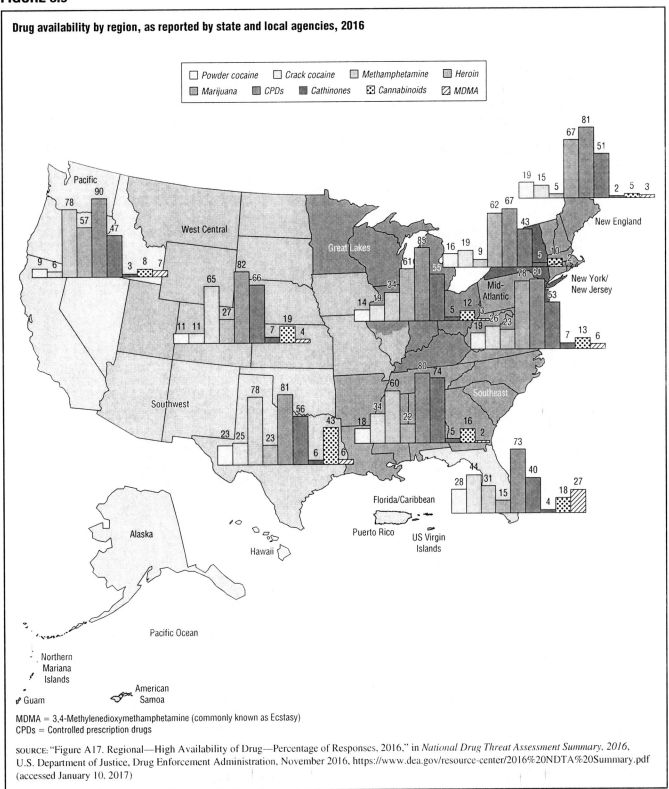

MDMA = 3,4-Methylenedioxymethamphetamine (commonly known as Ecstasy)
CPDs = Controlled prescription drugs

SOURCE: "Figure A17. Regional—High Availability of Drug—Percentage of Responses, 2016," in *National Drug Threat Assessment Summary, 2016*, U.S. Department of Justice, Drug Enforcement Administration, November 2016, https://www.dea.gov/resource-center/2016%20NDTA%20Summary.pdf (accessed January 10, 2017)

sales were not included. As a result, meth manufacturers simply bought ephedrine-containing products at drugstores and then used it to manufacture methamphetamine.

The passage of the Domestic Chemical Diversion Control Act of 1993 made it illegal to sell ephedrine over the counter as well, but pseudoephedrine, a substitute, was not included in the ban. The Comprehensive Methamphetamine Control Act of 1996 made it illegal to knowingly possess ephedrine and pseudoephedrine (called precursor chemicals) and doubled the possible penalty for manufacturing and/or distributing methamphetamine from 10 years

FIGURE 8.6

Methamphetamine seizures on southwestern U.S.-Mexico border, 2016

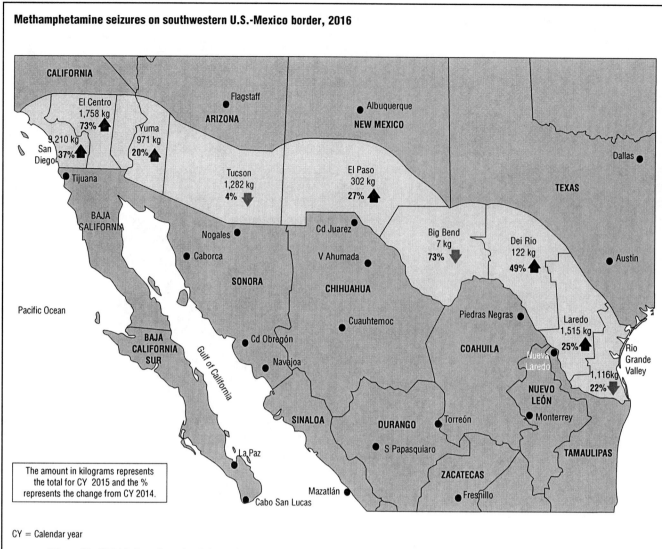

SOURCE: "Figure 89. CBP Methamphetamine Seizures by Southwest Border Corridor in 2016, with Percent Change from 2014," in *National Drug Threat Assessment Summary, 2016*, U.S. Department of Justice, Drug Enforcement Administration, November 2016, https://www.dea.gov/resource-center/2016%20NDTA%20Summary.pdf (accessed January 10, 2017)

to 20 years. The Methamphetamine Trafficking Penalty Enhancement Act of 1998 further increased penalties for trafficking in methamphetamine. The Combat Methamphetamine Epidemic Act of 2005 placed restrictions on the amount of ephedrine, pseudoephedrine, and phenylpropanolamine (another precursor drug to methamphetamine) that can be sold to an individual in one day or over a 30-day period, required vendors to verify the identity of purchasers of these drugs, and required vendors to keep these products inaccessible to customers without vendor help. Because of these restrictions on the purchase and sale of ephedrine and pseudoephedrine, the drug ephedra is often used as a substitute. Ephedra, also known as ma huang in traditional Chinese medicine, contains both ephedrine and pseudoephedrine. In addition, drug traffickers circumvent the law on restrictive sales by having many individuals purchase the drugs up to the daily and monthly limit, a practice that is called "smurfing."

Methamphetamine Prices, Purities, and Supply

The prices and purity of illicit drugs play an important role in understanding and analyzing drug markets. The purity of a drug refers to the extent to which it is diluted (mixed) with other substances. Determining the prices and purities of illicit drugs accurately is challenging because illicit drugs are not sold in standard quantities and are generally sold at varying purities. In addition, data can be collected only from seizures and purchases by undercover agents. Thus, the data gleaned from the samples collected must be used to estimate these factors for the total drug supply for that year.

According to the DEA, in *National Drug Threat Assessment Summary, 2016*, methamphetamine smuggled into the United States from Mexico had an average purity level of more than 95% in 2015. This high purity level, combined with steadily increasing supply, played a key role in driving down the price of methamphetamine in the United States.

COCAINE

Production and Distribution

The coca plant, from which cocaine is produced, is grown primarily in the Andean region of Colombia, Peru, and Bolivia, with Colombia being the largest producer. The first step in the production of cocaine is to mix the coca leaves with sulfuric acid in a plastic-lined hole in the ground. The leaves are then pounded to create an acidic juice. When this juice is filtered and neutralized, it forms a paste. The paste is purified into cocaine base by the addition of more chemicals and filtering. This cocaine base includes coca paste, freebase cocaine, and crack cocaine. It is typically transported from the jungles where it was produced to southern Colombia, where it is processed into cocaine hydrochloride (white powder) at clandestine drug laboratories. Small, independent Bolivian and Peruvian trafficking groups also process some cocaine. It takes 660 pounds to 1,100 pounds (300 kg to 500 kg) of coca leaf to make 2.2 pounds (1 kg) of cocaine.

After processing, cocaine is shipped to the United States and Europe. Mexico and other Caribbean and Central American countries serve as transit countries for the shipment of drugs into the United States. Drug traffickers shift routes according to law enforcement and interdiction pressures but, as with most drugs, cocaine is primarily smuggled into the United States across the southwestern border. The DEA also indicates that substantial amounts enter the country at New York City and Miami via maritime and commercial air smuggling.

Cocaine Prices, Purities, and Supply

According to the DEA, in *National Drug Threat Assessment Summary, 2016*, the availability of cocaine in the United States decreased steadily between 2007 and 2014. The supply of cocaine entering the United States subsequently rose between 2014 and 2015, driven largely by increased cultivation and production in Colombia. Meanwhile, cocaine seizures rose 56.7% between 2014 and 2015, reaching their highest levels since 2010. The DEA notes that cocaine-related deaths declined significantly between 2006 and 2010, falling from 7,448 to 4,183 over that span. Cocaine-related deaths rose to 4,681 in 2011, the dipped to 4,404 in 2012 before climbing again, topping 5,415 in 2014.

MARIJUANA

Production, Availability, and Distribution

Marijuana is made from the flowering tops and leaves of the cannabis plant; these are collected, trimmed, dried, and then most often smoked in a pipe or as a cigarette. Many users smoke "blunts," named after the inexpensive blunt cigars from which they are made. Blunt cigars are approximately 5 inches (12.7 cm) long and can be purchased at any store that sells tobacco products. A marijuana blunt is made from the emptied cigar casing, which is then stuffed with marijuana or a marijuana-tobacco mixture. A blunt may contain as much marijuana as six regular marijuana cigarettes. In some cases blunt users add crack cocaine or PCP to the mixture to make it more potent.

According to the DEA, in *National Drug Threat Assessment Summary, 2016*, marijuana was the most widely available drug in the United States in 2015. The drug's prevalence was due primarily to high importation levels from Mexico. Between 2010 and 2013 U.S. law enforcement agencies seized approximately 2.9 million pounds to 3.1 million pounds (1.3 million kg to 1.4 million kg) of marijuana annually along the nation's southwestern border with Mexico. A substantial proportion of this marijuana was entering the country via underground tunnels leading into Arizona, California, New Mexico, and Texas.

Marijuana seizures along the southwestern border decreased 3.7% between 2014 and 2015. Despite this decline, certain regions along the border saw an increase in the amount of marijuana seized during this span. The largest increase was in the Laredo area of Texas, where DEA agents seized 194,205 pounds (88,090 kg) in 2015, a 33% increase over totals from 2014. The highest volume of seizures in 2015 occurred in the Tucson region of Arizona (926,766 pounds [420,374 kg]) and in the Rio Grande valley in Texas (543,786 pounds [246,657 kg]), although both these areas saw declines from 2014. (See Figure 8.7.)

THC Content and Price

The active ingredient in marijuana is THC (delta-9-tetrahydrocannabinol), which is mostly concentrated in the flowering tops (colas or buds) of the cannabis plant. The flowering tops of female plants that have not yet been pollinated and, therefore, have not yet produced seeds, have the highest THC content. This plant part is called sinsemilla (literally, "without seed"). By contrast, feral hemp, commonly called ditchweed, contains a low THC content and is generally not a product drug users want.

The DEA reports in *National Drug Threat Assessment Summary, 2016* that average marijuana potency increased significantly between 1995 and 2014. In 1995 the THC content of marijuana in federal seizure samples was slightly less than 4%; by 2014 the THC content of marijuana had tripled, to 12%.

The DEA also indicates that the marijuana legalization movement has had a notable impact on marijuana use in the United States. The DEA suggests that although

FIGURE 8.7

Marijuana seizures on southwestern U.S.-Mexico border, 2015

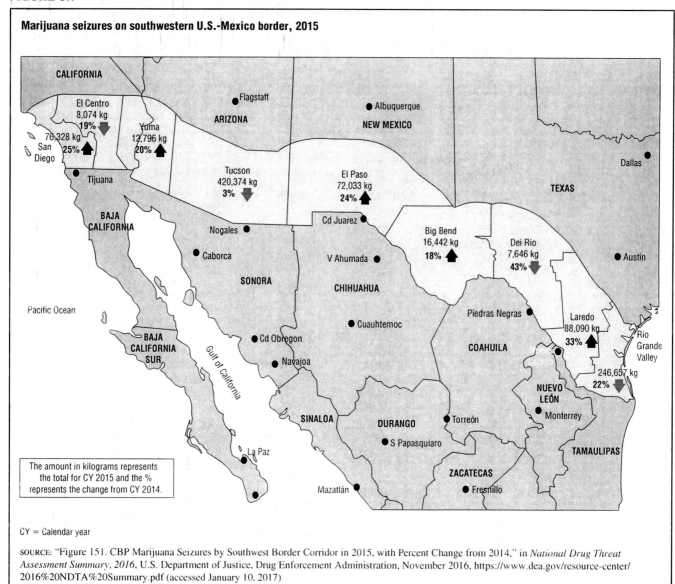

The amount in kilograms represents the total for CY 2015 and the % represents the change from CY 2014.

CY = Calendar year

SOURCE: "Figure 151. CBP Marijuana Seizures by Southwest Border Corridor in 2015, with Percent Change from 2014," in *National Drug Threat Assessment Summary, 2016*, U.S. Department of Justice, Drug Enforcement Administration, November 2016, https://www.dea.gov/resource-center/2016%20NDTA%20Summary.pdf (accessed January 10, 2017)

marijuana remained illegal at the federal level in 2016, the legalization of recreational marijuana in a handful of states will likely lead to an increase in both marijuana use (including among teens) and domestic cultivation of the drug. Despite legalization, much of this increased production will continue to be sold on the black market, as marijuana growers seek to circumvent costs related to state regulations or taxation. According to *National Drug Threat Assessment Summary, 2016*, groups and individuals have established operations in states such as Colorado and Washington, where recreational marijuana is legal, with the express goal of acquiring and shipping the drug into regions of the country where the drug remains illegal under state law.

In contrast, legalization advocates argue that eliminating prohibitions on marijuana has the potential to usher in a number of potential economic, legal, and health advantages for society as a whole. In "Marijuana Legalization and Regulation" (http://www.drugpolicy.org/marijuana-legalization-and-regulation), the Drug Policy Alliance contends that states and jurisdictions that legalize marijuana will reap considerable economic benefits from the new laws, both in the form of increased tax revenues and job creation and by reducing costs related to prosecuting marijuana offenses in the criminal justice system. It further notes that state regulation of marijuana has the capacity to impose tighter restrictions on the sale and use of the drug, thereby making it more difficult for underage individuals to acquire. Meanwhile, the implementation of testing protocols for marijuana would provide significant health benefits to users by increasing quality standards while reducing potential exposure to diseases and other harmful chemicals. The DEA notes in *National Drug Threat Assessment Summary, 2016* that revenues from legal marijuana sales topped $5.4 billion in 2015, a 17.4% increase over revenues of $4.6 billion in 2014.

HEROIN

Heroin users represent the smallest group using a major drug. In *Key Substance Use and Mental Health Indicators in the United States: Results from the 2015 National Survey on Drug Use and Health*, SAMHSA estimates that there were 329,000 current heroin users in the United States in 2015. (See Figure 4.2 in Chapter 4.)

Heroin Production and Distribution

PRODUCTION PROCESS. The source of heroin is the opium poppy. After the leaves of the poppy fall off, only the round poppy pods remain. Heroin production begins by scoring the poppy pod with a knife. A gummy substance begins to ooze out. The opium gum is scraped off, collected, and taken to a refinery where it is converted into morphine through a chemical process that involves dissolving the opium gum in boiling water and straining the liquid. The dried morphine is pressed into bricks, which are converted into heroin through a chemical process using acetic anhydride, sodium carbonate, activated charcoal, chloroform, ethyl alcohol, ether, and acetone. The resulting product is graded from 1 to 4, with No. 1 and No. 2 heroin being raw base forms, No. 3 the brown (smokable) form, and No. 4 being the white (injectable) form. Variations in the process are introduced as the heroin is diluted to increase its bulk and profits. Pure heroin might be mixed with various substances including caffeine, baking soda, powdered milk, and quinine.

OVERVIEW OF THE TRADE. Opium poppies are intensely cultivated in four regions of the world: Southeast Asia, Southwest Asia, Mexico, and South America. The INL reports in *International Narcotics Control Strategy Report* that in 2014 Afghanistan accounted for approximately 82% of the world's illicit opium, harvesting 521,392 acres (211,000 ha) of opium poppies to produce 6,945 tons (6,300 t) of raw opium.

Mexico produces a variety of heroin called black tar because it looks like roofing tar. It was once considered inferior to Colombian and Asian heroin, but it has reached a level of purity high enough that it can be snorted or smoked. Mexican heroin is targeted almost exclusively to the U.S. market. The long U.S.-Mexican land border provides many opportunities for drug smugglers to cross. Female couriers are used more frequently than male couriers. Mexican heroin is smuggled in cars, trucks, and buses and may also be hidden on or in the body of the smuggler. Many smugglers send their drugs by overnight-package express services.

The bulk of heroin from South America comes from Colombia. Many Colombian coca traffickers have been requiring their dealers to accept a small amount of heroin along with their normal deliveries of coca. This has allowed the Colombian producers to use an existing network to introduce a pure grade of heroin into the U.S. market. Much of Colombian heroin production is sent through Central America and Mexico by smugglers traveling on commercial airline flights into the United States. These smugglers hide the drugs in false-sided luggage, clothing, hollowed-out shoe soles, or inside their bodies. The DEA notes in *National Drug Threat Assessment Summary, 2016* that heroin from Latin America and Asia generally comes in white powder and is predominantly found in the eastern United States. Heroin from Mexico, which is typically available in the western United States, mostly appears in either brown powder or black tar form.

Purity

Purity is important to heroin addicts because low-purity heroin must be injected to get the most out of the drug. Many people feel uncomfortable using needles and fear contracting the human immunodeficiency virus, which can be spread by sharing a needle with an infected user. High-purity heroin can be smoked or snorted, which makes heroin more attractive to potential users who do not want to use needles. Despite these so-called advantages of high-purity heroin, an estimated three out of five heroin users continue to inject the drug no matter what its purity. However, in *National Drug Threat Assessment Summary, 2016*, the DEA indicates that the increased prevalence of high-purity heroin has led to increases in accidental overdoses. For example, heroin overdoses in the United States more than tripled from 3,306 in 2010 to 10,574 in 2014.

FENTANYL

Fentanyl is a powerful synthetic opioid that has elicited serious concern among law enforcement officials in the 21st century. Up to 50 times more potent than heroin, fentanyl is typically manufactured in China, and then smuggled to various points in North America. (See Figure 8.8.) The drug is then combined with heroin or other opioid powders and sold to unsuspecting users, who inject the drug without realizing how potent it is. According to the DEA, in *National Drug Threat Assessment Summary, 2016*, the increased prevalence of fentanyl played a role in the steep rise in opioid-related overdose deaths during the second decade of the 21st century. The DEA notes that synthetic opioids such as fentanyl and tramadol caused 5,544 overdose deaths in 2014. Indeed, fentanyl is so potent that it poses serious harm to agents who handle the drug during investigations. In "DEA Warning to Police and Public: Fentanyl Exposure Kills" (June 10, 2016, https://www.dea.gov/divisions/hq/2016/hq061016.shtml), the DEA warns that "touching fentanyl or accidentally inhaling the substance during enforcement activity or field testing the substance can result in absorption through the skin and that is one of the biggest dangers with fentanyl. The onset of adverse health effects, such as disorientation, coughing, sedation,

FIGURE 8.8

Fentanyl and fentanyl precursor traffic, from China and within North America

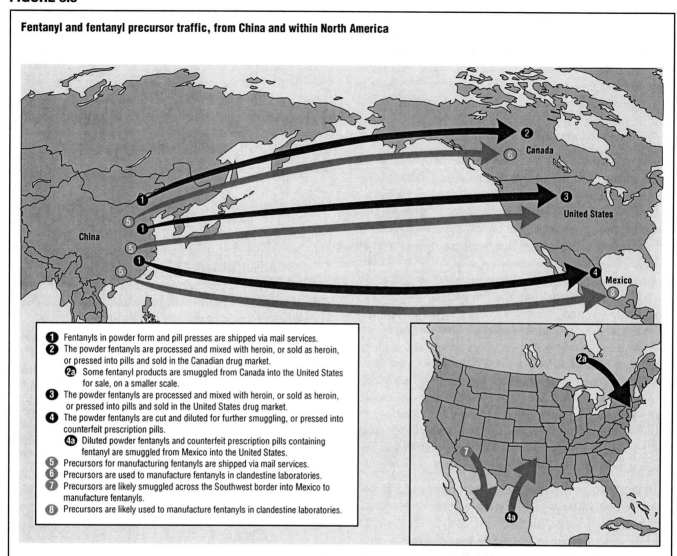

① Fentanyls in powder form and pill presses are shipped via mail services.
② The powder fentanyls are processed and mixed with heroin, or sold as heroin, or pressed into pills and sold in the Canadian drug market.
    ②ₐ Some fentanyl products are smuggled from Canada into the United States for sale, on a smaller scale.
③ The powder fentanyls are processed and mixed with heroin, or sold as heroin, or pressed into pills and sold in the United States drug market.
④ The powder fentanyls are cut and diluted for further smuggling, or pressed into counterfeit prescription pills.
    ④ₐ Diluted powder fentanyls and counterfeit prescription pills containing fentanyl are smuggled from Mexico into the United States.
⑤ Precursors for manufacturing fentanyls are shipped via mail services.
⑥ Precursors are used to manufacture fentanyls in clandestine laboratories.
⑦ Precursors are likely smuggled across the Southwest border into Mexico to manufacture fentanyls.
⑧ Precursors are likely used to manufacture fentanyls in clandestine laboratories.

SOURCE: "Figure 83. Illicit Fentanyl and Fentanyl Precursor Flow Originating in China," in *National Drug Threat Assessment Summary, 2016*, U.S. Department of Justice, Drug Enforcement Administration, November 2016, https://www.dea.gov/resource-center/2016%20NDTA%20Summary.pdf (accessed January 10, 2017)

respiratory distress or cardiac arrest is very rapid and profound, usually occurring within minutes of exposure." For these reasons, the DEA advises law enforcement officials not to attempt to conduct field tests on fentanyl.

PHARMACEUTICALS

The DEA estimates in *National Drug Threat Assessment Summary, 2016* that abuse of CPDs costs approximately $25 billion in health care costs and $25.5 billion in lost work productivity each year in the United States. Although there has traditionally been little trafficking in CPDs by drug trafficking organizations, law enforcement officials have noted a steady increase in organized distribution of prescription drugs by street gangs. The DEA reports that more than half (53%) of CPD users acquire the drugs for free from friends or relatives; a little more than one-fifth (21.2%) of CPD users obtain the drugs from one doctor, whereas 2.6% acquire the drugs from more than one doctor. According to the DEA, the number of CPD-related overdose deaths rose steadily between 2007 and 2014, from 19,601 to 25,760.

CHAPTER 9
ANTIDRUG EFFORTS AND THEIR CRITICISMS

The Harrison Narcotic Act of 1914, which outlawed opiates and cocaine, was the first legislation aimed at prohibiting the possession and use of mood-altering drugs in the United States. Following that act, laws were passed or amended at intervals, but the war on drugs did not begin in earnest until the early 1970s with the Comprehensive Drug Abuse Prevention and Control Act of 1970. The phrase "War on Drugs" was coined in 1971 during the administration of President Richard M. Nixon (1913–1994). A national effort was launched after that to bring illicit drug use under control, and it is still very much under way in the 21st century.

Not everyone agrees with governmental efforts to control or prohibit the use of mood-altering substances. Prohibition of alcohol came to an end in 1933 because of massive public disobedience. (See Chapter 1.) Data from the 2015 National Survey on Drug Use and Health, which are published in *Results from the 2015 National Survey on Drug Use and Health: Detailed Tables* (September 8, 2016, https://www.samhsa.gov/data/sites/default/files/NSDUH -DetTabs-2015/NSDUH-DetTabs-2015/NSDUH-DetTabs -2015.pdf) by the Substance Abuse and Mental Health Services Administration (SAMHSA), suggest a similar public response to laws that prohibit the use of drugs. In the report SAMHSA estimates that in 2015, 48.8% of people aged 12 years and older (130.6 million people) had used an illicit drug at some point during their life. Just fewer than 18% (47.7 million) of people aged 12 years and older had done so in the past 12 months, and 10.1% (27.1 million) had used an illicit drug during the past 30 days.

One criticism leveled at governmental efforts to control or prohibit the use of mood-altering substances is that they appear to be inconsistent with the public health issues they raise. Tobacco and alcohol cause many deaths per year, yet both are legal substances. In the fact sheet "Health Effects of Cigarette Smoking" (December 1, 2016, https://www .cdc.gov/tobacco/data_statistics/fact_sheets/health_effects/ effects_cig_smoking/), the Centers for Disease Control and Prevention (CDC) estimates that 480,000 premature deaths occur each year as a result of smoking and exposure to secondhand smoke. Kenneth D. Kochanek et al. of the CDC's Division of Vital Statistics report in "Deaths: Final Data for 2014" (*National Vital Statistics Report*, vol. 65, no. 4, June 30, 2016) that 30,722 people died of alcohol-related causes in 2014. The National Highway Traffic Safety Administration reports in "Traffic Safety Facts, 2015 Data: State Alcohol-Impaired Driving Estimates" (December 2016, https://crashstats.nhtsa.dot.gov/ Api/Public/Publication/812357) that in 2015, 10,265 people died from car crashes that involved alcohol-impaired driving. In comparison, drug abuse produced 49,714 deaths in 2014, according to the Office of National Drug Control Policy (ONDCP) in *National Drug Control Strategy: Data Supplement 2016* (January 2017, https://obamawhitehouse .archives.gov/sites/default/files/ondcp/policy-and-research/ 2016_ndcs_data_supplement_20170110.pdf).

NATIONAL DRUG CONTROL STRATEGY

The Anti-drug Abuse Act of 1988 established the creation of a drug-free nation as a U.S. policy goal. As part of this initiative, Congress created the ONDCP (https://clinton1 .nara.gov/White_House/EOP/ondcp/html/general.html) "to establish policies, priorities, and objectives for the Nation's drug control program, the goals of which are to reduce illicit drug use, manufacturing, and trafficking; drug-related crime and violence; and drug-related health consequences." The ONDCP director develops the National Drug Control Strategy annually, which describes the nation's antidrug program and puts forth the proposed budget of the ONDCP.

The first National Drug Control Strategy was prepared by William J. Bennett (1943–), the first ONDCP director, and submitted to Congress by President George

H. W. Bush (1924–) in 1989. Reduction of demand was a priority and has remained such over the years. The strategy also called for directing efforts at countries where cocaine originated, improving the targeting of interdiction (the interception of smuggled drugs), increasing the capacity of treatment providers, accelerating the efforts aimed at drug prevention, and focusing on the education of youth. In its details, the drug strategy laid emphasis on law enforcement activities and the expansion of the criminal justice system.

Since that time the basic building blocks of the National Drug Control Strategy have remained the same, but the specific emphases have changed. Some presidents lean more toward enforcement, others more toward fighting drug traffickers, and yet others more toward treatment and prevention. Whatever the model, all strategies to date have had the same components: prevention and treatment (together constituting demand reduction); and law enforcement, interdiction, and international efforts (together constituting supply disruption). The emphasis given to each of these components has been reflected in federal budgets.

In January 2009 President Barack Obama (1961–) appointed Edward H. Jurith (1951–2013), the former general counsel of the ONDCP, as the office's acting director. As early as the spring of 2009, only a few months into his presidency, President Obama had given indications of the direction his administration would take in the War on Drugs, including nominating a "drug czar" who favored treatment over incarceration and developing a major initiative to curtail violent drug trafficking on the U.S.-Mexican border. (See Chapter 1.) In May 2009 Gil Kerlikowske (1949–) was sworn in as director of the ONDCP, and shortly thereafter the phrase "War on Drugs" was dropped.

In *Epidemic: Responding to America's Prescription Drug Abuse Crisis* (2011, https://obamawhitehouse.archives .gov/sites/default/files/ondcp/policy-and-research/rx_abuse _plan.pdf), the ONDCP outlines a four-point "Action Plan" aimed at stemming prescription drug abuse, which includes a strategy for monitoring the distribution of prescription drugs on the state level, as well as programs to promote the safe disposal of unused medication. The *National Southwest Border Counternarcotics Strategy* (May 2016, https://obamawhitehouse.archives.gov/sites/ default/files/ondcp/policy-and-research/southwest_strategy -3.pdf) provides a detailed overview of the ONDCP's strategy for combating illegal drug trafficking along the nation's border with Mexico, which includes an emphasis on both bolstering border security and interdiction efforts, and on promoting drug treatment and prevention programs within border communities. In the *Caribbean Border Counternarcotics Strategy* (January 2015, http:// www.noticel.com/uploads/gallery/documents/25753ac71fd7 a89312e3fc76624bc76e.pdf), the Obama administration describes its plan to curtail drug smuggling into the

United States through the Caribbean. The report states that cocaine trafficking is the leading area of concern for law enforcement agencies monitoring the region, while noting that the islands are also a major launching point for the distribution of heroin, marijuana, and controlled prescription drugs. Among the objectives outlined in the report is the disruption of transnational drug cartels operating in the region, as well as curbing incidences of drug-related violence in Caribbean nations.

THE FEDERAL DRUG BUDGET

The national drug control budget for fiscal year (FY) 2017 is outlined in *FY 2017 Budget and Performance Summary: Companion to the National Drug Control Strategy* (December 2016, https://obamawhitehouse.archives .gov/sites/default/files/ondcp/policy-and-research/fy2017 _budget_summary-final.pdf). The total drug control budget grew to a projected $31.1 billion in FY 2017, up from $21.8 billion in 2008.

The national drug control budget is divided into two broad components: reducing the demand for drugs and disrupting their supply. Reducing the demand for drugs supports research and programs that help communities work toward a drug-free environment and encourage young people to reject drug use. Funding to disrupt the supply of drugs supports efforts to keep individuals and organizations from profiting from trafficking in illicit drugs, both domestically and internationally. Significant portions of the international budget are spent on supporting international eradication efforts that, in turn, depend on the cooperation of other countries and on the U.S. drug certification program, which may temporarily deny funding to certain regimes.

Table 9.1 shows the overall supply-and-demand proportions from FY 2015 to FY 2017. Nearly 51% of drug control spending in FY 2017 was allocated to drug abuse treatment and prevention, and about 49% was allocated to disrupting the drug supply. This ratio marks a shift from budget allocations for FY 2015, when 48% of drug control funding was devoted to demand reduction and 52% was slated for supply reduction.

Table 9.2 summarizes the drug control budget by agency. The agencies that work to reduce the demand for drugs include the ONDCP, the U.S. Departments of Education, Health and Human Services, Interior, Transportation, and Veterans Affairs, and the U.S. Small Business Administration. The agencies that work to disrupt the drug supply include the U.S. Departments of Defense, Homeland Security, Justice, State, and the Treasury.

Most domestic law enforcement funds are spent by the U.S. Department of Justice, or on its behalf, and underwrite the operations of the U.S. Drug Enforcement Administration (DEA), the chief domestic drug control

TABLE 9.1

Federal drug control spending, by function, fiscal years 2015–17

[Budget authority in millions]

Function	Fiscal year 2015 final	Fiscal year 2016 enacted	Fiscal year 2017 request	Fiscal year 2016–2017 dollars	Change percent
Treatment	$12,543.1	$13,248.6	$14,281.6	+$1,033.0	+7.8%
Percent	43.4%	43.4%	46.0%		
Prevention	1,341.5	1,496.2	1,544.7	+48.5	+3.2%
Percent	4.6%	4.9%	5.0%		
Domestic law enforcement	9,394.5	9,699.1	9,525.5	−173.6	−1.8%
Percent	32.5%	31.7%	30.7%		
Interdiction	3,960.9	4,479.9	4,138.5	−341.4	−7.6%
Percent	13.7%	14.7%	13.3%		
International	1,643.0	1,637.0	1,581.1	−55.9	−3.4%
Percent	5.7%	5.4%	5.1%		
Total	**$28,882.9**	**$30,560.8**	**$31,071.4**	**+$510.6**	**+1.7%**
Supply/demand					
Demand reduction	$13,884.6	$14,744.8	$15,826.3	+$1,081.5	+7.3%
Percent	48.1%	48.2%	50.9%		
Supply reduction	14,998.3	15,816.1	15,245.1	−571.0	−3.6%
Percent	51.9%	51.8%	49.1%		
Total	**$28,882.9**	**$30,560.8**	**$31,071.4**	**+$510.6**	**+1.7%**

Note: Detail may not add due to rounding.

SOURCE: "Table 1. Federal Drug Control Spending by Function," in *FY 2017 Budget and Performance Summary: Companion to the National Drug Control Strategy*, Executive Office of the President, Office of National Drug Control Policy, December 2016, https://obamawhitehouse.archives.gov/sites/default/files/ondcp/policy-and-research/fy2017_budget_summary-final.pdf (accessed March 13, 2017)

agency. Interdiction funds are managed by the U.S. Department of Homeland Security, which oversees all border-control functions and the U.S. Coast Guard. International funds are divided between the U.S. Departments of State and Defense. The Department of State's Bureau of International Narcotics and Law Enforcement Affairs (INL) is the lead agency that manages international programs. The Department of Defense is involved in supporting anti-insurgency programs in the Andean region and elsewhere. (Insurgencies are organized, armed rebellions against governments.)

INTERNATIONAL WAR ON DRUGS

The links among drugs, organized crime, and insurgencies outside the United States have long been known. A connection to terrorism is a contemporary emphasis that arose in the aftermath of the September 11, 2001 (9/11), terrorist attacks against the United States. In *Fiscal Year 2004 Budget: Congressional Justification* (May 20, 2003, https://www.state.gov/documents/organization/22061.pdf), the INL made a case for the convergence between the War on Drugs and the War on Terror:

> The September 11 attacks and their aftermath highlight the close connections and overlap among terrorists, drug traffickers, and organized crime groups. The nexus is far-reaching. In many instances, such as Colombia, the groups are the same. Drug traffickers benefit from terrorists' military skills, weapons supply, and access to clandestine organizations. Terrorists gain a source of revenue and expertise in the illicit transfer

and laundering of money for their operations. All three groups seek out weak states with feeble justice and regulatory sectors where they can corrupt and even dominate the government. September 11 demonstrated graphically the direct threat to the United States by a narco-terrorist state such as Afghanistan where such groups once operated with impunity. Although the political and security situation in Colombia is different from the Taliban period in Afghanistan (the central government is not allied with such groups but rather is engaged in a major effort to destroy them) the narco-terrorist linkage in Colombia poses perhaps the single greatest threat to the stability of Latin America and the Western Hemisphere. It also potentially threatens the security of the United States in the event of a victory by the insurgent groups. The bottom line is that such groups invariably jeopardize international peace and freedom, undermine the rule of law, menace local and regional stability, and threaten both the United States and our friends and allies.

The key to the international War on Drugs is disruption of the drug supply. The ONDCP states in *National Drug Control Strategy, 2006* (February 2006, https://www.ncjrs.gov/pdffiles1/ondcp/212940.pdf) that market disruption "contributes to the Global War on Terrorism, severing the links between drug traffickers and terrorist organizations in countries such as Afghanistan and Colombia, among others. It renders support to allies such as the administration of President Alvaro Uribe [1952–] in Colombia. Market disruption initiatives remove some of the most violent criminals from society, from kingpins such as the remnants of the Cali Cartel to common thugs

TABLE 9.2

Distribution of federal drug control spending, by agency, fiscal years 2015–17

[Budget authority in millions[a]]

	Fiscal year 2015 final	Fiscal year 2016 enacted	Fiscal year 2017 request
Department of Agriculture			
U.S. Forest Service	12.4	12.3	17.9
Court Services and Offender Supervision Agency for the District of Columbia	52.6	58.1	58.7
Department of Defense			
Drug Interdiction and Counterdrug Activities/OPTEMPO	1,409.3	1,343.3	1,222.0
Defense Health Program	73.5	75.5	75.5
Total Department of Defense	**1,482.8**	**1,418.8**	**1,297.5**
Department of Education			
Office of Elementary and Secondary Education	50.2	50.1	50.1
Federal Judiciary	1,158.9	1,210.6	1,246.7
Department of Health and Human Services			
Administration for Children and Families	18.6	18.5	60.0
Centers for Disease Control and Prevention	20.0	75.6	85.6
Centers for Medicare & Medicaid Services[b]	8,230.0	8,760.0	9,140.0
Health Resources and Services Administration	27.8	129.0	164.0
Indian Health Service	111.3	114.7	140.9
National Institute on Alcohol Abuse and Alcoholism	59.5	54.2	54.2
National Institute on Drug Abuse	1,015.7	1,050.6	1,050.6
Substance Abuse and Mental Health Services Administration[c]	2,460.4	2,512.2	2,986.0
Total Health and Human Services	**11,943.3**	**12,714.7**	**13,681.3**
Department of Homeland Security			
Customs and Border Protection	2,423.0	2,664.9	2,655.7
Federal Emergency Management Agency	8.3	8.3	6.2
Federal Law Enforcement Training Center	46.8	44.1	43.6
Immigration and Customs Enforcement	467.9	485.8	527.0
United States Coast Guard	1,265.7	1,616.1	1,269.0
Total Homeland Security	**4,211.5**	**4,819.1**	**4,501.6**
Department of Housing and Urban Development			
Community Planning and Development	463.5	486.9	589.1
Department of the Interior			
Bureau of Indian Affairs	9.7	9.7	9.7
Bureau of Land Management	5.1	5.1	5.1
National Park Service	3.3	3.3	3.3
Total Interior	**18.1**	**18.1**	**18.1**
Department of Justice			
Assets Forfeiture Fund	284.1	238.7	243.1
Bureau of Prisons	3,491.0	3,672.4	3,491.8
Criminal Division	40.0	39.0	39.9
Drug Enforcement Administration	2,373.1	2,426.5	2,485.6
Organized Crime Drug Enforcement Task Force Program	507.2	512.0	522.1
Office of Justice Programs	260.9	280.2	275.6
U.S. Attorneys	76.8	72.6	75.9
U.S. Marshals Service	270.4	278.1	289.9
U.S. Marshals Service—Federal Prisoner Detention	498.0	510.0	505.5
Total Justice	**7,801.7**	**8,029.6**	**7,929.4**
Department of Labor			
Employment and Training Administration	6.0	6.0	6.0
Office of National Drug Control Policy			
High Intensity Drug Trafficking Areas	245.0	250.0	196.4
Other Federal Drug Control Programs	107.2	109.8	98.5
Salaries and Expenses	22.6	20.0	19.3
Total Office of National Drug Control Policy	**374.8**	**379.9**	**314.2**
Department of State[d]			
Bureau of International Narcotics and Law Enforcement Affairs	446.1	434.7	382.4
United States Agency for International Development	95.5	136.2	131.9
Total State	**541.6**	**570.8**	**514.3**

such as the vicious MS-13 street gang." As outlined in *National Drug Control Strategy, 2012* (April 2012, https://obamawhitehouse.archives.gov/sites/default/files/ ondcp/2012_ndcs.pdf), the Obama administration emphasized a balanced approach to drug control efforts but remained committed to policies that would "increase

TABLE 9.2

Distribution of federal drug control spending, by agency, fiscal years 2015–17 [CONTINUED]

[Budget authority in millions[a]]

	Fiscal year 2015 final	Fiscal year 2016 enacted	Fiscal year 2017 request
Department of Transportation			
Federal Aviation Administration	30.7	31.5	31.6
National Highway Traffic Safety Administration	2.7	11.5	11.5
Total Transportation	**33.4**	**43.0**	**43.1**
Department of the Treasury			
Internal Revenue Service	60.3	60.3	95.8
Department of Veterans Affairs			
Veterans Health Administration[e]	671.8	682.4	707.6
	$28,882.9	**$30,560.8**	**$31,071.4**

OPTEMPO = Opearating/Operations Tempos

[a]Detail may not add due to rounding.

[b]The estimates of the Centers for Medicare and Medicaid Services (CMS) reflect Medicaid and Medicare benefit outlays for subsance use disorder treatment; they do not reflect budget authority. The estimates were developed by the CMS Office of the Actuary.

[c]Includes budget authority and funding through evaluation set-aside authorized by Section 241 of the Public Health Service (PHS) Act.

[d]The fiscal year 2016 funding level represents the fiscal year 2016 President's Budget request.

[e]VA Medical Care receives advance appropriations; fiscal year 2016 funding was provided in the Consolidated Appropriations Act, 2014 (Public Law No. 113–76).

SOURCE: "Table 2. Federal Drug Control Spending by Agency," *FY 2017 Budget and Performance Summary: Companion to the National Drug Control Strategy*, Executive Office of the President, Office of National Drug Control Policy, December 2016, https://obamawhitehouse.archives.gov/sites/default/files/ondcp/policy-and-research/fy2017_budget_summary-final.pdf (accessed March 13, 2017)

security along the Nation's borders and disrupt and dismantle the transnational criminal organizations that seek to traffic illicit drugs across them." In the *FY 2017 Budget and Performance Summary: Companion to the National Drug Control Strategy*, the Obama administration further noted that illegal drug trafficking is frequently a key source of funding for terrorist organizations, while also acting as a "powerful and corrosive force" with the capacity to undermine "the rule of law in affected countries." This destabilizing aspect of the drug trade ultimately hinders a government's ability to counter terrorist threats effectively.

DISRUPTING THE DRUG SUPPLY

Internationally, the federal effort is concentrated on what the INL calls the Andean ridge, the northwestern part of South America where Colombia, Ecuador, and Peru, running north to south, touch the Pacific and where landlocked Bolivia lies east of Peru. In *International Narcotics Control Strategy Report: Volume I, Drug and Chemical Control* (March 2016, https://www.state.gov/documents/organization/253655.pdf), the INL estimates that 90% of all cocaine seized by U.S. law enforcement officials in 2014 came from Colombia. The remaining cocaine came from Bolivia and Peru. Besides focusing on Colombia, the INL also concentrates on Mexico because the country is a major transmission route of drugs to the United States and because it is a significant source of heroin, marijuana, and methamphetamine.

The centerpiece of the disruption effort is the eradication of coca and poppy by providing airplanes and funds for spraying herbicides that kill the plants. Efforts also include assisting foreign law enforcement agencies and foreign governments with counternarcotics and anti-corruption activities, and providing financial support through the U.S. Agency for International Development (USAID) for the planting of legal crops and improving infrastructure (roads and bridges) so that farm goods can be delivered to market. The latter measures are necessary because many of the people who are involved in cultivating drug-producing plants live in remote and undeveloped regions, and this is the only source of income. The USAID programs are intended to give them alternatives.

Elsewhere, the INL is concentrating on Afghanistan and Pakistan. In all, INL programs extend to about 150 countries and involve assistance in law enforcement and in the fight against money laundering (making illegally acquired cash seem as though it was legally acquired). What follows is a brief encapsulation of the INL strategy in selected high-focus areas.

Colombia

The primary effort to disrupt the drug supply in Colombia is coca eradication. The coca tree (*Erythroxylon coca*) is a densely leafed plant that is native to the eastern slopes of the Andes Mountains and is heavily cultivated in Colombia.

Table 9.3 shows the amount of coca leaf that was cultivated in Colombia between 1986 and 2015. The area cultivated in Colombia increased from 46,200 acres (18,700 ha) in 1986 to 419,600 acres (169,800 ha) in

TABLE 9.3

Amount of coca leaf cultivated, by country, 1986–2015

Year	Net coca cultivation (hectares)				Potential pure cocaine production (metric tons)			
	Total	Bolivia	Colombia	Peru	Total	Bolivia	Colombia	Peru
1986	162,500	37,800	18,700	106,000	710	220	30	460
1987	175,700	41,300	25,600	108,800	740	220	40	480
1988	193,300	48,900	34,000	110,400	750	225	55	470
1989	215,700	52,900	42,400	120,400	755	220	70	465
1990	211,700	50,300	40,100	121,300	775	220	65	490
1991	206,200	47,900	37,500	120,800	805	220	60	525
1992	211,700	45,500	37,100	129,100	835	225	60	550
1993	195,700	47,200	39,700	108,800	720	240	65	415
1994	201,700	48,100	45,000	108,600	745	255	70	420
1995	203,900	48,600	50,900	104,400	900	240	210	450
1996	201,700	48,100	67,200	86,400	770	215	255	300
1997	187,100	45,800	79,500	61,800	680	200	265	215
1998	185,500	38,000	101,800	45,700	690	150	380	160
1999	179,900	21,800	122,500	34,700	650	70	460	120
2000	187,500	19,600	136,200	31,700	770	80	530	160
2001	221,800	19,900	169,800	32,100	1055	100	700	255
2002	200,750	21,600	144,450	34,700	975	110	585	280
2003	166,300	23,200	113,850	29,250	790	100	445	245
2004	166,200	24,600	114,100	27,500	755	115	410	230
2005	199,500	21,500	144,000	34,000	875	115	500	260
2006	220,500	21,500	157,000	42,000	890	115	510	265
2007	227,000	24,000	167,000	36,000	765	130	450	185
2008	186,500	26,500	119,000	41,000	600	150	265	185
2009	185,000	29,000	116,000	40,000	605	150	260	195
2010	182,000	29,000	100,000	53,000	690	160	240	290
2011	158,000	25,500	83,000	49,500	630	175	180	275
2012	153,500	25,000	78,000	50,500	570	145	165	260
2013	167,000	27,000	80,500	59,500	635	160	190	285
2014	193,500	35,000	112,000	46,500	740	185	250	305
2015	248,500	36,500	159,000	53,000	995	230	420	345

Notes: Based on new yield data, the U.S. government recalculated Colombian potential pure cocaine production from 2007 and do not match numbers published in International Narcotics Control Strategy Report (INCSR) for those years. The U.S. government also backcast potential pure production for Peru from 2007 to 2014 and do not match published INCSR numbers.

SOURCE: "Table 154. Andean Net Coca Cultivation and Potential Cocaine Hydrochloride Production, 1986–2015," in *National Drug Control Strategy: Data Supplement 2016*, Executive Office of the President, Office of National Drug Control Policy, 2016, https://obamawhitehouse.archives.gov/sites/default/files/ondcp/policy-and-research/2016_ndcs_data_supplement_20170110.pdf (accessed March 13, 2017)

2001. The area of cultivation then declined through 2003, rose again through 2007 to near-2001 levels, and then dropped dramatically in 2008 to 294,100 acres (119,000 ha). Coca leaf cultivation in Colombia continued to plummet through 2012, when it fell to 192,742 acres (78,000 ha), its lowest level since 1996. Coca leaf cultivation in Colombia increased slightly in 2013, to 198,920 acres (80,500 ha), before rising sharply to 276,758 acres (112,000 ha) in 2014 and to 392,898 acres (159,000 ha) in 2015.

Table 9.4 shows the amount of coca leaf that was eradicated between 1987 and 2015. U.S. aerial eradication efforts in Colombia increased dramatically, from 104,484 acres (42,283 ha) in 2000, to a high of 424,065 acres (171,613 ha) in 2006. This was a fourfold increase in eradication. Eradication then declined steadily over the next eight years. In 2014, the last year for which figures were available as of March 2017, manual eradication efforts eliminated 137,274 acres (55,553 ha) of coca leaf in Colombia, and aerial eradication efforts eliminated an additional 28,919 acres (11,703 ha) in that country for a combined total of 166,193.2 acres (67,256 ha).

Poppy eradication takes place in Colombia as well because that country supplies a great deal of the heroin entering the United States. Colombian opium poppy eradication is discussed in *National Drug Control Strategy: Data Supplement 2016*. In 2001 aerial eradication efforts removed 6,383 acres (2,583 ha) of the plants; in 2004 aerial and manual efforts together removed 11,261 acres (4,557 ha). Eradication then fell by about half in 2005 and 2006, as aerial eradication of poppies was discontinued in April 2006 to focus on the aerial eradication of coca. By 2010, the last year for which data were available as of March 2017, eradication efforts eliminated 1,347 acres (545 ha) of opium poppy in Colombia. Additionally, Colombian cultivation of opium poppy declined from 16,062 acres (6,500 ha) in 2001 to 1,977 acres (800 ha) in 2014.

Along with their efforts to eradicate coca and poppy in Colombia, USAID and other international organizations have conducted "alternative livelihoods" programs that provide farmers involved in cultivating coca and poppy with alternative crops. USAID began operating such programs in Colombia late in 2000 and in Afghanistan in 2004, although the idea had been implemented in other areas more than 30 years earlier.

Besides Colombia's aggressive seizure of drugs within its borders, the country is working with the United

TABLE 9.4

Amount of coca leaf eradicated, by country, 1987–2015

[Hectares]

Year	Bolivia[a]	Colombia[b] Manual	Colombia[b] Aerial	Peru
1987	1,040	460	—	355
1988	1,475	230	—	5,130
1989	2,500	640	—	1,285
1990	8,100	900	—	—
1991	5,486	972	—	—
1992	3,152	959	—	—
1993	2,397	793	—	0
1994	1,058	5,412	—	0
1995	5,493	32,432	—	0
1996	7,512	—	15,407	1,259
1997	7,026	—	31,663	3,462
1998	11,621	—	49,641	7,825
1999	16,999	—	39,113	13,800
2000	7,653	—	42,283	6,200
2001	9,435	84,251	1,745	6,436
2002	11,839	122,695	2,762	7,133
2003	10,000	127,112	4,220	7,022
2004	8,437	131,824	6,232	7,605
2005	6,073	134,474	37,540	8,966
2006	5,070	164,119	42,110	10,136
2007	6,269	148,435	64,979	11,056
2008	5,484	129,876	95,731	10,143
2009	6,341	101,573	60,954	10,025
2010	8,200	97,836	43,957	12,033
2011	10,509	103,302	34,592	10,290
2012	>10,000	100,549	30,486	14,171
2013	—	47,052	22,120	23,785
2014	—	55,553	11,703	31,205
2015	11,109	—	—	35,830

[a]Beginning in 2001, U.S. government surveys of Bolivian coca take place over the period June to June.
[b]Colombian eradication data for 1999–2001 were obtained from the Policia Nacional de Colombia (CNP)/US 22 Department of State Bureau of International Narcotics and Law Enforcement Affairs (INL) Air Wing unpublished data (February 2005). Estimates for 2001 to 2014 were published online by the Office of National Drug Control Policy (ONDCP) at https://www.whitehouse.gov/ondcp/targeting-cocaine-at-the-source, accessed on October 14, 2016.
Note: Black lines denote data not available.

SOURCE: "Table 155. Amount of Coca Leaf Eradicated, 1987–2015 (Hectares)," in *National Drug Control Strategy: Data Supplement 2016*, Executive Office of the President, Office of National Drug Control Policy, 2016, https://obamawhitehouse.archives.gov/sites/default/files/ondcp/policy-and-research/2016_ndcs_data_supplement_20170110.pdf (accessed March 13, 2017)

States in the resumption of the Air Bridge Denial program. This program works by forcing or shooting down aircraft that appear to be taking part in drug trafficking activities. The program was halted in 2001, when a civilian aircraft was downed in Peru and two U.S. citizens were killed. It was resumed in 2003. According to the INL, in *International Narcotics Control Strategy Report*, as of October 2015 the government of Colombia had suspended all aerial eradication programs, in order to implement "a new drug control strategy that reduces focus on forced coca eradication, and enhances efforts on interdiction; rural policing; prosecuting criminal organizations; anti-money laundering; alternative development, including crop substitution; market development for licit products; infrastructure and development projects; social investment; and protection of national parks."

Colombia, however, illustrates some of the fundamental dilemmas of interdiction. The drug trade there has been one symptom of a festering civil war. Through the 1990s and into the first decade of the 21st century, antigovernment insurgent groups and illegal paramilitary groups were heavily funded by the drug trade. Nonetheless, the Central Intelligence Agency (CIA) notes in *World Factbook: Colombia* (January 12, 2017, https://www.cia.gov/library/publications/the-world-factbook/geos/co.html) that "more than 31,000 former paramilitary troops had demobilized by the end of 2006 and the United Self Defense Forces of Colombia as a formal organization had ceased to function. In the wake of the paramilitary demobilization, emerging criminal groups arose, whose members include some former paramilitaries." The largest of the insurgent groups is the Fuerzas Armadas Revolucionarias de Colombia (FARC; Revolutionary Armed Forces of Colombia). The CIA reports that the Colombian government initiated formal peace talks with the FARC, with the goal of "reaching a definitive bilateral ceasefire and incorporating demobilized FARC members into mainstream society and politics." After Colombian voters rejected a proposed peace deal in an October 2016 referendum, the Colombian government and FARC struck a revised peace agreement in November 2016, formally ending more than 50 years of conflict. Joshua Partlow and Nick Miroff report in "Colombia's Congress Approves Historic Peace Deal with FARC Rebels" (WashingtonPost.com, November 30, 2016) that in signing the deal FARC rebels agreed to forfeit a portion of the assets acquired through the illegal drug trade, in order to provide reparations to victims of the civil unrest.

Bolivia and Peru

According to the INL, in *International Narcotics Control Strategy Report*, Bolivia is the third-largest producer of cocaine and is "a significant transit zone for Peruvian cocaine." Bolivia is poor and has had an unsettled history (nearly 200 coups since its independence in 1825). The country has been under democratic rule since the 1980s, but successive governments have been reluctant to support eradication programs energetically because coca cultivation (but not cocaine production) is legal in Bolivia. Coca is a traditional crop in this country, and the coca leaf is chewed by the inhabitants; eradication has resulted in a popular antiestablishment movement.

According to the *National Drug Control Strategy: Data Supplement 2016*, 42,005 acres (16,999 ha) of coca leaf were eradicated in Bolivia in 1999; a year later, the amount of coca leaf eradicated in the country fell by more than 50%, to 18,910 acres (7,653 ha). (See Table 9.4.) This figure fluctuated in the ensuing years, rising to 29,235 acres (11,839 ha) in 2002, before falling to 12,528 acres (5,070 ha) in 2006. In 2015, 27,451 acres (11,109 ha) of coca leaf were eradicated in Bolivia. These eradication efforts are offset by replanting, and eradication is sometimes violently opposed by the population. As a result, the amount of coca leaf that was cultivated in Bolivia increased for much of this period, from 53,375 acres (21,600 ha) in 2002 to 90,193 acres (36,500 ha) in 2015. (See Table 9.3.)

The INL explains that Peru is the second-largest producer of cocaine in the world and a major importer of cocaine precursor chemicals. Unlike the Bolivian government, however, the Peruvian government is committed to counternarcotics activities. Regardless, the government's actions are hampered by organized bodies of *cocaleros* (coca growers), who enjoy sufficient popular support. Thus, in Peru as in Bolivia, replanting frequently follows eradication efforts. Nonetheless, Table 9.3 shows that the cultivation of coca leaf in Peru decreased dramatically between the early 1990s and the first half of the first decade of the 21st century, from a peak of 319,013 acres (129,100 ha) in 1992 to a low of 67,954 acres (27,500 ha) in 2004. Peruvian coca leaf cultivation subsequently rose steadily over the next decade, climbing to 147,028 acres (59,500 ha) in 2013, before dropping to 114,904 acres (46,500 ha) in 2014 and rising again slightly to 130,966 acres (53,000 ha) in 2015. Eradication maintained a steady increase throughout this span, rising to 77,109 acres (31,205 ha) in 2014 and 88,538 acres (35,830 ha) in 2015. (See Table 9.4.)

Mexico

Mexico is one of the principal producers of marijuana, methamphetamine, and heroin entering the United States. It also serves as a thoroughfare for cocaine, which is produced in South America and sent north to the United States.

From 2000 to 2006 President Vicente Fox (1942–) and the Mexican government were energetic in the eradication of the cannabis and poppy crops. (Cannabis is the botanical name of the plant from which marijuana is derived.) Mexican officials were vigorous, as well, in the arrest and prosecution of members of drug cartels, even though these efforts were hampered by severe budget constraints, corruption, and inefficiencies within the law enforcement and criminal justice institutions. In 2006 Felipe Calderón (1962–) succeeded Fox as the president of Mexico. According to the INL, in *International Narcotics Control Strategy Report*, during the first two years of the Calderón administration significant progress was made in attacking drug trafficking and consumption. In October 2008 Presidents George W. Bush (1946–) and Calderón announced the Mérida Initiative, a plan to achieve stronger law enforcement cooperation between the United States and Mexico. During the Bush administration, the initiative was primarily focused on strengthening law enforcement capabilities, largely through arming and training Mexican counterdrug agencies.

In March 2010 President Obama implemented an overhaul of the Mérida Initiative. Clare Ribando Seelke and Kristin M. Finklea of the Congressional Research Service report in *U.S.-Mexican Security Cooperation: The Mérida Initiative and Beyond* (January 18, 2017, https://fas.org/sgp/crs/row/R41349.pdf) that the shift in policy was aimed primarily at strengthening political institutions in Mexico, both as a means of eliminating corruption in the criminal justice system and as a way of restoring public faith in government. According to Seelke and Finklea, President Obama's revised strategy was founded on "four pillars": "1) disrupting organized criminal groups; 2) institutionalizing the rule of law; 3) creating a 21st-century border; and 4) building strong and resilient communities." Highlights of the plan included a shift away from providing equipment to Mexican security personnel in favor of emphasizing training and technical assistance; helping promote new "criminal procedure code" with the aid of the Mexican Congress; and developing bilateral policies as a means of strengthening border security and rooting out corruption among border officials. Community building, with an emphasis on educational outreach and the development and strengthening of social institutions, was also a hallmark of President Obama's revised initiative. Seelke and Finklea report that between FY 2007 and FY 2016 the U.S. Congress appropriated $2.7 billion in funding for the Mérida Initiative.

Shortly after his election in November 2012, the new president, Enrique Peña Nieto (1966–), reaffirmed Mexico's commitment to the initiative, while stressing that his administration's top priority in further cooperation with the United States would be on reducing drug-related violence. According to Seelke and Finklea, the initiative began to show some signs of success between 2011 and 2016. Drug-related violence fell during this span, and in June 2016 the Mexican government implemented sweeping changes to the country's criminal justice system at both the state and federal level. That same month, Héctor "El Güero" Palma (1940–), a former figure in the Sinaloa cartel who had been held in the United States since 2007 on drug-related charges, was extradited to Mexico to face homicide charges.

Along with marijuana and heroin, one of the drugs imported to the United States over the U.S.-Mexican border is methamphetamine, a synthetic drug that is made in illegal laboratories. This drug has become an increasing problem in the United States. (See Chapter 4.) U.S. law enforcement agencies have done much to combat the spread of this drug domestically, but they are also active in stopping the flow of methamphetamine and its precursors (other substances that are used to make methamphetamine) into the country. In general, increased production of methamphetamine within Mexico is indicated by increased seizures at the U.S. southwest border. The Department of Justice reports in *National Drug Threat*

Assessment Summary, 2016 (November 2016, https://www .dea.gov/resource-center/2016%20NDTA%20Summary .pdf) that methamphetamine seizures on the southwestern border rose from 8,871 pounds (4,024 kg) in 2010 to 35,898 pounds (16,283 kg) in 2015, an increase of more than 400%.

Afghanistan

In *International Narcotics Control Strategy Report*, the INL indicates that Afghanistan produces more than 80% of the world's opium supply. When Afghanistan was under the control of the zealously religious and conservative Taliban regime, cultivated poppy acreage dropped precipitously. According to *National Drug Control Strategy: Data Supplement 2016*, opium poppy cultivation in Afghanistan declined from 159,408 acres (64,510 ha) in 2000 to 4,164 acres (1,685 ha) in 2001. The United States invaded Afghanistan in 2001, in a response to the 9/11 terrorist attacks, and the Taliban was driven from power. An unintended consequence of these events was that poppy cultivation resumed, rising to 75,985 acres (30,750 ha) in 2002. By 2004 poppy cultivation reached a staggering 510,767 acres (206,700 ha) but then dropped by nearly half to 265,391 acres (107,400 ha) in 2005. The recultivation of poppy was in part a response to a continuing drought in the region: opium poppy is hardy and can grow under adverse conditions, supplying income to farmers. By 2007 poppy cultivation in Afghanistan had nearly reached 2004 levels at 499,153 acres (202,000 ha). (See Table 8.3 in Chapter 8.) Poppy cultivation subsequently declined over the next four years, falling to 284,171 acres (115,000 ha) by 2011, before once again experiencing a steep rise. By 2014 the nation's poppy cultivation topped 521,392 acres (211,000 ha), the highest level on record. This increase was driven in part by the U.S. military's decision to adopt a nonintervention policy toward opium cultivation in Afghanistan, in the belief that the economic security offered by opium production had an overall stabilizing impact on the nation's population, many of whom were dependent on the crop for their livelihood. (See Chapter 1.) Poppy cultivation in Afghanistan fell slightly in 2015 to 496,682 acres (201,000 ha).

Afghanistan's post-Taliban government officially banned opium poppy cultivation and pressured its regional governors to suppress the drug trade. Despite these efforts, the situation in Afghanistan was, in the immediate post-Taliban era, similar to the situation in Colombia, with a weak central government unable to assert itself in areas where autonomous warlords hold de facto (virtual) power. Other countries and organizations have tried to help. For example, USAID has been active in establishing alternative development programs. According to the *FY 2017 Budget and Performance Summary: Companion to the National Drug Control Strategy*, a portion of USAID's budget of $131.9 million in FY 2017 was dedicated to ongoing efforts to promote alternative agricultural development initiatives in Afghanistan, with the aim of reducing the nation's dependence on revenues generated by opium production. Toward this effort, U.S. programs in FY 2015 had converted 9,845 acres (3,984 ha) to the production of licit alternative crops that provided agriculture and income to 55,926 households.

FOSTERING INTERNATIONAL COOPERATION: THE DRUG CERTIFICATION PROCESS

The United States uses a drug certification process to promote international cooperation in controlling drug production and trafficking. Section 490 of the Foreign Assistance Act of 1961 requires the president to annually submit to Congress a list of major drug-producing and drug-transiting countries. The president must also assess each country's performance in battling narcotics trade and trafficking based on the goals and objectives of the 1988 United Nations Convention against Illicit Traffic in Narcotic Drugs and Psychotropic Substances. Countries that have fully cooperated with the United States or that have taken adequate steps to reach the goals and objectives of the 1988 convention are "certified" by the president. U.S. aid is withheld from countries that are not certified. Many countries resent the process, but most work toward certification.

TRANSIT-ZONE AGREEMENTS

Other countries not on the list are frequently reluctant to cooperate with the United States to stop drug traffickers. The Caribbean basin, for example, is a major transit zone for drug trafficking. The Caribbean basin countries are those that border, or lie in, the Gulf of Mexico and the Caribbean Sea, such as the island nations of the West Indies, Mexico, Central American nations, and northern South American nations. Bermuda is also included, even though it is in the Atlantic Ocean. Most of the islands have bilateral agreements with the United States, but these agreements are limited to maritime matters that permit U.S. ships to seize traffickers in the territorial waters of particular Caribbean islands. Few transit-zone countries permit U.S. planes to fly in their airspace to force suspected traffickers to land. Some transit-zone countries have no maritime agreements with the United States.

DOMESTIC DRUG SEIZURES

The DEA is also at work within the United States to disrupt the drug supply. Table 9.5 shows annual marijuana plant eradications between 2002 and 2015, by state. During that span, total marijuana eradications increased by 27%, from 3.3 million plants to nearly 4.3 million plants destroyed. As Table 9.5 shows, California accounted for

TABLE 9.5

Marijuana plants eradicated, by state, 2002–15

State or jurisdiction	Total cultivated plants eradicated													
	2002	2003	2004	2005	2006	2007	2008	2009	2010	2011	2012	2013	2014	2015
Alabama	60,444	51,137	54,956	91,614	48,177	26,648	36,866	60,304	25,188	16,767	7,004	5,374	3,934	15,330
Alaska	8,616	7,350	5,337	5,836	6,163	5,180	4,259	4,612	3,304	7,540	4,383	2,709	2,624	249
Arizona	3,837	19,574	2,128	113,523	82,781	35,227	14,386	10,204	27,336	10,172	45,695	19,680	2,013	2,452
Arkansas	32,537	72,565	34,433	46,082	13,501	29,540	21,217	6,104	14,114	50,382	522	3,161	76,033	14,726
California	1,267,771	1,181,957	1,214,420	2,011,277	2,995,285	4,951,976	5,322,053	7,519,580	7,392,652	3,987,538	2,081,160	2,903,887	2,684,636	2,643,708
Colorado	15,127	13,981	6,158	7,383	7,486	4,928	30,033	29,890	11,823	26,024	23,304	16,604	8,056	27,072
Connecticut	2,935	3,027	4,095	1,349	1,543	2,155	2,940	1,859	3,641	2,430	1,253	1,096	1,927	867
Delaware	108	200	187	319	298	0	206	576	784	455	194	305	923	83
Florida	37,854	37,744	28,006	74,863	46,526	83,814	94,700	65,448	51,366	46,828	37,414	46,756	31,404	18,486
Georgia	75,770	46,985	18,738	27,709	66,605	21,436	50,447	49,716	67,163	23,556	70,986	10,130	15,674	49,148
Hawaii	435,789	392,422	379,644	255,113	201,100	139,089	102,771	51,532	97,333	83,578	84,611	32,289	29,463	15,852
Idaho	1,449	13,664	7,367	19,433	4,899	36,431	20,784	77,748	21,714	786	65,411	10,699	6,060	6,987
Illinois	15,852	41,806	27,888	14,461	7,669	55,967	16,311	10,056	47,601	14,930	8,769	7,765	14,326	3,890
Indiana	15,551	31,192	27,546	35,045	25,873	26,226	37,945	37,242	60,844	89,396	71,200	96,510	84,528	63,530
Iowa	1,036	1,257	417	5,244	169	3,161	676	3,540	4,262	536	1,878	181	1,359	454
Kansas	4,879	14,471	3,728	3,690	3,739	2,315	2,876	25,784	31,018	29,394	515	8,340	16,272	2,692
Kentucky	378,036	527,775	476,803	510,502	558,756	492,615	353,170	333,326	330,227	403,778	414,378	443,788	461,543	571,340
Louisiana	5,299	5,090	6,825	3,700	5,167	3,039	2,078	5,450	4,469	3,120	2,328	48,007	726	724
Maine	7,169	16,258	11,773	9,076	12,427	10,358	5,019	11,398	13,687	5,261	2,719	718	1,472	848
Maryland	2,582	3,445	2,601	1,953	4,510	3,780	2,839	3,680	3,912	3,647	2,792	2,606	5,638	2,834
Massachusetts	2,371	1,937	2,248	1,302	1,401	2,683	2,691	4,144	2,730	5,973	1,976	413	1,802	3,138
Michigan	26,443	24,524	30,805	29,902	26,813	35,746	62,549	42,329	60,240	75,102	48,898	56,086	75,427	18,942
Minnesota	6,929	2,967	3,632	7,371	4,762	8,925	18,498	10,797	4,736	3,315	14	6,534	1,304	601
Mississippi	3,973	2,984	2,487	3,104	2,399	2,400	1,737	1,215	1,164	1,166	602	2,187	1,374	2,736
Missouri	12,612	14,285	10,896	9,970	21,144	16,447	8,932	20,146	18,183	11,366	538	2,303	7,214	7,248
Montana	513	404	892	518	691	342	784	602	850	10,286	1,504	750	1,381	241
Nebraska	4,302	2,632	1,818	1,419	524	1,203	1,825	1,895	78,049	43,015	86,692	5,213	8,175	3,640
Nevada	1,513	1,877	3,375	1,148	1,836	6,090	10,011	15,116	32,015	96,916	47,870	12,954	6,310	5,153
New Hampshire	1,055	547	975	789	11,878	1,903	1,510	1,405	2,106	1,713	142	300	248	27
New Jersey	2,302	1,260	2,068	1,960	1,956	3,677	2,599	3,941	4,286	2,360	1,781			
New Mexico	2,568	1,507	2,621	5,065	3,255	3,804	965	1,094	8,404	9,230		1,737	1,048	115
New York	14,414	99,423	17,364	19,616	14,466	9,444	14,195	15,559	11,253	15,599	9,893	19,290	13,018	11,623
North Carolina	112,017	34,283	35,965	70,882	101,489	16,368	105,200	67,294	133,201	22,031	9,255	9,174	4,302	4,187
North Dakota	1,543	1,811	4,004	136	288	574	16							
Ohio	41,090	44,597	49,551	48,250	42,300	51,093	56,293	48,051	105,121	50,704	23,209	22,616	26,554	24,455
Oklahoma	5,149	4,297	7,154	13,682	12,776	22,394	21,067	66,000	61,055	28,016	13,248	11,182	28,925	23,387
Oregon	45,458	32,346	62,621	47,620	113,608	277,766	91,801	257,850	205,989	140,003	33,286	27,988	16,067	39,138
Pennsylvania	7,308	5,622	4,389	9,930	12,888	13,265	10,887	18,232	22,268	13,886	8,721	5,757	5,718	4,825
Rhode Island	551	76	187	79		0								
South Carolina	27,013	15,038	6,404	12,686	35,336	38,781	30,524	23,031	5,034	7,390	8,097	2,622	2,607	2,040
South Dakota		340	199	0	75	314	263	87	246	69	0	0	0	0
Tennessee	485,819	679,105	416,012	440,362	483,271	178,322	539,370	447,167	333,459	600,259	144,571	151,897	111,361	127,565
Texas	53,175	33,404	9,706	10,303	7,197	40,182	36,280	65,033	83,445	119,555	103,336	160,329	261,763	231,660
Utah	7,820	173	1,702	343	6,603	4,444	90,224	83,981	106,845	78,363	13,167	4,424	0	0
Vermont	2,302	3,427	2,126	1,171	1,710	2,864	925	1,877	4,063	2,020	1,495	1,032	2,454	1,196
Virginia	17,888	11,419	9,611	33,838	20,001	11,833	19,239	18,583	47,453	28,153	11,974	12,205	11,869	37,089
Washington	45,159	65,675	134,474	136,165	144,181	295,573	580,415	608,923	321,583	346,484	216,010	40,733	57,263	35,933
West Virginia	30,887	74,690	54,728	57,600	57,582	44,732	146,553	224,130	420,110	185,510	189,801	158,383	196,573	195,427
Wisconsin	6,993	8,523	9,009	5,353	8,425	9,324	36,348	37,613	42,556	30,841	26,321	8,347	6,625	32,320
Wyoming	32	33	48	350	129	149	23	588	303	76	22	0	0	0
United States*	3,341,840	3,651,106	3,200,121	4,209,086	5,231,658	7,034,327	8,013,308	10,394,642	10,329,185	6,735,519	3,928,943	4,385,788	4,300,833	4,253,958

*Does not include Puerto Rico or the Virgin Islands.

SOURCE: "Table 120. Eradicated Domestic Cannabis, Total Cultivated Plants, by State, 2002–2015," in *National Drug Control Strategy: Data Supplement 2016*, Executive Office of the President, Office of National Drug Control Policy, 2016, https://obamawhitehouse.archives.gov/sites/default/files/ondcp/policy-and-research/2016_ndcs_data_supplement_20170110.pdf (accessed March 13, 2017)

more than one-third (38%) of all marijuana plant eradications in 2002, with almost 1.3 million plants destroyed in the state that year. By 2015 nearly two-thirds (2.6 million, or 62%) of all domestic marijuana plant eradications occurred in California. By contrast, of the states for which data from 2015 were available, only Utah and Wyoming recorded no marijuana plant eradications that year.

Table 9.6 provides an overview of methamphetamine seizures in the United States between 2000 and 2015, by state. Early in the first decade of the 21st century the total number of methamphetamine seizures more than doubled nationwide, from 10,169 incidents in 2000 to 23,824 incidents in 2004. The number of methamphetamine seizures subsequently fell to 17,615 incidents in 2005, a one-year decline of 26%. Nationwide methamphetamine seizures fell sharply in 2006 and 2007, to 9,177 incidents and 6,856 incidents, respectively, before gradually rising again, reaching 15,217 incidents in 2010. Methamphetamine seizures then began to decline, and by 2015 there were 7,635 seizure incidents in the United States.

In 2000 California led the nation in methamphetamine seizures, accounting for more than one-fifth (2,209 out of 10,169, or 21.7%) of all incidents in the United States. (See Table 9.6.) Over the next 15 years, California experienced one of the most dramatic declines in methamphetamine seizures in the country, recording only 28 incidents in 2015. By contrast, methamphetamine seizures in Indiana rose from 358 in 2000 to a peak of 1,796 in 2013 before dropping to 1,378 in 2015, making it the state with the highest number of seizure incidents that year. Another state that experienced a significant increase in methamphetamine seizures during this period is Ohio, which saw incidents rise from 36 in 2000 to a peak of 1,157 in 2013 (an increase of 3,114%) before dropping to 810 in 2015. Tennessee also saw a dramatic increase in methamphetamine seizures during the first decade of the 21st century, with the number of incidents rising from 318 in 2000 to 2,333 in 2011 (an increase of 634%). Methamphetamine seizures in Tennessee subsequently experienced a steep decline over the next four years, dropping to 510 by 2015. The District of Columbia, Hawaii, Idaho, Massachusetts, Nebraska, Nevada, and Utah recorded no methamphetamine seizures in 2015.

ILLICIT DRUGS AND DRUG-RELATED CRIME

Production and trafficking are not the only criminal activities associated with the illegal drug trade. The Department of Justice reports in *National Drug Threat Assessment Summary, 2016* that the distribution and use of illicit drugs is frequently tied to theft and acts of violence. As Figure 9.1 shows, methamphetamine is a known factor in about one-third (33.7%) of all drug-related violent crimes. Other drugs with a strong link to

incidences of violent crime include heroin (20.2%) and crack cocaine (14.2%). Heroin is a known factor in more than one-third (35.6%) of all drug-related cases of property crime. Methamphetamine contributes to more than one-quarter (27.8%) of all drug-related property crimes, and controlled prescription drugs are known to be associated with roughly one in six (15.5%) of all drug-related property crimes. (See Figure 9.2.)

MARIJUANA LEGALIZATION MOVEMENT

In the United States the legalization of drugs almost invariably refers to the legalization of marijuana rather than, for example, heroin or cocaine. The use of "hard drugs" such as these is relatively limited, and most Americans consider them to be highly addictive and damaging to one's physical and mental health. Marijuana's situation is different. Some studies suggest significant harm from marijuana use, including effects on the heart, lungs, brain, and social and learning capabilities. Other studies find little or no harm from moderate marijuana use. Regardless of what the research says, marijuana is generally thought of as a relatively mild drug, an opinion that is supported in Canada by those who introduced repeated initiatives to decriminalize marijuana possession and in the Netherlands, where marijuana sales are tolerated in coffee shops.

Public Opinion

Polling data gathered by the Pew Research Center between 1969 and 2016 show public opinion increasingly favoring the legalization of marijuana. (See Figure 9.3.) In 1969, 84% of survey respondents opposed legalization, and 12% favored it. By 2016 those opposed had declined to 37% of the public, whereas 57% were in favor. Among millennials (those who were aged 18 to 35 years in 2016), support for legalization was particularly strong, with 71% of people in this age group expressing this opinion. Between 1969 and 2016, the percentage of Americans who had ever tried marijuana also increased dramatically. In 1969, only 4% of adults responded that they had tried marijuana; by 2016 this figure had risen to 43%. (See Figure 9.4.)

A number of initiatives and referenda attempting to legalize marijuana for medical purposes or to decriminalize possession of modest quantities have gained consideration on state ballots. Many states and local jurisdictions have decriminalized certain uses of specific amounts of marijuana. Decriminalization means that the state or local jurisdiction no longer considers uses of marijuana in the amounts and manners it specifies as illegal, but the jurisdiction may still consider these uses as civil infractions and may impose civil fines, drug education, or drug treatment. Nevertheless, the possession and use of marijuana is still illegal under federal law, and this law supersedes state and local marijuana decriminalization laws. Therefore, a

TABLE 9.6

Methamphetamine seizures, by state, 2000–15

State	2000	2001	2002	2003	2004	2005	2006	2007	2008	2009	2010	2011	2012	2013	2014	2015
Alabama	102	223	335	519	797	524	269	247	617	671	717	292	310	223	112	72
Alaska	28	14	35	53	121	66	19	7	18	13	22	5	4	2	0	1
Arizona	474	355	293	254	218	133	42	21	33	24	18	5	22	5	4	1
Arkansas	400	542	636	1,170	1,339	692	432	368	401	662	814	281	104	65	43	14
California	2,209	1,801	1,704	1,260	774	466	414	278	355	269	180	107	99	67	46	28
Colorado	206	303	517	507	411	268	133	72	60	48	31	13	14	9	7	6
Connecticut	0	1	2	1	0	4	3	0	1	2	1	0	4	1	2	2
Delaware	0	0	0	2	3	1	0	0	1	1	3	2	13	5	5	4
District of Columbia	0	0	0	0	1	0	0	0	0	0	3	1	0	0	0	0
Florida	20	43	189	322	441	471	200	185	216	416	527	161	332	527	525	328
Georgia	69	107	210	436	545	429	191	118	197	216	331	140	90	66	24	21
Hawaii	4	3	11	4	10	12	3	1	0	0	3	0	0	1	0	0
Idaho	160	144	133	119	75	35	23	23	13	17	19	8	3	4	3	0
Illinois	165	401	696	1,085	1,576	1,425	840	394	359	411	474	634	802	670	728	680
Indiana	358	518	750	1,032	1,377	1,488	800	813	739	1,328	1,229	1,437	1,698	1,796	1,471	1,378
Iowa	286	582	922	1,465	1,666	913	348	198	239	336	379	407	400	308	143	165
Kansas	682	841	782	675	636	410	183	101	159	181	239	194	149	69	48	23
Kentucky	113	181	382	504	608	606	334	305	441	741	1,359	1,745	999	476	468	188
Louisiana	16	17	139	136	176	135	28	54	44	162	222	79	117	52	11	13
Maine	2	3	0	0	4	5	5	1	4	1	4	5	11	22	33	56
Maryland	0	2	1	2	3	7	7	2	2	0	4	1	3	0	1	3
Massachusetts	0	2	2	2	1	8	2	4	3	3	2	2	3	6	9	0
Michigan	24	133	255	365	459	510	284	212	454	713	864	437	753	609	750	941
Minnesota	165	214	334	479	288	168	68	48	46	31	27	9	9	14	8	7
Mississippi	132	251	508	437	523	345	277	178	439	938	913	318	248	94	2	1
Missouri	929	2,178	2,754	2,884	2,913	2,313	1,317	1,277	1,510	1,793	1,945	2,071	1,963	1,484	1,034	503
Montana	36	76	104	129	104	35	13	10	10	18	21	11	8	14	17	11
Nebraska	37	208	368	287	321	283	32	29	65	40	27	18	11	6	7	0
Nevada	286	260	106	241	152	85	44	24	17	16	13	16	6	3	1	0
New Hampshire	1	3	1	2	2	9	4	3	1	7	8	15	13	20	11	13
New Jersey	0	1	3	1	2	3	6	1	4	0	1	0	2	4	2	2
New Mexico	81	146	170	308	224	102	51	44	73	66	66	22	20	10	6	2
New York	2	8	30	35	69	26	42	13	20	17	35	47	154	140	200	288
North Carolina	16	37	70	222	473	487	211	158	197	209	235	395	558	571	535	433
North Dakota	36	86	210	258	238	171	40	27	33	35	8	8	15	6	7	4
Ohio	36	99	141	224	533	657	357	230	258	336	375	352	802	1,157	936	810
Oklahoma	509	934	1,040	1,406	899	328	218	114	191	778	870	997	764	438	209	106
Oregon	394	631	606	583	632	232	66	41	46	17	21	11	10	5	7	10
Pennsylvania	9	18	29	64	134	95	63	17	24	42	38	10	127	208	209	276
Rhode Island	0	1	4	1	0	0	3	0	0	0	0	1	1	1	1	3
South Carolina	6	12	61	166	336	252	111	68	130	244	343	338	499	398	356	584
South Dakota	8	24	37	48	35	25	15	13	11	9	22	5	10	15	19	2
Tennessee	318	631	809	1,587	2,341	1,717	892	599	829	1,492	2,163	2,333	1,714	1,672	961	532
Texas	538	746	670	864	733	437	187	156	249	278	213	109	56	284	13	15
Utah	283	204	153	110	107	67	39	8	15	13	10	9	2	4	1	0
Vermont	0	0	0	0	1	2	0	2	0	0	4	0	4	3	1	2
Virginia	1	5	10	43	108	86	22	25	21	29	106	202	317	387	309	93
Washington	982	1,483	1,420	1,007	954	545	335	240	127	70	45	35	12	12	6	3
West Virginia	3	21	66	106	326	445	166	111	116	139	207	92	132	67	16	4
Wisconsin	31	51	95	127	108	79	33	7	16	26	45	41	46	44	14	3
Wyoming	12	39	67	36	27	13	5	9	6	0	11	2	6	5	9	4
U.S. total	10,169	14,583	17,860	21,568	23,824	17,615	9,177	6,856	8,810	12,858	15,217	13,423	13,442	12,057	9,384	7,635

Note: Incidents include laboratories, glassware, or dump sites; U.S. total includes specified states only.

SOURCE: "Table 125. Methamphetamine Seizure Incidents, by State, 2000–2015," in *National Drug Control Strategy: Data Supplement 2016*, Executive Office of the President, Office of National Drug Control Policy, 2016, https://obamawhitehouse.archives.gov/sites/default/files/ondcp/policy-and-research/2016_ndcs_data_supplement_20170110.pdf (accessed March 13, 2017)

person residing in a state that has decriminalized the possession and use of marijuana can still be arrested and prosecuted by federal officials under federal law.

In November 2012 this potential opposition between federal and state authority became an actuality, after voters in Colorado and Washington passed referenda legalizing possession of small quantities of marijuana for recreational purposes. Tim Dickinson reports in "The Next Seven States to Legalize Pot" (RollingStone.com, December 18, 2012) that the passage of these laws "fundamentally changed the national conversation about cannabis." In November 2014 Alaska, Oregon, and the District of Columbia passed initiatives legalizing the sale and use of marijuana for recreational purposes. Two years later, in November 2016, residents of California, Maine, Massachusetts, and Nevada also voted to legalize recreational marijuana.

Arguments for and against Legalization

FOR LEGALIZATION. Most of those who favor legalization promote two principal arguments. The first argument

FIGURE 9.1

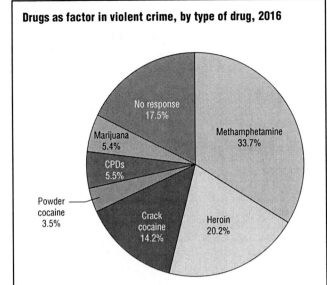

Drugs as factor in violent crime, by type of drug, 2016

CPDs = Controlled prescription drugs

Note: Percentages do not add up to 100% due to some survey recipients selecting "Don't Know" as a response to these questions and to some survey recipients failing to respond to these questions.

SOURCE: "Figures A3. Drug That Most Contributes to Violent Crime—Percentage of NDTS Responses, 2016," in *National Drug Threat Assessment Summary, 2016*, U.S. Department of Justice, Drug Enforcement Administration, November 2016, https://www.dea.gov/resource-center/2016%20NDTA%20Summary.pdf (accessed January 11, 2017)

FIGURE 9.2

Drugs as factor in property crime, by type of drug, 2016

CPDs = Controlled prescription drugs

Note: Percentages do not add up to 100% due to some survey recipients selecting "Don't Know" as a response to these questions and to some survey recipients failing to respond to these questions.

SOURCE: "Figures A4. Drug That Most Contributes to Property Crime—Percentage of NDTS Responses, 2016," in *National Drug Threat Assessment Summary, 2016*, U.S. Department of Justice, Drug Enforcement Administration, November 2016, https://www.dea.gov/resource-center/2016%20NDTA%20Summary.pdf (accessed January 11, 2017)

FIGURE 9.3

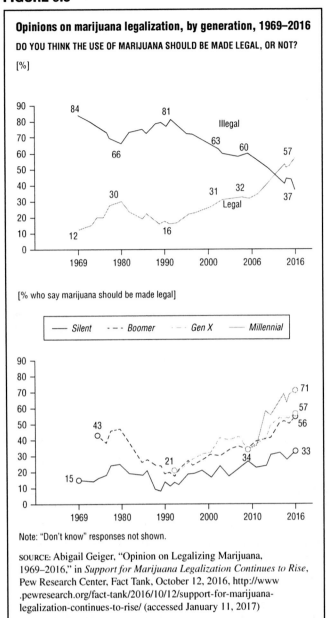

Opinions on marijuana legalization, by generation, 1969–2016

DO YOU THINK THE USE OF MARIJUANA SHOULD BE MADE LEGAL, OR NOT?

[% who say marijuana should be made legal]

Note: "Don't know" responses not shown.

SOURCE: Abigail Geiger, "Opinion on Legalizing Marijuana, 1969–2016," in *Support for Marijuana Legalization Continues to Rise*, Pew Research Center, Fact Tank, October 12, 2016, http://www.pewresearch.org/fact-tank/2016/10/12/support-for-marijuana-legalization-continues-to-rise/ (accessed January 11, 2017)

is that an approach to drugs based on prohibition and criminalization does not work, produces excessive rates of incarceration, and wastes money that could be more productively spent on treatment and prevention. The second argument is that drug use is an activity arbitrarily called a crime. It is imposed by law on some drugs and not on others, and can be seen as criminal at one time but perhaps not at another. Murder, rape, and robbery have always been considered inherently criminal acts, but drug use is simply a consumption of substances. For example, alcohol consumption was once prohibited but is now legal. Likewise, during the early 1900s opiates were legally sold in pharmacies, and the soft-drink Coca-Cola contained small quantities of cocaine.

Some who advocate the legalization of drugs believe the government has no right telling people what they may and may not ingest. Most legalization proponents,

FIGURE 9.4

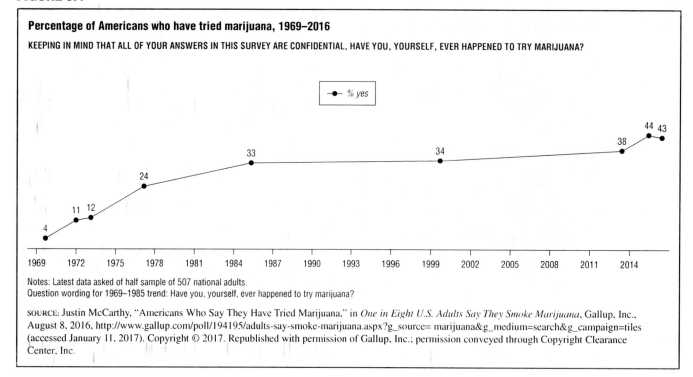

Percentage of Americans who have tried marijuana, 1969–2016

KEEPING IN MIND THAT ALL OF YOUR ANSWERS IN THIS SURVEY ARE CONFIDENTIAL, HAVE YOU, YOURSELF, EVER HAPPENED TO TRY MARIJUANA?

Notes: Latest data asked of half sample of 507 national adults.
Question wording for 1969–1985 trend: Have you, yourself, ever happened to try marijuana?

SOURCE: Justin McCarthy, "Americans Who Say They Have Tried Marijuana," in *One in Eight U.S. Adults Say They Smoke Marijuana*, Gallup, Inc., August 8, 2016, http://www.gallup.com/poll/194195/adults-say-smoke-marijuana.aspx?g_source= marijuana&g_medium=search&g_campaign=tiles (accessed January 11, 2017). Copyright © 2017. Republished with permission of Gallup, Inc.; permission conveyed through Copyright Clearance Center, Inc.

however, recognize that many drugs can be harmful, but they do not see this as a reason to make their use illegal. They point out that tobacco use and alcohol abuse are known to be harmful, but their use is legal. The policy these legalization advocates recommend is based on educational and public health approaches such as those used for tobacco and alcohol. They believe that a greater harm is imposed on society by prohibiting such substances, as evidenced by the consequences of the Prohibition period of the early 20th century, when alcohol was banned and crime, racketeering, and homicide rates soared.

Many proponents argue that legalization will result in decreased harm and crime from trafficking, gang wars, and illegal activities committed to obtain drugs; lower incarceration rates and associated cost savings; more funds available for treatment from savings and from taxes on legally distributed drugs; and the potential use of drugs like marijuana for medical purposes.

AGAINST LEGALIZATION. The federal government's case against legalization is summarized by the DEA in the brochure *Speaking Out against Drug Legalization* (2010, https://www.dea.gov/pr/multimedia-library/publications/speaking_out.pdf).

Like legalization proponents, the DEA's position is organized around the concept of harm. Certain drugs are illegal or controlled because they cause harm. In the DEA's view, the legalization of drugs, even if only marijuana, will increase the harm already suffered by the drug-using public by spreading use to ever larger numbers of people. The agency makes the point that drugs are much more addictive than alcohol and invites the public to contemplate a situation in which commercial interests might be enabled to promote the sale of currently illicit substances.

Would legalization reduce crime? The DEA does not believe it would. Under a regulated drug-use system, age restrictions would apply. A criminal enterprise would continue to supply those under age. If marijuana were legalized, trade in heroin and cocaine would continue. If all three of the major drugs were permitted to be sold legally, other substances, such as phencyclidine and methamphetamine, would still support a criminal trade. The DEA does not envision that a black market in drugs could be eliminated entirely because health authorities would never permit potent drugs to be sold freely on the open market.

For all these reasons, the DEA advocates the continuation of a balanced approach to the control of drugs including prevention, enforcement, and treatment. Still, by 2015 the Obama administration and the Department of Justice had begun to implement a more flexible approach to the issue of marijuana legalization, particularly as it pertained to legislation in individual states. A more in-depth discussion of this policy shift appears in Chapter 1.

MEDICAL MARIJUANA

THC (delta-9-tetrahydrocannabinol), the active ingredient in marijuana, has been shown to alleviate the nausea and vomiting caused by chemotherapy, which is used to treat many forms of cancer. Marijuana has also been found useful in alleviating pressure on the eye in glaucoma patients. Furthermore, the drug has been found effective in helping to fight the physical wasting that usually accompanies AIDS. AIDS patients lose their appetite and can slowly waste away because they do not eat. Marijuana has been found effective in restoring the appetite of some AIDS patients. This is not to say that all scientists agree that marijuana is healthful or useful. For example, some studies find that marijuana suppresses the immune system and contains a number of lung-damaging chemicals. Still, the potentially beneficial uses of marijuana as a medicine have led to an advocacy movement for it to be made legally available by prescription.

Opponents of the medical legalization of marijuana often point to Marinol (a laboratory-made form of THC) as a superior alternative. Marinol provides a standardized THC content and does not contain impurities, such as leaves, mold spores, and bacteria, which are generally found in marijuana. Many patients, however, do not respond to Marinol, and the determination of the right dosage is variable from patient to patient.

Marijuana has been used illegally by an unknown number of cancer, glaucoma, and AIDS patients on the recommendation of their doctors. Nonetheless, the medical use of marijuana is not without risk. The primary negative effect is diminished control over movement. In some cases users may experience unpleasant emotional states or feelings. In addition, the usefulness of medicinal marijuana is limited by the harmful effects of smoking, which can increase a person's risk of cancer, lung damage, and problems with pregnancies (such as low birth weight). However, these risks are usually not important for terminally ill patients or those with debilitating symptoms. Also, the drug can be eaten to be effective.

Some states and local jurisdictions have decriminalized the cultivation of marijuana for personal medical use. As mentioned previously, however, the cultivation of marijuana is still illegal under federal law, which supersedes state and local marijuana decriminalization laws. In addition, such state and local rulings do not necessarily establish that the use of marijuana is medically appropriate. That issue is hotly debated in the media and among Americans, but no nationally recognized medical organization (such as the American Academy of Pediatrics, the American Cancer Society, or the American Medical Association) has endorsed the medical use of smoked marijuana.

IMPORTANT NAMES
AND ADDRESSES

AAA Foundation for Traffic Safety
607 14th St. NW, Ste. 201
Washington, DC 20005
(202) 638-5944
FAX: (202) 638-5943
URL: https://www.aaafoundation.org/

Action on Smoking and Health
1250 Connecticut Ave. NW, 2nd Floor
Washington, DC 20036
(202) 659-4310
E-mail: info@ash.org
URL: http://ash.org/

Adult Children of Alcoholics
World Service Organization
PO Box 3216
Torrance, CA 90510
(310) 534-1815
URL: http://www.adultchildren.org/

Al-Anon Family Group Headquarters
1600 Corporate Landing Pkwy.
Virginia Beach, VA 23454-5617
(757) 563-1600
FAX: (757) 563-1656
E-mail: wso@al-anon.org
URL: http://www.al-anon.alateen.org/

Alcoholics Anonymous World Services
PO Box 459, Grand Central Station
New York, NY 10163
(212) 870-3400
URL: http://www.aa.org/

Beer Institute
440 First St. NW, Ste. 350
Washington, DC 20001
(202) 737-2337
1-800-379-2739
FAX: (202) 737-7004
URL: http://www.beerinstitute.org/

Bureau of International Narcotics and
Law Enforcement Affairs
U.S. Department of State
2201 C St. NW
Washington, DC 20520
URL: https://www.state.gov/j/inl/

Campaign for Tobacco-Free Kids
1400 I St. NW, Ste. 1200
Washington, DC 20005
(202) 296-5469
FAX: (202) 296-5427
URL: http://www.tobaccofreekids.org/
index.php

Cocaine Anonymous World Services
21720 S. Wilmington Ave., Ste. 304
Long Beach, CA 90810-1641
(310) 559-5833
FAX: (310) 559-2554
E-mail: cawso@ca.org
URL: https://ca.org/

Distilled Spirits Council of the
United States
1250 I St. NW, Ste. 400
Washington, DC 20005
(202) 628-3544
URL: http://www.discus.org/

Drug Policy Alliance
131 W. 33rd St., 15th Floor
New York, NY 10001
(212) 613-8020
FAX: (212) 613-8021
E-mail: nyc@drugpolicy.org
URL: http://www.drugpolicy.org/

Nar-Anon Family Groups
23110 Crenshaw Blvd., Ste. A
Torrance, CA 90505
(310) 534-8188
1-800-477-6291
E-mail: wso@nar-anon.org
URL: http://www.nar-anon.org/

Narcotics Anonymous World Services
PO Box 9999
Van Nuys, CA 91409
(818) 773-9999
FAX: (818) 700-0700
URL: http://www.na.org/

National Council on Alcoholism
and Drug Dependence
217 Broadway, Ste. 712
New York, NY 10007
(212) 269-7797
FAX: (212) 269-7510
E-mail: national@ncadd.org
URL: https://www.ncadd.org/

National Institute on Alcohol Abuse
and Alcoholism
9000 Rockville Pike
Bethesda, MD 20892
(301) 443-2857
E-mail: niaaaweb-r@exchange.nih.gov
URL: https://www.niaaa.nih.gov/

National Institute on Drug Abuse
6001 Executive Blvd., Rm. 5213, MSC 9561
Bethesda, MD 20892-9561
(301) 443-1124
URL: https://www.drugabuse.gov/

National Organization for the Reform
of Marijuana Laws
1100 H St. NW, Ste. 830
Washington, DC 20005
(202) 483-5500
FAX: (202) 483-0057
E-mail: norml@norml.org
URL: http://norml.org/

Office of National Drug Control Policy
750 17th St. NW
Washington, DC 20006
(202) 395-6700
URL: https://www.whitehouse.gov/ondcp

Office on Smoking and Health
Centers for Disease Control and
Prevention
1600 Clifton Rd.
Atlanta, GA 30329-4027
1-800-232-4636
URL: https://www.cdc.gov/tobacco/about/
osh/index.htm/

Substance Abuse and Mental Health Services Administration
5600 Fishers Ln.
Rockville, MD 20857
1-877-726-4727
URL: https://www.samhsa.gov/

U.S. Drug Enforcement Administration Office of Diversion Control
8701 Morrissette Dr.
Springfield, VA 22152
(202) 307-1000
URL: https://www.dea.gov/index.shtml

Wine Institute
425 Market St., Ste. 1000
San Francisco, CA 94105
(415) 512-0151
FAX: (415) 356-7569
URL: http://www.wineinstitute.org/

RESOURCES

The various agencies of the U.S. Department of Health and Human Services (HHS) produce important publications on the consumption of alcohol, tobacco, and illicit drugs in the United States and their health effects. Reports of the U.S. surgeon general and special reports to Congress are published through this office.

The Substance Abuse and Mental Health Services Administration (SAMHSA) produces the annual National Survey on Drug Use and Health. SAMHSA also tracks treatment services. The most recent report is *National Survey of Substance Abuse Treatment Services (N-SSATS): 2014* (March 2016). SAMHSA tracks reported episodes of drug abuse; the most recent published results are in *Treatment Episode Data Set (TEDS) 2003–2013: National Admissions to Substance Abuse Treatment Services* (December 2015). The agency also operates the Drug Abuse Warning Network, which collects data from emergency departments.

The HHS publishes the bimonthly *Public Health Reports*, the official journal of the U.S. Public Health Service. This journal is a helpful resource on health problems, including those that are caused by alcohol and tobacco. The Association of Schools of Public Health has been a partner in the publication of *Public Health Reports* since 1999.

The National Institute on Alcohol Abuse and Alcoholism (NIAAA) publishes the journal *Alcohol Research and Health*. This journal contains current scholarly research on alcohol addiction issues. The NIAAA also publishes the quarterly bulletin *Alcohol Alert*, which disseminates research findings on alcohol abuse and alcoholism.

The National Center for Health Statistics, in its annual *Health, United States*, reports on all aspects of the nation's health, including tobacco- and alcohol-related illnesses and deaths. The *Morbidity and Mortality Weekly Report* is published by the Centers for Disease Control and Prevention (CDC), which also publishes many studies on the trends and health risks of smoking and drinking. Additionally, the American Cancer Society and the American Lung Association provide many facts on cancer and heart disease.

The U.S. Department of Agriculture (USDA) was responsible for several helpful reports concerning tobacco up until 2005. Its publications *Tobacco Outlook* and *Tobacco Briefing Room* monitored tobacco production, consumption, sales, exports, and imports. These publications were discontinued in 2005 after the government ended the decades-old tobacco quota system. (See Chapter 7.) The USDA still publishes the annual *Agricultural Statistics*, which provides valuable information about farming, and *Food Consumption, Prices, and Expenditures*, which compiles data on how the nation spends its consumer dollars. Other useful information is provided by the USDA's Economic Research Service and the U.S. Department of Labor's Bureau of Labor Statistics, which examines how people spend their income, including spending on cigarettes and alcohol.

The National Highway Traffic Safety Administration of the U.S. Department of Transportation produces the annual *Traffic Safety Facts*, which includes data on alcohol-related accidents.

The Bureau of Justice Statistics monitors crime in the United States and focuses on criminal prosecutions, prisons, sentencing, and related subjects. Particularly helpful are *Drug Use and Dependence, State and Federal Prisoners, 2004* (Christopher J. Mumola and Jennifer C. Karberg, October 2006) and the annual publications *Compendium of Federal Justice Statistics* and *Sourcebook of Criminal Justice Statistics*. The Federal Bureau of Investigation's annual *Crime in the United States* provides arrest statistics for the United States. The U.S. Department of the Treasury's Alcohol and Tobacco Tax and Trade Bureau provides alcohol and tobacco tax information.

Other important annual surveys of alcohol, tobacco, and illicit drug use in the United States are conducted by both public and private organizations. The CDC's Youth Risk Behavior Surveillance monitors not only alcohol, tobacco, and illicit drug use but also other risk behaviors, such as teenage sexual activity and weapons possession. The Monitoring the Future survey of substance abuse among students from middle school through college is conducted by the National Institute on Drug Abuse and the University of Michigan, Ann Arbor, Institute for Social Research. The most recent reports are *Monitoring the Future National Survey Results on Drug Use, 1975–2015: Volume 1, Secondary School Students* (Richard A. Miech et al., June 2016) and *Monitoring the Future National Survey Results on Drug Use, 1975–2015: Volume 2, College Students and Adults Ages 19–55* (Lloyd D. Johnston et al., July 2016).

The Wine Institute, the Distilled Spirits Council of the United States, and the Beer Institute are private trade organizations that track alcoholic beverage sales and consumption, as well as political and regulatory issues. Action on Smoking and Health publishes reviews that are concerned with the problems of smoking and the rights of nonsmokers. The Campaign for Tobacco-Free Kids provides information on tobacco-related federal, state, and global initiatives; cigarette taxes; tobacco advertisements; tobacco and smoking statistics; and tobacco-related special reports.

Gallup, Inc., and the Pew Research Center provide important information about the attitudes and behaviors of the American public.

The national policy on combating drug abuse is centered in the Office of National Drug Control Policy (ONDCP). The ONDCP, which prepares a drug control policy each year for the president and coordinates efforts across the federal bureaucracy, is an excellent source for statistics that are collected from many other agencies. Publications consulted for this volume include *National Drug Control Strategy: Data Supplement 2015* (2015), *National Drug Control Strategy: Data Supplement 2016* (2016), *FY 2016 Budget and Performance Summary: Companion to the National Drug Control Strategy* (November 2015), *National Drug Control Strategy, 2016* (2016), and earlier reports.

Domestic law enforcement and interdiction activities fall under the U.S. Department of Justice. The U.S. Drug Enforcement Administration (DEA) oversees all domestic drug control activities. The DEA publishes *Drugs of Abuse* (2015), a resource tool that educates the public about drug facts and the inherent dangers of illegal drugs.

The effort to control drugs beyond the nation's borders is largely under the supervision of the U.S. Department of State. The agency within the Department of State in charge of the drug control effort is the Bureau of International Narcotics and Law Enforcement Affairs. An excellent source of information is the bureau's annual *International Narcotics Control Strategy Report*.

Gale, Cengage Learning, sincerely thanks all the organizations listed here for the valuable information they provide.

INDEX

Endocrine system, 24
Environmental factors in addiction, 71
Environmental Protection Agency (EPA), 46–47, 113
Environmental tobacco smoke. *See* Secondhand smoke
EPA (Environmental Protection Agency), 46–47, 113
Ephedrine, 130–131
Eradication, crop
    Afghanistan, 15
    Bolivia and Peru, 143–144
    as centerpiece of drug disruption effort, 141
    coca leaf, 143*t*
    Colombia, 143
    domestic eradication programs, 145, 146*t*, 147
    federal drug control budget, 138
    Mexico, 144
Erectile dysfunction, 27
Excise taxes, 110–111

F

Fair Packaging and Labeling Act, 113
Fair Sentencing Act, 16
Familial studies, 6, 21
Family history and alcoholism, 23
Family Smoking Prevention and Tobacco Control Act, 46, 49, 78, 113, 114
FARC (Fuerzas Armadas Revolucionarias de Colombia), 143
Farming. *See* Cultivation, drug
FAS (fetal alcohol syndrome), 27, 28
FASDs (fetal alcohol spectrum disorders), 27–28
Fatalities, traffic. *See* Traffic fatalities
FDA. *See* U.S. Food and Drug Administration
FDA v. Brown and Williamson Tobacco Corp., 114
Federal Bureau of Narcotics, 13
Federal Cigarette Labeling and Advertising Act, 46, 120
Federal Food, Drug, and Cosmetic Act, 13
Federal government
    alcohol regulation, 111–113
    drug control budget, 138–139, 140*t*–141*t*
    drug interdiction efforts, 126–127
    drug regulations, 13
    drug trafficking penalties, 123, 124*t*
    electronic cigarette regulations, 51
    history of drug policies, 13–16
    international drug supply disruption, 141–145
    National Drug Control Strategy, 137–138
    tobacco regulations, 113–114
Federal prisons, 67–68, 68*t*, 69–70, 70*t*
Federal Trade Commission, 113

Feinstein, Dianne, 16
Fentanyl, 135–136, 136*f*
Fetal alcohol spectrum disorders (FASDs), 27–28
Fetal alcohol syndrome (FAS), 27, 28
Firefighters' use of anabolic steroids, 65
Food, Drug, and Cosmetic Act, 13
Food and Drug Administration. *See* U.S. Food and Drug Administration
Food services industry, 118
Ford, Gerald, 14
Foreign Assistance Act, 145
Fox, Vicente, 144
Framework Convention on Tobacco Control, 49, 107–108
Freebasing, 61
Fuerzas Armadas Revolucionarias de Colombia (FARC), 143
Funding. *See* Costs and expenditures

G

Gender
    alcohol use, 17, 19(*t*2.2), 22–23, 74*t*, 77
    anabolic steroids, 65
    binge drinking, 19, 76
    cigar and smokeless tobacco use, 79*t*
    cigarette purchases by youth, 80*t*
    cigarette smokers, 38(*t*3.1)
    drug-related deaths, 114–115, 116*t*–118*t*
    federal prisoners, 70*t*
    heroin smugglers, 135
    pain reliever use, 58*t*
    preteen/teen substance use, 72, 72*t*, 73*t*
    state prisoners, 69*t*
    substance abuse treatment admissions, 93, 96*t*
    tobacco use, 79, 80–81
    tobacco-related deaths, 119
    treatment admissions, by substance, 97, 98*t*
Genetic factors
    addiction, 71
    alcohol use disorders, 21–22
    hangover symptoms, 25
    nicotine addiction, 42
Geographic location
    cigarette smokers, 39, 41*t*
    youth alcohol use, 77
    youth tobacco use, 81
Good cholesterol, 26
Government regulation
    alcohol, 111–113
    drugs, 13
    electronic cigarettes, 51, 52
    inconsistencies of government policies, 137
    tobacco, 113–114
Granholm v. Heald, 112
Grassley, Chuck, 16

H

Hallucinogens
    drug categories, 2
    history, 12
    by types, 61–63
    use by time of use and age, 63*f*
    youth use, 85–86, 87–89, 88*f*
Hangovers, 25
Harm, related to marijuana legalization, 150
Harmful use, definition of, 8
Harrison Narcotic Act, 13, 137
Hatch, Orrin G., 112
Hazardous Substances Act, 113
Health insurance, 51
Health issues
    alcohol, 25–26
    binge drinking, 74–75
    cigarette smoking, 11
    commonly abused drugs, 3*t*–4*t*, 5*t*
    fentanyl, 135–136
    maternal smoking, 50–51
    medical marijuana, 150–151
    secondhand smoke, 45*f*, 113
    surgeon general reports on smoking, 45*t*
    tobacco, 42–45, 44*f*, 46, 47*f*, 119, 122*t*
    youth tobacco use, 78
Heavy drinking, 19(*t*2.2)
Heroin
    drug trafficking, 135
    drug-related deaths, 115
    history, 12, 13, 14
    seizures, drug, 128*f*, 128*t*, 129*t*
    types and effects, 64
High school students. *See* Adolescents
High-density lipoproteins, 26
Holbrooke, Richard, 15
Holder, Eric, Jr., 16
Homeland Security Act, 1, 126
Hoover, Herbert, 13
Hydrocodone, 57
Hypertension, 26

I

Illicit drugs. *See* Drugs
Immigrants, 13
Impulsivity, 22
India, 12
Indiana, 147
Inhalants, 2, 63, 83, 83*f*
Injectable drugs
    cocaine, 60, 61
    heroin, 14, 64, 135
    methamphetamine, 59
    oxycodone, 57
INL (Bureau for International Narcotics and Law Enforcement Affairs), 125, 141, 143
An Inquiry into the Effects of Ardent Spirits on the Mind and Body (Rush), 9

CPSIA information can be obtained
at www.ICGtesting.com
Printed in the USA
FFOW01n2249230917
40285FF

9 781410 325389